THE ARRIVAL THE STRUGGLE THE ASCENDANCY

THE ARRIVAL THE STRUGGLE THE ASCENDANCY

E. A. CAROSI

Copyright © 2006 E. A. Carosi
All rights reserved.

ISBN: 1514735261
ISBN 13: 9781514735268
Library of Congress Control Number: 2015920198
CreateSpace Independent Publishing Platform
North Charleston, South Carolina

For Joann, my wife, my best friend my muse.

ACKNOWLEDGEMENTS AND THANKS

To my friend and editor, John Tessitore, who took my scribbling and turned it into a novel.

To Mary Anne Giansanti who took my handwritten pages, deciphered them and typed my story.

ABOUT THE STORY

Hugo Rossi, Jr, the main character in the story, lives in Rhode Island and is a retired educator. His introduction into the story as a young grade school student is factual as are the succeeding chapters culminating in India. All the other characters in the story up to the introduction of young Hugo are fictional but are based on the exploits of actual persons. Salvatore, Hugo's grandfather, is a legendary character, a myth in the Italian American community. Hugo, Sr. is a character based on the actual person. However, events, timelines and associated characters are taken out of context or are a creation by the author to enhance the story.

IN THE BEGINNING

Abruzzi, Italy, 1914

Salvatore Giuliano Rossi at nineteen-years old stood six-foot, two-inches tall, possessed chiseled Roman features, a three-foot span of massive shoulders, weighed 225 pounds, and was the strongest man in the village of Atri, population 1,500, one of the many small villages in the high plain Abruzzi region of Italy. Single, he lived with his father, Hugo, and his mother, Santina, on twenty acres in a stone, wooden floored farmhouse with no plumbing or electricity that his father sharecropped for the village mayor, the Barone Vitorio Santagatta.

Salvatore was educated by the dedicated local parish priests and nuns of the village. Poetic by nature, he had graduated at the top of his class of 25 students, spoke some French and German, and was eager to attend the University of Rome on scholarship provided by the village to its top student. For the past twelve months he had worked tirelessly for his father, who he loved and respected as no other man.

His father, Hugo, was legendary throughout the region. Built like a tree trunk, with powerful arms and legs, he had been an outstanding soccer player for the village of Atri and had gained celebrity status for his physical courage on and off the playing field. He was held in high regard and treated with great respect by every man in Atri. Hugo possessed a natural dignity, a love of people, and was a protector to those who were weak and needful. His life was his wife, his son, and his church. He assisted Monsignor Centofanti at Sunday mass and holy days of obligation. He insisted that Salvatore memorize the church liturgy in Latin, a daunting task that consumed hours of Salvatore's after school hours, but pleasing his father was more important than sporting with friends.

At thirty-seven years old his mother, Santina, was one of the most beautiful woman in Atri – Salvatore worshiped her. Tall, slender, cascading auburn hair, full-lips, high cheek bones, a perfectly shaped beautiful face and figure that had turned every head in Atri for many years.. Her every action, her every motive was to please her small family. The women in the village called her affectionately *la principessa*, "the princess."

In the boiling political cauldron that was then Italy, Salvatore had become a Marxist, a socialist free thinker who read extensively from Kropotkin, Marx, Engels, and Trotsky, books that were smuggled into the village by his mother's brother, Zio Antonio. Antonio was an outspoken socialist revolutionary and considered a dangerous enemy of the state by local officials and especially by Capt. Oreste Capuano of the posted carabiniere. At five-foot six-inches with a scraggly goatee, weighing 120 lbs., Antonio Tartaglia cut a chaplinesque figure as he would rant and rage against all government and all authority. Antonio was fearless and seemed constantly enraged at someone or something. His love was his sister Santina and her family. There was always a meal to be had, a joke to share and an apt student like Salvatore to instruct in the ways of bomb making and revolutionary rhetoric.

In the evenings they gathered at the village Center Square seated at tables in front of Fabio Potenza's small café discussing politics, the future of Italy, the lack of any power to change things. All this under the watchful eye of the local carabiniere Commander, "Captain Shithead" Capuano. The newspapers they read were communist and socialist shrieking's meant to arouse passion, and they did.

On May 14, 1914, while plowing his fields behind an ancient horse, Hugo Rossi at 40 years of age reared up and crashed to the ground of congenital heart failure. He died in the arms of his son, Salvatore gasping in Italian, *"take care of your mother... take care of your mother."*

The funeral was attended by the entire village of Atri and relatives from the entire Abruzzi region. His sudden death came as a stunning blow to friends and family alike. Monsignor Ritacco eulogized him as the strong, steady influence of goodness in this society slowly going the way of the devil. The burial cortege strung out for a mile. Amid the mourners, in a position of prominence befitting his stature, stood Mayor Barone Santagatta, resplendent in sashes and medallions. The Barone had always daydreamed of the beautiful Santina Tartaglia Rossi with genital warming results as the now widow Rossi, he assured himself, his time had come.

Salvatore was shattered by his father's death. He knew life only through his father's eyes, his father's strength, and his father's love. As they walked slowly toward the gravesite, he gripped his mother's hand tightly. Reassuringly, he looked at her youthful beautiful face and silently cried out for this man and woman who had shared so much love together. Santina Rossi's life had come to an emotional end. The one and only man she had given herself to in sacred matrimony, was dead, as was her soul. Salvatore sensed his enormous responsibility and heard the dying words of his father reverberating in his head. He placed his arm around Santina's shoulders tightly, protectively. The Barone Santagatta watched, genitals warming. The responsibility was now Salvatore's, twenty acres of seasonal vegetables, wheat, pigs, chickens and milk cows, with half the earnings from the cash crop sale of pigs and chickens going to the Barone as rent for the farm. With the help of a local village boy and encouragement from Santina, he broke into a daily rhythm, starting at dawn and finishing well at dusk. They managed. In time Salvatore resumed his visits to Potenza's Café for coffee and radical conversations, under the ever-watchful gaze of Captain "Shithead". The discussion raged: revolution in Russia, war with Germany, political upheaval in Italy. A bleak future for a young man in Atri in August of 1914.

On a warm September evening, after listening to Zio Antonio rant and rave about the assassination of Austrian Crown Prince Franz Ferdinand in Sarajevo, Yugoslavia and what that would now cause for two solid hours, Salvatore bid Zio Antonio, Potenza, and several friends *buona notte* and began the half-hour trek to his farm. From a distance he could make out the light from oil lamps in the windows facing the village.

The night was cloudless; a full moon bathed the landscape in light and shadows. He was three hundred feet away from the house when he saw a figure bolt from his house and leap upon a horse, galloping into the distance. He ran, heart pounding, breathless through the still open front door. His senses reeled when he saw his mother, naked from the waist down, bloodied, bruised, one bloody breast exposed. She sat huddled beneath the kitchen table, sobbing uncontrollably. He covered her with a blanket, picked her up from beneath the table, and carried her to bed.

He sat beside her. Her back was to him, trembling, convulsing. "Mama, Mama, who did this to you?"

She cried out, "Santaga...," then quickly caught herself. "No, Salvatore, no! Please, I don't want to lose you, too! It was nothing. It meant nothing. We can forget this. I need you!"

Her hand slipped from his pant leg. He walked slowly in hypnotic thought toward the woodshed, selected a razor-edged, short-handled axe, and began the long walk to Santagatta's villa. He walked in a trance, disembodied. The villa loomed ahead in the bright moonlight, a 15th century castle, always under the ownership of the Santagatta family. Spacious lawns, garden fountains, the winery. It was only now that Salvatore realized the magnificence of the estate. He paused. His excitement filling his bladder, he urinated purposely on the headstone of a deceased Santagatta in the small family cemetery at the outer rim of the property. Light shown from the Barone's bedroom. Salvatore knew every inch of the estate and the villa. He had spent many hours as a boy with his father tending gardens and repairing the interior. He knew in what room the Barone slept; in what room was his toilet and in what room he performed sex with young boys and girls. He climbed an apple tree for a better vantage point of the Barone's bedroom. He watched him in the dim light, his sinewy body reflected in a dresser mirror. He fondled himself, an expression of satisfied appraisal shaping his lips.

Salvatore gripped the handle of the instrument of vengeance. The lights went out in the bedroom. The villa was quiet. The fragrance of lilac and grapes clinging to the still air. Salvatore waited until he was sure Santagatta had succumbed to wine and sleep. He kept to the shadows as he made his way to a drainpipe affixed to the stonewalls and rising to the roofline. He had climbed the pipe dozens of times to reach the ancient slate roof in constant need of repair. He climbed quietly in bare feet, gripping the uneven stonewall with his toes. A narrow ledge ran beneath the bedroom window, open and screenless to the night air. Salvatore stepped from the drainpipe to the ledge, the bedroom window was 15 feet away. He pressed himself against the uneven stonewall, making handholds as he edged his way to the window.

Sweat poured profusely from his face; he became conscious of his pounding heart and rapid breathing. The sharpened axe was stuffed through his belt against his stomach, scraping ever so noiselessly against the uneven ancient stonewall. He was there. The window was covered with light gauze drapery as protection against mosquitoes. Gripping the windowsill, he peered into the room. The brilliant moon illuminates the sleeping, grunting snoring Barone. Salvatore slid silently through the window where he stood ten feet from the fornicating monster. He had never experienced the emotion he now felt: choking, eye-bulging rage. It was all he could do to restrain himself from charging across the room and leaping upon the sleeping Barone.

He walked to the side of the bed and stared down at the beast that had taken his mother in animal lust, his father's wife, his dead father's wife. He gripped the axe in two hands raised in front of his right shoulder, he called his name softly, "Wake up Barone. It's time to pay for being a filthy, evil pig."

The Barone awakened, eyes wide with shock. "What are you doing here, are you insane?" He struggled with the sheet trying to place one foot on the floor.

"Don't move another inch, Barone. *Porca di miseria, animale!*" Salvatore raised the axe above his head.

"What are you doing, Salvatore, what are you doing? I love you, my boy! I helped your father when he needed time to pay his rent. I've been good to you! What's wrong with you?"

Salvatore heard nothing but the roaring in his head. He brought the axe down with such powerful force one foot left the floor. The axe split Santagatta's sternum, sliced through his heart, and buried itself inside his chest. He remained mouth opened in half scream, eyes protruding from his head. It took all of Salvatore's strength to extricate the axe from the Barone's chest. With three sharp blows he severed his head from his body; it rolled slowly to one side of the bed, eyes still protruding. Salvatore stood with the axe in one hand by his side, dripping blood. He awakened from his trance. The sound of muffled voices and running footsteps reverberated in the huge stone courtyard. Salvatore dropped the axe, climbed through the windowsill to a handhold on the ledge beneath the window, and dropped fifteen feet to the ground in his bare feet. He quickly retrieved his shoes as cries echoed from the window above. Salvatore ran for the cover of trees as heads emerged from the bedroom window, scanning the estate for the intruder.

Sticking to the fields, he ran as only a man possessed of fear and exultation can run, lungs expanded, muscles contracted, feet barely touching the ground. He arrived at the rear of his house in minutes emerging from the field and cautiously approaching a window open to the night air. He heard the tear filled voice of his mother and the consoling voice of Si Antonio. He saw the Bugati automobile as he rounded the corner at the front of the house. A bright red streamlined racing car, gleaming in the moonlight, chrome spoke wheels, two seats and a beauty. It was Zarlenga, the racecar driver, but why was he here? Salvatore pushed open the door. Santina ran to him, wrapped her arms around placing her cheek to his chest. "You must leave Atri at once. They will know it was you. They will be here in an hour or two." She looked into his eyes, tears streaming from hers.

Knowing full well that this would be a long separation, Zio Antonio materialized from the bedroom, suitcase in hand. Cap pushed back at its usually cocky angle, furrowed brow, and cigarette dangling from his lips. *"Hai mazzarre il porco?"* (You killed the pig?) he asked, serious in his manner and speech, unusual for Zio Antonio. "You have the pig's blood all over you. You need to change clothes, no questions yet. C'mon, c'mon. subito, subito, hurry, hurry." In seconds he changed into fresh clothing that Santina had ready and waiting.

Zio Antonio grabbed the suitcase. "I'll be in the car. Kiss your mother good-bye. *Subito, subito!*" Santina clutched his face with her trembling hands, "Promise me you will let me know you are safe. Promise me."

"I promise you, Mama, I promise you. I love you, Mama."

Santina pressed a medal into his hands. "This was your father's St. Anthony medal. Wear it always."

"I promise, Mama."

"Go, go, go." She pushed him toward the door, the rumble of the Bugati in the background.

"Aayyy, andiamo!" Zio Anonio yelled as he raced the Bugati engine. Salvatore's hand slipped from his mother's as he leaped into

the Bugati's passenger seat. Zio Antonio, waiting on no further sentiment accelerated down the rutted, bumpy road toward the center of Atri.

"Where are we headed, Zio Antonio, and how did you get Zarlenga's car?" Salvatore asked over the roar of the Bugati's sixteen cylinders.

"Zarlenga owed me a big favor," yelled Zio Antonio. "I solved his problem with the Palumbos when he knocked up their youngest daughter last year." Zio Antonio downshifted into a sharp turn. "Listen, Salvatore, you have to get out of this region right now. Abruzzi is too hot for you...I have friends in Naples." He swerved wildly, missing a three-foot hole in the road by inches. "*Avon goola*, these roads are made for friggin' goats, not automobiles! These friends will get you a job on the docks. You're gonnna have a new name at least while your in Naples. *Hai capito?*" You understand?

"Yes, yes," yelled Salvatore. "So what's my new name?"

"Guiseppe Ferraio," said Zio Antonio. Joe Smith.

"What the hell kind of name is that for a guy on the run?"

"Don't worry, kid. There's a lot of Joe Smiths in Naples. You'll just be one more, and I betcha half of them are on the run from something."

"How did you know?" "I didn't, I drove up to see my sister to show her the Bugati, she told me, good thing."

The Bugati slowed at a fork in the road. The left fork heading south along the coast, the right fork into Atri. "Listen, Salvatore, we have to head down the coast to Foggia, then across country to Naples. Shithead will have the cops alerted, so we're gonna travel only at night. I made arrangements with some people to put us up for the next few nights, so don't worry. Zio Antonio's got everything taken care of and, by the way, just so you'll know, if you didn't kill that friggin' pig, the boys at Potenza's had already decided he had to go. It was planned for the Feast of St. Anthony. Domenic Disandro picked the short straw, but now you've taken care of that."

Not another word was mentioned about the Barone. It was over. Six hundred kilometers to Naples from Atri with terrible roads and few places to buy petrol. Somehow at dawn on the fourth morning of travel they arrived starving, unshaven, and almost out of petrol to a sleeping, soon to be alive and bustling with passionate activity, Naples.

Chapter 1

VITO THE ANARCHIST

Dawn was breaking as the Bugati rumbled down a cobblestone street named Via Delacroce. The city began to stir with activity as early morning workers emerged from apartments carrying lunch pails, satchels, and tools. These were the craftsmen and laborers, the bakers and the fishmongers. The clerks, shopkeepers, and city workers would follow them. Naples was a huge city, teaming with people who seemingly never stopped babbling and singing. It possessed the largest slum in all of Italy, with narrow winding streets, four and five story cement and stone tenement buildings hundreds of years old, decorated with laundry strung on clothes lines stretched across the street from building to building. From the *Spaccanapoli*, as it was known since ancient times, came the day laborers and unskilled, uneducated hump workers. The streets were redolent with the fragrance of garlic and the baking of bread for the day's meals. Via Delacroce turned into Via DeCesare, which ran on the perimeter of the enclave.

"Antonio, where the hell are we going?" asked Salvatore as he looked from side to side, taking in the enormity of the city.

"Worry about nuthin', kid. We're going to a friend of mine's house. He's going to help you out of this shit you got yourself into."

"What does he do? I mean, how can he help me? Help me do what?" asked Salvatore, an edge of impatience to his voice.

"*Sta' calmo, sta' calmo.* You can't give in to impatience," said Antonio. "You have to learn to control emotions. If you don't, you're gonna get nailed by the cops. *Hai capito?*"

Salvatore slumped in his seat. "Yeah, you're right. I just can't help it. It's not everyday that something like this happens in somebody's life."

Antonio smiled as he slowed, looking at houses and addresses on the cobbled street. He placed his hand on Salvatore's arm. "I understand. Don't forget, you're my blood…and here we are!" Antonio parked the Bugati in front of a two-story house, neatly white washed with a wrought iron balcony across the front covered with flowering vines. A herringbone brick walk wound behind the house.

"C'mon, let's go," said Antonio.

"Wait a minute, who is this mystery man? You know, I know some of the people you hang around with," said Salvatore sarcastically.

"Aayy, aayy!" protested Antonio. "Leave it to your uncle. You're about to meet the most interesting character of your life."

Salvatore extricated himself from the confine of the Bugati and followed Antonio toward the back of the house. They approached a solid wooden door with a massive doorknocker, shaped like a woman's breast. Antonia knocked twice. Within seconds the door exploded open.

THE ARRIVAL THE STRUGGLE THE ASCENDANCY

"What?" roared the apparition. He stood there, a gaunt giant of a man, Rasputin-like blazing black eyes shifting from Salvatore to Antonio. Recognition of Antonio creased his face with a smile. "Antonio, you son of a bitch, whadda you doing in Naples?"

"Vito, you crazy man," laughed Antonio as they hugged one another.

"Who's the kid with you? C'mon in, c'mon in." Vito instinctively scanned the area and bolted the door.

"So, Antonio, who is this kid?" Vito asked, cocking his head to one side and folding his arms.

Salvatore stood slightly behind Antonio. It was then that he took in the full measure of Vito. At least six-feet three inches tall, sinewy, broad shoulders, and an animal-like vitality that he exuded in every motion. His hands were monstrous in size, and when he spoke it was with a deep booming bass voice. A full black straggly beard and a shoulder-length head of hair added to his messianic appearance. Antonio smilingly turned to Salvatore, gesturing toward Vito.

"Salvatore—oh, excuse me. Giuseppe Ferraio, meet Vito 'The Anarchist' Romanelli."

Salvatore extended his hand and Vito enveloped it with his massive paw.

"*Piacere*, Giuseppe," boomed Vito. "*Vito, ti posso parlare da parte per un minuto?*" Vito, can we talk privately for a minute, asked Antonio.

"Yeah, c'mon, we'll go into the bedroom."

Salvatore sat at the kitchen table absorbing his surroundings. The apartment was sparse. Just the necessities, thought Salvatore, with the exception of one whole wall covered with books, with more books in boxes stacked in front of the rustic bookshelves. At twenty-nine-years old Vito the Anarchist was possessed of a photographic memory and an ability to transfer thought instantly into free-flowing, dynamic speech. He was known to speak for an hour as if reading a speech with not so much as a note. In fact, at the age of five Vito was kicked in the head by a horse and lay in a coma for ten days, and when he awoke he was thought to have been neurologically damaged. As Antonio and Vito emerged from the bedroom, Vito walked toward Salvatore with a solemn look on his face.

"Don't you worry, Salvatore, about a thing. We do in life what we must do. You stay with me for a while, Salva... Madonna! I mean, Giuseppe, Giuseppe." He beamed a broad smile, and characteristically never made the mistake again. "C'mon, you guys must be hungry after driving all that way on those shitty roads. I'll put some coffee on. Tina will be here in a few minutes."

No sooner had Vito ended his conversation, there came the sound of the apartment door being unlocked. Framed in the doorway was Tina Valetta, 32 years old, five-foot ten inches tall. Salvatore stood mesmerized as he took in her flaring hips, her over-full lips, the cascading hair that fell well below the curve of her perfectly rounded buttocks. "Aayy, Tina," boomed Vito. "Just in time. C'mon make us some eggs and whatever you can scrape up. I just put the coffee on."

"Aayy, *cafone*! What am I, some slave? Don't you introduce me to your friends?" Tina was looking directly at Salvatore. Her voice was coarse and sensual. As she walked to the kitchen sink she undulated.

"I'm sorry, sis," said Vito. He paused a millisecond. "Giuseppe, my sister, Tina. She makes sure I eat and have clean clothes. Obviously, she thinks I'm a helpless, stupid animal."

"No," said Tina, "just stupid," as she playfully tossed a dishcloth in his direction. "You're lucky. I just bought this loaf of bread at Vellucci's bakery. He was just taking it out of the oven," said Tina. "Give me a few minutes and we'll have some eggs and cheese."

Salvatore watched her every movement, fascinated by her beauty. Tina served espresso, soft-boiled eggs, and fresh provolone cheese. Vito never stopped talking even with his mouth full, crumbs tumbling from his lips.

"Listen, Giuseppe, tomorrow we visit Fabrizio Trombetti. He's the boss on the docks; he hires all the workers. They load ships, unload ships, fill the warehouses. Everything that goes on down on those docks has to be cleared by Fabrizio. He's a Communist, a union boss. And his brother is a big man in the Mafia down in Sicily."

They sat around the rough-hewn wooden table sipping espresso deep in conversation. Tina was detached and stared at Salvatore. "Where are you from?" she asked, looking steadily into Salvatore's eyes as he shifted his weight and gaze to Vito questioningly.

"It's okay, Giuseppe, she's seen it all and heard it all. Her ex-husband is down in Sicily somewhere hiding out with some Mafioso. If they ever catch him, he's going to jail for robbery, murder, and kidnapping. A real nice guy." There was no response from Tina as she continued her steady gaze at Salvatore.

"We're from a town called Atri up in Abruzzi," said Salvatore. "A small place, without many people." Antonio jumped in.

"Tina, I'm here on business, and Giuseppe is looking for a future. There's not a hell of a lot going on in Atri these days and, besides, I haven't seen this bastard brother of yours for almost a year now. If I knew his sister was so beautiful, I would have been here sooner!" Tina smiled, knowing there was something more to the story than Antonio let on.

"All right, listen. You guys will stay with me tonight. Tomorrow, Guiseppe will pay a visit to Fabrizio. Right now I have to get ready for a rally at Piazza St. Angelo in front of City Hall." Vito looked grim, determined.

"What's the rally all about?" asked Antonio.

"What's it all about!" boomed Vito, voice rising, face purpling. "I'll tell you what it's all about!" Vito rose to take the center of the kitchen. Clearly, this was his element. He began slowly, deliberately, quickening to a crescendo. "The thieving, rotten bastard city fathers want to tax the local fishermen. They want an annual tax on their boats," his voice now at a fever pitch. "Do you believe this shit? Most of these guys live from hand to mouth as it is. What they want to do is grab money from the little guy so the big *spacones* don't have to pay...the bastards!" he shouted.

Listen Vito," said Antonio, "I gotta get the Bugati back to Atri. My buddy Zarlenga is probably losing sleep over my using it to come to Naples. He knows why we're here." Vito nodded with pursed lips in understanding. "Giuseppe, come here and kiss your uncle goodbye." Salvatore threw his arms about Antonio, tears in his eyes.

"Aayy, no sadness. This is a new beginning for you, *hai capito*, you understand?" Salvatore, wiping a tear from his cheek, nodded. Antonio's head motioned to the apartment door. "C'mon outside, I want to talk with you. *Scusa, Tina! Vito, vieni per un momento.*"

Salvatore followed Antonio to the Bugati, gleaming in the morning sunlight. "Listen to me carefully, kid." Antonio pulled Salvatore toward him by his shoulders. "You can trust these people;

THE ARRIVAL THE STRUGGLE THE ASCENDANCY

they're good honest people. They'll get you out of Italy. We have friends in America. That is where you must go."

"But what about my mother, who'll take care of her?" Antonio cut him off abruptly.

"Don't worry about her, she's my sister. I'll take care of her. She'll be fine." Antonio held Salvatore's face as he spoke. "If you need to communicate with me or your mother for any reason while you're here or anywhere, write to Monsignor Ritacco and use this address as a return address. He'll get the letter to me or your mother. Remember who you are—Giuseppe Ferraio." Salvatore closed his eyes in weary resignation and nodded slowly. Antonio and the Bugati roared off to Atri.

Salvatore watched as the car careened around a distant corner and went out of sight. He stood rigid, almost catatonic, hands deep in his pockets, his mind drifting.... He sensed a presence and turned to find himself staring into Tina's large brown eyes.

"Hey, what are you doing out here? Are you coming with us or are you staying here?" she asked him with her head tilted to one side, a smile radiating from her full lips. The sight of her immediately revived his senses.

"Okay, okay, I'm coming with you, but what am I walking into, a riot?" he answered. At this moment emerging from the rear apartment with a powerful stride came Vito, arms flailing, mumbling his speech to himself.

"You want a riot, *figlio mio*? You might have one, Giuseppe'!" Vito's eyes darted left and right out of habit, checking his surroundings before continuing in a lowered voice. "This morning, my young friend, you're going to meet some dynamic people. I'm not sure, but we think Trotsky may be with us and a new guy, a

7

real comer, Benny Mussolini. He's good, a leader. Kind of a hack, but the people love him. All right, are we ready for this?" asked Vito rhetorically, pulling his trousers up and expanding his chest with a deep breath. "Let's go."

The walk to Piazza St. Angelo took twenty minutes. The streets were packed with people headed for the rally, calling to one another, fists clenched high, fingers parted in a V for victory, exuberance in the air.

"Aayy, Vito, we need you today! You gotta give them hell for us!" cried out a local fisherman. "Vito, Vito!" yelled someone in the crowd. "We depend on you today, don't back down."

Vito was relishing his position of leadership. Surrounded by admirers, he was carried away by emotion. He stopped, raised both his enormous hands, paused for effect as the crowd slowed, and boomed out, "Today is *your* day. Today is the *people's* day. Today we will be heard!" The crowd roared its approval, raised Vito to their shoulders, and walked into the vast Piazza St. Angelo.

The Piazza was choked with demonstrators. With no space for movement, the crowd moved as a single wave. Vito was shouldered to a small-elevated platform in the center of the square. The platform had been assembled and trundled into the square by the loyal following before dawn. The roar of the crowd was deafening as only a crowd in Naples with an axe to grind can be. As Vito was lowered to the platform, his smile became a cackle of glee as he embraced his fellow speakers, Gabrielle D'Anunzio and Benito Mussolini. The crowd roared in ear-splitting approval.

"Thank you, Vito, for inviting me to speak today," said the somber, intense D' Anunzio. "It's a fantastic crowd and they are primed and ready." Mussolini strode the same platform, eyes narrowed, jaw jutting out, the picture of a Caesar. The crowd loved it.

"Benny, Gabriele," yelled Vito over the din, "this is not about taxes or fishing boats, this you know. I promised you a crowd, now it's up to you two to convince these people to go to war against Germania. Listen, I'll start with the boat tax. Benny, you take over from me and turn your talk to the *risorgimento* and Italian pride." Vito snatched up a megaphone. Someone in the crowd elbowed his way to the platform with the flag of Italy and handed it to Vito. With the flag raised aloft and the crowd roaring, he brought the megaphone to his mouth waiting for a break in the pandemonium. Slowly, the crowd lowered its cacophony to a loud murmur. Vito took in a deep breath.

"People of Naples, citizens of Italy, my brothers and sisters! There comes a time in one's life when enough becomes enough." The crowd bellowed its approval, screaming "enough, enough, enough." Vito raised his hand to quell the chanting. His speech was meant to cut into the hearts of the crowd. He spoke of freedom from want. He quoted Julius Caesar, Cicero, Garibaldi, and Karl Marx. For thirty minutes he spoke with near hysterical passion, priming the crowd for his fellow orators, and only once mentioning the boat tax. Salvatore held Tina's hand gently as they edged and pushed their way to the platform in spite of the large crushing crowd, his mind focused only on Tina's soft, warm hand gripping his almost willingly. It thrilled him just to touch her skin.

They made it to the front of the platform just as Mussolini began his tirade for interventionism and the restoration of Italian dignity by going to war against Germany and joining the triple entente of Britain, France, and Russia. Salvatore held Tina by her shoulders. His head swam with ecstasy. Tina turned to look at him. He gazed into her eyes. They remained locked, unblinking, swaying with emotion. At that moment there was no crowd, no sound, only Tina's enormous brown eyes and Salvatore's thundering heart.

Mussolini was at full vocal throttle when Salvatore took in the first glimpse of the tri-cornered hats of the carabiniere. Carabiniere and local police lined the perimeter of the square, ringing the crowd. In the distance, Salvatore could see prison wagons with steel barred windows being pushed into position. The crowd sensed there was trouble. There were shouts and catcalls at the police and soldiers:

"Aayy, you fat salame!"

"Asshole, how many fathers do you have?"

"Bushel ass, get some pants that fit!"

Pockets of laughter erupted around the jokesters. Mussolini had seen it all before. As he spoke, he warily scanned the crowd for the best path out of the square. Vito patted his pant leg, assuring himself that the twelve-inch length of pipe was still strapped to his thigh. He was not about to leave his audience. From the corner of his eye Salvatore watched as the young man next to him unfolded a red beret and adjusted it to his head. At the same moment, a dozen others around the platform donned the same cap.

In a flash, Salvatore knew they were police and this was their badge of identification if trouble began. And began it did, with a hundred screaming whistles. The red berets rushed the platform groping for Mussolini, Vito, and D' Anunzio. The police and soldiers closed in from all sides. The crowd panicked frantically running in every direction. Heads were being cracked loudly with police batons. Demonstrators were being dragged into wagons. Fistfights raged throughout the square.

Mounted carabiniere charged through the crowd, sabers slashing indiscriminately. People fell mortally wounded left and right. Salvatore's first instinct was to protect Tina. He pulled her to the ground, huddling against the speakers' platform. Vito fought three red berets, pipe in hand, flailing like a wild beast, thoroughly enjoying every second of this impromptu combat. Teeth gnashing, feet kicking, roaring like a lion, he beat back the red berets.

Salvatore looked up to see the patent leather tri-corner cap of a carabiniere. Dark blue uniform, epaulettes, leather service straps and holster, black riding boot, and the insignia of captain. The captain shouted as he drew his revolver from its holster: "*Muova, muova!* Move, move!" He was aiming at Vito's chest.

Salvatore sprang upwards reflexively, quickly as a cat, left hand grasping the captain's right wrist forcing the revolver into the air, right hand holding the captain's left wrist. The captain was a powerful man, and against Salvatore's youthful strength he slowly gained the advantage. The muzzle of the revolver was slowly turning toward Salvatore. Their eyes finally met. Salvatore stopped breathing as he looked into the cold dark eyes of Captain Shithead.

A look of startled surprise came over Capuano's face as they stood locked in a struggle for the pistol. "*L'assassino del barone, Salvatore Rossi*," he blurted out, and with a renewed strength inclined the Beretta pistol closer to Salvatore's head. "*Aiutami, aiutami*, I have the murderer of the Barone Santagatta!" screamed the officer, but the roar of the crowd drowned out his cries for help.

Tina sprang from nowhere smashing Capuano in the right temple with a cobblestone loosened from the floor of the ancient piazza. Blood spurted from his temple as he instantly tumbled to the ground. Tina picked up the Beretta, stuffed it into her pocket, and grabbed Salvatore's hand. Salvatore was stunned by the presence of Capuano in Naples. He had been found out! All around him the rioting raged, the crowd refusing to give in to assaults by the carabiniere and local police. He felt the tugging at his hand and turned to meet Tina's frantic eyes. "C'mon Giuseppe', c'mon!"

They crouched low and ran for the outside perimeter of the piazza. Miraculously, they made it to a narrow street off the piazza with no interference. Most of the police were now defending themselves from the hostile crowd, which had the winning edge. As they raced away from the piazza they heard the first gun shots. They stopped and turned. The police were shooting randomly into the crowd. People were dropping to the ground, dead or wounded, by the dozens.

The crowd scattered in every direction, the police in pursuit. Tina pulled at Salvatore's hand. "Let's go. We have to get out of here. Your friend the carabiniere is going to come to and he'll be looking for us." They raced toward the *spaccanapoli*, the largest slum in Italy, as the panicked crowd streamed by them. Gradually, they slowed to a fast walk.

"Where are we going," asked Salvatore.

"To my house," she answered, glancing over her shoulder and quickening the pace.

They entered the spaccanapoli along with hundreds of rioters, all seeking anonymity and safety in a sprawling warren of streets lined with four, five, and six-level cement and stone buildings. Where there were sidewalks, they were no more than three feet wide. Garbage was everywhere. They turned a corner and crossed the street to a four-story cement tenement. On the first level a sign in the front window announced *La Bella Napoli Trattoria Pizza, Calzone and Pasta*. A doorway to the right of the Trattoria led to the upper level.

Tina pulled Salvatore through the entranceway into a completely alien existence. Salvatore had never entered a building that was not one level. The stairwell was dark and musty, and smelled of the thousand families that had lived and died in the tenement over the centuries. The stairs were steep, made of cement worn in the center from the millions of foot steps making their way in and out of the home of so many, at each level. Babies cried, men swore, food cooked—bringing the building to life.

Salvatore followed Tina to the fifth and top level. Pausing at the small landing outside the door, she turned to Salvatore, smiled ever so slightly, and pushed her way in. An old croaking voice from somewhere inside the apartment called out, "*Chi é?*"

"It's me, Mama," Tina called back. Salvatore followed Tina to a small parlor in the rear of the apartment where he came upon a small, angelic-faced woman in a black dress, black shoes, and black shawl. Her white hair was neatly tied into a bun, and she sat with rosary beads, rocking back and forth in an old wooden chair.

"Tina, *chi é quest'uomo?* Who is this man?" Her voice was soft and inquisitive, without any sense of unease.

Tina explained that Salvatore was a friend of Vito, and that he would be staying with them for a while. "He needs some help right now, Mamma."

"*Allora gli fai qualcosa de mangiare e bere.* Good, good," she said smiling at the handsome new arrival, "make something to eat and drink. He looks like he needs it."

Tina took Salvatore's arm and led him to the seated woman. "Salvatore, this is my mother-in-law, Julia Valetta. I live with her and take care of her."

Salvatore took the old woman's hand lightly in his. "*Piacere*, Signora Valetta," he said, bowing formally at the waist. The old woman nodded her head and motioned toward the kitchen with her hand.

Salvatore scanned the apartment. Wood, stone, exposed cold water pipes, oil lamps and candles, small kitchen with no food storage. One bedroom and a water closet retrofitted into one corner in recent years. Tina stood at the small sink in the kitchen, sunlight streaming in through one of the three windows carved out of the corner of the tenement.

"Well, what do you think?" she asked with a full smile. Salvatore seated himself at the large kitchen table.

"Is this my hideout?" he asked with a resigned tight smile.

"Aayy, c'mon, it could be worse, you know. You could be in the jail house right now, and besides it won't be long before you're out of Naples." Their eyes met and held at the thought of parting. "I'll make some pasta and ceci beans, you pour some wine for us. And don't forget my mother-in-law, she drinks all day long."

Captain Oreste Capuano came to his senses slowly, eyes and mind adjusting to his surroundings. For a moment he could not recall what had happened. Then it came crashing in on him. "Rossi, Rossi, Salvatore Rossi!" He tried to sit upright in his hospital bed but fell back from the pain emanating from his temple. He raised his hand and gently felt the gauze bandages wrapping his forehead. He looked to his left and right, rolling his head slowly. He was in a hospital ward: white ceiling, white floors, white beds. The other beds were empty, and he felt a curious comfort in the sterility of his surroundings. He heard footsteps and the rustling of female skirts. Turning his head slightly, he saw a nun in white habit approaching his bed.

"*Aahh Signore Capuano, é sveglio.* You are awake."

"Yes, sister," smiled the patient. "Where am I?"

"This is the Holy Apostles Hospital, *Capitano*. You were brought here by ambulance yesterday afternoon. You have been unconscious since your arrival. How do you feel?"

"Fine, Sister, fine, *grazie*. When can I leave?"

"Doctor Pella is on his way to examine you this afternoon. And you have distinguished visitors in the waiting room impatiently awaiting your awakening. Are you hungry, *Capitano*?"

"No, Sister, no, *grazie*. Who is in the waiting room?"

"I believe it is Colonel Raimondo of the state police with some other men. Do you feel up to seeing them?"

Capuano seemed to come to attention in his hospital bed. "Colonel Raimondo! Here, to see me? Yes, Sister, please bring them in!" Capuano could hear the echoing of muffled voices as the entourage came walking down the hollow corridor toward the ward. He heard the clicking of leather heels, the whipsaw of military trousers, and suddenly they were in the ward headed toward him.

Struggling to push himself up in his bed, the captain of the Atri carabiniere nearly pissed himself with excitement. Colonel Raimondo, here to see him! The legendary Silver Fox who captured the Pizzano gang in Palermo, single handedly fighting Antonio Pizzano to the death.

"Capitano Capuano, you have engaged in an act of great bravery and I came here personally to congratulate you on your heroic deeds." The voice of the Silver Fox echoed with great *basso profondo* dignity. Tall, with carefully coiffed silver hair, gold epaulettes, riding breeches, a pencil-thin moustache, and brilliantly polished cavalry boots, the Colonel cut an impressive figure.

"Thank you, Colonel, for this honor," said Capuano, literally lying at attention as he saluted the Fox gravely.

"Captain," said the Fox slowly, sitting now on the bedside. The Barone Santagatta was my brother-in-law and my closest friend. This man you claimed to be the assassin of the Barone, what is his name?" The Fox leaned in closely to Captain Capuano.

"Rossi, sir, Salvatore Rossi is his name. He's from Atri, sir, a radical anarchist and a troublemaker! I promise you, sir, he will not get away with this heinous crime.

The Silver Fox leaned back, a smiling grimace creasing his face as he reached for Capuano's hand.

"Captain, I am putting you in full charge of this investigation. You know this Salvatore Rossi better than anyone. I want your oath and commitment that you will bring this murderer to justice and his due, which shall be his execution by hanging." The Fox spoke with a solemn expression and a slow cadence to his deep voice. Capuano almost burst with pride and excitement. To be personally handed this singular honor over hundreds, no thousands of other investigators made his head swim with euphoria.

"Colonel Raimondo, I pledge to you today that I shall bring into custody Salvatore Rossi dead or alive. This I swear to you, so help me God!" he declared, his right hand held up in pledge fashion.

The Fox stood adjusting his jacket. "Good, then you will be permanently assigned here in Naples until we bring in Rossi. You can set up your office at our local headquarters on the Piazza DeCesare. Report to me there as soon as you are released from the hospital."

Vito "The Anarchist" Romanelli was released from a holding cell at carabiniere headquarters on the Piazza DeCesare at 5 a.m. on the day following the rally. In actuality, he was kicked out to silence his nonstop ranting on civil rights, his right to a lawyer, and his convoluted personal defense of his actions at the rally. The Silver Fox had ordered Musollini and D'Anunzio to be transported to Rome for further interrogation. Vito made his way home stopping at Dante Timpani's Café, where he was greeted as a returning hero.

"Aayy, Vito, Vito, *ecco nostro eroe!*" beamed Tampini as he turned to the others who were smiling and clapping their hands. "Our hero, Vito the Anarchist!" Timpani scraped a chair to the table as Vito hungrily devoured rolls and coffee. "Vito, you were great yesterday. I was there. I've never seen a crowd like that. Must have been three or four thousand people. They were waiting for you." Vito grunted in disgust. "What about your sister?" asked Timpani.

"What about my sister, Dante? Is she alright?" Vito's forehead was furrowed in anger. He sat back in his chair and stared blankly at Timpani waiting for an answer.

"All I know is what I saw," said Timpani hunched over the table, whispering now and shifting his eyes left and right. "Your sister smashed a carbanierre captain on the head with a cobblestone. He went down like a sack of beans." Vito sat backing his chair with a sigh of relief, covering his eyes with enormous hands.

"Who did she hit? Did you know the guy?"

Dante shook his head, murmuring his reply. "I never saw this cop before, and you know most of them come in to eat and scrounge from time to time. He might have been from out of town. They brought in a lot of cops from Abruzzi. Maybe he came from some town up there."

Vito clasped his hand around Tampini's wrist gripping it tightly. "Thank you, old friend, thank you. Tina must be at her house. I'll go there now."

Tina opened the apartment door as she heard Vito's voice mumbling on the stairs. Vito threw his arms around her kissing her forehead, rocking side to side. "What, are you a cop killer?" mocked Vito with a sardonic smile. "You know, you could wind up in jail. Who's gonna take care of Julia if you're not around?" As he spoke he turned his head to the parlor door and to the wide grinning face of Salvatore. "Giuseppe!" howled Vito, wrapping his arms around Salvatore and lifting him off his feet as he kissed his cheek. "I saw you battling that rat bastard cop that tried to shoot me. Thank you, thank you!"

Salvatore looked sheepishly aside. "Vito, if it weren't for Tina we'd both be dead. She knocked him out with a cobblestone."

Vito turned to Tina with an arched eyebrow. "Aaa, so that was the guy you clobbered. Is he alive or dead?"

"I don't know," said Tina turning her back to Vito as she closed the apartment door. She turned slowly searching for Salvatore's eyes, a questioning look in her own. There was a moment of complete silence.

"What? What?" said Vito, looking first at Tina, then at Salvatore. "C'mon, talk to me," said Vito, "what's the story?"

Salvatore cleared his throat. "The cop she hit is Captain Oreste Capuano," he said. "He was posted in Atri. He knows what I did. He's probably here looking for me."

"Oh, *Madonna mia*," Vito groaned and sank slowly into a kitchen chair. Let me think, let me think.

"*Vito, mio fanciullo, come stai?* How are you my boy?" asked Julia.

"Julia, you look wonderful," said Vito rising from the kitchen chair and walking the three paces to the parlor door. "Let me look at your beautiful face," he declared, cupping her face in his hands.

"*Vattene*, get out you big gorilla." She smiled up at Vito, obviously pleased at the attention. "Tina, make some coffee for Vito. I'm going back to my knitting. Say goodbye before you leave," smiled Julia, waving a finger at him in mock admonition.

"Lovely lady, Julia, good woman. I'll never know how she had a son like Nello. Tina, when was the last time you heard from him?" asked Vito straddling a kitchen chair. Salvatore's eyes searched Tina's face intently.

"I don't know, Vito, it's been months. Every now and then he sends one of his trained dogs over here with an envelope stuffed with money for Julia. But him, who knows."

"All right," said Vito, "we have to figure out what our next move will be. Giuseppe, did you see anyone else that you know with this Captain Capuano?"

"No, at least I didn't see anyone else. There could be other cops with him. I doubt he'd be the only cop from the Atri area."

"That's true, that's true," said Vito, index finger over his lips as he murmured. Tina poured espresso into cups on the kitchen table and carried one into the parlor for Julia. Vito sipped slowly from his cup, Salvatore waiting for words of reassurance.

Tina stood in the parlor doorway with her arms folded, leaning against one side of the archway, and said, "Well, genius, what do we do next?"

"He's got to get out of Naples. He's got to get out of Italy. He's a wanted man," said Vito bringing both palms down smacking his knees. Tina's eyes dropped to the floor, not wanting to look at Salvatore for fear of showing her pained expression.

"So, what do we do?" asked Salvatore.

"Nothing for now," said Vito rising from the table. "I want you to lie low until I can contact some people here and in America, hai capito?"

"I understand," said Salvatore. "Vito, get word to my Uncle Antonio. Let him know I'm all right."

"I will, don't worry. And remember, don't go outside," said Vito as he walked into the parlor to kiss the cheek of the now sleeping Julia.

Chapter 2

THE HUNTER

Captain Oreste Vincente Alfredo Capuano strode with purposeful intent across the vast expanse of the Piazza DeCesare. Boots gleaming in the morning light, navy blue trousers bloused perfectly above the boot tops, razor sharp trouser creases, and a bicorn cap glistening from an oil rub, he walked with an air of authority, his captain insignia burnished to a high importance. Lesser officers passed and saluted with rigid formality. He returned each salute smartly with a nod and a dignified smile. This was his domain, the ancient statues, the spraying fountain—a mountain of Renaissance statuary, an allegory of marble. This was civilization, not that back woods toilet Atri. But on the other hand, it was Atri that got him noticed by his majesty Colonel Raimondo, who in minutes he was about to visit for his new assignment.

He had arrived. The national headquarters for the carabinieri had been in Naples since its formation in 1814. He entered the marble and granite portico, the umbrella to two massive panel doors adorned with gleaming brass hinges and handles, and with the carabinieri insignia emblazoned on each. Two uniformed guards snapped to attention and saluted with a smile and a condescending, "*Buon giorno, Capitano.*" As the doors were pushed open for him, he ascended two stairs to a cathedral-domed atrium with ornate marble flooring. The cream-colored plaster walls were covered with pictorial deeds of the carabinieri from the late 1800s. Awards and flags were draped from balconies and flagpoles.

In the center of the atrium sat a receptionist behind a black desk, ornately engraved in gold with the seal of Italy carved in the front. Capuano removed his cap and walked briskly to the desk and announced, "Captain Oreste Capuano to see Colonel Raimondo." The receptionist was gathering together several stacks of papers together, totally absorbed with her task. Capuano caught his breath when she turned to him.

"*Scusi, Signore Capitano*, I've got to get this paperwork ready for delivery to Rome this afternoon and I'm not doing such a great job of it." She smiled at Capuano. "Can I help you, Captain?"

Capuano estimated she was about twenty-three, a stunning face with full lips framed by bales of golden hair. His eyes reflexively traveled her body. Large pointed breasts, small waist, a broad smile revealing large, even white teeth. "*Scusa, Signorina*, for a moment...." His voice trailed off, unable to focus his conversation. She smiled again, small dimples forming in her cheeks.

"Who are you here to see, Captain?" she asked.

She announced Capuano and gave him directions to a broad marble staircase at the far end of the atrium. He turned as he walked toward the staircase and smiled. She had been watching him. She continued to smile, throwing her head back and licking the corner of her upper lip. Capuano's heels reverberated click,

click, click on the terrazzo flooring as he advanced upon the fortress-like doors to Colonel Raimondo's office. One of the doors swung open revealing Raimondo in full glistening regalia, reeking of pomp and circumstance.

"Aay, Captain, good to see you! Come in, come in."

Capuano came to rigid attention and saluted: "Captain Oreste Capuano reporting for duty, sir." Raimondo smiled and returned the salute.

"You can dispense with the formality, Captain. Relax, a glass of wine? Some brandy?"

"No, thank you, sir, but coffee would be fine."

"Of course. Maria, please bring some coffee for us." A trim woman in her late sixties nodded and left the room. "Come, Oreste, let's talk." Capuano followed Raimondo as he led the way to a leather settee. Antique furnishings, Persian carpets, brass candelabra...an office befitting the head of the service, thought Capuano. "Now, my friend," said Raimondo, motioning his guest to be seated, "let's get down to the business of bringing in this little son of a whore, Salvatore Rossi."

The coffee quietly arrived as they spoke. "Maria..."

"Yes, Colonel?"

"No calls or interruptions for the rest of the morning."

"*Si*, Colonel," as she quietly closed the office door.

"Good woman, Maria. She's been with the service for over twenty years." He took a sip of his coffee. "All right, Oreste, down to business. This is going to be the most important assignment in your career." Raimondo spoke slowly, with dramatic emphasis, clearly relishing his roll as leader and motivator. "I want this son of a bitch. I want him to pay for my brother-in-law's murder. Am I understood, Captain?"

"Yes, Colonel, I understand completely," barked Capuano, bolting from his sitting position to a full stance at attention.

"Good, good," smiled Raimondo patting Capuano's cheek. I can see I have the right man for the job. You're up for the challenge?"

"*Si*, Colonel. I am ready and anxious to begin work. And I promise you, I will not fail."

"You will be headquartered here," continued Raimondo. "Your office will be down the hall from mine with a complete staff and anything you need to launch a full manhunt for this animal, Rossi. Anything you ask for will be provided—manpower, money, anything. I expect a plan on my desk in three days and implementation of that plan as soon as possible. I'm going to assign Lieutenant Coppa to you to act as your aide. He knows his way around headquarters and can facilitate all of your needs. Any questions?"

"No Colonel," snapped Capuano, "I'm just anxious to get started."

"Good. Maria will show you to your office and set you up with administrative staff," said Raimondo, placing his arm around Capuano's shoulder and walking him to the door.

Maria Calise at age sixty-seven was the essence of dignity – small, trim, hair tied tightly in a bun, invariably dressed in black. Never indulging in idle conversation, with an intense and rarely changing facial expression, she had earned the reputation of 'the oracle' at headquarters. She had served three commanders and knew everything there was to know about everything and everyone in the building, indeed, in the entire service. She was widowed at forty-two and since that time had made the service her life's vocation and avocation. To Colonel Raimondo she was indispensable and shared his every confidence.

THE ARRIVAL THE STRUGGLE THE ASCENDANCY

Capuano followed the elderly woman down the long, broad terrazzo corridor, their heel's clicking out of synch with Maria's short, swift steps and Capuano's long military stride. Maria turned the brass knob on the tall oaken door opening into a spacious office. Capuano almost yelped with joy. Surely, his career was now assured. All that remained was to bring in Salvatore Rossi.

"Captain Capuano, sir."

Capuano was brought out of his trance. Turning, he beheld a handsome young lieutenant standing at attention and holding a salute. Capuano returned the salute with rigid formality.

"Yes, Lieutenant, may I help you?"

"Lieutenant Giovanni Coppa reporting for duty, sir." Coppa flashed a friendly smile as he completed his salute.

"Ah, yes, of course. Happy to meet you," said Capuano mustering all of his dignity and self-importance. After all, he thought to himself, a slight smile creasing his mouth, one must look important to be treated as important.

"I've been assigned to you as your adjutant, Sir," Cappo explained in an eager voice, "along with detectives Nino Rocca and Paolo Zincone. Signorina Lucretia Buonano will act as your secretary, sir. Rocca and Zincone will be reporting this afternoon. Miss Buonano will be here at any moment." As he finished the last word the door swung open and a breathless Lucretia Buonano, breasts heaving, blond hair in wisps around her face, stepped into Capuano's office.

"I'm sorry I wasn't here sooner, Captain. I was helping out on the reception desk. One of the regular women is out today, so I did my best at filling in for awhile." She smiled as she spoke, fully aware of the effect she had on men.

"Captain, may I present your secretary, Lucretia Buonano," said Coppa turning one to the other. Capuano took Lucretia's extended hand. It seemed as if electricity coursed through his body when he felt her soft warm flesh.

"No...yes...please, don't worry about it, Miss Buonano." Capuano caught himself before he stammered another word. "I'm still trying to find my way around the office," he explained at last, struggling to look away from her chest.

"I'll set up my desk in the reception area and prepare a system for filing and record keeping. That is, once I find out what we are working on."

"Don't worry, Miss Buonano. By this afternoon I will demystify everything for you." He was speaking now with quiet authority, having regained his lost equilibrium. Capuano watched as Buonano made her way into the outer office, and he thought of his wife and four children at home in the city of L'Aquila.

"Well, Giovanni," continued Capuano, once again feeling in full control, "in my office we'll use first names. Of course, you will always refer to me as Captain. As soon as Rocca and Zincone arrive we will have our first staff meeting, but right now I need a few hours to draft a rough outline of the procedures I plan to use on this project. Can you get me some lunch, Giovanni, or do we go out for it?"

"Neither, Captain," replied the young Lieutenant smartly, "we have a staff officer's dining room on the first level. I'll show it to you. The chef is from Switzerland and he is a genius."

Detective Lieutenants Nino Rocca and Paolo Zincone were veterans of the Naples underworld. They had been partners for six years and had worked their way up into the ranks of respected investigators by working the streets as rookie carabinieri and non-commissioned officers. Both thirty years old, they waited for the appearance of their new commander with yawning indifference. After all, he came from some backwater toilet called Atri, and who the hell knew where that was.

Paolo scraped his chair closer to the conference table and leaned his elbows on its polished surface. Tall, muscular, with a broken nose bent out of shape, he was known as 'il Selvaggio'— the Savage— for his brutal interrogations. Rocca, by contrast, had left the seminary at age eighteen and joined the service. Quiet, analytical, slight of build, he was the problem solver of the pair. Paolo slapped his hand on the conference table.

"What the frig does this guy think we are, shit heels? How long do we have to wait to meet this new genius?"

Nino bolted upright in his chair smiling slightly as he put his finger to his lips. "Shhh...*stare zitto!*" His eyes darted toward the door leading from Capuano's office. "You're gonna get us both in trouble." Paolo waved his hand in disgust and looked out a window.

Captain Oreste Capuano sat behind his new massive desk savoring the moment. He knew he must not fail in his mission. His plan had to work. It would require the assistance and confidence of a solid team. Most importantly, they had to respect him and admire him. Let them wait, he thought, reviewing his plan step by step. Besides, he told himself, this would set the tone. After all, I'm the commander and they must learn from the beginning who is in charge. At last he felt ready. He stood, straightening his tie and adjusting his jacket. He gripped the brass knob, pushed opened the door, and strode into the adjoining room.

Zincone, Rocca, and Coppa all sprang stiffly to attention. Lucretia Buonano sat demurely, legs crossed, pad and pen in hand ready to take notes.

"At ease, gentlemen. We will from this moment forward conduct ourselves informally, of course with the exception of when we are in the company of ranking officers." Capuano was impressed with himself, his delivery, form, he was a leader of men.

"Excuse me, Captain," said Giovanni, stepping forward, "may I introduce detectives Lieutenant Nino Rocca and Paolo Zincone." Capuano shook their hands with a firm grip.

"I've heard a lot about you two. I'm happy to have you on this investigation. As you know, the Colonel has given the case the highest priority and we are to be denied nothing that will make our task go quickly and efficiently—money, people, equipment... nothing."

Lucretia uncrossed and crossed her legs. Several strands of blond hair fell across her face. Capuano was drawn to look at her as she brushed them away.

"Gentlemen," he continued, "this is the plan that I have conceived, the plan that will deliver Salvatore Rossi into our hands. It is my belief that Rossi is still in Naples, hiding somewhere, perhaps in the *Spaccanapoli* with his anarchist friends. We want him alive, remember this. We want him alive to stand trial and be hung for the heinous crime he has committed." Capuano referred to a large map of Naples affixed to a blackboard. "We will divide the city into twenty major grids and each major grid will be further divided into ten minor grids. You will assemble a team of twenty men each. Zincone, you will start at the southern end and work toward the middle of the city. Every house, every business, every church, *everything* must be searched. Everyone will be interrogated. You will assign people to the docks in street clothes. I want every avenue of escape covered. You have informants, use them. Money is no object. We have a drawing of Rossi. It is an exact likeness. It also lists his height, weight, eye color, and other information you will need. We have copies for everyone connected with the search. You will work grid by grid. As each minor grid is completed, we will check it off until we have completed a major grid. In this way we will miss nothing. Every Wednesday morning and every Friday morning we will meet here at 0800 hours for a status report. Our first meeting will be in one week."

Zincone and Rocca looked at each other in disbelief. "But Captain," began Zincone, "we need to assemble our teams…"

Capuano cut him off abruptly with a wave of his hand. "Gentlemen, that's an order. Carry it out. I don't care if you work twenty hours a day. Carry it out!"

The two officers saluted smartly and left Capuano's office, Zincone shaking his head in resignation.

"Will you be needing anything else, Captain?" Giovanni Coppa asked.

"No, Giovanni, you can go, but check back with me first thing in the morning. I want to take a tour of the docks."

"*Si, Capitano.* I'll requisition a vehicle now and I'll be here right after breakfast tomorrow morning." Giovanni saluted Capuano, flashed his boyish smile, and nodded toward Lucretia. "*Signorina*," he said, taking his leave and stepping into the corridor.

"Will you be needing me for anything else today, Captain?" asked Lucretia with a playful tilt to her head, hair falling over one eye. Capuano smiled, broadly aware of some hint of suggestiveness.

He was exulting in the way he had just conducted his staff meeting. He felt gigantic, a force of life. Now this force was focused solely on the lone figure of Lucretia Buonano, and he felt something within him stir at the sight of this beautiful young woman so obviously baiting him.

"No, *Signorina*, not right now, but soon." Lucretia arched her eyebrows and walked slowly toward the door, looking over her shoulder at Capuano. "*Signorina...*"

She stopped in the doorway, her back still to the room. "Yes, Captain?"

"You are one of the most beautiful woman I have ever seen in my entire life. You absolutely decompose me."

"Why, Captain, that is so very sweet of you to say that. Thank you very much."

Capuano's breath came a little faster. "I'll be seeing you in the morning, then?"

"*Si*, Captain, in the morning. Lucretia bent down to adjust a shoe strap. The sight of her heart-shaped buttocks caused Capuano to gasp audibly. "Good night, Captain."

"Good night, Lucretia." Capuano knew it was only a matter of time before he made love to this woman. He turned to his desk and placed the picture of his family in the bottom drawer.

Chapter 3

THE HUNTED

A ngela Mia briskly entered the ancient apartment building. From each hand hung a cloth bag filled with cheeses, prosciutto, olives, wine, olive oil, eggs, and bread. In spite of her obvious age, the wiry, neatly dressed woman quickly ascended the stairs with no noticeable fatigue. She reached the landing on the fifth level and called out, "*Julia, Julia, apri la porta!* Open the door!" There was no answer.

Angela Mia turned the doorknob and entered the apartment. Placing the grocery bags on the kitchen table she walked with familiarity into the small parlor where her sister slept soundly in her chair, knitting needles in her lap and a small empty glass on a table next to her. "*Julia, svegliate.*"

Julia's eyes opened slowly, staring for a moment as recognition set in. She opened her arms, her mouth breaking into a partially toothless smile. "*Oh, Angela Mia, mia bella sorella!* I'm so happy you came. How are you?" Julia arose from her chair to embrace Angela Mia. They hugged and kissed one another, and Julia held her sister's hand as they walked into the kitchen. "So tell me," Julia began again, "how are you, my dearest?"

"Fine sister, fine. I work too hard, don't make enough money, and my daughter's not married yet, but there's still time and you know she's very beautiful. Other than that, life is about the same as it has been since Armando died twenty-five years ago." "Has it been that long, Angela Mia?"

"Yes, it has, but it seems as if it were only yesterday." Julia nodded her head in sympathy as she brought coffee to the table. "Tell me, sister," continued Angela Mia, taking a cup in her hand, "how have you been? Is Tina working? How have you been feeling? You know, I would like it much better if you didn't drink so much wine."

The sound of laughter and footsteps on the landing turned their heads to the door as the knob turned and the door burst open to reveal Tina looking over her shoulder at Salvatore, both laughing as if in a childish moment. Tina turned, mouth dropping open in wide-eyed surprise.

"Angela Mia!" Tina rushed to embrace her aunt. They stood and hugged for a long moment. Tina held her at arms length. "How have you been, Auntie, it's been months."

"I know, sweetheart. I wish we lived a little closer. It would make it a lot simpler to get together."

"How's my beautiful cousin? Has she found anyone she can stand yet?"

"You know your cousin. She's a little coquette. Just when the boy thinks he has her she drops him!" They both laughed knowingly. Salvatore stood awkwardly in the open doorway, smiling expectantly. Angela Mia took in his manly frame and good looks, asking, "And who is this handsome young man?"

"Oh, I'm sorry, Auntie." There was an excited edge to Tina's voice. I would like you to meet Salvatore…" Tina caught herself and threw her arms up in mock amazement. "What am I saying!"

Salvatore stepped forward, hand extended. "*Mi chiamo Giuseppe Ferraio, Signora, piacere della conoscenza.*" My name is Joseph Smith, Signora. It is a pleasure to make your acquaintance, Salvatore said smiling, exposing large white even teeth.

"Ah, Giuseppe, are you sure it is not Salvatore?"

"I'm sorry, Auntie," said Tina, face fully flushed. "Just tongue-tied, I guess." She exchanged a side-glance with Salvatore, a glimmer of a smile on her lips.

"Well, Giuseppe, what do you do here in Naples?" asked Angela Mia. "I don't think I've seen you before."

Salvatore eased into a kitchen chair. Tina stood nervously with her hands clasped in front of her. "I'm a friend of Tina's brother, Vito. I'm visiting for a while. I have some family here. It's more like a holiday. I don't get to Naples often."

Angela Mia studied Salvatore's face and hands. "Well, I'm glad you're keeping company with Tina. Vito will only get you locked up in jail, that scoundrel," said Angela Mia with obvious affection in her voice. "You're staying with the anarchist then," a prying shadow to her voice.

Salvatore hesitated a second too long. "Yes, I am. He's a good cook when he's home."

Angela Mia continued studying Salvatore. "Where do you live, Giuseppe Ferraio?" asked the old woman, the prying shadow still in her voice.

"In the Abbruzzo, Signora, L'Acquila."

"Aah, L'Acquila, I've been there. A good-sized town. Are all the Ferraios from L'Acquila, Giuseppe?"

"All that I know of," smiled Salvatore.

"Well, enjoy your holiday in Naples, Giuseppe, and I hope to see you again soon," said Angela Mia as she arose from the kitchen table signaling her departure.

"*Dammi un bacio, Angela Mia.*" Give me a kiss, said Julia, "and don't be such a stranger."

"I will, I will sister. I promise." She kissed and hugged Tina good-bye, paused and extended her hand to Salvatore. "Good-bye, Giuseppe."

"Good-bye, Signora."

Julia returned to her parlor smiling, happy to have seen her younger sister. Placing her knitting on her lap, she called to Tina. "*Tina, portami un bicchiere di vino, per piacere.*" Julia sipped her wine and in a matter of minutes was once again asleep.

Salvatore drummed his fingers on the kitchen tabletop. "She seems like a very intelligent woman. She wasn't just asking curious questions, she was almost interrogating me". He rubbed his hands across his face. "Does she work? What does she do?"

Tina sat down at the kitchen table. "I don't know for sure. She really doesn't talk much about herself. I think she works for the city in some office…administration, bookkeeper, I'm not certain."

Salvatore leaned back in his chair, crossing his arms over his chest. "Do you think she suspects anything?"

Tina smiled reassuringly. "How could she, she just met you and I can tell she likes you."

"Tina." Julia called from her parlor.

"*Si, Mamma.*"

"*Aiutomi a andare aletto, mi sento un po' male.* Help me to bed, I feel a little sick."

Tina lifted Julia's feet into her bed, covering her with a light blanket and handing her a set of worn rosary beads.

"Is she all right?" asked Salvatore, concern in his voice.

Tina smiled, "She's fine, she drinks too much wine and she doesn't eat enough. Actually, she has the constitution of a horse." They both laughed, Salvatore nodding his head in understanding.

Salvatore leaned forward in his chair. "Tina, you are a remarkable woman. You're beautiful, intelligent, what happened to you and your husband?"

Tina crossed her legs, looking off into a corner of the room. "We were kids. He was exciting, always doing things the other young guys wouldn't dream of doing. He was fun; he was the first and only man I ever made love with. I was twenty-years old, he was twenty-two. We had a small wedding. My mother and father were both alive at the time. My father always knew him for what he was; he called him a buccaneer, a pirate. He was always with a gang of friends. He had a job as a waiter at the Excelsior Hotel; we lived with Julia on the other side of the city.

"At first we were typical newlyweds. It didn't last long. He would be out all night with his friends, he quit his job. He said he was never going to serve another fat German tourist again as long as he lived. He's big; he's tough. It didn't take long for the local mafia don to take notice of him. He started hanging out with the mafia people. He did small things for them, then bigger things. Little by little he gained a reputation as a tough, ruthless man. They sent him to Sicily to do a job. It seems one of the mafia *capi* was taking a little too much for his cut of the pie and he told everyone to go and screw themselves. His name was Nicandro 'The Animal' Stefano. He had a gang of renegades that used to gather at a bar just off the Via di Mare on the waterfront. Nello walked in one Wednesday afternoon and killed the Animal and six of his gang in cold blood. His reputation was sealed. He came back to Naples a mafia hero. He was rewarded with money and the status of *capo*.

"It was never much of a marriage. I loved him and he loved his freedom. Hanging out with his friends. And there were women, a lot of women. I stopped sleeping with him. I didn't want to be with a man, a man who was my husband who had been sleeping with who knows how many sluts." Tina arose from the kitchen table not looking at Salvatore. Salvatore's eyes followed her every movement as she leaned against the small kitchen sink staring off into space.

"Tell me what else happened," Salvatore said in a matter of fact tone. Tina smiled, resigned to her fate.

"So, you want my life story? I'll tell you my life story." She reached for two glasses and the half-empty bottle of wine. From the cupboard she withdrew an open pack of French cigarettes. She slowly seated herself as she lit a cigarette. Salvatore poured two glasses of wine.

"I didn't know you smoked."

"I don't normally, only when I talk about depressing things, and Nello is a depressing thing."

"What happened after his return to Naples?" Salvatore leaned forward, both elbows resting on the table.

"He expected me to be there for him when he wanted me. He beat me a few times. Julia tried to intervene, but nothing was going to stop him from doing what he wanted to do. I ran away one night and wound up at Vito's house. He was enraged when he saw the bruises on my face. I had all I could do to stop him from looking for Nello to confront him and take revenge.

"I stayed at Vito's that night. The next morning very early there was a pounding on the door. Vito leapt from bed, grasped his Lupari shotgun, looked out a side window and started cursing. He ran for the door, threw it open and slammed the muzzle into Nello's face. Nello turned pale and raised his hands. Vito was so enraged he was choking on his words and mucous was dripping from his nose. 'You fucken' whore master, you fucken' gutter rat, I'm going to kill you today.' He was screaming like a madman." Tina chuckled and took a long drag on her cigarette.

"I didn't want Nello dead. I didn't want Vito in trouble. I knew I couldn't physically stop him. I had to do something quickly. 'He's a worthless pig,' Vito snarled, and spit in Nellos face. 'What, do you think I'm afraid of you, you asshole! I'm crazier than you and don't give a shit what happens to me.' Then Vito pushed the Lupari deeper into Nello's face.

"I said, 'Vito, Vito please, wait there's something you need to know, it's important.'

'What, what do you have to tell me,' he yelled. Suddenly, there was a moment of silence, and I said to him in a steady voice, 'If you kill him, you kill the father of my baby.'

"Vito's shoulders drooped, his face lost all expression. He backed a pace away from Nello, lowered the Lupari, and turned and walked into the apartment, staring at the floor. I closed the door behind Vito and turned to Nello. 'Everything he said about you was true,' I told him. Nello had regained his calm. 'I know,

I know it is true,' he said. 'I do what I have to do. I make no excuses. It's all I know how to do. I make no apologies for my style of life to anyone. I wish you had married a lawyer, an accountant, a good man—someone who would appreciate you.' Nello stepped forward to embrace me, but I moved back and folded my arms across my chest. He just looked at me and in a quiet voice he asked, 'Is it true what you told Vito? Tell me the truth, I need to know.'"

Tina suddenly broke off her story, arose from the table, and leaned against the kitchen counter.

"And what did you respond?" asked Salvatore in a voice eager for an answer.

"I told him the truth, that I had lied to save his worthless life. He nodded, turned and walked out of my life. Vito never mentioned the incident again. I think he knew all along that I had fabricated the pregnancy story. I choose to live here with Julia; she needs me. I work for a seamstress three or four days a week. Jobs are tough to find in Naples, you know."

Salvatore nodded his head. He stood and walked the two paces to the kitchen counter. He reached for her hands and kissed them as he looked into her eyes. "You are like no one I've ever met in my entire life." Tina laughed softly, looking into Salvatore's warm eyes. "Is this the part where you kiss me?" mocked Tina.

Their lips devoured one another. He took her standing in the kitchen, Tina with one foot placed on a chair. The arousal was so intense and euphoric that in a matter of minutes they exploded in climax together. They giggled like children and clung to one another. "I love you, Tina Valetta, I've loved you from the moment I saw you on my first day in Naples."

Tina's arms were around Salvatore's neck. "You fall in love easily, Salvatore. Are there any girls in Atri who you also fell in love with after making love to them?"

"No, there's no girl in Atri who I love," said Salvatore seriously. "Do you have feelings for me Tina, tell me."

"Sleep in my bed tonight, my sweet boy," said Tina, a subtle mocking tone in her voice.

"What about Julia?" said Salvatore in a lowered voice.

Tina's face glowed with girlish delight. "Don't worry," she said, running her palm gently down her lover's cheek. "She sleeps long and deep from all of the wine she drinks!"

For the next two weeks they made love every day, either in the afternoon or in the evening when Julia was asleep. Tina displayed a passion that drove Salvatore to heights of furious, powerful lovemaking. Vito came by once or twice a week to visit and update Salvatore on what had become a full-scale manhunt for the fugitive, Salvatore Rossi. He cautioned Salvatore to stay indoors until he could make arrangements to get him out of Naples. Forced to remain in the small apartment, Salvatore's boredom was made enjoyable by the incessant attention of Tina and the wonderful peasant dishes that Julia or Tina prepared every evening.

"Salvatore," called Tina, "come eat, the pasta is ready!" The fragrant aroma of warm garlic and olive oil wafted through the apartment. "Wake Julia, please."

"Tina," called Salvatore from the parlor.

"Yes, what is it?"

"Come here for a minute, Julia doesn't look good and I can't wake her up."

Tina knelt beside Julia's rocker and felt her cheeks. "She has a fever. Help me get her into bed."

Salvatore picked up the sleeping Julia and placed her gently on their bed. "What is it?" he asked.

"I don't know," said Tina. "This has happened before. She needs a compound from Zanni's pharmacia. He makes a medicine for her."

"I'll get it," said Salvatore, rising from the bedside. "Where is the pharmacia?"

"No, you can't go. You heard what Vito said, you're a hunted man in Naples."

"Don't worry about me. I'm like a cat, no one will see me. Besides, you need to stay with Julia, you know what to do. And by the way, keep the pasta hot!" smiled Salvatore reassuringly.

"I'll write a note to Zanni. I know he's open till seven. I'll tell him you're a nephew of Julia's. He's a nice man, there shouldn't be any problem." Tina scribbled a note and handed it to Salvatore. "The pharmacia is three streets over on a corner, you can't miss it. And please be careful. Don't talk to anyone." Salvatore took the note and kissed Tina lightly on the lips.

"Stop worrying," said Salvatore as he quietly left the apartment.

Nino Rocca and Paolo Zincone sat stone faced at the conference table, eyes riveted on Captain Capuano, their stomach's churning.

"Two goddamned weeks and we have nothing, absolutely nothing! What did this guy do, disappear into thin air? Or is it that you two with two hundred other cops can't find your asses with your own hands!" Capuano turned in disgust and looked out his office window, then returned his gaze to Rocca and Zincone. "Look we're under an enormous amount of pressure. Raimondo has a hard on for this guy Rossi, and guess who's in charge of this investigation! All right, Zincone, tell me where we are right now."

Zincone rifled through some papers on the conference table before him. "My team has covered ten grids to date, we're working twelve-hour days. We have his picture in every tratoria, meat market, bakery, every business in every grid we covered to date."

"And you, Rocca?"

"Captain, we also covered ten grids and did exactly the same things Zincone has done. None of our informants has any information we can use—not even bad information."

"All right, all right," said Capuano throwing his hands in the air. "Next week same time. Remember, no leaves, no time off for anyone on this case. Am I understood?"

"Yes, Captain," said Zincone and Rocca in unison as they rose from the conference table and rushed out of the office.

Capuano turned to see Lucretia sitting at her desk in the outer office, long blond hair draped over one eye. She sensed his presence and looked up smiling. "Ah, Lucretia, thought you'd be gone by now," said Capuano walking toward her and returning the smile. Lucretia leaned back in her chair, stretched her arms and yawned, pushing her chest out against a high-collared white starched shirt.

"Oh, excuse me, Captain, it's been a long day," she sighed. Capuano's nostrils flared, his eyes glued to her breasts. "Captain?" said Lucretia in an inquiring tone.

Capuano snapped out of his trance. He shuffled his feet and placed his hands behind his back. "Listen, Lucretia." There was a slight tremor to his voice. "Would you have an early dinner with me? I, uh, really don't like eating alone and, well, I know a nice little place not far from here. We could walk, if that's all right with you."

Lucretia stood and adjusted her skirt. "Why Captain, I would be happy and proud to have dinner with you."

Capuano beamed with joy.

They arrived at La Vongola, a small family-run restaurant on the bay of Naples. The staff knew Capuano as a steady diner, and with professional instinct they seated him and his guest at a secluded table in a quiet corner. Menus arrived, a bottle of the best house wine was brought, compliments of the owner. The baked whitefish proved exquisite, the service was impeccable and anonymous. Capuano told his life story over dinner, his ambitions, his hopes, his dreams. Lucretia, eyes glimmering in candlelight, sat entranced, full heart-shaped lips now smiling, now oohing and aahing, captivating Capuano with her beauty.

"*Signorina*, shall we stroll along the docks for a while," asked Capuano.

"Why, yes, Captain, I'd like that." They strolled the wooden planking of the dock, the scent of salt air, fish, and tar hanging in the early evening air. Hundreds of large and small boats bobbed at anchor, awaiting their masters at dawn. They made small talk, Capuano preoccupied with the possibilities of the evening.

Their hands brushed. Her small hand folded into his. They walked slowly, silently, Capuano's stomach full of butterflies, heart beating rapidly. Finally he blurted out, "Lucretia, would you like to see where I live? I mean, can I offer you an after dinner liquor at my apartment? It's only minutes away and it's still early." There was a pleading hopefulness in his voice, and at that moment he felt like a fool.

"I'd love to see your apartment, Captain." Lucretia squeezed Capuano's hand as she spoke. Capuano tightened his buttocks with joy as he turned and headed for his apartment.

Raimondo had seen to it that Capuano would lack for nothing in his search for Rossi. The apartment was within ten minutes walking distance from headquarters on the second floor of a building housing an antique shop on the first level—two large bedrooms, a marble bathroom with the latest in fixtures, and electrical lighting throughout. A spacious kitchen pantry with ice cabinets for refrigeration made it one of the better apartments in Naples.

Capuano's hands trembled as he unlocked the apartment door; his heart beat rapidly as he flicked on the light. "*Bella, Signorina.*" He bowed majestically. "Allow me to show you my abode. Well, what do you think," he asked, beginning to feel more confident, "is it grand enough for me?"

Lucretia sat on a silken covered Louis XIV sofa in the expansive living room. "Why, Captain, I think it's only befitting a man of your stature." She smiled and looked up at Capuano with an expression of total, serene vulnerability.

"Well, let me get us a glass of Asti Spumante. I just happen to have some in the icebox. Don't move, I'll be right back." Alone in the kitchen, Capuano fumbled for glasses, pulled desperately at the stubborn cork, and struggled to calm himself before returning to the living room. As he crossed the threshold, glasses in hand, he froze in mid-step and stopped breathing. Lucretia was naked on the sofa, her soft golden curls spread out upon two silk pillows, left knee crossed over right knee. Capuano took in her flawless rounded bottom and moistened smiling lips. Not a word was spoken.

He placed the wine on a coffee table and fell to his knees, his face sliding between Lucretia's warm pink breasts. "I want all of you in my mouth," groaned Capuano as he searched for Lucretia's nipples with his tongue. "I love you, I love you, Lucretia."

"Oh, now my lover, now," moaned Lucretia as she wrapped one leg around Capuano's back.

Salvatore left the building just as dusk was settling. As he reached the street, he paused for a moment to get his bearings. He turned right and approached the corner, then turned left along a narrow street, keeping close to the tenement buildings as he made his way in the half-darkness. The neighborhood was awake with activity—mothers calling, kitchen pans clanking, voices arguing, voices laughing.... Another block, his senses alert, and he was there. A small bell jingled his arrival. A dozen gas lamps brightened the interior, and the pungent aroma of herbs, spices, and elixirs filled the air.

"May I help you, young man?" The wrinkled face of the pharmacist conveyed an expression of almost fatherly concern.

"*Si, Signore*," smiled Salvatore as he handed the note to Zanni. The old man donned his spectacles, scanned the note, and mumbled "*Aspetta un minuto*," as he retired to the rear of the pharmacy. Alone in the shop, Salvatore took in the well-stocked shelves, the many bottles of various colored liquids, the calendar of feast days tacked to the wall just above the cash drawer. And then he saw it—his own likeness in a line drawing, together with his name, and age. Nervously, he paced before the pharmacy counter. Had he been recognized? Should he leave? Zanni emerged from the rear of the store.

"All set young man," said Zanni. "Two tablespoons of this concoction four times a day. It will take a while, but she'll be all right."

Salvatore paid with a warm "*grazie*" and hurriedly left the store. If there had been recognition, the pharmacist certainly hadn't shown any.

Julia's fever had heightened; her forehead was beaded with sweat. Salvatore uncorked the bottle and handed it to Tina. She held the spoonful of tonic to Julia's lips and forced her to take it into her mouth.

"Thank you, Salvatore, without this who knows what would happen to her. You know, at her age I worry about every little thing that she complains about." Tina sat by Julia's side with a basin of cold water and alcohol, swabbing Julia's forehead and face with a small face cloth to bring down her temperature.

"Tina," said Salvatore softly, "please, get some rest. I'll watch Julia, just show me how much alcohol to mix with the water.

Tina stood and kissed Salvatore lightly on the lips. "You're a good man, Salvatore Rossi. Come, I'll show."

Salvatore stayed awake the entire evening, swabbing Julia's forehead, neck, and face until finally at dawn Julia's fever broke.

"Why didn't you wake me?" scolded Tina as she padded barefoot into the bedroom just as the sun came up over Naples.

"You looked so peaceful sleeping. Besides, I think the fever is down."

Tina placed her hand on Julia's forehead. "Yes, thank God it's almost gone. C'mon, doctor Rossi," laughed Tina, "I'll make you some breakfast. You've earned it."

They lingered over coffee and rolls. "Salvatore, I think Julia will be all right. I'll fix her some pastina and egg, if she's back to normal. I need to go to work today. Can you stay with her and watch her?"

Salvatore chuckled. "Why, where do you think I'll be going, to visit my lawyer? Don't worry, I'll be busy writing some letters to my mother and Antonio. By the way, do you think you could stop at Vito's and check to see if I have any mail from Atri?"

"Of course I will," said Tina, "if my crazy brother is home. With him you never know."

"Tinahhhh!" The robust voice of Julia confirmed her return to the living.

Nino Rocha pounded up the stairs, threw open the huge oaken door, and stood at the threshold gasping for breath. Capuano turned from a wall map, a startled look on his face.

"Well Lieutenant? What's so important?"

"We know where the son of a bitch is!" Rocha entered the office smiling broadly.

Capuano could not contain himself. "Where? Where is he?"

"He's somewhere in the vicinity of Zanni's pharmacia, in that jungle of tenements in the north end of the district."

"Wait a minute," said Capuano, his elation waning as quickly as it had risen. "What do you mean 'somewhere'?" He slowly sat down, never losing eye contact with Rocha.

"We had his picture in Zanni's pharmacia," the policeman explained, speaking quickly. "Zanni recognized him right away, as soon as he walked in. He had a note for some medicine for…" Rocha fumbled for his notebook and flipped to the right page. "Ah, yes, ah…Jesus, I can't read my own writing! I guess I was so excited…the medicine was for Julia Valetta, she's an old woman who lives in the area. She's also the mother of the mafia capo who killed Stefano the Animal in his bar about two years ago. Okay if I smoke, Capt?"

"Of course, Nino." Capuano leaned back in his chair, fingers forming a spire touching the tip of his nose. "Do you have any idea where she lives?" he asked, his voice measured and low.

"No, Captain, but it's a contained area. The whole area is sort of a pocket. If we bring in a group of our people for a house to house, I'm sure we'll trap him." Capuano tapped his fingers together, eyelids half closed. The silence in the room became deafening. "Well, Captain, do I have a go ahead?" Rocca leaned forward, cigarette dangling from his mouth.

Capuano rose and walked to the map of Naples on his wall. "Nino, show me the area where you assume he is."

Rocca approached, his eyes squinting, bending down to look at the bottom of the map. He removed the cigarette from his mouth. "Right there, in this pocket, Capt." His finger drew a 'V' shape in one corner of the map. Capuano pondered the map, rubbing his chin. His adrenaline was rushing. He had to urinate. The feeling was delicious.

"There must be two or three hundred tenements in that enclave," he murmured almost to himself.

Rocca nodded. "Yes, Captain, but we can flush him out with enough people."

"No," said Capuano, waving an extended finger in the air. No, here's what we're going to do." He backed away from the map to pick up a pointer. "We'll have our people in street clothes near the pharmacia and patrolling each street as inconspicuously as possible. Every major entrance or exit form the area will have a least two men posted. Everyone will have Rossi's picture. We will work twelve-hour shifts, no days off. If we do a house to house he could find out about it and escape. You know how people in that slum talk."

"Captain, I think you're right," said Rocca as he scratched at the back of his neck. "I'll fill Paolo in and we'll implement the plan by this evening."

Capuano placed his hands on the younger man's shoulders. Their eyes met. "Don't fail me, Rocca," he said, almost in a whisper, "we have him in our grasp."

"'Don't worry, my Captain," responded Rocca, stiffening to a smart salute, "we won't let you down!"

Tina heard the footfalls first. "Who's coming here at this time?" she said in a lowered tone of voice, forehead wrinkled in a frown. Salvatore stopped writing, pencil in air, listening to the echoing stairwell. Before they could move, a knock came softly on the apartment door. Tina rose cautiously, approaching the door.

"*Chi é?*" she asked, motioning Salvatore into Julia's bedroom.

"*Tina, cara mia, sono Io, Angela Mia.*"

Tina exhaled and ran to open the door. Salvatore emerged at the doorway of the bedroom where Julia slept soundly. Tina threw her arms around the midnight visitor.

"Angela, what are you doing out so late and alone? It must be midnight."

Angela Mia seated herself at the kitchen table. Salvatore bent down to kiss her cheek.

"I like that, Salvatore, you're a very respectable young man."

"No, Auntie," protested Tina unconvincingly, "it's Giuseppe, not Salvatore." Angela Mia looked at both of them, the hint of a sad smile on her face.

"Listen to me, both of you. That's why I'm here. Don't ask me any questions. I can't answer any, just do as I say." Tina and Salvatore looked at one another in wide-eyed amazement. "The police know you're here. The Naples police force and the Carabinieri have the area surrounded with plainclothes men. They're waiting for you to show your face on the street and when you do they will arrest you. When you went to Zanni's pharmacia two nights ago he recognized you and immediately ran to one of the detectives working on your investigation."

Salvatore fell into a kitchen chair, his face buried in his hands. Tina moved to his side and began rubbing his neck.

"How do you know all these things?" Tina's voice was flat, monotone.

"I told you sweetheart, I can't tell you anything. It's best for you not to know." Angela Mia stood, placing the palms of her hands on the kitchen table and staring first at Salvatore and then at Tina. "This is what you will do to escape this trap they have set for you. Tomorrow morning at seven Mariani's funeral home will send a hearse here to pick up a dead person. No one knows who lives in most of these tenements, and no one cares. That dead person will be you, Salvatore. They will carry you out and deliver you to the funeral home. When you arrive there will be someone there to give you further instructions."

"Where will they take me?"

"I don't know. Don't worry, these people are professionals at what they do." Salvatore nodded grimly. "Now I must go home, I'm tired and this city is full of crazy people."

"Auntie, let me walk you home, please," said Tina reaching for a sweater.

"No, no sweetheart. Mr. Beretta will accompany me home." Angela Mia smiled as she spoke. Tina shook her head quizzically.

"Who is Mr. Beretta?"

Angela Mia opened her large purse and removed a 32-caliber pistol. "And don't you worry, I know how to use it," she laughed. She kissed Tina and Salvatore and then was gone, footsteps fading into the dark street.

Salvatore shook his head in amazement. "How does she know these things? Is she right?" He rose from the table, pacing the floor. "Tina, what will become of me? What about my mother? What about you, I love you! I don't want to leave you."

Tina silenced his worries with her lips. She looked steadily into his eyes. "First, if she said there's a trap waiting for you, she knows, she's not a silly woman. Second, I'll visit your mother and reassure her that you are all right. Third, we will never be apart. I love you more than anything in the world, and no matter what, we will be together always. And number four, I want to carry your baby." Salvatore pulled her to him and kissed her neck and mouth. "Can we start number four now?" he whispered and pressed her against the kitchen counter.

Salvatore awoke at five. He lay motionless, staring at the rough ceiling. He turned to Tina, resting his head in his hand. He watched Tina's chest rise and fall with each breath. Tina's eyes fluttered; she sensed Salvatore's gaze.

"What are you looking at, little boy? Didn't you see enough of me last night?" Tina sat upright, pulling the sheet above her nakedness, smiling coquettishly.

Salvatore reached for her, pulling her warm naked body to his own. "I want to make sure we made a baby last night," he said in a husky voice.

Tina's mouth devoured Salvatore's. She straddled his hips. Reaching for his erect penis and sliding onto it they rocked in unison, exploding in orgasm together. They both muffled a chuckle of euphoria and hugged one another.

"What was that called," said Tina laughing lowly, "an insurance fuck?"

Salvatore pulled her to him for a long, warm kiss.

"C'mon," urged Tina. "Mariani's people will be here in an hour, and you have to be ready to go."

The clattering of hooves on stone and the clanking of brass ornamentation awakened a number of first-floor tenants. On the street the black lacquered hearse was lettered in gold, discreetly announcing Mariani Mortuary. The carriage was windowless, with two paneled doors at the rear and an open landau cab with seating for eight up front. Mariani himself was driving, with four assistants as passengers. The hearse came to a clattering halt in front of the apartment building, sounds echoing off the canyon-like tenements. The assistants leaped down, scurrying to the rear of the hearse with Mariani fast behind.

"*Subito, subito*, get the box up the stairs." The assistants quickly pulled the simple pine box from the hearse and hurriedly ascended to the top landing. Tina opened the apartment door to greet them. Mariani was in the lead.

"*Signorina*, I'm here for the body," said the stately mortician with a courteous bow.

"*Buon giorno, Signore Mariani*," smiled Tina. "Here is the body." Salvatore stepped forward and grasped Mariani's hand.

"Good, good my young friend. Get in the box and don't even breathe. I'll take care of everything else." The last thing Salvatore saw before the box was screwed shut was Tina mouthing the words "I love you."

Salvatore weighed well over two hundred pounds. Mariani's burly crew struggled down the narrow stairwell, cursing all the way. Inside the coffin, Salvatore was tossed around like a doll. They emerged from the stairwell onto the street to be confronted by Nino Rocca and two plainclothes policemen. The five men froze in their tracks, staring at Rocca.

"Aay, Mr. Mariani, you got another customer," said Rocca unsmilingly. "Who is it?"

Mariani needed time to think. "Put the body down, boys, take a break." The men moved to the rear of the hearse, happy to be away from the policemen. Mariani turned to face Rocca and his question.

"You want to show me some identification, Officer? These are very personal matters." His voice was clear, unwavering.

Rocca drew his badge from a coat pocket, glaring at Mariani with contempt. The mortician appeared to study the badge, then took a step back.

"A pleasure to meet you, Lieutenant Rocca, "said Mariani with a slight bow. "How may I help you?"

"Who's in the box?" snapped Rocca, pointing at the coffin that now rested on the rough cobbled street.

"Aah, Lieutenant, this is Attilio Gizzarelli, he was eighty-three years old, lived on the second floor here. He died late last night."

Rocca nodded his head, listening for a hint of nervousness, anxiety.

"Open the box, undertaker, I want a look."

Mariani gave breath to a faint sigh, just audible. "Lieutenant, we have the body in an oil cloth bag. The doctor said it looked like small pox. He wasn't sure. If you want to look inside, I'll give you the tools, but I'm not going to expose myself or my men to the body again until we can disinfect it. I'm sorry." Mariani turned to his men and waved a hand in the air. "Roberto, bring the tools so the Lieutenant can examine the body."

Rocca stood unmoving, a look of bewilderment spreading across his dull face. Finally, in a half stutter, he shouted "No, no, that's all right. Just get this fucking body out of here!"

"Of course, Lieutenant, I understand, and thank you. Oh, by the way, let me give you some business cards in case you should ever need our services." Rocca took the cards halfheartedly and motioned Mariani away. He waited, hands on hips, as the hearse pulled away, the four black, sleek cantering horses clattering over the cobblestone and gravel. Mariani turned and gave a final wave of his grey gloved hand.

"All right, men, back to patrolling the streets," said Rocca stifling a yawn and massaging his lower back with his other hand. This was going to be a long, drawn out hunt, he thought.

The carriage rocked wildly side to side on the rough road leading to the funeral home. Salvatore felt bruised and battered, he needed to urinate, he was starving, and he was completely helpless. It seemed as though the carriage would go on forever when suddenly it slowed and came to a stop. The doors were flung open and Salvatore could hear voices as the casket was pulled from the hearse. He felt himself being carried on flat terrain and then tilted downward as the bearers descended a staircase, muttering and cursing.

"All right, boys, place it right here on the floor next to the wall." It was the voice of Mariani. Voices and footsteps receded beyond hearing, a door slammed shut, and he knew he was alone. A moment later a door opened and the sound of multiple footsteps approached the casket. The cover to the casket was being pried off, falling to the floor with a heavy thud. Salvatore sat upright to the glare of gas lamps illuminating the room with harsh yellow light. He stared at Mariani questioningly. Two sullen-faced figures in spats and Borsolino hats seemed to be studying him.

Mariani beamed with satisfaction. "How do you feel, my boy, after your long ride?"

Salvatore scratched the back of his neck. "Mr. Mariani, I feel like I'm about to piss my pants unless you have a toilet." Nervously, Salvatore smiled as he climbed from the box.

"Of course, of course, my boy," said Mariani motioning to a door in the far corner of the room. The two sullen-faced observers moved a few steps back as Salvatore raced to the bathroom.

Emerging a few minutes later, his eyes took in the contents of the large room: three marble-topped tables with a trough indented, a variety of pumps, rubber hoses, gallons of amber colored liquid, low sinks, high sinks, and the unmistakable odor of formaldehyde.

Mariani, hands clasped in front of him, smiled at Salvatore and motioned to a stairway. "Come, my boy, I have a small conference room upstairs. There is someone else joining us." Salvatore ascended the stairway into a mahogany room, comfortably appointed. The two other men entered behind him. Mariani pointed to a table that had been set before their arrival. "I thought you might be hungry so I ordered a salami and pepper sandwich for you with a bottle of my favorite wine."

Salvatore devoured the sandwich without speaking a word. He quickly consumed two glasses of wine and was now beginning to feel more relaxed. He sat back in his chair and wiped at some crumbs with his napkin. Mariani left the room leaving the two strangers sitting silently, like a pair of grotesque figurines, at the far end of the table. Salvatore heard footsteps ascending from the embalming room. The door to the conference room opened to reveal a brutishly handsome man of perhaps forty-two years, impeccably attired in a perfectly fitted suit, a diamond stick pin, kid gloves, and a gold-knob walking stick. The two men leaped to their feet and advanced to kiss his hand.

"*Don Leone, questo é un onore, molto lieta della conoscenza.*" Bowing low, the smaller of the two men spoke emotionally of the honor it was to finally meet their employer.

Don Leone smiled and clapped each man on the shoulder, "*Bravo, bravo, grazie!* You did a good job, boys, relax. Take a break. I'm going to talk with our friend Salvatore here." Salvatore was drawn to the hawkish features and black, deeply set eyes that now stared at him unblinking as the new visitor took the seat directly across from him. The figure remained silent and unsmiling, the only movement his fingers drumming rhythmically on the table. Salvatore sat uncomfortably under this cold gaze. A feeling of anger welled up within him. Who was this actor playing the role of tough guy?

"Why are you staring at me?" he blurted out at last. "What is this, some foolish game you want to play? You want to toy with me?" Salvatore leaned forward in his chair, face flushing, anger in his voice and in his eyes. The older man met the anger with a sardonic smile. He stopped drumming his fingers, casting the room in tomb-like silence.

"I just wanted to see the man—I mean the boy—who is fucking my wife."

Salvatore's brow furrowed, eyes narrowed, "What the hell are you talking about!" he shouted, hands upraised in a gesture of incredulousness.

Don Leone smiled broadly. "You don't know who I am, do you?"

"No, I don't know who you are," said Salvatore. "And I don't give a shit who you are. You sit there and insult me with your tough guy act. Why should I take your crap?"

"Why? I'll tell you why, because in two seconds those two buffoons who just left us will come in here and kill you on my command, *vuoi capire*, you understand?"

At that instant it became clear. "You're Nello Valetta," said Salvatore almost in a whisper, and he fell back in his chair staring at his visitor with a look of wonder and confusion.

"Well, well, you're not so stupid after all."

Salvatore closed his eyes and sighed. "Why are you here," he asked, still struggling to grasp the meaning of this extraordinary encounter. "What do you want with me?"

"Why? Because I was asked to be here."

"Stop talking in riddles," protested Salvatore, what do you mean you were asked to be here?"

Don Leone leaned back, crossed his legs carefully, and straightened the crease in his trousers. In a slow, lazy gesture, he reached inside his jacket for a package of cigarettes, lit one, inhaled and blew perfect smoke rings toward the ceiling. Salvatore watched every move with mounting impatience, determined not to allow himself to be baited by this poseur. Finally, Don Leone leaned across the table, looking Salvatore directly in the eyes.

"You saved my mother's life. You were good to her. You were good to Tina. I treated both of them like shit. They deserved better than me." He ran his hands over his face looking at Salvatore over his fingertips. "Marriage was never for me. I tried for Tina. She's a good woman, but it wasn't meant to be. The streets are where I belong, this is my natural habitat." He sat upright and appeared to study Salvatore. "Tina needs somebody like you, a nice country boy. One of these days we'll get divorced so she can remarry and be happy with some one. Who knows, maybe she'll invite me to the wedding." The sharp features gave way to a boyish grin. He stood and reached for his gold knobbed walking stick. "In a few days, Giuseppe Ferraio, you will be on your way to America and a new life."

Salvatore sat stunned for a moment, eyes wide, his mouth slightly open. He leaped to his feet. "America? What about my mother, what about…" He paused. Don Leone chuckled and beckoned with his hand for Salvatore to continue.

"Come on, come on, say it—what about Tina? That's up to Tina. The best place for you to start a new life is America. We have friends there. There are *paisani* in Boston and New York. You have to get safe first, and then you can make decisions. This cop who's chasing you, what's his name…ah, yes, Capuano. He wants your balls nailed to his office wall, *capisci?*"

Salvatore clenched his fists, staring at the floor. He nodded his head. "I understand."

"Good. You'll stay here until were ready. I'll talk with my man on the docks, he'll decide when you go. Until then Mariani has a room set up in the attic. You'll stay there and you'll stay hidden."

Salvatore nodded in agreement, bristling at the thought that he was being chastised like a schoolboy, and yet aware that he had no alternative other than to obey. It was the end of their audience. Stick in hand, the man he knew as Nello left the room without another word. Left alone with his thoughts the meeting seemed almost surreal, like something out of a dream. But it was real enough, he knew. The cigarette of Don Leone still smoldered in the ashtray before him.

A few years earlier Mariani had fixed up a small bedroom in the attic of the funeral home. When his wife questioned him about it, he told her it was for an occasional afternoon nap. "After all," he said, "I'm not getting any younger you know, and I want to come home to you well rested." He smiled slyly and winked at his round, middle-aged wife who accepted his reasoning with a proud smile.

The reality was that Mariani's was regularly enjoying his young secretary on the small hard bed that Salvatore now sat on, looking forlornly through a small octagon shaped window, his thoughts drifting to Tina, his mother, and his trip to America. A small wooden desk was pushed against the wall, and Salvatore seated himself, picked up pen and paper, and began writing to his mother. He wrote of his anxiety over his upcoming journey and of his fierce love for Tina. He spoke of his father and of the farm and the plans that they had made as a family, and he concluded with the promise that he would write often from America, and that he would return to her as soon as God would allow him. Then he sealed the envelope, kissed it, and addressed it to Monsignor Rittaco.

There was a soft knock and the door opened. It was Tina, arms loaded with bags of food and wine. Salvatore's heart leapt with excitement at the sight of her.

"Hi, little boy! I came to play with you in your hide out." She dropped the bags on the table and threw herself into Salvatore arm, hearts crashing together in rapid unison.

"How did you know I was still here?" He was beside himself with joy, holding her two hands and staring at her with eyes wide like a child on Christmas morning.

"Nello came to the house. He told me everything."

Salvatore's smile vanished at the sound of his rival's name. "He told me to wait here until he could make arrangements on the docks," he explained in a flat, awkward tone, working to control his jealousy. "I don't know how long I'll be here."

Tina took his hand and led him to the small bed. She sat and playfully patted the mattress with her palm. "Sit down, little boy, I'm going to chase your worries away everyday that you're here."

Captain Oreste Capuano, feet apart, a pointer in his hand, stood in front of the map of Naples and the expanded map of the *Spaccanapoli*. Before him sat Nino Rocca, Paolo Zincone, and six plainclothes officers. Capuano lowered his head looking directly at Rocca and Zincone. "You screwed up like amateurs!" His voice rose to a screaming crescendo. He paced in front of his audience, everyone staring at the floor. He stopped, turned, and thrust the pointer toward Rocca. "What happened? Tell me how the hell you let him slip away!"

Rocca leaped to attention. "Captain, we had every street covered. We concentrated over twenty men on two streets and four intersections. Nothing, absolutely nothing happened out of the ordinary."

Capuano put his face just inches from that of his junior man. "Find out where his girl lives. Go house to house, if you have to. If he's on the street, he's on his way out of the city. Zincone!"

"*Si, capitano.*"

"I want the train station covered, the docks, all roads leading out of the city—immediately. As a matter of fact, leave now! We don't have a minute to lose.

Zincone saluted hastily and rushed out of the office with two men in tow. Capuano returned his attention to Rocca. "Did anything, absolutely *anything* happen that was out of the ordinary. Think man, think."

Rocca put his hand to his chin, slowly began to shake his head, then paused. "There was something, but I don't think its anything important." Capuano leaned forward motioning for Rocca to continue. "It's just that some undertaker picked up a body. He said it was an old man who died of small pox…he wasn't sure, but that's what the doctor thought it might be."

"Did you see the body?"

"No, Captain, I didn't want to expose my men to the disease."

Capuano stared at Rocca, his thoughts elsewhere. "Who was this undertaker?"

Rocca rubbed the back of his neck. Shaking his head he turned to the other men in his team. Two of them threw up their hands in a gesture of helplessness. "Captain, I…" He stopped. Reaching into his jacket pocket he fished out a creased business card. Smiling broadly he announced, "Captain, his name is Mariani. Mariani's Mortuary."

Capuano grunted. "We can't overlook this. Go over to his place and ask some questions; look around, see what you come up with." Rocca saluted and performed a pirouette all in one motion, anxious to take his leave. In an instant he and his men were gone.

Capuano walked to his office window, chin in hand. The capture of Rossi would seal career; he would be promoted, perhaps permanently stationed in Naples, or even Rome! But to fail…

"What are you cooking for me tonight, Captain, or is it going to be just champagne and dessert?" Lucretia's voice snapped him out of deep thought. He turned smiling, striding toward her as she locked the office door.

Mariani came pounding up to the attic bedroom breathlessly bursting through the door.

Salvatore sat bolt upright in the small bed while Tina covered herself with a sheet.

"Mi *scuzi, signore*, I'm terribly sorry to barge in on you like this, but it's an emergency." He paused to catch his breath. "You must leave now, immediately! My carriage is waiting for you at the rear entrance."

Salvatore sprang from the bed naked. "What's is it, Signore Mariani, what has happened?"

Mariani threw his hands up. "The police are on their way." His voice was now at fever pitch, his arms flailed wildly. "If they catch you here, I'm in deep shit. C'mon, c'mon, *supito, supito*! Put your clothes on, Signorina, you're coming too. We can't take any chances that they pick you up. Quickly, down the stairs, to the left."

Mariani showed them out, searching frantically for any sign that the police had arrived. He slammed the rear door shut and scurried down the stairway following Tina and Salvatore, who were already in the back of the hearse. Salvatore wrapped his arms tightly around Tina in a protective embrace. Mariani spoke briefly with the driver and backed away as the hearse turned on the gravel driveway and made for a short stretch of road leading away from the rear of the mortuary.

In minutes Mariani saw them coming. Three vans rolled to a stop beneath the second-story porch of the mortuary. The mortician recognized the policeman who stepped out of the lead vehicle. Mariani adjusted his tie, brushed his jacket lapels, exposed his starched white cuffs, and advanced to open his front door. As the policeman raised his fist to knock, the thick black doors opened to reveal the dapper Mr. Mariani smiling in recognition.

"Ah, Lieutenant...*ma dio mio*! I'm so sorry, I've forgotten your name. But welcome, welcome. This is certainly a surprise. Please, how may I be of assistance?"

Rocca pulled himself up to his full height, extracted his badge from his inside pocket, and pushed it almost into Mariani's face. He spit the words out slowly. "The name is Lieutenant Rocca, senior detective, Carabinieri."

"Ah, yes, of course, Lieutenant Rocca. How foolish of my. My apologies. Please, come in."

Rocca stepped into the receiving room and motioned his team members to follow. "Undertaker," he half growled, "we're going to take a look around."

"But Lieutenant, what's this all about?" the little mortician protested with all the indignation he could muster. "I'm a respectable business man, and I'm also a member of the City Counsel." Rocca snorted and continued his walk through the funeral home, Mariani shadowing him.

It took only minutes for the policemen to discover the attic stairway. As Rocca opened the bedroom door his eyes went immediately to the unmade bed. "And what is this, undertaker? Who sleeps here?"

Mariani, looking and sounding as sheepish as possible, said, "I do, Lieutenant. I'm afraid at my age I find I need an afternoon nap once in a while."

Rocca's hand emerged from beneath a sheet. "Well, it looks like you left your shorts here the last nap you took, undertaker," said Rocca as he dangled a pair of Tina's silk underpants from one finger."

Mariani hesitated only for a moment as he moved closer to Rocca. "Lieutenant, I'm a mortician, yes, but I am a man just like any other. Naturally, there are times when I don't nap alone." Mariani raised his eyebrows and glanced at the ceiling. "I'm sure you understand, Lieutenant."

Rocca chuckled as he threw the underpants on the bed. "So this is where you bury your stiffs, Signore Mariani, in a manner of speaking." He laughed freely, obviously pleased with the wit of his joke, and the other policemen joined in, adding lewd comments of their own.

"Yes, Lieutenant, in a manner of speaking," said the little mortician, laughing pleasantly along with them.

The hearse rattled to a jolting halt. Salvatore had held Tina tightly about the shoulders, neither of them speaking a word in the near total darkness. Tina stared up at Salvatore, his face just visible from the thin rays of light penetrating the seams of the door.

"Hey, wake up, little boy, we're here, wherever that is."

Salvatore broke out of his thoughts and smiled down at Tina. The rear doors suddenly sprang open, and in the harsh light of the open doorway the familiar figures of Nello's men motioned them to hurry and follow. The carriage had stopped at the rear entrance of a warehouse. The smells were almost overpowering— cheese, olives, fish, leather, all piled on pallets in a vast building within walking distance to the commercial wharf. Nello's men led the way through the labyrinth of towering pallets. The warehouse was empty with the exception of a single guard, who nodded respectfully as the little party passed by on its way to an open wooden stairway. At the top of stairway they entered an enclosed office with a large window overlooking the entire ground floor.

"Sit down and wait," said one of the men pointing to a pair of wooden chairs. "He'll be here in a little while." Then they left. Salvatore sat, hands on knees, scanning the office. Tina sat impassively staring at Salvatore, knowing he would be leaving Italy soon.

"Who the hell will be here soon?" "Those guys are with Nello," motioned Tina.

"Nello?" Tina shrugged her shoulders, palms upraised. "I don't know, they operate in a shadow world I don't understand." Tina was about to say more, but sound of footsteps froze them in mid speech. The door opened to reveal Nello, eyes focused on Tina, a wry smile about his lips.

"*Aayy, ragazzi!*" It was Vito. He pushed past Nello, embracing Tina and bringing a huge arm around Salvatore, kissing them on both cheeks. "Well, my friend," said Vito holding Salvatore by both shoulders, "You are about to embark on a great adventure, eh!"

Nello approached, taking Tina's hand and bending to kiss her fingertips. "Hello my lovely wife, you're surprised to see me?" Tina shook her head and looked toward the ceiling, saying nothing. Nello pointed to the office chairs. "All right, let's sit down. We need to discuss some details." Nello remained standing, pacing the room. "Tina, you will leave with your brother. The police will be looking for you once the trail goes cold on Salvatore. You can stay with him. They don't know your brother and sister." Nello stopped directly in front of Salvatore. "You're leaving tomorrow morning on the freighter *Garibaldi*." Salvatore leaped to his feet; Tina covered her mouth with her hands.

"I can't go tomorrow! What about my mother? Arrangements…I have no money. Where will I stay…" Vito interrupted him with a raised hand.

"*Calmati, calmati*, listen to me. If you stay in Italy you're a dead man. There will never be a trial; they'll kill you in prison, do you understand me?" Salvatore sat down again, his head nodding in silent understanding. Nello continued pacing.

"I have my men on the docks; we won't have a problem getting on board. Unfortunately, you won't be walking up the boarding ramp. Tomorrow morning you get packed in a wooden crate with very few possessions and you'll be loaded aboard with the rest of the cargo. Don't worry, they won't bury you on the bottom of the hold. When the ship gets underway someone will uncrate you and tell you what to do." Nello walked to a small closet in the office and removed what appeared to be an inner tube. "Take this, there's a thousand dollars in US money in here, it's waterproof. Wrap it around your waist before you leave the ship. Needless to say, you won't be going down the debarkation ramp either." Nello extended his hand. "Good luck in America. We have friends there, they'll take care of you."

He turned to Tina, who this time returned his gaze. If her lips didn't speak, her eyes did, and Nello bent to kiss her gently on the cheek while pressing money into her hands, then quickly left the office. Tina watched him as he tread his way across the warehouse floor with his two bodyguards trailing behind. Vito moved next to Salvatore, wrapping a huge arm around his shoulders.

"Hey, don't worry. I'll take a little trip up to Atri. I'll see your mother and Uncle Antonio. Tina will come with me. We'll spend some time there—two maybe three weeks, until things cool down here, you understand?"

Salvatore nodded, eyes not leaving Tina. Vito prepared to leave and stopped in the doorway. "All right, I'm gonna get you some food for your trip. They'll be here to pack you up at five tomorrow morning. See you in about an hour."

Left to themselves, Salvatore spoke first. "I'll come back as soon as I can. I don't know how I'm going to live without you." Tina ran to him throwing herself to his knees, sobbing compulsively. Salvatore slid from the chair into her arms, his face buried into her neck, tears streaming down his cheeks. "I love you! I'll always love you! I'll be back for you. I won't have to stay in America forever. Maybe you'll come to America." Their lips, wet with tears, crushed together, devouring one another. They remained on the floor, locked in their embrace, unmoving, unspeaking. It seemed like only minutes had passed when they were shaken out of their reverie by a heavy pounding of the door.

"Hey, I'm coming in. Are you done saying good bye?" Tina and Salvatore looked at one another and burst into laughter. "Come in Vito, we're decent," called out Tina. Vito banged open the door, his arms laden with food.

"All right, this is for us to eat right now," he said, placing a large bag on top of a desk, "and this is for you to take on board ship." He set the rest of the bags on the floor by the door. "Tina, find some glasses; we'll have some of this wine—a toast before departure!"

Nello's men arrived at dawn along with two workers in striped overalls. They spotted Salvatore peering from the office window and motioned him to come down. At the bottom of the stairs the workmen finished screwing and nailing together a heavy wooden crate. The cover, propped up against a loaded pallet, was inked with 'L. Verducci Leather Goods, Naples, Italy, to Feinstein Distributing, 43 East 23rd Street, New York, NY, USA.'

The taller of the two men spoke in an accent that Salvatore didn't recognize. "Take a leak, kid, you're gonna be in this box for a little while. And get your stuff. You're gonna need it."

Salvatore returned with his valise and the provisions from Vito. The rubber inner tube was snug around his waist. "All right, c'mon, get in, we have to be on the dock in ten minutes." Salvatore climbed into the crate and lay down. Quickly, the workmen sealed the top down.

"Don't worry, it ain't tight." Salvatore recognized the voice. "But there's a hammer and pry bar near your feet, just in case. And keep your ears open. One of our people will find you after the ship sails."

Salvatore felt the crate being loaded onto a warehouse truck; others were piled on top of him. The feeling was strange and exhilarating. He heard muffled voices and shouts giving direction, the growling, hissing, and clanking of a steam-powered loading hoist. He felt the crate rising, twisting and jerking from left to right, top to bottom. Then he was descending, his body stiff with anticipation until suddenly the crate came to a hard thud that sent him sprawling. There were no more voices. A moment later the crate was being dragged or pushed, he wasn't sure, until it struck something with a loud bang and, once again, there was complete silence.

He took a sip of wine, thinking that he would do well to save his water for emergency. God knew when he would get any more.

He groped in the darkness for the pry bar and hammer. His fingers touched the hard metal and he eagerly pulled them to him, their bulk and weight giving him a welcomed sense of reassurance. The air was hot and stale, and he found it difficult to stay awake. He dozed, only to jerk awake with the movement of the freighter and the blasting of the steam horns, signaling to all in dock that the ship was underway.

He had no way to judge time, but it seemed as if he had already been in the crate for hours. His back was sore from lying in one position for so long; and just as he was telling himself that he would lose his mind if he had to stay cooped up much longer he heard the voice faintly calling, "*Ay, paisano, paisano, dove stai?* Where are you?"

Salvatore banged on the crate with the hammer. A moment later he head the screech of ripping nails as the lid was pulled up and back, revealing the faintly visible face of a smiling teenage boy. Salvatore sat up, groaning and rubbing his neck. "*Ay, paisano*, you all right?" The boy held up a lantern illuminating a thin face with a shock of black thick wavy hair.

"I'm fine, *grazie*," said Salvatore, his eyes squinting in the glare of the lantern. He pulled himself out of the crate and peered through the darkness as best as he could. The hold was solidly packed with crates, barrels, and sacks of all sorts, including various foods, leather goods, clothes, and machinery. His own crate rested alone against a bulkhead at the bottom of a steel stairwell.

"Follow me," said the boy as he handed Salvatore an oil lamp and lit it with a taper.

"Where are we going?" said Salvatore. "And where the hell is there a toilet?"

The boy laughed. "C'mon, I'll show you." They threaded their way through the forest of exports, squeezing through openings and climbing over towering pallets. As they made their way through the maze Salvatore noticed the glinting of what appeared to be small eyes, hundreds of them.

"Hey, kid, are those rats?" The boy stopped laughing.

"This ship is loaded with them. Don't worry, they have enough to eat. Just don't walk around down here without a lantern. A guy I know got drunk and fell asleep on top of a crate. They chewed his shoe off. Took a couple of his toes, too." The boy continued to lead and then stopped. "All right, Mr. Rossi, this is where you're going to live for the next three weeks."

They stood in front of a large crate marked 'MACHINERY—HANDLE WITH CARE.' The boy pulled open a side panel that had obviously been provided for them, revealing a small space at the base of what appeared to be an electric generator. In the space was a stool, blankets, two lanterns, bottles of wine and water, and a large hamper of food.

"Well, what do you think?" said the boy smiling, his hands on hips.

"I'll tell you what I think," said Salvatore, shaking his head in disblief, "I think this is a hell of a lot better than being in jail."

The boy led the way into the crate and lit both lanterns. "All right, Mr. Rossi, welcome to the Hotel Excelsior. Put your bag in a corner but, be careful, the floors get a little wet from the bilges."

Salvatore's face went blank. "What are bilges?"

"Oh, you'll find out soon enough, Mr. Rossi. The bilges hold the seawater that seeps into the ship through the hull and who knows from where else. After a couple of weeks it gets pretty wet down here. But don't worry, your crate's on a pallet."

Salvatore glanced around, "So where's the toilet!"

The boy pointed. "Go to the hull. That's where the bilge water gathers. Be careful when you take your pecker out, some rat might grab it and run away." The boy grinned as he spoke, showing even white teeth. "Go ahead, I'll wait here for you."

Salvatore edged his way to the bilges holding a lantern aloft and warily looking for the glinting eyes and listening for the rustle of feet. He returned to find the boy perched on the stool chewing on a crust of bread.

"All right, Mr. Rossi, you're on your own till tomorrow. I'll try to get you some hot soup or coffee. Just stay in the crate until you hear me, *capisci?*"

Salvatore nodded. As the boy turned to leave, Salvatore asked, "Hey, I forgot to ask, what's your name?" The boy grinned again, a big sheepish grin that reminded Salvatore of all the small town boys that he had known back in Atri, boys who lived each day with open hearts and endless dreams.

"My name is Charlie Luciano. When we get to New York, I'm going over the side with you. It's all set; Nello spoke with people in New York. They're going to take care of us." In another moment he disappeared into the maze of pallets. Salvatore closed the packing crate and sat on the stool, taking inventory of his possessions by the glow of the oil lamps sitting on the floor. His thoughts drifted to Tina, his mother. When would he ever see either of them again? He clasped his hands together and prayed, dozing off into a sound sleep sitting upright on the stool.

Captain Capuano stood at attention as he saluted Colonel Raimondo, who was seated behind his massive cherry wood desk. "Well, Captain, where the hell are we with the investigation? I thought we had him trapped — stand at ease, Captain. Please, sit down. Some coffee?"

"No thank you, Colonel. My men trailed him to the waterfront and then the trail went cold. No one knows anything. You know how they are down there—half of them are Mafioso, the other half are afraid to talk." The Silver Fox drummed his fingers on his desk. He rose noiselessly, slowly walking to the window, hands clasped behind his back. The silence made the Captain nervous.

"Capuano, I took you from a small dung hill of a town specifically to run this investigation." Raimondo's voice was soft and measured. "I gave you carte blanche—people, money—and you give me…nothing." Capuano stared crimson faced at the floor. "Captain, you have one more week to find this piece of garbage and bring him in. I promise you, if you don't you'll be back in Atri as quickly as I took you from Atri. Am, I understood?"

Capuano leapt to his feet, saluting Raimondo's back. "Yes, Colonel, fully understood."

"You may leave now, Captain, and remember what I said."

Back in his office, Capuano instructed a uniformed officer to track down Nino Rocca and Paolo Zincone and bring them to him immediately. When they received the message the expression on the messenger's face said it all. The two officers met outside Capuano's office. Rocca—his hands raised palms up, shoulders shrugged—spoke first in a whisper. "What is this, Paolo? What's he pissed off about now?"

"He's pissed off because now he knows *we* know we lost him." Zincone exhaled through pursed lips. "C'mon, let's go face the music."

Lucretia Buonano escorted them into Capuano's office. As usual, he stood studying the map of Naples and the blow up of the *Spacanappoli*. The officers snapped to attention. Capuano turned, waved them to seats. "So, you two geniuses, the flowers of the Carabinieri, the cream of the crop, and you couldn't catch a goddamn hayseed from Atri!"

"But captain…"

"Shut up, Rocca! I'll let you know when you can talk." Capuano began pacing, then abruptly stopped. "All right, Rocca, where do you think he is?"

"I don't know, Captain, my best guess is that he's on a ship sailing who knows where."

"And you, Zincone?"

"I'm with Nino, sir. That's the only way he could get out of Naples. Every other avenue is blocked or under observation."

Capuano paused, running his hands over his face, dark circles pronounced under his weary eyes. "All right, here's what I want you to do. Take your men down to the docks and question everyone, and I mean everyone! Check all the manifests. Anything looks unusual, follow up on it. And I want the sailing times of all the ships that departed in the last twenty-four hours and the names of all crewmembers, and I want you back here by four pm. You've got six hours, am I understood?"

"Yes, captain!" They spoke in unison, stepping on each other's shoes in their haste to exit the office.

Lucretia peered around the doorway of the adjoining office. "Don't be so unhappy, my little stallion." She flashed an enormous smile. "Wait until you see the costume I'm going to wear for you tonight." Capuano was immediately resurrected from his misery as he felt himself hardening.

Rocca and Zincone had failed. There was nothing—no information, no leads...nothing. Salvatore Rossi had escaped their grasp and had probably escaped Italy. Four days later Capuano once again stood in front of his Colonel.

"The case will remain open, Captain Capuano; you will remain here temporarily until I decide what other course of action I intend to take. Disband your team, send them back to their duty stations." The Fox spoke in a flat, matter-of-fact voice, and returned to the work on his desk. "That will be all Captain, for now."

"Yes, Colonel."

Three weeks had seemed like three years to Salvatore. The hold was covered with two inches of water; bilge pumps could hardly keep pace with the leaking, porous hull. He had spent most of his time reading his Bible, writing long letters to his mother and Tina, and hoping somehow they would finally get to their destination. He had slept slumped in a corner of his crate, listening to the rats trying to eat their way through the soft wood. He stank, everything stank. He was constipated, reluctant to expose himself in the bilges only in extreme emergency, and then very quickly by the light of the two lanterns.

Charlie Luciano brought him a hot meal every evening accompanied from time to time by a handsome German boy, Heinrich Schiller, who was sworn to secrecy and happy to be part of the conspiracy. Many in the crew knew he was there but they knew better than to say anything to the ship's captain for fear of the Mafia's retaliation upon return to Naples or, for that matter, on the ship itself.

"Aay, *paisano*, it's me." Luciano pried open the crate and climbed in. "You know, *paisano*, I don't know what stinks worse, the shit in this hold or you." He laughed, holding his nose.

"I can only imagine. I can't tell," said Salvatore good naturedly, "I've been living with it for three weeks."

"Well, you're not going to have to live with it anymore. We'll be In New York harbor by tonight. Pack your stuff up; take only what you can swim with. Oh, *Madonna mia*, you can swim can't you?"

"Yes, yes, I can swim, don't worry," chuckled Salvatore.

"All right, I'll be back in four or five hours. We'll wait up on deck until midnight and then we swim for shore. To the left of the docks there's going to be two automobiles; they'll be flashing their lights. We'll swim for the lights, *capisci*?"

"Are these people helping us, Charlie?"

"I really don't know, Salvatore. Their friends of Nello. They're from Sicily, big shots in New York. I'm gonna be working for them as a runner."

"What's a runner do?"

"Who knows, maybe I run for things," smiled Luciano. "Anyway, it beats living in Naples, that I'm sure of. Remember, only what you can swim with." Luciano closed the crate and was gone. Salvatore surveyed his worldly possessions. He took the rubber inner tube that Nello had given him with one thousand American dollars inside. He counted the money and replaced it carefully into the sealed end of the tube. He packed his letters and his Bible in the tube and sealed the open end with a small can of cement used for repairing flat tires, also supplied by Nello.

Luciano returned. They made their way up to the fore deck crouching behind smoke stacks and air funnels. Schiller was their waiting for them. He shook Salvatore's hand. Luciano, eyes darting back and forth, whispered to Schiller: "Heinrich, you have to watch and lower the rope into the water as soon as you see the light? You signal me and we go over one at a time, you got it?"

Heinrich was grinning, flushed with excitement. "Don't worry, I got it Charlie." He walked nonchalantly from behind the stacks, strolling the railing of the foredeck. The midnight watch stopped him, they chatted, and he continued on his rounds. Heinrich looked back toward the smoke stacks, wiping imaginary sweat from his brow.

There was a full moon, bathing the ship in an almost phosphorous blue-green light. This would have to be quick. There came a low whistle. It was Heinrich, signaling furiously. Luciano dashed for the railing and was over the side in seconds. Salvatore checked his rubber tube and waited for the whistle. It came, and he dashed for the railing. Heinrich handed him a round cork life preserver.

"Put your arm through this and shimmy down the rope. There are toeholds on the way down. When you're in the water look that way—see, over there, the lights flashing. Good luck!" Salvatore glimpsed the lights as he clambered over the railing and in seconds was up to his neck in the chill saltiness of the Hudson River. Luciano was twenty feet away, waiting for Salvatore. Salvatore bobbed beneath the black water and emerged with the life preserver under his armpits. Wordlessly, they kicked toward the now intermittent lights.

They swam for twenty-five minutes until, rigid with cold, they stumbled onto a muddy low-lying marsh. From out of nowhere came swinging lanterns and the sound of a familiar language. Three men appearing to be in their late twenties in caps and workmen's clothing came out of the darkness, a cigarette in each mouth. One of them draped heavy woolen blankets over the shivering bathers.

"*Buona sera, ragazzi, e benvenuto in America!*" They grasped hands, shaking vigorously.

"*Grazie, grazie amici.*" The words spilled out of Salvatore's mouth. He was grateful to be out of the water and on dry land.

The smallest of the three men motioned them toward the vehicles. "My name is Massimo Gentile," he said, the obvious leader of the group. "That's Antonio and Remo." The two men touched the brim of their caps in greeting as they trudged through the thick marsh grasses and spongy earth. Remo held the door open to the chugging Model-T and Salvatore and Charlie Luciano piled into the back seat, clutching their blankets tightly about themselves. Remo drove as Massimo gave him instructions. Antonio drove the car following them. "Welcome to New York, boys. We'll get you some food and a hot bath and a decent place to steep tonight. Charlie, your father is waiting for you in Manhattan. Salvatore, we're going to get you to Providence. That's in Rhode Island, about two hundred miles north. You have some cousins there on your mother's side that you probably didn't know you had. They live in an Italian section. They call it Silver Lake.

Chapter 3

THE ARRIVAL

Salvatore nodded dumbly, eyes wide looking left and right as they drove into Manhattan. The city was throbbing with activity and it was 1:30 in the morning. He gaped at the buildings, at the lighted signs, at the automobiles blanketing the wide streets. His thoughts drifted to Tina; she would love to see this. The memory of their last kiss engulfed him. The car slowed and came to a stop at the rear of a wooden tenement building.

"This is it, kid." Massimo swung open the back door. "Fifth floor, rear apartment."

Charlie and Salvatore exchanged kisses on both cheeks and vowed to see one another in the coming months. Salvatore watched as his young guardian disappeared inside the tenement. "Next stop, Providence," said Massimo leaning into the back seat. "Remo and Antonio will drive you. I stay here. *Buona fortuna,* my young friend."

The drive to Providence seemed to take forever, a succession of small towns and bad roads. They drove in silence, occasionally making an attempt at small talk. The men in the front seat seemed to know their way to Providence, as if this were a trip they had taken many times. Massimo had given Salvatore the name of his mother's cousin who had emigrated from Italy more than ten years earlier. Remo was to drive him to Saint Bartholomew's Church and deliver him to Monsignor Cavalaro, who would know where the cousin lived and worked.

Salvatore awoke in the rear of the Ford as it came to a stop in front of a small red brick church. It was still early, just a little past seven, but already a dozen children were at play in the church schoolyard under the watchful eye of the nuns. Remo led the way to the front door of the rectory, which was opened by an elderly woman who directed them to a small sitting room. Monsignor Cavalaro entered the room and motioned for Remo and Antonio to follow him. Salvatore remained seated on a comfortable divan. In moments Remo and Antonio returned to the sitting room grasping Salvatore's hand and shaking it vigorously. "Good luck, my friend. Monsignor Cavalaro will take good care of you. He is a friend of our friends in Italy." And they were gone.

Monsignor Cavalaro entered the room with his arms extended and a look of warmth and greeting. He appeared to be about fifty, a big man, round faced, balding, with kindly eyes and a pink complextion. Salvatore liked him instantly. Monsignor Cavalaro offered his hand in greeting and Salvatore rose in respect. "No, no, my son, please stay seated, you've had a long journey."

Salvatore smiled, nodded. "Thank you, Father, it has been a long trip."

Cavalaro sat across from Salvatore adjusting his cassock. "Well, my son, we're glad to have you here. Our friends in Italy have informed me of your plight and we're here to help you. Do you speak any English?"

"No, Father, I wish I did. I can't speak a word."

Cavalaro stroked at his chin. "Well, that's not a large problem. We have English classes in our school next door. You will start soon." Cavalaro leaned forward in his chair placing a hand on Salvatore's shoulder. "Unfortunately, my son, your mother's cousin Assunta was killed six months ago in a fire at the textile mill where she worked, not far from here. It was tragic; no escape routes, no safety regulations, no concern for their employees who they treat like slaves. Well, what can one expect, they're Yankees; they own everything, they run everything, even the government. She was only thirty-nine years old. Her husband was devastated. He couldn't live here any longer. A month ago he moved to Brockton, Maassachusetts."

Salvatore sat bewildered, searching for words. He was alone in America. The Monsignor smiled, knowing what was coursing through the young man's mind. "Don't worry, you will be living here with me at the school next door. We have a room set up for you. Nothing fancy, you understand, but we have showers there and you'll be safe. After all, you are here illegally." Salvatore exhaled a sigh of relief and nodded in gratitude. "You will take your meals with me here at the rectory. My housekeeper will take care of this. You won't be paid much. You'll be assisting our janitorial staff, Nemo and Federico." The Monsignor stood. "Come, you must be starving. There is a large bowl of pasta waiting for us in the kitchen."

The room was in the basement of the school next to a boiler room. There was a bed, a small-mirrored dresser, a writing table and a chair, an electric lamp, and wall pegs for hanging clothes. To Salvatore it was better than the Excelsior Hotel in Rome. He used the boys' room toilet and showered in the boys' locker room either early in the morning or after school closed for the day. Mrs. Almonte, the Monsignor's housekeeper, fawned over Salvatore as if he were her own son. She prepared special treats for him and wouldn't let him wash or iron his own clothes. Nemo and Federico took a liking to the polite, serious, hard working young man. They began inviting him for dinner at their homes which, combined, consisted of twelve very noisy children. Salvatore spent most of his evenings writing to his mother and Tina. He saved the letters, unsure if he should involve the Monsignor in his use of Father Rittaco as the go-between for his correspondence. He had been at Saint Bart's for six weeks; he was feeling comfortable in his surroundings. Many evenings he walked the neighborhood standing aloof, watching the men play bocce on Sunday afternoons or watching a new sport called baseball being played in a park not far from the church. He missed his mother; he missed Tina passionately, spending sleepless nights thinking of their lovemaking. One morning Mrs. Almonte informed Salvatore that the Monsignor wanted to speak with him about something.

"Monsignor?" Salvatore called softly into the small front office of the rectory.

"Ah, Salvatore, my son, come in. Please, sit."

Salvatore sat rigid in a high-backed wooden chair, his face serious and fearful. The monsignor smiled and patted his knee. "Don't worry, my son, you have done nothing wrong. In fact, you are doing an excellent job. But I think it's time for you to take lessons in English. You will learn the language much more quickly than you do on the street, and in the correct manner. How do you feel about this?"

Salvatore broke into a broad grin. "Oh, yes, monsignor, this is what I want to do. When can I start and where do I go?"

"Good, my boy. I knew you would be excited by this news. I know you were an honor student in Atri and you were ready to attend the University, isn't that so?"

"Yes, monsignor, but how did you know this?"

"Well, my son, I'm still in contact with friends in the old country—especially one old friend I was in seminary with. His name is Rittaco, Monsignor Rittaco." The Monsignor spoke with raised eyebrows and an expression of feigned innocence. "Have you ever heard of him, Salvatore?" Salvatore's mouth dropped open. He began to stammer an answer. From beneath his desk the Monsignor lifted a small canvas bag. "I believe these letters are for you, my son." Salvatore opened the bag, slowly reaching for the letters. Hands shaking, tears welling up in his eyes, his lips began to tremble. He could not speak for fear of crying.

The monsignor stood and placed both hands on Salvatore's shoulder. "It's all right, my son, I understand how much you miss your loved ones." The words touched his heart, and Salvatore broke into heaving sobs. The Monsignor waited, allowing his young charge to regain his composure. After a moment he asked, "Do you feel better, my boy?"

"Yes, Monsignor," said Salvatore, shaking his head and drying his eyes with his palms, "but how did you know? How did they know where I was?"

THE ARRIVAL THE STRUGGLE THE ASCENDANCY

The Monsignor seated himself behind his desk. "Salvatore," he began, speaking almost in a whisper, "Father Rittaco is a friend of mine. He wrote me and told me the whole story of what happened in Atri. I also know that he is your confessor and your priest."

"But how did he know I was with you?"

"He has friends in Naples and Sicily who knew where you would be going. Once he found out where you were, he mailed the letters to me all in one box. Now, my son, take the letters to your room and read them to your heart's content. Oh, and by the way, you start your English classes tomorrow night at seven o'clock at the school, in room 201."

Salvatore fairly flew to his room. Sitting on his bed he carefully opened the first letter from Tina. He devoured every word. The scent of her perfume made him heady with excitement and longing. There were letters from his mother and Si Antonio. Tina was still in Atri. Angela Mia was looking after Julia. Tina would be returning to Naples the next day. Julia was not well. Si Antonio had returned to Naples with Vito to feel out the situation. There were eight letters, five of them from Tina. He reread each of Tina's letters, clutching them to his chest, eyes closed, overcome with the thought of her kisses. The next day he brought a packet of letters to Tina and his mother, addressed to Father Rittaco, to the Monsignor for mailing.

There was a chill in the night air. Snow dusted the sidewalk as Salvatore walked from the rectory to his first English class at St. Bart School, determined to learn the language as quickly as possible and having promised himself that he would be a model student. It was two weeks before Christmas. Pangs of loneliness swept over him as he lapsed into thoughts of Tina and his mother, of the Christmases when his father was alive—the family together for *la notte della vigiglia di natale,* midnight mass, and the simple gifts on Christmas morning. Tears welled up in his eyes as he strapped the collar of his hand-me-down woolen coat up about his cheeks. As he entered the classroom he forced himself to dismiss the bittersweet thoughts from his mind, and he vowed to return to Italy as soon as possible.

The English teacher was a handsome, well-dressed man named Mr. Capasso, an Italian teacher at Mt. Pleasant High School. Mr. Capasso had arrived from Italy as a teenager and had earned his undergraduate degree from Brown University, the only Italian-American in his class. His English was flawless, speaking with almost theatrical preciseness. All his work at St. Bart's was voluntary. Because the need was so great, classes met three nights a week every week for the entire year. Each group attended for twelve weeks; it was then up to the student to continue on his own. Mr. Capasso took a special interest in Salvatore. He knew of his scholarship in Italy and was impressed with his quiet, studious demeanor. In addition to his class work, Salvatore made a point of memorizing ten new English words a day. To his enormous delight, at the conclusion of the twelve weeks of classes he was speaking a halting brand of English with remarkable pronunciation.

That Christmas Eve, Salvatore served at midnight Mass— the liturgy, the fragrance of incense, the ringing of bells all familiar to him from his time with Monsignor Rittaco in Atri. He continued to assist at Mass three mornings a week, and soon he gained the respect of the parish regulars, especially the mothers and grandmothers with marriage-age daughters and granddaughters. He lived for the next day's mail and ached with longing for Tina. His letters became more and more passionate, and she responded with a lock of hair, perfumed stationary, and allusions to the lovemaking they would enjoy once they were reunited.

Zio Antonio had joined the Italian Army only after Italy had broken away from Germany and Austria-Hungry. It was rumored that the Italians would join with the allies against the former triple alliance. Salvatore read this at the breakfast table smiling to himself, imaging Si Antonio in uniform taking orders from superiors and standing at attention. Monsignor Cavalaro held his coffee up to his lips with two hands, examining Salvatore. He had filled out well, he thought, a fine broad shouldered physique admired by all the young men in the area. A natural athlete, he was much in demand on Sundays for the new game of American football. Salvatore looked up from his plate of bacon and eggs, prepared lovingly by Mrs. Almonte, sensing something was to come.

"Salvatore."

"Yes, Monsignor?"

"It's time for you to learn a trade. You will still live at the school, for the time being, and you will still take your meals with me."

"Yes, Monsignor; thank you, Monsignor."

"Tomorrow morning you will meet with Pasco LoFredo, a parishioner. He works for the Gilbane Building Company. They build houses, churches, small buildings. They're a good company and they hire a lot of our people. You must be ready at six tomorrow morning, *capisci?*"

"Sí, Monsignor, I'll be ready."

Salvatore was at the rear door of the rectory at 5:30. Mrs. Almonte had coffee and buttered toast waiting for him. She had packed a lunch pail with two large sandwiches and a ball jar of hot coffee that would remain warm until lunchtime. Pat LoFredo was a small, congenial, ruddy-faced man who had emigrated from Carrara several years earlier. An expert with tile and marble, he was a torrent of conversation and hand motions all the way from St. Barts to the job site on North Main Street in Providence.

Overseeing the sight was William Gilborne, the caricature of an Irish immigrant—red-faced, barrel-chested, a mop of black hair slightly tinged grey at the temples. He stood at a roughly assembled table, construction blueprints spread from end to end, as he directed the construction.

"Meesta Gilborne." Pat LoFredo led Salvatore to the makeshift headquarters. Gilborne turned at the sound of his name and responded with a toothy smile.

"Good morning to ye, Patsy!" Bill Gilborne's melodious brogue seemed to burst into the cool morning air, and his broad grin seemed to belie his tough, aggressive nature. "And who's this good-looking young man with ye? Ye got another good man for me?"

"Yessa, Meesta Gilborne. This is a Salvatore Rossi. He's a from the old country. He's a good man." Gilborne extended his hand. Salvatore's large hand was enveloped by Gilborne's.

"I am pleased to make your acquaintance, Mister Gilborne." Salvatore spoke slowly, shyly, unsure of the effect of his newly acquired English. Gilborne sized up Salvatore in a practiced glance.

"All right, Salvatore, I could use another good worker. And if Patsy sez you're a good man, that's good enough for me. Ye start off as a learner at learner's pay. Patsy will show you the ropes. The more ye learn and the better ye get, the more money I pay you. Understand?" Salvatore nodded and looked at LoFredo for help.

"Yessa, Meesta Gilborne, I'll explain everything to him," assured LoFredo.

"Thank ye, Pat, he'll be working with you on the cement gang. Let's go, we got a building to put up here."

Salvatore followed LoFredo across the lumber-strewn building site to one side of the brick building surrounded by wooden staging. LoFredo explained what Gilborne had said. "Listen, Salvatore, he's a good Irishman. He's tough but he's fair. And he pays more than the Italian house builders." Salvatore nodded in understanding. LoFredo pointed to four men mixing cement in large flat troughs, shoveling sand and cement in proportion and adding a set number of buckets of water to create a thick grey mortar. The mixture was then shoveled into a hod—a wooden V-shaped vessel open on one end—and hoisted on the shoulders of the hod carriers to the masons setting redbrick at various levels on the staging around the building. When the call came for more brick, the hod carrier took up another hod designed for brick carrying. It was backbreaking labor, and it went on for ten hours a day, six days a week, with a break at midday for lunch. The cement mixers and hod carriers came to a halt as LoFredo ushered Salvatore into a circle of men.

"Awrighta, listena to me. This isa my friend, Salvatore Rossi. He's a justa come over froma the old country and he no speaka the language too good."

The men howled with laughter. "Hey, Patsy, whaddaya you speakin, the King's English!" It was Stash Polanski, a large, round-face Pole. He took off his leather glove and extended his hand to the newcomer. "Glad to have you with us, Salvatore, or should we call you Sally?" They all laughed, and one by one they put down their tools and shook Salvatore's hand.

The crew consisted of four Italians, two Irishmen, a Pole, and one Armenian, all immigrants and all having arrived within the past five years. The winter was unusually mild, and the bricklayers set brick in the cold as long as it wasn't freezing. Salvatore became a hod carrier and cement mixer. At the end of his fist week he couldn't feel his legs; climbing the ladders to deliver mortar and bricks all day took its toll. By day's end he was exhausted, his body aching as never before. But it was good work, and he was proud of the fact that he was helping to build something with his own hands. His humble demeanor, his willingness to help anyone, his physical stature, and his quiet dignity drew people to him, especially the Italians on the crew. He was a natural leader. He learned everything he could from each job he was given. Soon he was an apprentice bricklayer. In no time at all he became proficient and was setting brick as rapidly as the old pros. But he respected seniority, and they in turn gave him respect.

"I been watchin' your work over the last couple of months" Gilborne told him over coffee one morning. "You're a smart young man. I want you to learn a little bit more about this business, d'ye understand?"

"Yes, Mister Gilborne." Salvatore looked directly into his employer's eyes. "I understand you very well."

"Good. Everyday I want ye to spend an hour with me. I'm goin' to teach ye how to read the blue prints for this job. Ye start with me tomorrow. I'll let Patsy know what ye'll be doin'. Keep up the good work. And Salvatore"—the Irishman grinned—"thank you."

"Thank *you*, Mister Gilborne," said Salvatore, moved by the sincerity of the words.

THE ARRIVAL THE STRUGGLE THE ASCENDANCY

Gilborne was amazed at the young Italian's quick mind and natural ability to absorb the reams of almost abstract drawings that were the nature of commercial blue prints. Salvatore stayed late each evening, confirming measurements and placement for the next day's work. It all came easily to him, and he found himself totally engrossed in the building trade. He studied the plumbers and electricians; he assisted the carpenter, absorbing information and skills like a sponge. Pat LoFredo became his closest friend and confidant. They ate lunch together, and Salvatore became a fixture in Patsy's home, which consisted of his robust, cheerful wife and their seven children. Every Friday the company bookkeeper delivered the pay envelopes that were distributed by Gilborne himself. Friday nights were reserved for the workingmen of Silver Lake and all the other working neighborhoods in Providence, a time to socialize with their countrymen in bars and taverns, where free food was served to attract the hard drinking, free-spending Friday night crowd. In Silver Lake there was Gentiles Tavern, Father and Sons Café, and a half-dozen bars and social clubs. The Polish neighborhoods, the Irish, the French—they all had similar locations. Salvatore would join Patsy and some of the other laborers for a glass of wine, a dish of snails, and small talk about work and family. The younger men would stay into the night; the married men would leave early, their wives expecting the pay envelop that would provide survival for another week. The winter stayed unusually warm. The men were able to work through February, losing few days to snow or freezing weather.

One evening in early March a packet of mail was waiting for Salvatore when he arrived at the rectory after work. Mrs. Almonte always presented the packet with a wistful, understanding smile. He sat on the edge of his bed and opened the envelopes, hungry for words from the two women he loved and longed for. Things were well at the farm; the winter wasn't too cold, Tina was a treasure and worked too hard; she was wonderful company and they had grown very close. "I know she loves you, and I'm sure you love her," his mother wrote. "I approve of this, and I'm sure your father would have approved."

Next he selected Tina's letter and held it to his nostrils. The scent of her perfume made him light-headed. Vito had been in jail and released. He went to Rome to live with Mussolini and some of the other young radical politicians. They were constantly hounded by the Carabinieri. Zio Antonio sent money every month—not much, but it helped. Salvatore slammed his fist into the mattress. He should be in Atri taking care of Tina and his mother! Things were well, the weather was good, and they were in good spirits. "I miss you so much. I need to feel your body next to mine. I need to touch you." Salvatore fell backward onto a pillow groaning with frustration. He opened the second letter from Tina as he lay on his bed. "My dearest darling sweetheart, I'm pregnant with your child…." The words didn't register. He re-read the opening lines slowly until finally they slammed into his consciousness. He lay absolutely still, clutching the letter to his chest. Tears sprang from his eyes. He kissed the letter and sprang from his bed, running next door to the rectory. As he burst through the rear door a smiling Mrs. Almonte was removing the Monsignor's dinner from the oven.

"Ah, my sweet Salvatore, you're having dinner with us tonight? You have so many invitations!" Salvatore smiled, wiping the remnants of tears from his eyes. "*Cara mia*, why are you crying?" He handed her the letter. "Oh, *Jesu*! Oh, *Jesu*, how wonderful!" She embraced him.

"Is the Monsignor in?"

"Yes, yes, in the study, go."

Monsignor Cavalaro looked up from his book as Salvatore entered the study. "Ah, my boy, you had a good day?" Salvatore handed him the letter. Cavalaro smiled broadly as he read the letter. "This is wonderful, Salvatore, wonderful!"

Salvatore sat down wringing his hands. 'Monsignor, I must get back to Italy. I must be there for the baby, for Tina and my mother." He paused awkwardly, looking at the floor. "You know we're not married?"

"Yes, my boy, I know this and I understand these things happen."

"Monsignor, she's four months pregnant. It took a month to get this letter; she's now five months pregnant. Please help me."

Cavalaro held his chin in his hand, staring into a corner of the study. "There is no way to get you back to Italy, Salvatore. You have no passport. You're a wanted man. There is a war on. Every ship is searched for stowaways. It's impossible." He paused only briefly, pained by the young man's look of dejection. "However," he continued, "there's a chance that we can get Tina and your mother here, if luck is on our side, and if we can call in a few favors."

Salvatore's heart raced with excitement. "Monsignor, when do you think we can get them here? How long?"

"I can't promise you anything, my boy. Remember this, I will do my best. Do you understand?"

"Yes, Monsignor."

"Good. Leave it to me. I'll talk with the Bishop in Boston; he's very strong with the Irish politicians and we are very close. For now work hard. You must save money for their passage here."

"Yes, monsignor." His spirits soared; he could tell no one, not even Patsy LoFredo. On the job site he was a dynamo, working with new enthusiasm. He had noticed a large black sedan at the job site on most Fridays after the payroll was delivered. There would be three or four men in long overcoats and Borsolino fedoras or caps—big men, tough looking. Some of the laborers would work their way down to the sedan, hold brief conversation, and then return. Pat LoFredo was one of the laborers who would visit the sedan every Friday and would return, obviously depressed.

One Friday evening the two friends sat over a glass of wine at Gentile's. Salvatore could see that something was troubling his companion.

"Pasquale, who are these men?" he asked. "I see you and some of the others visiting the big black sedan every Friday. Why? What do they do?" He sat back, a frowned expression begging an answer.

"They are scum of the earth! Vultures! Robbers! They are shit." Salvatore was startled by the force of the response. LoFredo looked left and right and leaned across the table. He motioned for Salvatore to come closer. "They are *Mano Nera* - Mafia. They prey on us, their own people. Do you believe this, Salvatore?"

Salvatore shook his head in disbelief. "I thought we left this foolishness back in Italy. What do they want from you?"

A waiter interrupted the conversation as he placed two glasses of wine on the table. "These are on Bartolomeo." He pointed to the far side of the smoky café. LoFredo and Salvatore looked across the room to a gap-toothed smile as a figure seated at the bar raised his wine glass in a toast. LoFredo raised his own glass in a half-hearted response.

"That's one of them," he said in murmured voice.

THE ARRIVAL THE STRUGGLE THE ASCENDANCY

"One of who, Pasquale?"

"One of the collectors."

"Pasquale, what do they collect every Friday. I don't understand."

LoFredo leaned back in his chair and rotated his wine glass on the table. "Six months ago I borrowed one hundred dollars from them. My youngest daughter was sick, we needed to take her to the hospital, to buy medicine. I didn't have the money. I have paid them back three hundred dollars in interest. The only way I can stop paying is if I give them the one hundred dollars all in one lump sum."

"Have you gone to the police?"

"Ha! They're all paid off. They do nothing."

Salvatore looked across the room at the smiling gap-toothed Bartolomeo. His hands unconsciously clenched into fists, his rage expressed only in his icy gaze and taught expression. "Don' you worry, my friend, I'll take care of this for you. How many others on the job owe them money?"

"There are five of us all in the same predicament. Why?"

"I want you to find out for me how much money they originally borrowed, do you understand?"

"Salvatore, I don't want you to get into any trouble. They will kill you in a minute."

"I'll work this out. Pasquale, please do as I ask. I want you to do this for me." LoFredo threw his hands up and nodded his head yes.

The week flew by uneventfully. Friday arrived. In the late morning Salvatore was nowhere to be seen. The payroll was delivered, followed minutes later by the black sedan containing Bartolomeo and two other henchmen. The men walked down the slight embankment to the ridicule of the loan sharks. In a thicket twenty-five feet away Salvatore crouched on his knees, a baseball bat in his right hand and a black hood over his head. His breathing came rapidly; his heart pounded like a sledgehammer. Revenge for the injustice paid his friend had emerged as a blood rage that he neither understood nor could control. It heightened his senses, his power; he became a jungle animal.

The last man to visit the sedan was LoFredo. As he turned to return to the job site Salvatore exploded from the thicket, covering the twenty-five feet in seconds. The men were stunned to see a hooded madman with a raised club charging at them. There was time for nothing. Salvatore fell upon them with a savage fury, smashing first one head, then another, then finally the face of Bartolomeo as he yanked his pistol from his jacket. He stood panting, muscles still taught, staring down at the three prostrate bodies. LoFredo remained transfixed, frozen by fear and awe. He knew it was Salvatore, the clothes, the brawny size.

Salvatore looked from the men to LoFredo. He motioned for him to go. LoFredo slowly moved away, climbing the embankment backward. As he watched, Salvatore pulled an ice pick from his pocket. LoFredo's mouth fell open. No! The word stuck in his throat as he scrambled back toward the sedan. Then he stopped as Salvatore walked to the rear of the sedan and jammed the ice pick into the two rear tires. He motioned again to LoFredo, this time violently, to return to the work site. He reached into the front seat of the sedan and took out a small black leather satchel. He rifled the pockets of the still unconscious men, taking out all the green backs in their possession. Then he was gone, not to return that day.

At seven o'clock the next morning the entire construction crew, hats in hand, waited as Salvatore walked toward the site. They advanced upon as a group, extending their hands and embracing him. The Italian men kissed his hands, his cheeks, all crowding tightly around him. Salvatore was surprised and confused by the attention, and then it occurred to him—LoFredo had seen everything and had told them. Salvatore was uncomfortable with the attention and smilingly insisted that everyone return to their work. LoFredo continued to re-tell the incident throughout the day, embellishing the story at each telling until Salvatore insisted that he stop. From that day on he was looked upon as their supreme leader and was treated with the utmost deference and respect.

Federal Hill overlooking the City of Providence was the site of bivouacked Civil War troops in training under the command of the infamous General Ambrose Burnside. Over the years it was transformed into a forest of three and four tenement dwellings. Populated first by the Irish immigrants and slowly as the century turned by Italian immigrants most of who arrived from Southern Italy and Sicily. By 1914, it was a bona fide Italian village in America, with shops, meat markets, poultry stores, and push carts hauling fresh produce and seafood all hours of the day. There were six Catholic Churches in the immediate area serving the multitude of families. All churches held mass in Italian as well as English. The streets were teaming with children of all ages. Young men held sway on their particular corner of Atwells Ave., which served as the main drag through the center of the "Hill," as it became known. There were numerous barrooms, cafes, and social clubs serving the mostly working class Italian's of the hill. The cacophony of sounds reverberating from the tenements and surrounding businesses was made up of mothers calling children, peddlers hawking their wares, and people hailing one another across the narrow streets.

On one of the narrow back streets sat the Imperial club, a social club popular with Sicilian immigrants. The owner, Domenico Zarraga, immigrated from Sicily at age fifteen, and now he was the most powerful underworld figure in Southern New England. He held court and received his vassals and visitors which included politicians, police and members of the clergy. "Dom" as he was called, presided from two spacious rooms in the rear of the social club with its own entrance. The club was constantly busy, populated by some of the most vicious criminals and underworld associates not yet in jail, all currying favor with Zarraga.

At forty-five years old, he was of average height, with dark olive complexion, slicked back jet-black hair, and sinewy build. His face was narrow, with full lips and a perpetual expression of sneering hostility. He had killed his first man at age seventeen in a knife fight with a thirty-five year old immigrant who had attempted to violate his fifteen-year-old sister. It was rumored that after he had cut the man's throat he had severed his genitals and stuffed them into his mouth and left him on a back street for the police to find. He was brutal, and ruled with fear. He was also leader of the Mano Nera in New England with a hundred men at his disposal. He controlled all gambling activities, all prostitution, and sanctioned all robberies and various criminal activities, including murders and beatings.

On a Friday evening a week after the attack on the loan shark's, Salvatore entered the front door of the Imperial Club known to all as the bucket of blood. The room was packed with Italian workingmen and thugs of every specialty. They were three deep at the bar. Salvatore strode to the bar, cap in hand. The men sized up this stranger in their midst with curious glances. Out of the corner of his eye he saw Bartolomeo, face bandaged, eyes swollen, in a game of cards with four other men.

"Whatayou gonna have my friend?" The bartender shouted over the heads of the bar crowd.

Salvatore lifted his head and raised his voice "I'm here to see Mr. Zarraga." A hush fell at the bar, an opening parted as he approached the bar.

"Who are you?" The bartender looked him up and down.

"I have some business with Mr. Zarraga, is he here?" The bartender pointed behind him. Salvatore turned to see two men behind him, one leveling a small derringer at his chest. They motioned for him to move to the rear of the building. He walked through the crowded room, one man in front leading the way. The man with the derringer pressing the nozzle into the small of his back as they walked. They drew little attention as they made their way through the noisy smoky room. He was ushered into a large plain room dominated by a huge ornate desk. Behind the desk sat Zarraga working his way through a large plate of linguine with clam sauce, a bottle of Chianti at his elbow. He looked up, removed the large napkin from his neck, wiped his mouth, refreshed his glass, poured a glass for Salvatore, slid it across the desk and motioned to the chair in front of the desk. The other men in the room sat haphazardly about, all eyes on Salvatore.

Zarraga leaned back in his kingly chair. "What can I do for you my friend? Who are you and why are you here?" Salvatore reached into his jacket outer pocket; five pistols were immediately pointed at him the sound of safeties off, hammers cocking and chambers loading the only sound in the room. Salvatore slowly withdrew a packet of greenbacks bound with elastic bands and laid it on the desk. The pistols were lowered.

"What's this?" asked Zarraga, a faint smile on his face. "You brought me a gift."

"No, Mr. Zarraga, I came to pay off some loans for my friends, the names and the amounts are on this paper."

Zarraga sat forward, reaching for the note and read the names slowly, eyes narrowing as he read. He motioned to one of the men against the wall and murmured something behind his hand. In seconds the gap toothed and bandaged Bartolomeo was in the room standing at the desk. Zarraga pointed at Salvatore.

"Does this look like the guy?" Bartolomeo motioned for Salvatore to stand. He stood, hat in hand looking from Zarraga to Bartolomeo. "Well, what do you think, Bartolomeo?"

Bartolomeo pursed his lips and shook his head. "I don't know Dom, I can't tell. This guy's a kid, I think he was older."

"Awright, go back to your card game." Zarraga pointed to the chair, and Salvatore reseated himself.

"Where did you get this money…what is your name, my friend, you never told me.

"Salvatore, Mr. Zarraga, Salvatore Rossi." Zarraga sat back in his chair a frown on his face, one finger pressed against his lips. "Aahh, yes, yes, of course. Our friends in Sicily told us about what you did in that small town in Abruzzi, what was the name. It escapes me…"

"Atri" interjected Salvatore.

"Yes, Atri, a small shit hole of a town." The men in the room chuckled. "Well now, Salvatore, you do have balls. I like that, I like that. Now tell me where you got this money." Zarraga's voice

THE ARRIVAL THE STRUGGLE THE ASCENDANCY

and expression turned cold as he leaned back, fingers drumming on his desk.

"I took up a collection from all the Paisani, they all wanted to help." Salvatore fingered his cap nervously, a strange anger building against this defiler of every virtue his mother and father had taught him. Zarraga smiled smugly, now toying with his visitor.

"The paisani, eh. Tell me, who were these paisani, I want to thank them myself." The men in the room exchanged laughter. Salvatore rose from his chair slowly with an expression of disgust and rising anger.

"The paisani who you screw, the paisani who work for a living, the paisani who grow families, the paisani who contribute to society. The paisani who attend mass. Your countrymen, who you take advantage of with scum like Bartolomeo." The words came out hoarsely, the tendons in his neck taught, face flushed, fists clenched. The men along the walls advanced toward the desk. Zarraga motioned them away. He stared at Salvatore with narrowed eyes, unblinking, unmoving. Salvatore turned and walked toward the office door donning his cap as he walked. There was a movement to stop him. Zarraga shook his head no.

"Aayyy, paisan." Salvatore slowed, not turning. "Tell the good and decent paisani that if they need help, I'm always good for a loan. They'll never get one from the Yankee bankers!"

Salvatore retraced his steps through the smoky, beer soaked room and exited into the cold night to begin the long walk home.

The letters from Tina came weekly in packets of four or five. She wrote almost daily, keeping Salvatore appraised of every kick and movement the baby made. She knew it was a boy. She could tell because she was carrying so low, at least that is what Salvatore's mother had sagely predicted. Julia Valetta was dead. She had succumbed to diphtheria at eighty-five years of age, her body unable to fight off the infection. Salvatore had opened the second letter to be greeted with the news of her passing. Nello had sent two women to live with her while Tina was in Atri. Angela Mia stopped by every other day to check on her sister as she declined day by day and on the tenth day rattled her last breath. Nello had made arrangements with Mariani to bury her. There was a small graveside service. Antonio was home on leave; he had driven Tina and Salvatore's mother to Naples for the service and had quickly turned around to return them to Atri. Salvatore lowered the letter to his lap and closed his eyes trying to recall Julia's angelic face, praying silently for the repose of her soul.

He slit open the final letter with a small penknife. Small pox was ravaging all of central Italy; there had been two cases discovered in Atri. Dr. Albanese, the only doctor in the town, had come down with the fever. No one was venturing into the town square, the small shops were shuttered. Fabio Potenza's Café was closed, the situation was turning grim. Tina assured him they would not venture from the farm until this menace had passed. A knot of fear gripped Salvatore's stomach. He felt powerless, unable to protect the two people he loved most in life. He gathered the letters together, tied them with a piece of twine, and stored them with all the other letters in the bottom dresser draw. He left the school and walked quickly to the rectory.

Mrs. Almonte directed him to the study. Father Cavalaro was asleep in a chair, an open book in his hands. He called the Monsignor softly. "Aah, Salvatore, my son, just resting my eyes for a moment. Come in, come in, you look worried, what's the matter?"

"Monsignor, what is the news from Abruzzi, the small pox, how bad is it?"

"It's not good my son, many lives have been lost. I know that it's in Atri, I received a letter from Monsignor Rittaco last week. He told me that Dr. Albanese was sick and unable to tend to anyone. This is a terrible tragedy. Only God can intervene in this illness. I know you're worried about your mother and Tina. I'm sure they will take all the necessary precautions."

"Monsignor, what about bringing them to America, can we do this?"

"This is possible, my son, but it will take some time even with the friends we have in Boston. You must trust in God and prayer that the evil disease is eradicated from Atri."

Salvatore walked slowly back to the school, hands in pocket, collar up, cap pulled low. He pondered his helplessness, his worries, the cold fear that something would happen to his mother or his pregnant soon to be wife. He abruptly turned and walked back to the church. The church was empty; the only illumination came from the half dozen votive candles that worshipers had lit, their red and yellow glow casting shadows across the altar. He knelt and clasped his hands tightly. He looked above the altar and spoke out loud to the crucifix, asking for Jesus to protect his loved ones and he in turn would forever be devoted to the word of the church. He prayed the Rosary several times with so much passion he began to sweat. That night he dreamt of Tina holding their newly born infant – a small, chubby, smiling boy holding his hands out to Salvatore. Try as he might, he could not reach the baby's hands.

The huge three-smokestack ship was of Swiss registry. It arrived in Boston harbor at 6:55 a.m. and, upon securing a berth, immediately began debarking passengers. Among the groups of passengers was a tall man, mustached with hawk like features and an arrogant demeanor. He wore a black broad-brimmed fedora pulled low over one eye, a long black overcoat of the latest European fashion, black trousers, and hand crafted black boots. He descended the gangway and stood on the quay. He lit a cigarette, exhaled, and looked left and right expectantly. In moments, a black sedan pulled onto the quay. Three men emerged from the sedan and approached the tall man. There was a brief conversation and a shaking of hands all round. The smallest of the three men carried a leather portfolio and acted as interpreter for the tall visitor. They entered the sedan and it slowly blended into Boston traffic, making its way south onto Route One, the Boston Post Road, toward Providence, Rhode Island.

Salvatore cut the twine on the numerous bundles of palm reeds to be distributed at mass the next day, Palm Sunday. The ladies auxiliary and the nuns of St. Bart's had finished decorating the church with a dozen large bouquets of lilies and sprays of blood red roses on either side of the white marble altar. The whole chapel was fragrant with incense and lillies. Monsignor Cavalaro sat at his desk in the vestry at the rear of the church, putting the finishing touches to his Sunday sermon. Salvatore separated the palm reeds for easy distribution and packed them in a large brass cradle next to the altar rail. The front door of the church squeaked open. Salvatore turned instinctively. The sun had not yet set and the figure of a man was silhouetted against the brightness of the day. Salvatore returned to his task. Many people came to pray or light candles at all hours of the day. The sound of leather heels on the terrazzo aisle was a common one. Salvatore continued his work, his back to the center aisle. The clicking heels came to a halt. Salvatore sensed someone standing. He turned, still in a stooped position, and slowly stood upright.

It was a tall man in a broad-brimmed black fedora, both hands deep inside the pockets of a long skirted overcoat. "Salvatore Rossi?"

"Yes, that's me." Salvatore moved closer to the altar railing. The man raised the brim of his Fedora, exposing his face. They stood facing one another, unmoving. Salvatore's first thoughts were of Zarraga and his men, and then slowly the face became familiar.

"You, Capuano!" He shook his head in disbelief.

"Yes, Rossi, it's me, who you thought you could escape, who you thought you made a fool of." Capuano drew a long-barreled .38-caliber revolver from his overcoat pocket and leveled it at Salvatore's chest. "Salvatore Rossi, you're under arrest for the slaying of Barone Vitorio Santagatta. On your knees, now!"

Salvatore hesitated. Capuano advanced onto the altar. "I said, on your knees!" Salvatore sank to his knees, his eyes never leaving Capuano's. "You are also an illegal alien in this country. There will be no American law stopping your deportation, my friend. I'm taking you back to Italy, and I'm going to watch you hang, you son of a bitch!."

Capuano moved behind Salvatore, preparing to manacle his hands behind his back.

"One moment, please." It was Monsignor Cavalaro, who had overheard everything.

"Don't interfere, priest." Capuano pointed the revolver at Cavalaro. "This murderer, this scum is coming back to Naples with me, and if I have to shoot you, I will. Do you understand, priest?"

"Yes, my son, I understand. But there is something you must know, something terribly important. You must listen for one moment, please."

"You have two minutes. Then I'm leaving for Boston with this trash."

"Yes, yes, I understand." Cavalaro advanced into the flickering light of the votive candles. "Captain, I know you are not aware of the circumstances that preceded the Barone's death, and this you must know." Capuano kept the revolver leveled at Salvatore.

"Be quick about it, priest. I have people waiting for me."

"The truth in this matter, Captain, is that following the untimely death of Salvatore's father, Hugo, Santagata went to the still grieving widow's home three weeks later—just three weeks, mind you. The body was not cold yet. There, Santagata raped and beat the widow Rossi. This, so help me God, is the truth."

Capuano remained expressionless, the pistol unwavering. "I think you're a liar, priest, and your time is now up."

"No, my son, there is one more important thing you must hear." Capuano rolled his eyes toward the ceiling, motioning for Cavalaro to continue. "The reason Colonel Raimondo is so anxious to capture Salvatore is because the Barone was his lover. Yes, they were lovers when Raimondo was still a boy, and they continued their relationship throughout their lives."

Salvatore's mouth fell open as he shifted on his knees. Capuano eyes narrowed as he pointed the pistol at Cavalaro. "You're a goddamned liar, priest. You'd say anything to save his ass from justice."

"No, Captain, I am not a liar," said Cavalaro almost in a whisper. He took the strand of beads that dangled from the cord of his tunic and clutched them tightly to his heart. "But I have forsaken my vows of silence of those whose confessions I take, and so has Monsignor Ritacco in Atri. He was the Barone's confessor and confidant for many years, and may God forgive us both."

Capuano's face paled in the candlelight. He lowered the pistol to his side. He began to speak, stopped, staring blankly at Salvatore. For a full minute he stood drifting in thought; there was not a sound in the church. Finally, with an audible sigh he slid the pistol into his pocket, adjusted his fedora, and walked back toward the church door, buttoning his coat as he made his way down the center aisle. Salvatore rose from his knees and stood next to Monsignor Cavalaro as they watched him disappear into the glint of sunlight.

The interpreter and the two immigration officials were waiting in the sedan. As he entered the rear door the immigration men turned to the back seat.

"Mario, ask him what happened? Where's the guy we came for?" The interpreter held a brief conversation with Capuano, who turned and looked out the side window. "What'd he say, Mario?"

"He said it was the wrong man. He looked like him and his name is Rossi, but it's not his man." The immigration men looked at one another, shaking their heads in disgust, the driver cursing to himself as the engine came to life.

As they drove through the streets of Providence, Capuano leaned toward the interpreter and asked: "How do you like living in America?"

The priest and his disciple stood motionless for several moments. They could hear the roar of an engine and the fading sound of its departure as Capuano's car pulled away. The priest moved first, putting his arm around Salvatore's shoulders. He turned and embraced Cavalaro. They rocked to and fro. A great exhale passed Salvatore's lips; his knees were weak. The priest held him by the shoulders at arms length.

"My son, I think for once and for all you are now free of the law."

Salvatore's face was creased with a gleeful grin. "You saved my life. I will never forget this day, and I will always be in your service." He knelt and kissed the priest's hand.

"Stand up, my son, you have a life to live. You're now a free man. And with our friends in Boston, we will start you on the road to citizenship."

"But, Monsignor, how did you know about Raimondo and the Barone? Why did you bother to seek this information? Why did Monsignor Rittaco write a letter to you?"

The priest smiled and raised his eyebrows. "Well, my son, it appears that now I really do have to go to confession, for you see, my boy, there was no letter, and Raimondo and the Barone were not lovers. Not, at least, that I know of."

Salvatore was stunned. "But what will happen when he gets back to Italy and finds out that this is not the truth?"

"First of all, Salvatore, I don't believe he will be going back to Italy, not without you. And if he does go back, what do you think he will tell Raimondo—that he found you and let you go because of the story I told him? No, my boy, you are a free man."

The words all made sense, but still Salvatore could not quite grasp the enormity of what had just occurred. "Monsignor," he continued, "what would you have done if he had asked to see the letter?"

"Well, my boy," and now the priest actually laughed aloud, "I never thought of that. But I can guarantee you, if you did leave with him, his car would never have made it out of Rhode Island thanks to your friend Dom Zarraga."

Spring arrived, bringing with it the joys and scents of the early flowers and the fresh young foliage that transformed the tidy little rectory garden. Tina was in her ninth month of pregnancy. Salvatore's every waking thought was of his bride-to-be and the coming baby, and how to get them to America. Every evening he rushed into Mrs. Almonte's kitchen expecting a packet of letters. It had been three weeks since he last received letters from Atri. He buried himself in his work; there was a building boom in Rhode Island and Bill Gilborne was aggressively seeking new contracts. Salvatore had become invaluable as a job superintendent. The laborers wanted to work on his projects. He had grown close with Pasco LoFredo and regularly enjoyed Sunday dinners at his home. Pasco's youngest daughter, Lucia, was a particular delight, and he doted upon her, bringing special small gifts he would make by hand. At only five, Lucia dazzled Salvatore with saucer blue eyes and blond pigtails that bounced wildly as she ran into his open arms. She loved Salvatore as much as she loved her family and screamed with delight upon his arrival, calling him "*Zio* Salvatore," *Uncle*, which made Salvatore's chest swell with love and pride.

It had been two months since his last letters; he was frantic and frustrated. He returned from work on a Tuesday afternoon to find Monsignor Cavalaro waiting for him on the rectory's front steps. Salvatore noticed that the priest was not wearing his usual benevolent smile.

"Salvatore, please, come into my study. I need to talk with you about something important."

"All right, Monsignor, what is it, news from Atri?" The slight quiver in his voice revealed the depth of his concern.

"Yes, my son, it is news from Atri." They had entered his study. "Please, Salvatore, sit down." He walked to the window overlooking the schoolyard, the long rosary beads at his side rattling against his vestments. He turned and drew a chair close to Salvatore.

Salvatore's voice was a dull monotone. "What is it, Monsignor?"

Cavalaro stroked his face with his hands, exhaled, reached into his pocket, and handed a letter to him. As Salvatore removed the already opened letter from its envelope, Cavalaro spoke. "Half of Atri has been wiped out because of the small pox. There was nothing that could be done. Even Dr. Albanese was taken from us."

Salvatore's lips moved as he read Monsignor Rittaco's letter. "*My heart goes out to young Salvatore. Please inform him that we tried*

THE ARRIVAL THE STRUGGLE THE ASCENDANCY

everything, but we were unable to save his mother and Tina, who as you know was close to child birth. Unfortunately, we had to bury them in lime immediately to prevent any further spread of this pestilence. We will have services for everyone as soon as we can...." The letter fell from his hand. Cavalaro reached out to place a hand on the younger man's shoulder. He was trembling, stuttering, agony etched into his face.

"Why, why, why!" Salvatore's voice rose to a thunderous roar. "Why did this happen, God, tell me why?" He bolted from his chair and ran to the church. There was no stopping him. He burst through the front door and ran down the aisle to confront the altar. Monsignor Cavalaro followed behind, as did Mrs. Almonte in her apron. With his arms spread wide, he roared at the crucifix above the altar.

"You have taken all in life that I love! You have ruined my life on earth, there is nothing left for me. I hate you for this, I piss on you for this, you mean nothing to me any longer! You're not my god!" He turned and brushed past Cavalaro and Mrs. Almonte, who was convulsed in tears. Father Cavalaro sat wearily in the first pew, head back, eyes closed. Mrs. Almonte knelt at the altar sobbing and praying out loud, her Rosary beads scratching at the altar railing. There came a wail from the basement of the school, choking and sobbing as if from a wounded animal. It lasted for a full minute and then silence.

Salvatore did not report to work the next day or the next. He lay on his bed red eyed and unblinking. He contemplated how he would take his life. Cavalaro knocked on his door accompanied by Mrs. Almonte, who carried a bowl of soup and a half-loaf of fresh baked bread, but there was no sound, no reply. On the second day Pat LoFredo came by to see his friend, thinking he was ill. He learned of the tragedy with visible anguish. He left the rectory and walked to the schoolyard a few yards from the door to the basement and Salvatore's room. He paced slowly, seeking to accompany his best friend in his grief while not intruding in his sorrow.

The next evening there were several men in the schoolyard. LoFredo had bought a basket of food that he left at the outside door. At the end of seven days there were twenty-five men smoking and talking softly amongst themselves, clustered in groups outside the basement door. LoFredo had taken his Lucia with him to the schoolyard. She carried a small basket of cookies that she insisted she give to Salvatore herself. At five she had a mind of her own. She tugged at LoFredo's hand, banana curls bobbing about, blue eyes pleading, small heart-shaped lips set in determination. LoFredo hesitated and gave in, opening the heavy door to the school basement. They stood for a moment in front of Salvatore's room. There was no sound. The little girl took two steps to the door and knocked, calling out: "*Zio* Salvatore, *Zio* Salvatore, it's me, Lucia. I have some of my favorite cookies for you." Still there was no sound. "Please, *Zio* Salvatore! Why don't you come to our house anymore? Don't you love me anymore?" she squeaked, the little voice tapering off in sadness.

There was a stirring from the room; the door slowly opened. "Oh, *Zio* Salvatore, you have a beard and your eyes are all red. I have to take you home so Mommy can make you something to eat, Mommy said so. Come on with me and Daddy." She reached for Salvatore's hand, a serious expression on her face. He bent down and picked up the little girl who smilingly threw her arms around his neck and softly said, "I love you, *Zio* Salvatore."

"I love you too, my little angel," said Salvatore, his voice a hoarse whisper. Pat LoFredo's eyes moistened as he placed his arm around

THE ARRIVAL THE STRUGGLE THE ASCENDANCY

his friend's waist and led him up to the schoolyard. All eyes turned as the heavy door opened, Salvatore emerging, the little girl snug in his arms. The crowd parted, murmuring as he walked toward the rectory. Reassuring hands reached out to pat his shoulder or squeeze his arm as he walked. He handed the smiling little girl to her father. They spoke in low voices. Salvatore took LoFredo's free hand and kissed his cheek. He walked into the kitchen door of Mrs. Almonte's kitchen; she awaited him with a steaming bowl of chicken soup, a tall glass of wine, and a tearful embrace. The next morning he was at the construction site, the men solemnly greeting him, respectful of his privacy. He never spoke again of his mother or Tina.

He threw himself into his work—arriving at the job site before dawn, the last to leave in the evening. He had changed, everyone could see that. Gone was the quick, easy smile. There was little laughter. Even so, he became even more compassionate toward the men who labored on his crews. It was as if this motley group of swearing, smoking, hard-working immigrants was his own family and it was his duty to protect every one of them from harms way. The men sensed his care and responded by working harder, wanting to please him. Bill Gilborne knew of his loss but said nothing. Instead, he allowed him more and more responsibility and assigned him to even larger construction projects.

The payroll was delivered each Friday by Gilborne's bookkeeper and manager, Abe Ratsky, a young, stout, smiling Jew who had been in America for two years. When the men saw the old Ford pull up to the job site the word would quickly pass along that "Abe the Rat was here with the cheese." Ratsky took the ribbing good-naturedly, giving as good as he got, especially toward the Italians. The men would howl with delight at his endless string of clever ethnic slights, keenly aware that they were all struggling for the same thing— a piece of land, a future for their families, a sense of decency. Salvatore had always liked Abe, and Abe saw in the serious young Italian someone with great potential in life.

On the first Friday of Salvatore's return, Ratsky intentionally held Salvatore's pay envelope until last, motioning him to follow to the Ford. He handed the pay envelope to Salvatore, removed his cap, and extended his hand, gripping Salvatore's tightly. "I vant you should know that me end my family, my vife and my children, offer to you our deepest sympathy. I vant you should know that ve pray for you on shabbos; this is like Sunday."

Salvatore bowed his head, humbled by the little man's sincerity. "Thank you, Abe, I appreciate your thoughts and your prayers. Please thank your wife and children for me."

The bookkeeper stepped closer and gripped Salvatore by the arm. "Leesin, Salvatore," he continued, speaking softly, as though imparting a great secret, "my vife vants you should come to our howz for dinner maybe Saturday at six o'clock. Ve vill not take no for an answer, so vata ya say?"

Salvatore smiled and nodded. "All right, Abe, yes I would be happy to come to dinner at your house."

"Goot! Leesin, vun other thing. Salvatore, I go to Roger Villaims College at the YMCA on Broad Street, downtown. I take courses in accounting. Vy don't you come vit me to enroll. I know you like dis business. They have courses on architecture; dis I know you vould like. Any vay, you think about it, it vill be good for you, and I know Mr. Gilborne vill pay for your books. And, *oyy*, how could I forget! The tuition is very, very cheap. You let me know."

THE ARRIVAL THE STRUGGLE THE ASCENDANCY

From that moment Salvatore struck up a friendship with Abe Ratsky that would last a lifetime. At the suggestion of his friend, he enrolled in Roger Williams College, taking courses in drafting, accounting, and English literature. He crowded his days with activity. He had returned to the church, giving his confession to Monsignor Cavalaro and once again assisting at Mass on Sundays and holy days of obligation. The days passed, one following the other, his love for Tina never diminishing.

Fourteen years passed; he was thirty-three years old. He had become one of the youngest construction superintendents in the country, known for his ability to bring in a job on time and on budget. He had moved from his apartment at the school to a third-floor tenement, eventually buying the three-decker home on Silver Lake Avenue. He had purchased a new Ford coupe and from time to time would drive Pat LoFredo and his wife to Boston to visit relatives. LoFredo's family had become his family in America. The children called him "Uncle" and respected him as another father. Little Lucia had blossomed into a tall, willowy, beautiful young woman—willful, capricious, and spoiled. Salvatore defended her every action. There had been women in his life, women who had loved him. But he had found that it was impossible for him to give all of his emotions to any woman. He had matured physically, more handsome than ever. Pat LoFredo's wife, Philomena, was desperate to find him a suitable wife. Ratsky's wife had introduced him to several young Jewish women, all to no avail.

It was on a Sunday drive to LoFredo's sister's house in Boston's North End that it happened. There were other visitors at the Boston home on this particular Sunday. LoFredo's cousin Attilio's wife, Gilda, had cousins in nearby Revere. They had arrived a short while earlier with their children and their oldest daughter, Francesca. Francesca had huge aquamarine eyes and soft full lips set against high cheekbones, with cascades of long auburn hair that fell almost to her waist. Shy and lady like, she was nineteen years old and the apple of her father's eye. Salvatore stood up upon introduction, took her hand, and stared dumb struck as their eyes locked upon one another in an awkward, fumbling moment. Their hands refusing to leave one another's, the room fell silent, he murmuring, "It's my pleasure to meet you" and she responding, "The pleasure is mine." Philomena and LoFredo exchanged knowing glances. Attilio and Gilda observed the obvious electricity with discomfort.

From that day the Ford coup spent every weekend in Boston or Revere. Attilio had warmed to Salvatore after learning of his financial success and his standing in St. Bart's parish, and LoFredo lost no time in embellishing Salvatore's background and outstanding character. As for Francesca and Salvatore, they were wildly and passionately in love. For the first time in fourteen years he was able to free himself of feelings of guilt for loving another woman. Tina would always have a place in his heart, but that would now become a loving memory.

They were married in April of nineteen thirty at the church of St. Anthony in Revere. Pat LoFredo was best man. Francesca moved to Silver Lake, settling into Salvatore's triple-decker. Their life was full of love and playfulness. She was an excellent homemaker in the Old World tradition, and quickly endeared herself to all the women of the parish. Salvatore was reborn. He had a new zest for life, a buoyancy to his every activity. Exactly nine months later she gave birth to an eleven-pound four-ounce wailing, crimson-faced baby boy. They named him Hugo after his father. Hugo Salvatore Rossi.

Chapter 4

THE STREET GUY

May, 1950

He had the physique of a Greek god, possessed chiseled features, a mop of unruly hair, and devastating blue eyes. At nineteen years of age he was known throughout Silver Lake and Federal Hill as a lady-killer. He had starred in football and baseball at Mt. Pleasant High School, developing a reputation as a tough kid. He had a temper. There were many Friday and Saturday night fist fights at dance halls and cafes in Providence and on occasion in Boston. He reveled in the violence. He was a leader. His band of followers were all equally tough young Italian men, distinguished by their pegged pants, suede shoes, silk shirts, and the gold crosses or oversized saintly medals that they wore around their necks more as jewelry than for any sense of reverence.

It was only a matter of time before a local mafia captain took note of the tough good-looking kid from "the Lake." Vito

Ferruccio was the local *capo*, operating out of a back room in a small shop called Nick's Variety. He ran a book making and loan sharking operation as well as an outlet for stolen goods. A call went out for Hugo to visit with Vito; he wanted to talk about things.

The only entrance to Ferruccio's office was through the front door of the variety store and through a maze of shelving and counters. Ferruccio's private back door was always locked and was used only for the shipment or delivery of stolen goods. The small bell on the front door jingled as Hugo entered the store. The young man behind the counter had delivered the message for Ferruccio and now he motioned Hugo to the back room.

Hugo stood in the open doorway. A broad smile creased Ferruccio's face. "Ay, Oogo!" he bellowed, pronouncing the name in Italian. "Come in, sit down. You want some coffee, a drink?"

"No, thank you, Mr. Ferruccio, not right now." Hugo moved to the chair that Ferruccio pointed to and sat down.

"Ay, what's this 'Mr. Ferruccio' stuff! That's what the prosecuting attorneys and the Yankee bankers call me! Call me Vito."

Hugo nodded. "Thank you, Vito." Ferruccio was short, fat, and had a face like a pig. His thick hair was slicked with pomade and his teeth were large square pieces of ivory spaced a quarter of an inch apart.

"Ya know, Hugo, I been watchin' you." Ferruccio leaned far back in his chair, his voice suddenly turning serious, his hands clasped in front of him like a man at prayer. "You're a tough young guy. You got your own little gang and you keep 'em in line. I like that. You outta school?"

Hugo was listening intently, wondering where this conversation was going to lead. The question seemed a simple one and he gave a simple answer. "Yea, I graduated last year from Mt. Pleasant."

"So you got a high school diploma. That's good. I like a smart man. So what are you doin' for a living, Hugo?"

"I work for my father as a laborer with Gilborne. He's a job superintendent. I'm on a job now in Attleboro."

Again, Ferruccio sat back in his chair crossing his hands over his ample stomach. He studied Hugo, the open shirt revealing a gold chain with a large Saint Anthony medal. When he spoke it was softly, with the solicitous tone of a close friend or a priest in the confessional. "Tell me, Hugo, what do you do on this job, what kind of work do you do?"

"Well I, ah, do a lot of things. I mix cement, I carry brick, I carry mortar—you know, construction."

"Sounds to me like you're working your ass off!" cried Ferruccio and he flashed a wide-toothed grin.

"Well, I guess I am," admitted Hugo, grinning too, and he sat back and crossed his legs, beginning to feel more comfortable with Ferruccio.

"So what do they pay you for all this work, Hugo, a couple a hundred a week?"

Hugo sat upright. "Are you kiddin', I make about sixty bucks a week, and that's gross before taxes."

"Holy shit, that's all you make for all that work?"

"That's it."

Ferruccio shook his head from side to side, his face wearing a look of painful injustice. "You got a girl friend, you know what I mean, somebody special?"

"Yeah, I do, she's special."

"Well, what the hell can you buy her with forty or forty five bucks a week? Whadaya do, take her to the Rainbow show down the street on Saturday night?"

"Yeah, that's about it. Once in awhile we go downtown to the Fay's Theatre to see a live show."

Ferruccio sat forward leaning his elbows on the desk, forming a tent of his chubby fingers. "Listen, Hugo, I can use a sharp young guy like you working for me. The works not hard; your not gonna get your hands dirty. You get to meet a lot of good people, and you also get a lot of respect. The job pays two hundred a week to start. That's with no deductions—cash. Waddya say?"

Hugo pulled his chair closer to the desk and leaned across forward so that the faces of the two men were just inches apart. "What do I do on this job, Vito? What about the hours, stuff like that?"

"Hugo, the job you got now is for assholes and greenhorns. What I got for you doesn't have any fuckin hours. A lot of days you do what you wanna do. I'll tell you what you need to know. You'll make more money than you can spend, *capece*?"

"When do you want me to start?"

"You can start today if you want, or next week. I think you might wanna give your father some notice, right?"

Salvatore sat biting his lower lip while Ferruccio waited for an answer. He stood, slowly extending his hand across the desk.

"Thank you, Vito, I'll take the job, but I can't start for two weeks."

Ferruccio grabbed the outstretched hand with both of his pudgy hands and shook it vigorously, smiling broadly. "Good boy, you made the right decision." Ferruccio reached into his pocket extracting a wad of cash and peeled off five twenty-dollar bills, holding the money out to Hugo. "Take this, we'll call it a sign-up bonus. Give you some pocket money so you can take that special girl some place besides the Rainbow show. You wanna take her up to the Ranch House in Johnston? It's a classy nightclub, friends of mine owns it. Frankie Lane's there for the next two weeks. Whadaya say, I'll call my friend George and get you a front table right near the band. You wanna go?"

Hugo stood feeling flush with cash, and now this! Only big shots went to the Ranch House. He felt as if he had arrived. "Yeah, Vito, I'd love to go, my girl's a big Frankie Lane fan."

"Awright, this Saturday night, seven o'clock for two people. I'll make the reservation for you. I'll call my friend Georgy, just go in and ask for him, you got it?"

"Okay, Vito, thank you, I appreciate it."

The *capo* wrapped his arm around Hugo's broad shoulders. "You're gonna do okay, make some money with us, have a good time. And I want you to stop by and see me every day, understand? I wanna fill you in a little more on some of the things you're gonna be doin'."

Hugo sat behind the wheel of his '41 Pontiac coupe. Since picking it up a year earlier he had had it painted a dark maroon and equipped it with a flashy set of white wall tires. The interior was immaculate, smelling strongly of Mennen after-shave, which he sprinkled liberally on the upholstery and floor mats. He tapped

THE ARRIVAL THE STRUGGLE THE ASCENDANCY

a Lucky Strike out of the pack and lit it. Inhaling deeply he ran Vito's conversation through his mind. He knew Vito was connected to the Mafia, everybody did. He knew that association with Vito was association with Dom Zarraga. He also knew that there was much prestige attached to this association. It meant power and respect on the streets of the Italian neighborhoods—power and respect born of fear. He smiled to himself, flicked the cigarette onto the street, and started the engine, the guttural rumblings of the dual glass-packed mufflers accentuating the powerful engine.

The Pontiac rumbled to a stop in front of a neat white bungalow just out of Silver Lake on Hartford Avenue. To the right of the bungalow a quarter-acre lot was under cultivation, with tall tomato stakes standing row after row. At the rear of the house stood a large grape arbor. Gardening tools rested against a wheelbarrow waiting for use. Most of the houses in the neat Italian neighborhood had similar gardens. On the front porch of the bungalow sat Angelina Natale, hands clasped about her knees, her dark hair in tangles about her face. She was seventeen, the youngest of nine children. Her face was heart shaped with matching full lips.

She wore an angora sweater, bobby sox, penny loafers, and a wide pleated skirt. She turned her head, nose in the air, refusing to acknowledge Hugo's arrival. He was late, again. Hugo craned his neck to view the porch from the driver's seat. He pushed his sunglasses over his forehead and turned the volume up on the A.M. radio that was blasting rock and roll. He raced the rumbling engine, the glass pack's reverberating through the neighborhood. Still, she refused to turn her head. He smiled, head tilted to one side like he'd seen in a James Dean movie.

"Aangieee, c'mon, I'm sorry! I had a meeting with somebody. He held me up. C'mon, let me see that beautiful smile." It worked. Angelina broke into an irrepressible smile, shaking her head as she opened the front gate. Hugo opened the passenger door from inside and she slid into the car.

"You know, I shouldn't even talk to you. You're always late, you don't call, your friends are more important than me..." He cut off her conversation with a kiss. "Hugo, we're in front of my house, my father would kill me!"

"No he won't, he likes me."

"No, you got it all wrong, he likes your father. He thinks you're a little cocky."

Hugo feigned an expression of surprise. "Me, cocky? It's not cocky, it's self-confidence. I'll show your father what I'm made of. After all, I'm gonna be his son-in-law." She nestled her head on his shoulder and looked into his eyes, smiling.

"C'mon," said Hugo, edging the Pontiac away from the curb, "let's go up the Hill and get a pizza at Iavazzo's. Some of the guys are gonna be there with their girls."

"So, who did you have to meet with that was so important, your stock broker?" There was a half-teasing tone to Angelina's voice.

"No, smart ass, I met with Vito Ferruccio. He offered me a job." Angelina sat bolt upright and stared at Hugo.

"What's wrong with you, your mouth's open."

"You know what's wrong, he's part of the Mafia, he's been in jail. You can't go to work for him. Besides, you've got a job, a good one, and your father is going to be really pissed off at you if you even think about leaving his company."

"Number one, Vito runs a legitimate business."

"Yeah, really, what does he do?"

"He runs a wholesale business."

"Oh, yeah, what does he wholesale?"

"Stuff, jewelry, housewares, things like that, plus he owns real estate."

"Well," said Angelina, sliding still further away from Hugo, "I don't think it's a good idea for you to work for someone who has a reputation as a Mafia guy."

"Listen, he's a good guy, and I'll make three times what I make with my father." To Hugo's relief they arrived at the pizza parlor, cutting off the conversation. "C'mon, I'm starved, what about you?"

"No, I'm just gonna have a Coke, I feel bloated." They exchanged glances.

"Did you, ah, you know what I mean, did you..."

"No, I didn't get it yet. I'm late."

"How late?"

"About a week."

"Is that normal?" They stood in front of Iavazzos' plate glass window. Chuckie Vileno was making faces at them as he gobbled down a dripping triangle of tomato and cheese.

"Yes, it's normal, but I better get it soon. I don't even want to think about it."

They entered Iavazzo's and headed to the noisy crowd in the side room. Four couples were gathered around the doubled-up table listening to Chuckie Vileno holding forth, as usual.

"Aay, look everybody, Mr. And Mrs. America are here! And guess what, Mr. America's going to pick up the check! Hugo, you're the greatest!" Chuckie exaggerated a sweeping bow as Hugo and

Angie found seats. Vinnie Marfeo, Hugo's closest friend, caught his eye and moved toward the men's room. Hugo followed. There was excitement in Vinny's voice as they entered the ancient toilet.

"I heard your gonna be with Ferruccio, you fuck you. I can't believe it!" He wrapped his arms around Hugo and gave him a bear hug.

"Hey, watch it, you're wrinkling my twenty dollar shirt." Hugo straightened his collar with mock seriousness breaking into a grin.

"My uncle says you're gonna come up pretty quick with Ferruccio. Just remember, the guy respects big balls, know what I mean?"

Hugo nodded his head. "Don't worry, I got balls, you know that."

"My uncle told me Zarraga was interested in you, asked questions about you."

"Yeah? C'mon, I don't believe it."

"I'm telling you it's the truth, swear on my mother."

"Vin, what are you doin' for your uncle?"

He shrugged. "I collect money. He's got a bunch of vending machines, I help out with that. I deliver stuff. He's got a book. I payoff the winners and collect from the losers. I'm doin' good. Whatta you gonna be doin'?"

"I don't know yet. I guess stuff like your doin'."

"Tell your old man yet?"

There was a pause. Hugo rolled his eyes toward the ceiling and exhaled through pursed lips, shaking his head. "No, I didn't tell him yet. You know my father, black is black, white is white, nothin' in between. I gotta talk to him over the next few days. C'mon, let's get outta this friggin' toilet."

THE ARRIVAL THE STRUGGLE THE ASCENDANCY

"Aay, what are you guys doin' in there, holding each others weenies?" Chuckie Vileno held himself by the crotch as he taunted Hugo and Vinny.

"Vinny," said Hugo grinning wildly, "let's take his pants off so we can show everybody his giant sausage." Vileno tried to get past them by climbing over the high-backed wooden booths.

"C'mon you guys, I was only kiddin." He was cornered against a jukebox sandwiched by two wooden booths.

"Awright, Chuckie, you got two choices," declared Hugo. "Either you drop your pants right now or me and Vinny are gonna take them off for you." The girls were giggling hysterically.

"Awright, awright, you got me cornered. I don't want you girls or any of you guys getting too excited." Vileno's pants fell to his ankles revealing baggy polka dot boxer shorts to howls of laughter and catcalls. "Awright, asshole, pull up your pants, time to go." Hugo turned and the noisy group exited the pizzeria while old man Iavazzo made the sign of the cross in relief as they trouped out the front door.

The Pontiac roared to life as Angie climbed into the passenger seat. She sat with her jaw clenched. "Well, where are we going now?" she asked as Hugo was in the process of a U-turn on Atwells Avenue.

"C'mon, Ang', it's Friday night, you know I go with the guys on Friday nights. It's only one night a week, were gonna go to Coffee's Cafe for a couple of beers, maybe play some cards." Angie sat rigid staring straight ahead. "You know you're acting like a two-year old, you do this all the time. Whataya gonna do if I have to work some nights for Vito?"

"Well," snapped Angelina, "I knew that was coming! Those guys live by night so no one can see what they're doing."

"See what I mean!" Hugo smashed the steering wheel with the palm of his hand and goosed the throttle so that the car leaped forward. "Geese, you already have me in the can! You gotta stop this shit. Listen, tomorrow night I have a surprise for you, I'm taking you somewhere special." She turned to look at him, features softening.

"Oh, really, and where is this special place?" Hugo smiled and pulled a Lucky Strike from his shirt pocket, tapped it on the steering wheel, and pushed in the cigarette lighter. The tide, he knew, had suddenly turned in his favor. "Well, are you going to tell me where this special place is or are we going to play twenty questions?"

Hugo inhaled deeply and blew smoke rings at her. "I'm taking you the Ranch House to see Frankie Lane, how's that?" Angie sat up and turned in her seat, mouth ajar.

"The Ranch House!" She shouted the words incredulously. "How can you afford that, it's expensive and they only let money people make reservations there?"

"Listen, we're all set, I have connections. We have a table right by the stage and we're gonna have steak and lobster and anything you want, whaddaya think?"

"What will I wear? How did you get reservations? Where did you get the money? What do you mean connections?" The words poured out of her mouth.

Hugo laughed aloud. "Never mind why or how, we'll have a great time."

"I can't tell my mother, she won't like the idea."

"Tell her were gonna go to a party at Rhodes. There's a band there every week and everybody dresses up." The Pontiac rumbled to a stop in front of Angie's house, engine idling. "C'mere, give me a kiss." She slid across the seat and kissed him quickly on the lips. "Hey, that's it?"

"You'll get the rest tomorrow night." She smiled and climbed out of the Pontiac, then leaned back into the car. "You have to tell your father about Ferruccio, you know that."

"Yeah, yeah, I am, I am."

"When?"

He paused, tapping the steering wheel with a drum roll of fingers. "Sunday, I'll tell him Sunday before dinner."

Hugo awoke at 10:15 Sunday morning, fuzzy headed from the previous night. When they had arrived at the Ranch House the parking lot was jammed with Caddies, Lincolns, and tail-finned Chrysler Imperials. Hugo pulled the Pontiac under the portico at the front of the Spanish motif entrance with its wide double wooden doors. Two uniformed attendants were scurrying from car to car, opening doors and mumbling a welcome to the Ranch House.

As Hugo and Angie approached the maitre'd station they were greeted by George Mosaff, a dapper, silvery haired, theatrical figure who appeared to be somewhere in his fifties. Born and raised on the Hill, George knew every Mafioso and associate in Rhode Island and Massachusetts. Menus in hand, he opened his arms in a welcoming gesture. "Ah, Mr. Rossi and *la bella signorina*, welcome, welcome, we've been expecting you. Mr. Ferruccio would be pleased to have you as a guest at his table. Please follow me."

They worked their way through the crowded room, the glitter of diamonds and glint of gold at every table. For the men, silk and mohair suits were the uniform of the evening. The crowd was overwhelmingly Italian, and it seemed as if everyone knew each other. The room echoed with nonstop chatter and laughter and champagne popping in every corner. Ferruccio looked up from a plate of linguine with clams, strands of linguine dangling from his overstuffed mouth. He motioned with his head and eyes to the empty seats at the table, washed the pasta down with a large glass of Chianti, and wiped his mouth two-handed with a napkin the size of a pillowcase. To his left sat a woman obviously twenty years his junior dripping in jewelry, her peroxide blonde hair arranged in a tall beehive. Hugo took note of her eyes that had been made up to the size of fifty-cent pieces and the ruby red lipstick that had been applied over her lip line. The black sequin dress was painted on a voluptuous body with large breasts about to explode from her low cut bodice.

"Ah, look at dese kids!" One arm swept out wide as a means of introduction. "Hugo, you look like a movie star. I'm glad you came. And what's this be-yootiful young lady's name?"

Responding, Angie blushed, looked down at the table, looked up and caught the eye of the blond smiling and sipping champagne. Ferruccio motioned for the waiter. "Nicky, drinks all around, and bring another bottle of Dom Perignon."

"Right away, Mr. Ferruccio," replied the waiter with a bow.

"Hugo, Angie, meet my friend, Peggy Staziak." Ferruccio grinned with pride as the blonde woman extended her hand as if presenting it to be kissed.

"Pleased to meet you, Hugo, Angie. Hugo, Vito told me so much about you. I wish you luck in the business." Hugo felt a slight stirring as she greeted him. As he took her hand he struggled to keep from gazing into the inviting depths of her impressive cleavage.

"Thank you, Peggy," he managed to reply. "I'm looking forward to getting started."

Ferruccio leaned over the table. "You talk with your old man yet? You give him notice?"

Hugo turned to look at the crowd as he responded. "No, tomorrow, I'm gonna tell him tomorrow." When the waiter came Hugo ordered stuffed lobster, Angie a filet mignon well done. While they ate a steady procession of silk and mohair suits came by to pay their respects to Ferruccio. There was much embracing and slapping of shoulders, and Ferruccio introduced Hugo to each of them by name and territory. To Hugo's surprise, they were from all over New England.

At ten o'clock the house lights dimmed and Frankie Lane made his way to the microphone to a standing round of applause. He opened with his big hit, *That's My Desire*. The crowd went wild. A suit came to the table and whispered into Ferruccio's ear. He abruptly got up and worked his way to a far corner of the room. Hugo could just make out a group of figures seated at a round table. He watched Ferruccio bend down and kiss someone on the cheek. There were handshakes all around. A moment later he worked his way back to Hugo, his large stomach impeding his progress as he squeezed his way through the tables.

"Hugo, come with me, the old man wants to see ya." The women sat mesmerized as Frankie Lane belted out *Mule Train*. They never turned their heads as Hugo rose, buttoned his jacket, and walked with his new boss back to the corner table. The candle in the center cast enough light to reveal the faces of Domenic Zarraga and four other men. Cigar smoke enveloping the table. Zarraga motioned to a chair next to him.

"So you're Salvatore Rossi's kid?"

Hugo had heard much about the man who was now addressing him—knew that men, even tough men, feared him. And finding himself suddenly sitting and speaking with this man made Hugo fearful, too, at least a little. But he was determined not to show it. "Yes, Mr. Zarraga," he replied simply, "Salvatore is my father."

Zarraga waved his hand side to side. "None of that, my friends call me Dom. You can call me Dom, *capece*?"

Hugo smiled imperceptibly. "Yes, thank you, Dom." The silk suits around the table sat back in their chairs puffing on cigars, staring at Hugo impassively.

"So you're going to work for Vito, is that right?"

"Yes, Dom. I'm looking forward to being with Vito very shortly."

"You know when you work for Vito, you work for me. You understand this?"

Yes, I do Dom." Zarraga studied Hugo for what seemed like an eternity to Hugo. Finally he pulled the cigar from his mouth. "We need young guys like you. You're a tough young guy. I know you take no shit on the street, and I like that. I like it that you got balls. You understand?"

"Yes, Dom, I do." Hugo smiled to himself, remembering his conversation with Vinnie Marfeo the day before.

"Good, I want you to meet some men who are with me." Zarraga pointed to each man in turn. "This is my right-hand man, Giusto Rotondo. This is Buster Zito, he's from Worcester, Mass. We've got a lotta good guys up in Worcester." Zito stood and extended his hand to Hugo. "Glad to have you with us, Hugo."

"This is Vinny Theresa," continued Zarraga pointing to a man who weighed close to thee hundred pounds. The enormous figure smiled and nodded a greeting. "And this is Nunzio Martella. We call him the Hammer. When we need to hammer somebody,

Nunzio is the best in the business." The men around the table erupted in loud laughter, coded comments filling the air. The Hammer starred at Hugo, eyes narrowed, unsmiling.

Hugo acknowledged each man and concluded with, "It's nice to meet all of you, a pleasure."

Zarraga slapped Hugo on the back. "All right, Hugo, go back to your pretty little girl friend. I can see she's anxious to see you. I'll be talking with you soon. And remember what I said."

"Yes, Dom, I will. And thank you for seeing me tonight."

Ferruccio had already returned to the table. When Hugo arrived he was in the midst of devouring a strawberry short cake, whipped cream covering his upper lip and chin. Frankie Lane was wrapping up his act as the crowd came to its feet. Ferruccio stood clapping, napkin tucked into his shirt collar.

"The old man, he likes you," Ferruccio shouted over the noise of the crowd. "I never seen anything like it." Ferruccio continued clapping as he spoke. "Something about your father, he says your father is one of the most stand-up guys he ever met."

Hugo nodded in appreciation. "He is, Vito, sometimes he's too stand-up."

The Pontiac glided to a stop in front of Angie's house shortly after one-thirty and seconds later the porch light came on. "Well, do I get a goodnight kiss?"

"Yes, a quick one, you know my mother's peeking out the window." The light from the dashboard and radio illuminated the front seat.

"Ang', you looked beautiful tonight. I saw all the guys looking at you."

She wrinkled her nose. "You're crazy, you know that, don't you? I didn't see any guys looking at me."

Hugo smiled and lowered his head to kiss her softly on the lips. "I love you, sweetheart, you know that, don't you."

Angie looked up into Hugo's eyes. "And I love you more than anything in the world." The porch light blinked on and off three times.

Hugo shook his head in amusement. "Three times, are you in trouble?"

Angie slapped him playfully on the shoulder and slid across the vinyl seat. "Don't forget about your father. If he finds out before you tell him, he'll really be pissed."

Hugo raised his hands in mock surrender. "All right, all right, enough, I'll talk with him tomorrow, I promise."

Hugo padded bare footed into the sunny kitchen. Francesca was picking clothes from a line strung from the first-floor apartment to a steel pole twenty feet away. Every apartment had similar clotheslines with pulleys on each end for reeling out wet, freshly washed clothes and reeling in when dry. The stovetop was crowded with a large pot of tomato sauce and two fry pans—one for browning meat balls, the other sizzling with sausage and pork ribs. The kitchen was large; the beaded wainscoting was painted a dark creamy corn contrasted by colorful kitchen wallpaper embossed with teapots, cookie jars, and laying hens. The floor was covered in the latest design linoleum.

Hugo poured a cup of coffee from the still warm pot and filled a dish, set aside for drippings, with two large meatballs. He tore off the end of a fresh loaf of crusty bread and dipped it into the bubbling pot of sauce, guiding the sauce soaked bread into his mouth using his free hand to catch any drippings.

"Hey, *vagabondo*, what time did you get in last night? And stop eating, you know dinner is at twelve-thirty sharp and Uncle Pat and Auntie Philomena are coming over."

Hugo looked at his mother, his mouth stuffed with food, and smiled. At forty-years old she was still a head-turner. She stood at the window, her arms full of clothes fresh from the line. "Ma, you look beautiful like that, especially those slippers. I like the way the heels cave in."

Francesca laughed in spite of herself. "Hey, wise guy, you'd better get dressed and get over to church, your father expects you at eleven o'clock mass and he won't be happy if you're late."

"Ma, please, he's a fanatic. If I'm two minutes late I hear about it for a week."

"Your father is not a fanatic. He believes that you can make one sacrifice a week; he doesn't ask for more than that and you know it."

"Okay, you're right." He swallowed the last gulp of coffee. "But you have to iron a shirt for me if you want me to wear a tie."

She looked at him shaking her head in frustration and exhaling through pursed lips. "All right, set the ironing board up and get me the shirt, and hurry up, it's now ten-forty!"

He arrived at St. Bart's at five past eleven and slid into the pew next to his father. Salvatore glanced sideways as he settled into the pew, his face expressionless.

Salvatore left his seat, genuflecting as he emerged from the pew. He still served at mass from time to time, and on most

Sundays passed a collection basket. That morning he had assisted Father Cavalaro at the eight o'clock mass and afterward had busied himself in the church basement hall, setting up tables and chairs for the afternoon communion parties. Every Sunday he waited for Hugo's arrival at the eleven o'clock mass. He instinctively knew that this was a guarantee of Hugo's attendance, and he had a sense of deep parental pride at watching his strikingly handsome son enter St. Bart's, invariably creating a stir of interest among the young women of the parish.

Mass had ended. Salvatore was in conversation with Monsignor Cavalaro and some of the parish elders. Hugo stood slightly apart smoking, making small talk with Chuckie Vileno. Hugo joined his father as good-byes were being said and the men broke off, walking in different directions.

"I don't ask much of you, Hugo," began Salvatore as the two of them made their way homeward. "I don't push you, don't ask you to pay board, your mother treats you like a little prince. Why can't you come to mass on time?" They walked slowly. The sky was a brilliant spring blue, not a cloud in sight; trees were in bloom or budding; the scent of lilac was in the air. The crack of a baseball bat could be heard from the baseball field. "Hey, I'm talking to you, are you listening?"

Hugo walked hands in pockets looking everywhere but in his father's direction. "I'm sorry, Pa, you're right, there's no excuse. I promise it won't happen again."

"You know, Hugo, if I had a dollar for every one of your promises, I'd be a rich man."

"No, Pa, I mean it. You're right this time. I won't disappoint you."

Salvatore looked at the brilliant sky and muttered under his breath. "*A voglio spettare*, when will this happen? Hugo, I know I'm tough on you. This is because I want you to grow into a man of good-standing, a man who's reliable, who believes in things, a man who is self-disciplined, a man who will command respect from other men." Salvatore stopped and placed his hand on Hugo's shoulder, turning and speaking earnestly and softly. "You're my only child, my son. When people look at you they see me and your mother and what we have produced for a man. I love you and want the best for you, only the best. Do you understand this?"

Hugo held his father's gaze, this man he loved and respected more than God himself, this man he knew to be fearful of no other man, this man who had lost so much and worked so hard. "Yes, Pa, I do understand, and you and Ma are very important to me and you know I love you both and respect you both above all else."

Salvatore threw his arms around Hugo's shoulders and hugged him. "C'mon, we got a great Sunday dinner almost on the table and Uncle Pat and Auntie Phil are coming over. They're probably already there."

There was no way, Hugo thought. There was no way to tell his father about leaving. Tomorrow he would tell him on the job. It would be better tomorrow; this way it wouldn't spoil Sunday dinner.

The crew was working on a ten-story office building in downtown Providence. Hugo arrived at the construction site twenty minutes after Salvatore set the men to their day's tasks. When Hugo entered the construction shed Salvatore was hunched over a set of plans and enjoying one of Abe Ratsky's many stories.

"Vell, vell, look at dis bik handsome young man! Howwa you, Hugo? You getting married soon?" Ratsky was beaming a thousand watt smile.

"No, Mr. Ratsky, not yet, but you never know. How is Mrs. Ratsky?"

"She's vell, Hugo, I'll tell her you're asking, she'll be heppy. Vell, I got to get bek to the office, the papervork keeps piling up. Salvatore, I'll talk vit you next veek. Hugo, it vas good to see you." Ratsky left the construction shack trading quips with some of the old-time employees, stopping to chat and swap jokes with old friends who had arrived at Gilborne when he did. The construction shack was suddenly silent. Salvatore had returned to the plans, speaking to Hugo as he leafed through long rolls of blueprints.

"What's the matter with you, you don't feel good? How come you're late?"

"Pa...I, uh...don't know how to tell you this...but, uh, I'm tired of the construction business. I want to do something else." The words came out in spurts, but finally he had said it.

Salvatore became rigid in mid-motion, letting the plans slip from his hands. He turned slowly toward Hugo removing the newly prescribed reading glasses. "What are you talking about, you want to quit the company? Am I hearing you right?" Salvatore's voice was calm and matter of fact; he stood waiting for an answer, arms folded across his chest.

Hugo stared out of the construction shack door, shifting his gaze to the floor. "Look, Pa, I want to do something else, something I like. I don't want to make a career of this business. What's wrong with that decision?"

Salvatore settled himself slowly into his old office chair, the back of his hand pressed against his lips. "And so, what do you want to do for a living, do you know?"

"Yeah, I was offered a job with…" Hugo abruptly stopped. He knew his father would never accept Vito Ferruccio as a legitimate businessman. "…with an insurance company, Metropolitan Life Insurance. They have a training program; they, uh, need somebody who can speak Italian to sell to the Italian people - you know - on the Hill, Charles Street, the Lake."

Salvatore nodded his head, lips puckered. "Insurance, what makes you think you are cut out for being a salesman? I can't see you trying to sell life insurance or selling anything to anybody, that's not your make-up, that's for your friend, what his name, the one who's always talking and clowning? Vileno, Chuckie Vileno, yes that's him. This insurance business is not for you. I'm surprised you can't see this."

"Look, Pa, I want to try it." He almost had himself convinced that his argument was sincere. "I don't have anything to lose, I'll learn something new."

Salvatore leaned forward, elbows on knees, hands covering his face. He stood slowly turning once again to the plan table. There was a moment of silence as he adjusted the blueprints. "Hugo, I can't live your life and I don't expect you to live my life. Whatever you decide will be all right with me and your mother. Have you told her yet?"

"No, Pa, but I will when I get home."

"All right, I'll terminate you as of today. You'll have one more check coming next week."

"Well…uhh…don't you want my two week notice?"

"What for? There are people on the job who can fill your job for now, and I have a stack of applications from people looking for work. No, you don't have to give notice, say goodbye to your friends. I'll see you at home tonight." Salvatore busied himself with a ruler and triangle. Hugo stood awkwardly for a moment before turning and walking out the shack door to the men now on coffee break.

The maroon Pontiac rumbled at the curb outside Mt. Pleasant High School. It was two forty-five. In a moment twelve hundred students would come crashing through the doors into the warm spring air. Hugo sat left arm draped over the driver's side door, cigarette dangling from the corner of his mouth, dark aviator sunglasses firmly in place, collar carefully turned up on the latest style gaucho shirt, navy blue pegged pants, matching navy blue suede shoes. The radio blared out the top fifty rock and roll hits. He knew he looked good, he felt good, he would see Ferruccio tonight, let him know he was ready to start work.

The young men walking by the car all knew the Pontiac and its occupant. His reputation for toughness and skill on the football field was legendary. So, too, was his reputation with his fists. Everyone knew he was not a man to trifle with. As a freshman he had run afoul of Chang Dimarco, a senior, and the toughest kid in school. At the end of the class day several hundred students had turned out to watch the confrontation, forming a vast circle around the two combatants. The fight raged for nearly a half hour, the circle shifting from one side of a large grassy field to the other. Finally, drenched in sweat, blood soaked, and exhausted, Hugo landed an overhand right, caving in Chang's nose, bringing him crashing to his knees and finally flat on his face. At that moment his legend was made forever. Sitting in the Pontiac he acknowledged the familiar passersby with a nod of the head or a brief show of his palm. Finally, he saw her running for the car, clutching books and notebooks, hair and breasts bouncing as she ran. She opened the car door and slid beside him.

"Hi, what are you doing here at this time? Didn't you go to work today?" He craned his neck to kiss her upturned lips, simultaneously shifting the car into gear.

"I gave my notice to my father today." He accelerated into traffic, the roar of hot rods and squealing of tires filling the air as students retrieved their cars.

"Yea, well, what did he say?"

"He surprised me, he didn't try to stop me. He said he couldn't live my life and if this is what I wanted to do, it was all right with him."

Angie studied his expression. "You're not telling me everything. You mean to tell me that you told him all about Ferruccio and working for him? C'mon, did you?"

The car glided to a stop in front of her house. He turned the ignition off and sat staring straight ahead. "I told him I was taking a job with the Metropolitan Life Insurance Company."

Angelina shouted. "I don't believe you did a thing like that! You know he's going to find out. What do you do then?"

He mumbled, drumming his fingers on the steering wheel and shaking his head. "I don't know, but I do know that I'm not going back to construction and I know that I can make some serious escarole working for Ferruccio and Zarraga."

"Yeah, sure," she retorted, jumping out of the car and slamming the door closed, "as long as you don't wind up in the can."

"Ay, Oogo, c'mon in, howarya?" Ferruccio hoisted his corpulent frame from a rickety office chair, extending his hand.

"I'm good, Vito, I'm good." "Well, what's up, you stop by to say hello, you need anything?"

"No, thanks, I just came by to let you know that I'm ready to start any time you want me to."

Ferruccio's face broke into a Cheshire grin. "This is good, this is very good. Tell you what, you be here tomorrow about nine o'clock. You gonna be working with another young guy, name is Steve Marfeo, you know him?"

Hugo smiled and hunched his shoulders in surprise. "Do I know him, he's my best friend. We're always together, he's a good kid."

"This is good, very good. You two will make a great team together."

Hugo stood to leave, still wearing a grin. "All right then, Vito, I'll see you tomorrow at nine am."

"Be on time, you got a little travelin' to do. Awright, be a good boy."

Hugo couldn't believe it, he'd be working with Stevie! What a deal this was, working with your best friend. He was still smiling when he pulled into the oil stained cement driveway of the tenement house on Silver Lake Avenue. He cut the engine and sat for a moment watching his father's powerful back and arms as he tilled the plot of earth that in a few months would produce enormous bright red Big Boy tomatoes. Hugo opened the old gate made of heavy chain-link fencing. It clanged behind him. Salvatore turned, wiping his brow with a small towel as Hugo walked toward the rear of the house on the newly laid cement walkway.

"Hi, Pa, you want a hand with this, I'll get the other hoe."

"No, son, that's all right. I'm done now. But Saturday I need you to help me put the tomatoes and the stakes in, okay?"

"Yeah, sure, Pa. What about the chicken manure, you want me to pick it up?"

"No, Uncle Pat is gonna take a truck from the job and pick up his and mine and drop it off Saturday morning. Go ahead, go upstairs, I'll be up in a minute. Your mother's got some roasted chicken for us."

Hugo opened the door into the fragrant kitchen, redolent of garlic and roasting chicken. Francesca busied herself at the sink preparing a salad. Hugo slowly and quietly closed the door and tiptoed behind his mother to within her grasp.

"Don't even think about it, Mr. Smarty Pants, I know it's you." There was mirth in her voice. He quickly encircled her waist, lifted her off the floor, and spun her in a circle around the kitchen, both laughing at his antics. "Put me down or you're going to have burnt chicken, smarty pants."

"You know, Ma," he said with a grin, "you're starting to get a little heavy, what do you weigh now, anyway?"

"None of your business, wise guy, and by the way, how come you don't have work clothes on? Didn't you work today?" Hugo pulled a chrome vinyl padded chair out from the kitchen table and sat down, resting one elbow on the table. "Well, what's wrong? Why didn't you work today?"

"Ma, I'm changing jobs. I already talked with Pa, I'm…"

"What are you talking about, what do you mean another job? Gilborne is a future for you, it was a future for your father, how can you think like this?"

Hugo held up both hands palm forward. "Wait, wait, let me talk. Please, sit down for a minute." Francesca sat down, shaking her head with an exasperated expression. "All right," Hugo began, "now listen to me without interruption, okay?"

"Okay, talk."

"I don't like construction, I never did. I did it for Pa and you, you have to understand this. I don't want to do this for the rest of my life, can you understand my feelings."

"What will you be doing for a job?" Francesca's gaze was level, her voice monotone. Hugo knew she could see through any excuse or exaggeration, she called it a mother's intuition. He looked at her squarely in the eyes.

"I'm going to work for the Metropolitan Insurance Company."

"*Gesù Cristo Mio!*" Francesca threw both hands in the air. "You, an insurance salesman? Impossible, I don't believe it. Something is up here, you're not telling me something."

"Ma, I just told you what I'm doing. I start tomorrow and I don't want to talk about it anymore, it's what I want to do."

For a long moment Francesca sat immobile, slowly nodding her head. Then she arose, muttered "*che sarà sarà*," and returned to her sink.

Chapter 5

THE WISE GUYS

"Awright, youse guys are gonna go up to Worcester and do some collection work." Ferruccio let out a loud belch, made a series of vile sounds in his throat, then spit into his wastebasket. "I make loans to certain business people around here, and I got a lot of customers up in Worcester and Brockton. I got restaurant owners, car dealers, markets, all kinds of people. Half of the assholes are behind payin me, and I'm good to them. I only charge twenty percent a week on the unpaid balance. Most guys get thirty percent or even more."

"Vito, how do you want us to collect the money, checks, cash? Do these people know we're coming up there to collect?"

"I was just getting to that, Hugo." Ferruccio shuffled to his desk drawer and extracted a large black ledger. He stood behind the desk flipping through pages and muttering to himself absentmindedly, settling his meaty buttocks into the creaking office chair. He glanced up, removing his eyeglasses. "Awright, I'm gonna write down ten or twelve names and addresses of what they owe and what I want today. Youse guys understand?" Steve Marfeo nodded, Hugo grunted yes.

Hugo wore a puzzled expression. "Vito, suppose they don't have the money, then what?"

"Don't listen to that shit, there's always money! So they don't pay somebody else, you understand me?" Hugo and Steve nodded in understanding. Ferruccio's face became flushed as he wrote names and amounts, suddenly exploding in anger. "This fucken asshole's got a wife and two girlfriends, he spends all his fucken money on broads and having a good time and the scum bag won't pay me! I'm putting a star next to his name, make sure you collect from this piece of shit." He finished writing and looked up from his desk. "Awright, this is how you do it. You go up to the guy, be a gentleman and tell him that you work for me and you're there to collect a payment. You show him the balance, you tell him what you want to have today. If he tells you he doesn't have it, you tell him he has to get it because your orders are to get the payment today and you don't leave until you get a payment, *capece?*"

"Vito, suppose the guy doesn't want to come up with the money, you know, refuses?"

"Stevie boy, I been doin this for thirty-five years, we used to make loans to green horns, you know, businesses people in trouble. Believe me, they will pay. Sometimes you have to apply a little pressure, you know what I mean? You can push a little, but not too much. We don't need any cops on the scene. Awright, get going, I want you guys back here at five. *Aay*, you know how to get there? You go straight up Route 146, okay?"

Hugo nodded as he folded the list and placed it in his shirt pocket. "Yeah, we got cousins up there, I been up there a hundred times."

The Pontiac nosed up Route 146, the two occupants clad in pegged suit trousers and suede shoes, the collars on their silk shirts open to the third button. Marfeo turned the radio up to the voices of the Golden Greek and his rock n' roll revue. He beat the dashboard to the rhythm of Etta James as she belted out *Annie Had a Baby*.

"Hugo," began Marfeo, "I can't fucken believe we're working together. And this isn't even work, it's like going for a ride to Worcester." Hugo tapped a Lucky Strike out of the package keeping his left hand on the wheel. He offered one to Marfeo. He wore a grin from ear to ear as Marfeo lit both of their cigarettes.

Hugo inhaled deeply. "Cheap bastard, at least he could have filled my tank with gas." They both laughed hysterically for two miles. "Steve, what the frig is this name? He writes like a fucken Jap. I wonder if he even went to school." They had parked the Pontiac in downtown Worcester and quickly found 415 North Main Street, a doctor's building.

"I dunno, Hugo, looks like Doctor Caruso or Carrozza. Look on the building directory, maybe we can find a name there." They scanned the building directory, Hugo's finger acting as a pointer. "Here it is, Caruso. Dr. Thomas Caruso. He's a dentist on the fourth floor."

The young receptionist greeted them pleasantly as they approached her desk. "May I help you, gentlemen?"

Hugo's eyes were riveted on a pair of pointed breasts pushing out of her tight crew-neck sweater. "Yeah, Miss, tell the doctor that we're here to see him from Providence at the request of Mr. Ferruccio."

The receptionist motioned to a row of chairs. "Please, have a seat, gentlemen, the doctor is with a patient and he will see you as soon as he can."

145

Marfeo edged his way past Hugo to the front of the desk and, bending over to within inches of the blonde's face, said in a hoarse whisper, "listen, you go in there and tell him what we just told you . . . now!"

The startled receptionist leapt from her chair casting a glance over her shoulder as she entered the doctor's inner office, the sound of teeth being drilled curling Hugo's toes. The drilling stopped almost immediately. When the door opened again a small balding man appeared, an obvious look of fear on his face and in his eyes.

"Gentlemen, please, we can talk in this other examining room." He held the door open as Hugo and Marfeo, stone faced, ambled into the room with the doctor following.

"How can I help you gentlemen?" Beads of sweat had become visible on his brow. Marfeo fingered the debtor list.

"Yea, Doc, Mr. Ferruccio sent us up here to collect the money you owe him. It says here you owe him eight hundred dollars, and we can't leave till we get it." Caruso went pale, biting his lower lip. "Listen, fellas, I'll have to go to the bank, I don't have that kind of money here. Can you come back?"

Marfeo glanced toward Hugo with eyebrows raised. "No, you listen, Doc, here's what you gotta do. Finish with your patient, then we'll all go to the bank together and we'll be gone. How's that, okay?"

Less than an hour later Caruso emerged from the Shawmut Bank clutching a brown envelope, his white lab coat flapping in the breeze. He approached the driver's window and handed the envelope to Hugo. "It's all there, eight hundred dollars, do I get a receipt?"

Hugo smirked. "Sorry, Doc, we don't do receipts. Don't worry, Mr. Ferruccio will mark your account paid." The doctor stood shaking his head in the middle of the bank parking lot as the Pontiac pulled out and disappeared into the stream of traffic.

Hugo turned to his friend suppressing a howl of laughter which suddenly burst forth at the same time that Marfeo did the same. "Madonna, I thought the guy was gonna shit his pants. You see him sweat in the office?"

Marfeo, choking back laughter, nodded his head, tears in his eyes. "Hugo, if this is all we have to do, we're gonna make a lot of frigin' money!

"Awright, now I'm in the mood," declared Hugo, flushed with the first taste of success. "Where else do we have to go?"

"Lemme see, the next guy is Manny's Auto Body on Mill Street, he owes five hundred."

The cement block building was in the center of the manufacturing district flanked by two used car dealerships and surrounded by an assortment of body shops, a welding shop, and a junkyard. The building's white paint—what was left of it—had long ago turned a brownish yellow. The double garage doors stood open. Hugo pulled the Pontiac off to one side of the building. A collection of cars—hoods up, tires flat—littered the property. As they approached the front entrance the brilliant white light of an acetylene torch lit up the rear of the darkened garage. They paused for a moment checking to see who else was present in the building. The welder was alone.

They walked to the rear of the garage, the smell of grease, gasoline, and fumes from the acetylene torch assailing their nostrils. They stood several feet away staring at the welder's mask as he continued welding a chrome bumper into place. He sensed their presence, cut off the acetylene torch with a popping sound, raised his mask and lazily came to his feet. He was a large man, better than six feet tall, bull necked, with powerful arms and an immense chest. He removed a pair of leather gloves as he spoke, instinctively knowing these were not customers.

"What can I do for you boys?" The voice was low, flat. Marfeo consulted the collection sheet looking at the welder. "Mr. Amaral, Manny Amaral?"

"Yeah, what can I do for ya?"

Hugo remained motionless slightly behind Marfeo. "We work for Mr. Ferruccio, he sent us up here to pick up the five hundred you owe him."

Amaral's nostrils flared visibly, moving a full heavy mustache. It was evident that his face had participated in a number of barroom brawls. He walked slowly toward them, carelessly snatching the welder's mask from his head and tossing it aside. "You tell that fucken rat bastard that I already paid him two thousand on a one thousand dollar loan, and he'll never get another dime out of me, you understand me?"

Marfeo glanced at Hugo who was staring motionlessly at Amaral, hands loosely at his side. "Listen, Mr. Amaral, we're under instructions not to leave unless we collect the full amount owed to Mr. Ferruccio."

"You fucken wops are all alike," growled the big Portuguese, "all wise guys. You think I give a shit about anybody on the Hill? I buried a few of you wop assholes, and I'll bury both of you if you don't get the fuck outta here." Amaral reached down and grabbed a tire iron from the floor as he walked menacingly toward them, slapping the tire iron into his palm as he advanced. Marfeo looked at Hugo, eyebrows raised in consternation and doubt. Hugo suddenly rocketed the three paces to Amaral smashing into his cheekbone with a powerful overhand right, momentarily stunning the enraged bull. Amaral swung the tire iron wildly with the force of a sledgehammer. Hugo ducked, falling to one knee and rising with a roundhouse uppercut to Amaral's groin. Amaral gripped his testicles and fell with a thud to the cement floor. Hugo stepped back a pace and began compulsively kicking him in the face and head. He emitted wild animal sounds as he kicked, blood dribbling from one nostril, eyes glaring wildly. He had no consciousness of Marfeo pulling him away from Amaral's body. As he regained his senses he heard Marfeo's voice as from a distance.

"C'mon, Hugo, enough, enough, you're gonna kill him!" He stood chest heaving, sweat covering his forehead. He wiped his forehead with the sleeve of his right arm, examining his bruised knuckles. Amaral's head lay in a pool of blood; he moaned in his unconsciousness. Marfeo was frantic, looking toward busy Mill Street. "C'mon, Hugo, let's get the fuck out of here now!"

Hugo's eyes scanned the dim interior of the garage. "No, we're not going anywhere until we get some money from this Portagee prick."

"Hugo, we're gonna get nailed, I'm telling ya."

"C'mon, his office is in the corner over there." The office was closet sized and greasy; outdated girlie calendars covered the walls.

"Hugo, there's no cash registers here, we're wasting time, this guy deals with checks from insurance companies."

"Yeah, I know, but I want to make sure, just another minute. Get in the car. Here, take the keys, get it started, I'll be right out." The exterior office door led to the side of the building where the Pontiac was parked. Marfeo scampered to the car quickly, starting the engine and slowly gunning it. Hugo scanned the office. He moved toward the bill-laden desk, his toe stubbing on an object. He looked under the lip of the desk. It was a floor mounted safe barely visible ensconced in the greasy floor.

He reached down, lifted the faceplate and spun the dial to zero. He grasped the handle and turned. He was shocked when the safe popped open. He reached in and pulled out an old bank night-deposit bag. It was stuffed with cash. Hugo heard muttering and cursing from the garage. He slowly raised himself from a crouching position to peer over the edge of the glass-paned office door. Amaral had groggily risen to his feet and was headed for the office, holding his head in both hands and staggering as he walked. Hugo crept to the still opened side door and dashed to the car.

"Don't race the engine. Go out slow, we don't want him to get a look at the car." Marfeo slowly exited the littered lot, blending with traffic as Hugo stared through the rear window at the rear office door. Amaral did not appear. Marfeo jockeyed into the outside lane accelerating past a line of traffic. "Steve, slow down, we don't want to get stopped by some Worcester cop."

"Yeah, you're right." The car slowed to the speed limit. Marfeo glanced at Hugo. "You know you coulda killed that guy. That's not why we came up here."

Hugo sat staring straight ahead, then said tightly, "Yeah, I know. He just pissed me off with the tire iron. I can't help it...you know me, sometimes I lose my head."

The car turned onto Route 146 headed south for Providence. Marfeo laughed shaking his head in disbelief. "I can't fucking believe you found his money! Where was it?"

"Stevie, I found it by accident, it was in a friggin floor safe. I turned the dial to zero and it opened. I almost fell over! I don't even know how much is in here. Take the next side road and we'll count it."

The Pontiac grumbled to a stop in a small wooded thicket. Hugo unzipped the overstuffed bag and began counting. "Holy shit, there's seven hundred fifty bucks here!" Their eyes locked, a smile spreading over their faces. "Naw, Steve, we can't, we gotta bring it all back, he's gonna find out one way or another." Marfeo grimaced, nodded, and nosed the car out onto the highway toward Providence.

"Where the hell youse guys been? My phone's been ringing off the friggen wall! I got calls from the old man, Vinny Theresa. Whad youse guys do up there, start a friggen war?" Ferruccio stared at one and then the other, shaking his head side to side.

"Vito, the guy came at me with a tire iron. All I did was ask him for the money he owed you, and Stevie didn't say two words to him. The guys a screwball. He swung at me with the tire iron, and I swung back. And by the way, he's a big bastard."

Ferruccio looked down at the bank bag and rubbed his chin. "How much did you collect?"

Marfeo stepped forward. "We got the eight hundred from the doctor and we uh…uh…took seven hundred and fifty bucks from the guy, Manny."

"What?" Ferruccio's eyebrows raised, his palms outstretched by his side questioningly. "You guys were supposed to collect five hundred dollars. What the hell…"

"Vito, I was in the guy's office looking for the money. I found the bag by accident. I didn't have time to count it, he was comin' at us again."

Ferruccio threw his hands up in exasperation. "Listen, you guys did a good job, the only mistake you made was you almost killed the guy. You gotta be more careful, *capito?*" They both nodded with relief. "Awright, tomorrow morning, Stevie, you come here around nine. Hugo, the ol' man wants to see you at ten o'clock, you got it?"

"Yeah, Vito, ten o"clock, I'll be there."

It was mid-June and unseasonably warm. Angelina sat on the top porch step peering nervously down Laurel Hill Avenue. She cupped her chin in her hands. Her hair, freshly shampooed, fell in ringlets about her youthful face. She wore a peasant blouse off the shoulders and the latest style khaki colored knee-length Bermuda shorts. She recognized the sound of the engine before she saw the Pontiac. She walked to the gate as the car pulled up. Hugo sat smiling, sunglasses in place, cigarette dangling from his lips. She was visibly nervous and unsmiling as she entered the car. Hugo frowned as he accelerated away from the curb.

"What did I do now?"

Angelina exhaled audibly. "I'm pregnant."

His knuckles whitened visibly on the steering wheel. He slowly edged the car to a halt by the side of the street. "How do you know? Are you sure?"

Tears welled up at the corners of her eyes. She looked small and vulnerable. Hugo slid across the vinyl seat and embraced her gently. She pressed her cheek into his chest. "I went to a doctor in Massachusetts, in Seekonk. I'm almost three months pregnant."

He held her quietly for several minutes, neither speaking. He lifted her chin and kissed her softly. "We'll get married. We were going to get married anyway, we'll just do it a little early."

She wiped the tears from her eyes, smearing mascara. "What about my father, your father?" Her voice was dejected, forlorn.

"Angie, we have two choices, either we go to Seekonk and get married by a Justice of the Peace or we sit down and tell them and have a small wedding. You make the decision."

She turned her head to look out the passenger window. "Or I could have an abortion."

He grabbed her by both shoulders and turned her to him. "Listen, the baby you're carrying is my baby too, and I don't want that."

She threw her arms around his neck smothering his face with kisses. "I wanted to hear you say that, I needed to hear you say that."

"Well, Mrs. Rossi, what do you want to do?"

The meeting took place at Salvatore's house. Francesca had made coffee, served with her biscotti. They sat in the parlor. Lorenzo and Francesca Delbusso, Angelina's parents, sat on one sofa, Hugo's parents sat on another. Hugo and Angelina sat on dining room chairs; the mood was congenial. There was an air of expectance in the room. The women especially anticipating news of an engagement, the announcement of wedding plans. The men smoked cigars and sipped at Lorenzo's homemade wine.

"Well, Hugo, Angelina, what's this big secret?" Francesca Delbusso was smiling broadly as she asked the question. Angelina fidgeted in her chair staring glumly at the carpet.

Hugo clasped his hands together, leaning forward in his chair and looking at his mother. He sighed deeply. It became evident that something was amiss. The mood suddenly turned solemn. "You know that Angie and me love each other very much, and we would never do anything to disgrace you or hurt you?" His eyes traveled from one set of parents to another. Francesca Delbusso was prescient as she muttered under her breath, "*Dio Mio!*" Hugo straightened in the chair, hands on hips. "We're going to have a baby," he declared matter-of-factly.

The room fell deadly silent. Lorenzo looked at Salvatore with a grim expression. Francesca covered her face with her hands sobbing quietly. Hugo's mother sat arms crossed, glaring at her son. Only Salvatore appeared undisturbed, his face calm, even serene, as though his thoughts were not of this moment but of another time now long ago in a land now far away. Finally he stood up and walked to Angelina who sat dejectedly and relieved, staring out the parlor window. She turned, looking up at him as he stood in front of her and reached for her hands.

"Angelina, sweetheart, I am happy for you and Hugo." He was smiling, eyes moistened with tears.

"How many months are you?" Francesca Delbusso was excited to know.

"Two or three, the doctor's not sure." Lorenzo Delbusso slapped his knee and stood. "Well, we can still have a wedding. It might be a little rushed, but who's to know? I know my wife's had an invitation list put together for months. What do you say, Salvatore?"

"Well Lorenzo, I think it's up to Angelina and Hugo, what do you two think?"

Francesca was on her feet, crossing to Angelina. "*Cara mia*, I would like you to have a church wedding." There were tears in her eyes as she spoke. "I have always dreamed of seeing you in a wedding gown, of having a big celebration with everyone there." Angelina turned to Hugo questioningly.

"Whatever you want, Angie, is what I want. I don't want to deprive you of a big wedding, you understand me?"

Angelina nodded, turning to Hugo's mother who out of old world respect she called Ma. "Ma, what do you think? I don't want to bring disgrace to you and Salvatore or to my mother and father."

Francesca moved to the parlor chair, knelt and embraced Angelina. "Listen, you little rabbit, we love you. There is no way you could disgrace us. This pregnancy was brought about by love. Half the people we know were conceived before their parents were married. This is not something so unusual."

The marriage ceremony took place at St. Bart's Church on Labor Day. It was a sparkling late summer day, high blue skies, not a cloud in sight. Monsignor Cavalaro performed the ceremony with full knowledge that Angelina was three months pregnant. He beamed with pride as he announced to the packed church, "I now pronounce you man and wife" to the sounds of raucous applause and loud salutations. Stevie Marfeo and Anna Tedesco were Best Man and Maid of Honor. Angelina looked stunning as they stepped from the altar. The gown had been custom made by Bianca of Boston, the most exclusive wedding shop catering to the Italian community. Pure white and sequined, with a form-fitting bodice, the train was six feet long. Angelina looked slim and showed not at all.

Three hundred fifty people packed the reception at Caruso's on Valley Street in Providence, with guests driving from as far as

Revere and Worcester. Dinner was traditional pasta and chicken with music supplied by the Traveler's, a five-piece group specializing in Italian wedding songs. Mr. and Mrs. Delbusso sat at the head table beaming and accepting congratulations from well-wishers. The head table was twenty-four feet long in order to accommodate the five bridesmaids and groomsmen in addition to the four parents, Cavalaro, and Angelina's grandmother who stood guard over the basket of envelopes containing cash wedding gifts. Vito Ferruccio and Giusto Rotondo, Zarraga's right hand man, came with their girlfriends. Vito presented a fat envelope to Hugo and Angelina with Domenic Zarraga's best wishes.

They left Angelina's house, still packed with celebrating relatives, at seven that evening to begin a honeymoon of five days in Niagara Falls followed by two days in New York City. Vito Ferruccio offered his new Cadillac Fleetwood for the trip, which Hugo eagerly accepted. Upon their return they moved into a newly renovated third floor tenement two streets over from Salvatore. The furnishings were sparse and were gifts from Salvatore, Francesca, and the Delbussos. It was a cozy four-room apartment heated by a four-burner gas range with a blower attachment. It would be the best time of their married life.

Chapter 6

"Where are you going? I promised my mother we would come over tonight to decorate the tree. I told you two days ago and you said you'd come. You're never home, you're never around when I need you."

Hugo stood in front of the bedroom mirror cursing under his breath at the length of his tie as he unfurled the knot to begin again.

"Hugo, I'm talking to you. Is it too much to give me an answer?"

"Angie." His voice was exasperated and tense. "I told you, I can't help it if Vito wants me to drive him somewhere tonight, and I can't turn him down. He pays me well; we're living good. I got my eye on a house in that new plat going up near the Alpine Country Club. You'd like that, wouldn't you?"

"Of course I would, but I worry about you. I don't even know what you do for a living, and I'm tired of lying to my friends that you sell insurance, it sounds stupid."

Hugo seated the knot into the Mr. "B" shirt collar, turned and held Angie by the shoulders looking down into her eyes. "Listen, I'm not going to be doing this forever. This will give us a start, a house, who knows, a business…"

"What kind of business, what experience do you have at anything?"

"It doesn't make any difference. I know guys that have shit for brains who own big businesses. If they can do it, I can do it." He turned to put on a topcoat. "Hey, give me a kiss. I won't be late, promise." He rubbed his hand across her protruding stomach. "Take care of little Hugo for me. Do you want me to drop you off at your mother's?"

"No, I'm not ready, my father will pick me up." He turned, kissed her on the lips, and was halfway out the tenement door. "Hey, what do I tell my mother and father?"

"Tell them I had to make a sales call." He spoke over his shoulder as he raced down the stairs.

When Hugo arrived at the grocery shop Ferruccio was pacing his cluttered office floor, a large cigar stuck between his corpulent lips, an oversized belt buckled beneath his protruding stomach.

"Aay, where the frig have you been, we can't be late. We gotta pick up a couple of guys and a panel truck."

"Vito, I'm sorry, you know my wife's pregnant. I had to do a few things, you know what I mean?"

"Yeah, yeah, awright." Ferruccio spoke as he struggled into a black topcoat. "C'mon, we're taking my car. Here, take the keys, you drive."

"Where we goin.

"Up the Hill, the club on Acorn Street. We gotta pick up a couple 'a guys." The Cadillac pulled to a stop next to the Acorn

Club known as the "bucket of blood" for the number of killings that took place there. "Awright, come on in, we gotta talk about tonight."

The club was packed with the usual Friday night crowd of workingmen, assorted wise guys, and wanna be wise guys awaiting their opportunity to prove how tough they were. Friday night was free food night—snail salad, squid salad, and *pasta fagioli* were on the house. Vito entered the club with Hugo behind. They worked their way to the back of the room. Behind the bar a television was turned to the Cavalcade of Sports for the Friday night fights. Small-time bookies took action from the crowd.

Several men called out greetings to them. Vito traded crude insults with some of the older men to coarse laughter. Steve Marfeo sat at the corner round table with two other men in their mid-twenties. Hugo looked with surprise at Marfeo and made a questioning sign with his hand as they approached the table. Marfeo raised his eyebrows and shrugged his shoulders in answer. Ferruccio collapsed into a wooden chair and yelled for snails and wine.

The food arrived almost immediately. "Awright, c'mon, let's eat. I want youse guys to get to know each other." Vito loaded two forkfuls of snails into his mouth and proceeded to talk, pausing to sip wine and swallow. "Hugo, you know Stevie, and these guys next to you come from East Boston. Meet Genaro Antonelli and Dante Ianelli. They're good guys; they're with our friends in Boston. And this is Steve Marfeo and Hugo Rossi." Hands were shaken around the table.

Vito wiped the snail sauce from his lower lip. "Awright, we're gonna do a little job tonight. We're gonna knock off the Howard Johnsons on North Main Street. There's gonna be three or four thousand bucks on the premises, which we're gonna grab after they close at eleven o'clock. There's a piece for you guys. We'll figure that out after we get the money, you got me?" Everyone around the table nodded in agreement.

The robbery went off like clockwork. Ferruccio watched from his Cadillac across the street from the restaurant as the black panel truck pulled into the empty parking lot at eleven fifteen with Marfeo at the wheel. Hugo approached the rear kitchen entrance carrying plumbing tools, as did Antonelli and Ianelli, masquerading as water department employees. The heist was easy. They forced all the employees except the manager into a walk-in cooler. The manager was so nervous his teeth were chattering. He led the way to the office safe, which was still open, and pointed to the night deposit bag.

They had a stroke of good fortune. The bag contained Friday, Saturday, and Sunday's deposits that were to be made the next morning. They tied the manager's hands to a waste pipe and ran from the rear door of the restaurant. As the stolen truck drove past Ferruccio's Cadillac, Hugo tossed the bank bag into the car window. They ditched the truck on a nearby side street and drove off slowly in cars parked nearby. Their instructions were to return home and report to Vito individually an hour apart the next afternoon.

The headline in the Monday *Providence Journal* announced in one-inch typeface: "Howard Johnson Robbed." The story went on to say that there was little to go on; the robbers "wore masks and dark glasses. Witnesses were being sought throughout the area." The haul proved even larger than Vito had predicted—nearly six thousand dollars, all in small bills. Hugo's share was five hundred.

THE ARRIVAL THE STRUGGLE THE ASCENDANCY

Ferruccio was pleased at the way Hugo had executed the quick in-and-out plan and promised him more creative ventures for the future.

Salvatore called Monday morning and left a message for Hugo to stop by that evening. Hugo arrived at seven to find his mother at her usual place at the sink clearing away the remains of dinner. Salvatore sat in the living room puffing on a full pipe and leafing through the evening paper. The console radio was turned to H. V. Caltenborn and his evening news broadcast. Hugo quietly crept up behind Fancesca and covered her eyes with the palms of hands. She was startled for a second, turned and received his kiss on the cheek. She seemed tired, even somber.

"How's Angie feeling, is she all right? I want you to take some chicken soup home for her, make sure you take it when you leave."

"Yeah, sure, Ma, what's wrong?"

"Your father wants to talk with you."

He turned to see Salvatore through a haze of pipe smoke, paper now on the living room floor. "Hi, Pa, what's going on?"

Salvatore removed the pipe from his mouth. "How's the insurance business, Hugo, are you doing good?"

Hugo's brow furrowed as he sat down warily across from his father. "What do you mean, Pa? It's fine, why do you ask?"

"Hugo, I told you a long time ago that I would never try to run your life, so there's no need to lie to me, do you understand me."

"Yes, understand."

"I know you're working with those people from the Hill, those people who preyed upon their own kind thirty and forty years ago and still do. These are people who bring nothing to society except trouble and unhappiness to everybody they touch. And now they have you." Hugo stared at the design in the living room carpeting. "Does your wife know that you're not an insurance salesman?"

"Yes, she does."

"How does she feel about this?"

"Not good."

Salvatore sat back in his chair, circles of pipe smoke wreathing around his head. He studied his son. The silence was painful for Hugo; he realized his father was waiting for a response. Francesca listened from the next room, pretending to clean her kitchen.

"Listen, Pa, it's not what you think. Ferruccio's not a bad person, he's got two or three different businesses. He needs someone like me to handle some of the debtors. It's more money than I have ever made anywhere, and I'm not going to be doing this job for the rest of my life. I want a house next year, maybe a business in a few years, you know, something I can buy."

Salvatore puffed on his pipe and nodded passively. Once again the room dropped into silence. Rising, Salvatore walked to a window to watch a heavy snow begin to fall. He stood with his back to Hugo. "So, then, this is your decision?"

"Pa, try to understand…"

"Hugo, I do understand. We all have to make our way in life and we all must pay for bad decisions. And we can also collect for good decisions." He turned to face Hugo, emphasizing his words with the stem of his pipe. "Remember this, I know all about those men, I fought those men, they are all cowards, they are like a pack of rats. These are the men you associate with, a pack of rats."

"But Pa…!"

"'No, you listen to me. If you get into trouble with the police, I will not be there for you, am I understood?"

Hugo pursed his lips and nodded. Salvatore turned back toward the window, silently watching the snowfall. Hugo stood awkwardly on the center of the room. Francesca appeared beside him and gently tugged him into the kitchen. She had prepared a cardboard box full of chicken soup and her home made preserves.

"Here, take this to Angie, tell her I'll be over in the morning. And remember, stay close. She's only got a couple of months to go." She opened the kitchen door to the stairway down to the first floor. Hugo stood in the open doorway, box in hand. Francesca buttoned his topcoat.

"Ma, talk with him, please." She nodded perfunctorily and kissed his cheek. She knew there would be no way to discuss Hugo's new found associates with her husband. The best she could do, she knew, was to keep peace between them.

Angie knew the baby was coming that night. She packed her small suitcase. It was two a.m. The only light was a small wall lamp illuminating the ironing board; the apartment was silent. She could hear the occasional snoring from the bedroom as Hugo slept. At two fifteen she gently shook Hugo's shoulder.

"It's time, we have to go to the hospital." He sat bolt upright reaching for his trousers and shoes, stumbling in the dark against the dresser.

A northeaster had dropped six inches of fresh snow on the still unplowed streets. Hugo, at his father's suggestion, had equipped the Pontiac with tire chains. They clunked rhythmically as they churned through the drifting snow.

The pains had started. Hugo's heart raced. "Are you okay, Angie? Is it all right?"

"Yes, I'm okay, just be careful driving. We don't want to get stuck in a snow drift."

The thought only added to his anxiety as he slowed imperceptibly, leaned into the steering wheel, adrenaline peaking his senses as he scanned the road for dangerous snowdrifts. At last he pulled the car into the hospital parking lot and held Angie by the shoulders as together they crunched through the snow and through the Admissions door He held both her hands as they wheeled her gurney into a delivery room, and he kissed her lightly on the lips as she disappeared behind a pair of swinging doors, leaving him standing alone in the deserted corridor.

Hugo Rossi, Jr. arrived at five-fifteen that morning, his legs and arms jerking in unfettered freedom. Hours later, Angelina lay propped up in the hospital bed looking exhausted but happy. The room was crowded with relatives, flowers, and gifts. Salvatore held the baby in his arms staring into large blue eyes. Deep feelings welled up in his chest as he thought of his own mother and father and what he had left years before in Italy. His mind drifted to Tina and to the child that was not to be. Tears misted his eyes.

A loud voice suddenly shattered his reverie. "Hey, Sal, you're only the grandfather. The grandmothers want to hold him too!" It was Pat Lofredo hiding a bottle of champagne, which he had obviously consumed much of before arriving at the hospital, and which he now proceeded to pass around in wax paper cups. The duty nurse diplomatically turned a blind eye to the champagne as well as to the overcrowded room.

Lofredo looked around. "Aay, where's the proud papa, where's Hugo?" Salvatore stared flatly in his direction. LoFredo raised his eyebrows, shrugging his shoulders.

"He's working, Uncle Pat," said Angelina, looking knowingly at Salvatore. "He had to make a sales call. He'll be here later."

Vito Ferruccio sat in his old wooden chair behind a desk piled high with invoices, orders, and food samples. His shirtfront had the usual oil stains in the usual spots. The stuffy back room was redolent with the scent of aged cheese, ripe olives, and dried meats. Ferruccio leaned back in the creaking chair scratching at an itchy crotch, ashes falling from a fat White Owl cigar. Across from the desk sitting in rickety folding chairs were Hugo, Steve Marfeo, and Dante Ianelli.

"I betcha youse guys never knew I owned this place. We sell to restaurants, hotels, grocery stores, a lotta people. I'm a wholesale distributor. It's a good business. Listen to me, save your money, buy into a business. That's the route to take, understand?" The three young men nodded in unison. "Awright youse guys did a good job at the restaurant and you been doin' a good job at collecting my bad debts, but I gotta break up the team. Stevie, you're staying with me. Dante, you gotta move down here from Boston; take your wife or leave her up there, whatever ya wanna do." He slapped his fat palm on the desktop and snorted a laugh. "But you'll have a better time down here with the broads without her, know what I mean?" The mood instantly turned light as the young men joined in Vito's laughter. "Hugo," Vito began again, this time his voice thick with the tone of business, "the old man wants you to work directly from his office on the Hill." A small smile split his lips. "I think he likes you. He likes guys with balls, and there's do doubt you got a big pair. So tomorrow you go see him at ten o'clock, *capece?*"

Hugo could hardly contain himself, but he maintained an expressionless face. Steve Marfeo turned and winked. This was it; he had worked himself up to the attention of the old man. The money would be much better, but more importantly he was now with Dom Zarraga and he would be allocated great respect and deference from wise guys all over New England.

"Aay, Hugo, how's your wife, she have the baby yet?" Vito had relit the White Owl and was sending out plumes of stale smoke.

"Yeah, we had a baby boy."

"Aw, that's wonderful! Whattaya gonna call him?"

"Hugo, were gonna name him Hugo."

"Aay, lemme know when you do the baptism. I wanna bring the baby a gift."

"Yea, I will, Vito, thank you."

The hospital corridors were empty. There were faint cries from the nursery. The charge nurse looked up from behind her station and smiled at Hugo as he made his way to Room 202. The door was half closed as he entered. Angie was sleeping, a nightlight illuminating her soft features. He bent to kiss her lips. Her eyes fluttered open.

"Where were you? Everyone was asking for you. Your father was not happy."

He settled himself on the edge of the bed. "I know, I know, I couldn't help it. We had an important meeting. I'll be making more money, things will be a hell of a lot better, you'll see. How did you feel today, how's the baby?"

She smiled up at him, shining with excitement. "He is a hungry little devil, and feisty. His little fists are constantly in motion."

He gazed at her, his heart swelling with love for this woman, the mother of his son. "I'll see him tomorrow, I'll be back in the afternoon. Do you want me to bring you anything?"

"Yes, a strawberry sundae with whipped cream and nuts."

He laughed, shaking his head. "You gotta be careful Angelina, your gonna look like an elephant!"

"How old are you, Hugo?"

"I'm twenty, Mr. Zarraga, I just turned twenty."

Domenico Zarraga leaned back in a plush high-backed chair. The top of his expensive walnut desk was empty with the exception of a telephone, ashtray, and lamp. "Twenty, that's a good age. I'd like to be twenty again."

Zarraga had not aged well; he looked more brutal with each passing year. His face was deeply creased, his blue-tinged lips held the look of a natural sneer, his heavy-lidded eyes had seen much. He had survived two murder attempts by rival factions. The leadership of the insurgent group was slaughtered in violent blood baths in Boston and Providence, leaving him the uncontested boss of New England.

"You know why I asked for you to work directly for me, Hugo?"

"No, Mr. Zarraga, I don't."

"Call me Dom, everybody does, even the papers." He twitched a smile. "I'll tell you why, because your Salvatore's son and he's one of toughest men both physically and mentally that I ever met. He's also a highly principled man. Does he know you're with me?"

Hugo instinctively looked down at his hands. "Yeah, Dom, he knows and he's not happy about it."

"Tell me what he said."

"He said he couldn't live my life and that I had to make my own way."

Zarraga grinned, showing large square teeth. "Yeah, that's your father all right—smart, tough, big balls. And that's what I think you got like your old man, you know what I mean?"

"Yeah, Dom, thank you for the compliment."

"You're gonna be doing a lot of different jobs for me, and the money's going to be lot more than Vito was paying you, but for that you have to deliver, *capito*?"

Hugo nodded. "I understand, Dom."

"One of the first things I want you to do is deliver these two envelopes to Carmine's restaurant down the street." Zarraga reached into a desk drawer and pulled out two small brown pay envelopes, obviously stuffed with money. "In the back room, last booth on the right-hand side, will be two cops in uniform. One guy is a major, Major Sullivan, the other is a captain, his name is Laforge. You got it?"

"Yeah, Dom, Sullivan and LaForge."

You sit down with them and you slip them the envelopes. Make sure no one is looking or in the area when you do this. This is very important, you got that?"

"I know what you mean, Dom, I know what I'm doing."

"Good, these guys are with us; they have been for some time. We got the mayor, four or five judges, politicians.... I pay, but it's a hell of a lot less than paying legal fees." Zarraga winked. "And by the way, get yourself a better car. You're gonna be pulling down around five hundred a week, you can afford it. Go see Iggy Lally at American Bank down the street. You know where it is?" Hugo

THE ARRIVAL THE STRUGGLE THE ASCENDANCY

nodded. Everyone in the Italian community knew American Bank. It had been founded by immigrants and specialized in small loans and mortgages, mainly loans based on character. "That's my bank," continued Zarraga, "that's one of my other businesses. Come back after you finish with Lollipop. That's his nickname, but he doesn't like it. We'll talk more about what you'll be doing."

Hugo emerged from the inner office to the front of the building. There was a showroom and storage area for vending machines, pinball machines, jukeboxes, and other games. This was Modern Vending. Everyone knew Zarraga owned Modern Vending, and many restaurants and bars were anxious to do business with him. For one thing, you could get an advance on future income from the machines; for another, you had the security of doing business with Dom Zarraga.

"Aay, Hugo, good to see you!" It was Giusto Rotondo, Zarraga's top lieutenant. Hugo shook the extended hand. "Hugo, you remember Buster Zito and Nunzio Martella from that time at the Ranch House." The three men were seated at a small table in the front window of the building drinking coffee. Buster Zito stood and extended his hand. Martella partially raised a hand in an expressionless greeting. Hugo nodded in his direction, a sudden feeling of anger clouding his mind. He knew that in time this miserable bastard and he would be at odds.

"Good to see you, Giusto, Buster." He nodded in Nunzio's direction who was watching passing traffic on Atwells Avenue. "I gotta do some business for Dom. I'll be back later." Rotondo smiled and gave him a thumbs-up sign.

Carmine's was opened in 1915 by two young immigrants and continued to remain one of the most popular family-style restaurants on the Hill. The original black and white octagonal ceramic tile floor was worn at the main entrance and the kitchen door from the many years of patronage. The tabletops were white enamel, still in good condition; the walls were hung with black and white photographs of local Italian-American sports figures, politicians, family members, and pictures of the Hill at the turn of the century. The menu was a chalkboard and consisted of whatever the chef was pushing that day. Three of the waiters had been there since the day the restaurant opened. They treated every customer with tired indifference, shuffling about in ankle length white aprons.

Hugo walked through the busy lunch crowd to the rear table, instantly recognizing the Providence Police uniforms. Major William Sullivan and Lieutenant Walter LaForge were engrossed in the veal special of the day as Hugo approached the table. Sullivan was a large man, red faced and prematurely gray. He wiped his mouth with a paper napkin and looked at Hugo with narrowed eyes.

"You must be Hugo, right?"

"Yeah, that's me."

"Sullivan pointed to the chair next to LaForge. "Sit down, how about some lunch."

"No thanks, I just have to leave something with you from a friend of yours."

Sullivan smiled with tight lips, nodding in understanding. "Just give it to Walter and tell our friend all's quiet on the Western front."

Hugo passed the two envelopes under the table to LaForge, who continued to finish his meal. Then he stood to leave.

Sullivan leaned back in his chair, head cocked to one side, a half smile on his ruddy face. "You know, sonny, all you have to do is keep your nose clean, show some respect, and you'll go a long way in the business. You know what I mean?" Hugo looked down at him for a second and wordlessly left the table. As he walked toward the main entrance he heard Sullivan speak loud enough for him to hear, "Just another punk ginny kid." His stomach knotted at the insult, his face reddened. He slowed a moment and then he realized who he was dealing with. They were crooked cops, the scum of the earth; you bought their service like you bought a hooker. He continued on his way, smiling to himself with the knowledge that he owned them.

Ignazzio Lally had been generous with Hugo and provided financing for a new black Ford Fairlane convertible with gold striping, a black nylon top, and spanking whitewall tires.

"Where did you get this car, it's beautiful." Angelina walked around the Ford holding baby Hugo, her mouth agape in wonder. "Hugo, we can't afford this kind of luxury. How will you pay for this?"

"Stop worrying, I got a raise. A good one, too. I'm making more than most lawyers or doctors." He reached into his pocket and pulled out a wad of cash. "Here, take this, buy something for yourself and the baby."

"How much is here?" She held the money, staring at it in wonder.

"Two hundred, and next week I'll give you more. I told you I would be making some serious money, didn't I?"

"Hugo, is this legitimate money?"

"Of course it's legitimate money, why shouldn't it be legitimate." He reached for the baby, holding him above his head at arms length. The baby gurgled and giggled, kicking his feet furiously. "Our son is going to have a good life, that I promise you." He handed the squealing baby back to Angelina.

"We're supposed to be at your father's for dinner at five-thirty, are you ready?"

Hugo made a face. "Angie, I can't come. I told you I have to meet with some people tonight, it's important."

"What do I tell your father, that you're up the Hill with Dom Zarraga and his gang, that's why you can't be at his house for dinner?"

"I'll talk with my father later. Come on, I'll drive you over there. I promise I won't be home late."

Domenico Zarraga sat at the rear corner table of the Gaslight restaurant in downtown Providence with Giusto Rotondo. They were having dinner and quiet conversation as Hugo approached the table. Out of the comer of his eye he noticed that Buster Zito and Nunzio Martella sat at the opposite end of the room, carefully surveying the crowd for potential trouble from a rival faction or perhaps from some snooping police reporter from the *Providence Journal*, which was once again engaged in their version of an organized crime expose.

"Hugo, good to see you. Sit down, we just ordered some dinner. The food's terrific here. You been here before?"

"No, Giusto, I heard about it but I've never been here. "

Dom Zarraga smiled his crooked smile and said, "Well, Hugo, now you can afford to eat here whenever you want with the money you're making—and the money you're going to make. Giusto, get Mary McKenna over here for a drink order. Hugo, what are you drinking?"

As Zarraga spoke the cocktail waitress appeared. Hugo's mouth dropped slightly open as he turned in his chair to place his order. The young woman standing before him was about his own age, perhaps twenty or twenty-one. Her strawberry blond hair was pulled back tightly in a long braid; her face angular and beautifully Irish, set off by large turquoise eyes. The cut of the cocktail uniform revealed long shapely legs and a hint of full, well shaped breasts.

"May I get you something to drink, sir?" Her smile was dazzling and inviting. Their eyes locked. Hugo was mesmerized and unmoving for several seconds. The sexual charge in the air was palpable. She blushed and fumbled with the order pad. Rotondo and Zarraga exchanged knowing smiles.

"I'll have, ah, I'll have a seven and seven...please." Their eyes never left one another's. She almost curtsied.

"Thank you, sir, I'll be right back." His eyes automatically followed her as she walked to the service bar. She glanced back, quickly averting her eyes from his gaze.

"Hey, Hugo, wake up and come down off cloud nine." Rotondo spoke with a grin from ear to hear. "That happens to everybody who meets Mary for the first time. She's beautiful, isn't she."

"She's more than beautiful, she looks like a movie star. What's she doing here working as a waitress?"

Zarraga broke in. "She's a student at Pembroke College, she's working her way through school. She makes more money here than she can anywhere else. And she's a good girl; she's no *putana*."

Rotondo nodded in agreement and glanced in the direction of Martella and Zito. "Yeah, Martella's in love with her, but she won't give him a second look."

Mary McKenna returned. She stood close to Hugo as she placed the drinks on the table. Their hands brushed as he placed a five-dollar tip on her tray, electricity surged through his body.

Nunzio Martella watched intently from his corner table, taking in the interplay between Hugo and Mary McKenna. His fists clenched and unclenched.

Hugo lived by night. Zarraga and Rotondo entrusted him with the task of ensuring that all crap games, card games, prostitution, loan sharking, and shake downs were sanctioned by the office on the Hill and that the office got its share. He had teamed up with Steve Marfeo and Buster Zito. They were an imposing trio when they entered a room. Tailored one-button rolled lapel suits, suede shoes or feather weight Florsheims, and custom made shirts marked them as successful wise guys. Everybody paid. They knew the consequence of not paying: broken windows, fires, burnt cars, and the occasional vicious beating—usually administered to bookies who wouldn't pay off on winning bets or tried to cheat on their kickbacks. He was totally enmeshed in the Mafia; his life was now in the hands of Dom Zarraga.

He had never had so much money in his life. It flowed in, and he spent it on gambling, clothes, and restaurants—especially the Gaslight, where he could be found most evenings huddled in conversation with Mary McKenna.

She was a good Catholic girl, educated by the nuns at parochial schools in South Boston. Her father and brothers were firemen in the city, her mother a pious woman who insisted on mass every Sunday and holy days of obligation. Her oldest sister was in a convent having recently taken her final vows. Still, she knew she would give herself to Hugo. He was all she thought about. They had never dated or even been together outside the Gaslight. That would end, and it did on a Tuesday evening in her small East Side apartment. They were in a naked embrace, tongues fencing as he penetrated her. She was a virgin. Her eyes rolled back. She moaned unintelligibly, arched her back, and exploded in orgasm in two spastic movements. She was consumed with lust as she thrust forward and again reached orgasm. As they lay spent and exhausted, she whispered, "I love you." He didn't respond.

"You're never home! I live alone. How long is this going to go on?" Angie was holding baby Hugo, who was using his tiny fingers to explore the openings of his mother's nose and ears. She placed him on the floor and he immediately crawled toward his father's shoes. Hugo stood before the dresser mirror knotting his tie. "Are you going to talk to me or what? We don't even do that any more. I don't like this. My friend's husbands don't live like this."

He bent down to pick up the baby, nuzzling his cheek. "Your friend's husbands don't make the kind of money I make, either. Your friends are not gonna have a new house next year, probably with no mortgage. Would you like that?"

"Not if it means that we go on like this forever. I want a husband. You haven't even kissed me in a week."

He flashed her a dismissive grin and lightly brushed her lips while handing her the baby all in one motion. "Listen, Angie, this won't go on forever. I need to work these long hours to make the good money I'm making. Suppose I had a job working the night shift, what's the difference?"

"The difference is that I wouldn't have to worry about you being locked up in jail or getting shot by some crazy cop."

"Listen, that's not going to happen. I don't do anything dangerous. I pick up money, I drive Dom places…you know, stuff like that. And I promise you I'll take some time off next week, okay?"

"All right," she replied tiredly. "When was the last time you saw your father? The baby spends more time with him than he does with you."

"I know, I know, I'll see him on Sunday. I gotta go, I'm late. Don't wait up for me. I have to drive Dom to Boston."

The long black Fleetwood glided onto Route One and headed north for Boston. Traffic was light. The powerful engine purred as Hugo accelerated into traffic. Domenico Zarraga sat next to Hugo in the front seat. Giusto Rotondo sat in the rear with Zarraga's lawyer, Thomas Stone. Stone's given name was Tommaso Sasso. He had changed it before entering Harvard College and had since acquired all the affectations of an English barrister. Tall and handsomely gray, he belied his sixty-three years by a decade or more.

Zarraga leaned over and placed a hand on Hugo's shoulder. "Hugo, you're the youngest guy I ever put so much faith in, do you know this?"

"Yes, Dom," replied Hugo with deep sincerity, "and you know how much I respect that and how I will always give you one hundred percent."

"I know you will, Hugo, I know you will. Listen, I'm moving you up. You're going to have your own crew of guys. I think you can be a real moneymaker. You pick out four or five guys, good guys. I want to know who they are, *capito?*"

"Yes, Dom." Hugo's heart raced. A crew of his own meant not only money but also respect; and in the dark underworld that he now inhabited, respect was the most valuable commodity.

"Listen, I want you to go up to Charles Street. I got a club up there, you take it over, work out of there with your crew." Zarraga chuckled. "It's called the Cadillac Club!"

They arrived at La Bella Napoli Ristorante in the North End, a Boston fixture frequented by the Archbishop, politicians, Boston Brahmins, and the wise guys. The Italian cuisine was the best in New England prepared by a kitchen full of newly arrived Italian immigrants, many of whom were illegal. Hugo pulled up to the front door. A valet opened the car doors and sped the Caddy into a parking area across the narrow street.

The owner, a short Neapolitan, greeted Zarraga in Italian and escorted them down to a subterranean function room that was as grand as the main dining room but had the added advantage of no windows or unprotected doors. The room was expansive. The table had been set in a horseshoe arrangement to accommodate fifty guests. A private bar was staffed by two men in white dinner jackets busily filling orders for the press of thirsty guests.

As soon as Zarraga entered the room men began to peel away from the bar to greet him. Each in turn embraced him, kissing him lightly on one cheek and then the other in a stylized ritual that reminded Hugo of alter boys genuflecting before their priest. Through it all Zarraga, like some holy father, maintained a patrician detachment.

Three men waited off to one side for the crowd to disperse. At one moment they and Zarraga walked toward one another. For the first time he smiled broadly, exchanging kisses and embraces.

These men, thought Hugo, are more important than the rest. Giusto Rotondo went through a similar exchange of greetings. Then, to Hugo's amazement, Zarraga turned and motioned to him.

Nervously, Hugo approached the small knot of men. Zarraga seized his elbow and pulled him close to his side. "Hugo, I want you to meet some very important people in our organization." Hugo smiled somewhat uncomfortably at these strangers. They were all expensively attired, silver haired, except for one who was balding; they exuded an air of confidence and importance. "Say hello to Carlo Gambino, Lucky Luciano, Joe Buonnano, all from New York, Vito Antonucci from Chicago, Sal Fria from California, and Leno Paglia from Sicily." Hugo advanced to each man and nervously shook their hands, overwhelmed to meet men whose names were legendary.

Leno Paglia, smiling, winked at Zarraga and spoke in heavily accented English. "Dom, thisa younga man looks strong, tough, he's a good man?"

"The best," said Zarraga shaking Hugo's arm like a boxing trainer, "Leno, he's on the way up."

"Atsa good, we need smart, tough young men to fill the ranks. I wish you alla the best of luck."

Luciano appraised Hugo with a narrowing of his eyes and his left hand holding his mouth and chin. "Hugo, what's your father's name?"

"Salvatore, Mr. Luciano."

"When did he leave Italy?"

"I think it was 1914, yes it was 1914." Luciano broke into a broad smile.

"I think I know your father, a good man, a man with coglione, we jumped ship together and swam to this country. Tell him I send my regards."

"I will, Mr. Luciano, thank you."

Hugo was heady with excitement. This was a special moment. He felt anointed and chosen; he knew his time had come. The men began taking their seats. Giusto Rotondo placed his arm around Hugo's shoulder. "Listen, Hugo, you can't stay for the meeting. Go upstairs, there's a private room for drivers and bodyguards up there. You're going to have a great meal. Try the veal spitzata, it's the best in Boston. I'll see you after the meeting. And, ay, don't worry about the check, it's all taken care of."

Chapter 7

MOVING UP

The Cadillac Club began life as a storefront grocery store specializing in imported Italian foods. Some of the patrons jokingly referred to it as the Baccalla Club, referring to a peasant dish made from dried cod, the smell of which still clung to the walls. Evolution turned it into the Cadillac Club. Now two large plate glass windows, painted over with exaggerated images of sleek, large-finned Cadillacs, flanked the main entrance. The glass concealed thick cement blocks fortifying the walls. The door had been reinforced with steel plate on the inside, and a peephole had been added for patron security.

Inside an antique bar ran the length of one sidewall; various sized tables were scattered about. At the rear of the room a small kitchen was tucked into one corner, and a small office had been built in the other. Two retired construction workers staffed the club, opening at seven a.m. and serving coffee royals to early morning card players and wise guy associates. Every wise guy in the North End of Providence frequented the place at one time or another. It was rumored that Zarraga's former associate, who used to use the club as his headquarters, had held back on the take. It was also rumored that Zarraga had him weighted with dumb bells and dumped into an old water-filled lime rock quarry off Route 146 on the way to Worcester. It was further rumored that he was trussed up and alive when he was dumped.

Hugo's reputation preceded him; he was Zarraga's chosen successor. It was a perfect fit. With Marfeo as his right hand, they wasted no time engineering tractor-trailer heists loaded with cigarettes and liquor, and boxcars full of silver ingots and gold wire ready for the vast Rhode Island jewelry industry. He was a moneymaker, and Zarraga got a third of everything.

It was a quiet Tuesday morning when Joey "The Mop" Moppelina took the call from Giusto Rotondo. Zarrago wanted to see Hugo right away. When Hugo arrived at the familiar club on the Hill, Zarraga was sitting back in his swivel chair, his fingertips joined in a spire touching his blue-tinged lips.

"You got some guys takin' action in a couple clubs and bars in your neck of the woods and we get fucken nothin'!" Zarrago suddenly jerked forward so that his body leaned over the desk. "One guy is Willie Nardo and his partner is Frenchy Sarault. Sarault hangs out at Ramps Tap, and the other guy goes from place to place but you can usually catch him at the V.F.W. Club on Volturno Street up in Marieville. You know where these joints are?"

Hugo nodded his head. "Yeah, Dom, I've been in both of them."

"Good, what I want you to do is grab both of these shits and do a number on them—you break an arm, you break a leg, you bust a nose, you understand?" Zarraga did not wait for a response. "These fucken bastards operate in my backyard! They were told three times already. You make it so they finally get my message, *capece?*"

"Yeah, Dom, I understand. When do you want this done?"

"Tonight! I want it done tonight. And make sure you take two or three good guys with you. Willie Nardo has buried a few people."

Hugo's mind raced, his pulse quickened. He would need Vinnie and Buster, that was enough. They had balls, and they knew how to handle themselves in a tough situation. The V.F.W. Club catered to working men of the North End, situated on a side street at the end of Charles Street. It received little attention from the police or neighbors in the area. It hosted card games, supported a softball team, and like most clubs offered free food on Friday nights. The walls were knotty pine, the floor pea-green asphalt tile. There were ten tables in the main room with a small private room in the rear for high stakes cards or craps. Three pinball machines lined one wall, a long bar covered another. On the back wall a television was mounted on a high shelf blaring the Friday night fights, the crowd around the bar grumbling and cursing as Carmine Basilio, the onion farmer from Canastoga, New York, battered the brains out of some second rate pug.

At the far end of the bar next to the fire exit and the pay phone sat Willie Nardo taking calls and jotting down bets on slips of paper. Vinnie Marfeo entered the club shortly after nine and walked to the far end of the bar. Some of the men called out greetings or waved in recognition. Both bartenders knew he was with Zarraga and showed appropriate respect.

Nardo was a big man. His huge torso obscured the wall-mounted pay phone as he hunched over taking action from bettors around the state. Around fifty, he was as tough as nails and cared little for Zarraga or for splitting his take with anyone. He openly referred to Zarraga as "the old asshole on the Hill." Nardo replaced the receiver and turned to see Vinny Marfeo standing a few feet away, one hand on the bar rail.

"Aay, Vinnie, whaddaya doin'? How's your uncles, I haven't seen those guys in months. You want something to drink? Some snail salad? They do a great job here."

"Naw, Willie, listen, I need to talk with you privately." The pay phone rang shrilly.

"Yeah, kid, wait a minute, I got some action coming in." He finished the call. "Awright, what's up?"

"I need to talk with you, it's important. Let's go outside." With a tilt of his head he indicated the exit door.

"Vinny, I'm busy, I can't leave the action, you know that."

"Listen, Willie, if it wasn't important I wouldn't ask you to leave the phone."

Nardo stared at the phone, as if waiting for it to ring. "Awright c'mon, we'll go out here for two minutes. You're interrupting my profession."

Hugo and Buster Zito leaned against the fender of a dilapidated black Buick with two flat tires parked at the rear of the club. Zito was obviously nervous, cracking his knuckles and breathing heavily, looking toward the street with the sound of every car engine. Hugo stared motionlessly at the fire exit door; he knew exactly what he would do and how he would do it.

The fire exit door opened, casting light and sound into the darkened rear of the building. As the door slammed shut and Nardo's eyes adjusted to the blackness, Vinnie Marfeo turned to stand next to Hugo. Nardo's eyes narrowed as he studied the three men.

"What the fucks goin' on here!"

Hugo's right foot shot into Nardo's groin with the force of a punted football. He gurgled a scream and fell to the ground clutching his scrotum, folded into a fetal position. The next kick caved in his prominent nose and mercifully knocked him unconscious. Zito produced a baseball bat that Hugo wrenched from his hands and with wild ferocity smashed Nardo's right leg, snapping bone. Saliva dripped from his lips and mucous from his nostrils as he smashed the bat into his forearm. The sickening sound of shattering bone woke Marfeo from his mesmerized state.

"All right, all right, Hugo!" He grabbed Hugo's arms as he raised the bat for another crashing blow. "Enough, enough, you're gonna kill the fucken guy!"

Hugo stood, chest heaving, sweat dripping from his face. Buster Zito reached for the bat. "C'mon, Hugo, let's get the fuck outta here. Somebody's gonna be looking for this guy."

For a long while no one spoke as they drove back toward Providence. "You should have told him why we were there," said Marfeo, breaking the silence.

Hugo turned from the front seat with a look of disgust on his face. "C'mon, Vinnie, you think he didn't know why we were there?"

"Yeah, I guess you're right."

Zito looked at Hugo from behind the steering wheel. "Hugo, if I were you I would definitely get myself a gun, he's a crazy bastard. And when he gets better, guess who he's gonna be lookin' for."

Domenico Zarraga rarely smiled; it was not in his nature. He sat back in the swivel chair, fingers interlaced, and smiled broadly.

"You did good, Hugo. That piece of shit will now get my message. And don't you worry about him trying to get back at you guys. He knows the next time he'll be in Berraducci's Funeral Home. How are you doing with the club, everything all right? No problem with the law of anything? We pay enough so there shouldn't be any nosey cops around."

"No, Dom, everything is good. I got some good deals coming that I need your approval on."

"Let me know, we'll talk about it. And remember, no drugs. None of that shit, understand?"

"Yeah, Dom, of course not. I don't want to be involved in any of that poison."

"All right, good, see me in a few days, *capece*?"

"Yes, Dom, I understand."

The Cardi's furniture truck was parked half on the sidewalk and half on the street as the workmen unloaded a large carton and commenced to haul it up to the third-floor apartment. Angelina opened the door to the sound of a loud knock.

"Mrs. Rossi? I got a delivery of a television for you. Were do you want it?" Angelina was stunned. She placed her hands over her mouth as the two deliverymen stood, carton in hand, impatient to set it down.

"Oh, I'm sorry, right in here in the den, in that corner please." She pointed to a far corner of the room and watched as the men opened the carton and removed a large square box with the name RCA Victor inscribed in the upper right hand corner and a small black screen in the middle. One of the men connected the rabbit-ears antennae while the other adjusted the picture using a pattern that appeared on the screen by way of the National Broadcasting Company. Programming, they explained, would not begin until four that afternoon.

"Well, whaddaya think, you like it?" Hugo had entered the apartment silenly, startling her. He handed the workmen a tip and walked them to the door. When he returned to the living room Angie was unsmiling.

"It doesn't make up for you not being home for the past two nights. And last week it was three nights. But then again the week's not over yet, so it might be four nights this week." She turned her back to him and walked into sleeping baby Hugo's room. Hugo followed her, speaking in tones of injured pride.

"Listen, what do you think I do when I'm not here, have fun? I have to travel out of town; that's how I can afford the little extras like a sixteen-inch television. You like that, don't you?"

"You can throw it out the window for all I care. I want a husband and I want a father for our son, and you're none of those things."

"Angie, Angie, that's just for now, I have to work these hours for a while. You want that house in Johnston, don't you? Well, don't you? C'mon talk to me!" Baby Hugo awakened, gurgling and kicking, his eyes following his father's movements.

She bent down and picked up the child, who stretched out his arms in Hugo's direction. "You know, there will come a time when you will realize what the important things are in life. I just hope that time will be soon."

"All right, I gotta go to work. I won't be late tonight, I promise." He turned to leave, ignoring her aloofness and the entreaties of his infant son.

"Your father wants you to stop by and see him."

He stopped in the bedroom doorway. "When did you talk to him?"

"This morning, he called me from work."

Hugo hesitated, a hand on the doorknob. As he turned he muttered, "I'll stop by and see him now, see what he wants."

Salvatore sat alone in his favorite reading chair puffing gently on his pipe as he turned the pages of the evening paper. The mahogany Philco radio played a classical melody; the fragrance of roasting meat filled the tenement apartment. Hugo entered quietly, looking first for Francesca. Salvatore folded the paper and placed it on the floor next to the chair. Knocking the ashes from his pipe he called out to Hugo: "Come into the parlor, son, have a seat." It was an unsmiling greeting.

Hugo entered the parlor and kissed Salvatore on the cheek. "How are you, Pa, where's Ma?"

"I'm fine, Hugo, your mother's at your house, you just missed her. She brought a dish for Angie and the baby. Sit down, I want to talk with you about something." Hugo's back stiffened at the prospect of what was to come. Salvatore sat back and refilled the pipe. "Angie was here last night crying her eyes out," he continued. His voice was flat, without accusation or judgment. "She says you're never home, you stay out all night, sometimes days at a time. Is this true?"

"Listen. Pa, I work out of town a lot, my job calls for this. I'm making good money, a lot of money. I'm taking care of my wife and son and next year we'll be in our own house. She has to understand that I do all this for her and the baby."

Salvatore observed his son with a steady unblinking gaze, puffing slowly on the pipe. "So tell me, Hugo, just what do you do that keeps you so busy, what kind of work is this?"

Hugo stared down at the floor, his hands resting on the crease of his trouser. "I do a lot of things, Pa. I run a bar, I handle investments, I oversee other businesses. It's not a nine-to-five bankers job, but I'm doing very well, she shouldn't complain. I'm doing this for her and the baby."

Salvatore removed the pipe from his mouth and pointed toward Hugo, jabbing the air as he spoke. "I know what you do, Hugo, I've always known what you do. And what you do is against everything I stand for. I came to this country with nothing but my integrity and honor and they were tested many times, but I still have them. I taught you this as a boy; I guess I was a poor teacher. Let me tell you this: if you do anything to hurt your wife or your son you will not be welcome in my house, do you understand?"

"Pa, I would never do anything. . ."

"Do you understand me?"

"Yes, yes, I understand you."

"Good, now you can go to your work, as you call it."

Hugo stood awkwardly, not wanting to leave the conversation on a sour note. "I'll see you Sunday then?"

"Yes, Hugo, Sunday. Uncle Pat will be here, twelve o'clock sharp." Salvatore retrieved the paper as Hugo wavered in his departure.

"All right, Pa, I'll see you Sunday." There was no response from behind the newspaper.

The Gas Light restaurant and lounge was in the center of downtown Providence. It boasted antique pole lighting on the cobblestone

THE ARRIVAL THE STRUGGLE THE ASCENDANCY

sidewalk surrounding the white antique brick building. The interior gave off a plush Gay Nineties look, and the menu and food we're some of the best in the city. The owner, Tommy Hoogasian, was a childhood friend of Domenico Zarraga and had no problems with shakedowns or troublesome wise guys.

Hugo could be found at the bar every evening that Mary McKenna worked. He was obsessed: obsessed with her beauty, her innocence, and her lustfulness. She reciprocated the obsession and could not wait for his arrival. She had blossomed into an even more sensual woman with the constant love making that took place at her small East Side apartment two or three nights a week. Her grades at Pembroke were slipping; her parents were demanding answers as to why they hadn't heard from her in weeks. When he would arrive at the restaurant her heart would leap in expectation. They were magnetized by one another.

"Why are you so late?" she whispered as she delivered drinks to a table.

"I had to do some business before I left my club," he responded as she returned to the bar. It had become common knowledge that Hugo and Mary were seeing one another. Although they were as discreet as possible, it was inevitable that they would be found out. Not an eyebrow raised, not a snide remark was ever uttered. At the Gas Light he maintained a respectful distance and she did her best at maintaining an aloofness that masked her desire to wrap her body around him.

The Hammer knew. Nunzio Martella had followed them to her apartment; had seen the lights turn on; had seen him leaving early in the morning. His jealous rage overcame all other emotions. He was in physical pain. He lay awake staring at the cracked ceiling of his one-bedroom Federal Hill apartment. He will kill them both, this is what he thought. She, the dirty little Irish slut who didn't think he was good enough even to talk to. And Zarraga's ass wipe, who was probably sticking it to her right now. He growled in the darkness as like a madman, gripping the mattress with his hands trembling as the night gave way to dawn.

Richard Tamborelli and Billy Devlin were the two young rookie cops assigned to the Charles Street beat, checking doors, dealing with domestic disputes, and tolerating the mistrust and stares from the patrons of the Cadillac Club. They were used to it. Tamborelli had grown up on Federal Hill, and Billy Devlin had grown up on Smith Hill—an Italian and an Irish enclave, both sharing the same culture of tight lips when it came to the police.

"Billy, what do you think? Should we just charge in there and bust them for illegal gambling some Friday night or what?" Tamborelli was a tall, slim, handsome young man anxious to climb the ladder of the Providence Police Department, despite its nepotism and corruption. His partner was a dimple-chinned good-looking kid who wore the map of Ireland on his face.

"Listen, Richard, I think we should wait until they have some hot stuff in there with a few of the heavy hitters, you know what I mean. That way we can grab them all."

Tamborelli stared at the front door of the club from the black Ford patrol car, drumming his fingers on the steering wheel and nodding in agreement. "Hey, Billy, look at the two fat assholes going into the Cadillac, fat Ferruccio and his brother-in-law, Nicky 'the Booster' Taglione."

Devlin grinned. "See what I mean, Rich, we wait and grab all the fish when the time is right."

The time was right the following Wednesday night. The club was in full swing with two crap games in progress, one of them with unlimited stakes that had drawn a large-cash crowd. In the back office Vito Ferruccio and Nicky the Booster where seated with a well-known fence, examining the contents of the black velvet bag recently stolen from a Providence jewelry manufacturer. The club's doorman, "Hercules" Baffoni, tended the heavy steel front door. A loud banging resounded on the steel door. Hercules slid the peep hole cover aside to reveal a young man in his early twenties holding large pizza boxes. He cracked open the door with the one inch chain still in place.

"Whaddaya want kid?"

"Somebody called for two large pizzas, that's what I got."

Hercules turned to the crowded, noisy room. "Aay, any youse guys order pizza?" There was no response. He looked through the opening of the door and shrugged. "Nobody here ordered pizza, kid, take a hike."

"Wait a minute, somebody from this club ordered this pizza and I'm not leaving until I get paid."

"Aay, what'a you, a wise guy?"

"No, I'm just doing a job, that's all."

The huge doorman hesitated, and then relented. "Awright, come on in and ask at the tables, maybe the guy was in the toilet." As he spoke he unlatched the heavy security chain. The door crashed open with the force of an explosion sending Hercules sprawling against tables as all heads turned and conversation abruptly stopped. In the center of the room stood Tamborelli and Devlin, their thirty-eight caliber police revolvers fanning the room.

"All right now, everybody on the floor. Down now, goddamit, on the floor!" Devlin's voice was loud and commanding. Bodies dropped to the floor in rapid succession leaving money and gambling paraphernalia on the tables. The pizza deliveryman reappeared with a flash camera and began photographing the tables and the men on the floor in rapid succession. Tamborelli headed for the small rear office, treading his way through the bodies and ignoring the babble of mumbled profanities as he passed.

The office door was locked. "Rossi, open the door. Why fuck around, I know there's no other way out. Let's not waste time." There was no response except the sound of scraping chairs. A chair slipped, someone tumbled, and Vito Ferruccio's voice could be clearly heard shouting obscenities.

Tamborelli's patience was wearing thin. "Ferruccio, you fat-assed bastard, you're pissing me off. Do I have to blow this door off and probably shoot you in the ass, is that what you want?" The door slowly cracked open. It was Hugo.

"All right, calm down, relax. Why are you guys doin' this? Do they know what you're up to downtown?"

Tamborelli ignored the question. "C'mon, get out here, I don't have all night."

Ferruccio and his brother-in-law, followed by Myer Kaplan, emerged from the office, all of them scowling in outrage and disbelief. Ferruccio's mouth curled in contempt. "Does Major Sullivan know what you guys are up to? Do you know who we are?"

Tamborelli smiled broadly and ignored the question. Devlin called from the middle of the room: "Rich, check the ceiling, there's a panel to the attic, see what's up there. Jimmy, jump on the desk and check the ceiling for any evidence." The pizza man turned photographer scurried into the room, leaped onto the dilapidated desk, and in seconds retrieved the velvet bag of diamonds.

Sergeant Connie O'Neil pulled open the rear door's of the paddy wagon and directed Hugo, Ferruccio, Nicky the Booster, and Meyer Kaplan onto the wooden seats, slamming and locking the doors behind them.

"I hope you guys know what the hell your doin'," O'Neil said, shaking his head. "This could lead to a lot of shit downtown, you know that."

Devlin spoke up, squaring his broad shoulders. "Listen, Sarge', we're the cops, they're the robbers. We did the job we're entrusted to do, is there something wrong with that?"

"Not as far as I'm concerned, rookie, I think it was a damn good job." Tamborelli leaned into the open doorway of the club. "All right, girls, you can go back to playing with your jacks."

Major William Sullivan, Deputy Chief of Police, was livid as he paced his office. Devlin and Tamborelli stood at attention along one wall. "Who the frig gave you authorization to conduct that raid?" His voice boomed across the room. Billy Devlin spoke first.

"Sir, we had them under surveillance for weeks. We knew what was going on inside the club."

"I don't give a shit what you knew, rookie, you needed my permission for that raid, do you understand me?"

"Yes, sir," they replied in unison.

He glared at Tamborelli and then at Devlin. "Get the hell out of my office! I'll deal with you two later."

T'homas Stone, Esquire, arrived at the Providence police station precisely ten minutes after the arrival of the paddy wagon carrying Hugo and his associates. He approached desk Sergeant Leo Zenowitz, his silver hair carefully coifed, his monogrammed attaché case in hand.

"Well, well, if it ain't Tommy Stone, how did I know you'd be here, counselor, and so soon, too! You must have your own private detectives following your clients around. What can I do for you, counselor?"

"Good evening, Sergeant Zenowitz, always a pleasure to see you. And, yes, I am here to see my clients, Mr. Rossi, Mr. Ferruccio, Mr. Kaplan, and Mr. Taglione, if I may, Sergeant."

"Yeah, well, Tommy, I'll see if they're booked yet and then you can go down to the holding cells to see your clients. I think you know the way."

"Yes, Sergeant, I do, and I would appreciate it if I could speak privately with Mr. Rossi in one of the conference rooms, if that's possible."

"Sure, counselor, I'll bring him up here for you."

Hugo was disheveled and obviously agitated as he was led into the small conference room on the second floor of the police station. A look of surprise changed to pleasure as he recognized Tommy.

"How are you, Hugo, are they treating you all right?"

"I'm fine, Mr. Stone," said the younger man, taking the offered hand, "it's good to see you."

"Mr. Zarraga doesn't abandon his friends and associates when they're in need, Hugo, you can rest assured of that. Now, tell me exactly what happened."

Hugo related in detail the events of the evening as Stone made an occasional note on a yellow legal pad.

"Well, Hugo," said Stone, rising from his chair and tucking the pad back into his case, "I don't think we have anything to worry about. It appears there was no probable cause for the invasion of the club, and this act was perpetrated without a search warrant. I've put a call into Major Sullivan, I'm sure he can resolve this entire matter this very evening."

Hugo, Vito, Nick, and Myer were released that evening to the chagrin of Devlin and Tamborelli, and to the cynical shrug of Sgt. Zenowitz, who had seen it all before. Myer Kaplan even got his diamonds back with an apology.

The door to the apartment was open. Hugo walked into the neat, cozy kitchen and threw his jacket over a chair, reaching for the refrigerator door as Angie appeared in the bedroom doorway.

"Well, if it isn't Jesse James. You decided to pay your wife and son a visit or do you just need a change of clothes? Ah, yes, you would need a fresh shirt. No doubt there's lipstick on the collar of the one you've got on." She turned and went to the baby, who had just awakened and was wailing for attention and a bottle.

Hugo spoke with anger as he bent over rummaging through the refrigerator. "You know, Angie, you're getting nuttier and nuttier every day. And, by the way, put some goddamned food in this house! I give you enough money."

She reappeared in the bedroom doorway holding baby Hugo, who was happily sucking on a bottle of formula. Her tone was bitter and sullen. "Why should I buy food, you're never here for dinner. I make special dishes and I wind up throwing the food away.

I guess your girlfriends have better things to offer you than pork chops and potatoes."

He leaned against the closed refrigerator door, arms folded across his chest. His voice was cold and menacing. "Enough, you hear me, enough! What, I don't give you enough money? You're girlfriends should live so well."

"My girl friends have husbands, real men who have jobs and come home at night and make love to them."

His right hand lashed out spontaneously, the backhand splitting her lip and snapping her head backward. The bottle slipped from her fingers to the discontented wail of the baby. She was too stunned to cry, her mouth open in shock. Hugo turned hesitantly to retrieve his jacket.

"You son of a bitch!" Tears streamed across her cheeks. "I won't put up with this kind of half life, this abuse, and I won't expose my son to this crap. Don't bother coming here anymore." Her voice escalated to a scream. *"Do you hear me?"*

Hugo stopped at the front door. "I'll be here whenever I feel like being here, and don't you forget it." He slammed the door and was gone. She leaned against the wall sobbing and mumbling to herself, baby Hugo happily kicking his feet and clapping his hands.

She lay next to him naked, her creamy skin and taut breasts a constant attraction to him. He ran his hands over her warm, moist body, then raised himself and kissed the strawberry blond crescent inviting his mouth. She arched her back and uttered an animal like moan. They made love for the second time that afternoon.

Mary McKenna had become the focus of his life. He was consumed by her and the Cadillac Club and little else. The sun had already set as he left Mary's apartment and walked across the pea-stone parking area to the Ford Fairlane and inserted the key into the door lock. There was a chill in the air. It was October. He turned to look up, finding Mary framed by the third-floor window waving good-bye.

The figure charged out of the darkness from behind the shrubs, his feet smashing into the pea stones with every footfall. Hugo's gaze swiveled quickly toward the sound, to be confronted with a cursing, wild-eyed Nunzio Martella lunging toward him, an enormous knife in his raised hand. He slashed at Hugo's head, missing by a fraction of an inch. Hugo leapt backward, not turning his back to Martella, frantically searching for some sort of weapon.

Martella advanced slowly toward the retreating Hugo. "You miserable pig," he cursed, choking on his words as mucus dripped from his nostrils, "you rotten fuck! I'll fix your pretty boy face!" His eyes glowed with wild hatred. Again he charged, as only a madman would, slashing the air haphazardly with the knife. There was no retreat for Hugo. In his scrambling to avoid the "Hammer" he quickly reached down and scooped up a handful of pea stone and dirt and hurled it into Martella's wild eyes, momentarily blinding him. The extraordinary power of Hugo's kick to Martella's mid section came from fear and rage. As Martella writhed on the ground Hugo wrenched the knife from his hand and without a moments hesitation plunged it through Martella's neck and into the ground beneath. His eyes bulged; he gurgled, gasped his final breath, and lay still. Hugo stood over the body, heaving in exhaustion. He looked from right to left; the neighborhood was quiet. He looked up to the third floor window. She had seen it all.

He dragged the body, gushing blood, to the trunk of the Ford and with super human effort threw it into the trunk, hastily wiping blood from his hands and the chrome bumper with an old rag. There was no time to go back to the apartment. He needed to act immediately. Once more he looked up at the window, and once more he saw the frozen form of his Mary, no doubt horrified by the scene she'd just witnessed. There was nothing he could do about that now. All he could do now was take care of business. There'd be time for other things later.

Hugo sped out of the parking lot and drove to an industrial area off North Main Street in Providence. He turned off the headlights, kept the engine running, and quickly ran to the trunk. The limp body was heavy and awkward. Pulling it by the arms he dragged it to behind a darkened trailer truck parked against a loading dock. Adrenaline quickened his actions. He turned from the body fearful of discovery, hesitated, then extracted the butcher knife from Martella's neck, blood still pumping from the wound. Glancing around he bent beneath the trailer and forced the knife into an opening in the metal undercarriage, leaving only a small piece of the handle exposed.

Chapter 8

DESTINY

"Salvatore, I want you to meet my wife's cousin, Julio. He runs a small restaurant in North Providence. Father Cavalaro helped him get into business. He would like to talk to you about something important"

"Yes, of course." Salvatore extended his hand in greeting to a small, shy man, dressed in an old but still respectable Sunday suit. "How are you, Julio?" he asked, at the same time staring at the man's battered face, which was severely discolored, cut, and swollen. "What happened to you? Did you have some sort of accident, Julio?" Salvatore's voice was full of genuine concern.

The newcomer appeared awkward in front of Salvatore, and he nervously looked to LoFredo for support. Pat LoFredo motioned for Julio to go on. "Salvatore," he began, speaking in a slow, timid voice, "three weeks ago I'm in the kitchen in my restaurant when two big young Mafioso come in the back door. They tell me they are there to protect me from any troublemakers who might want to break my windows or cause fights in my restaurant or bother my wife or daughter. They said for this kind of insurance it would cost one hundred dollars a week. I don't have that kind of money, but I didn't want any trouble. I know these types. I remember from the old country what they would do, so I started to pay. But then I just couldn't do it anymore. I couldn't pay my bills, I was behind on my taxes." He paused and looked down at the sidewalk, choking back tears. Pat Lofredo wrapped an arm around his shoulders.

"Go on, my friend, finish your story," Salvatore urged gently.

Julio composed himself and continued in a stronger voice. "This past Wednesday they came back with another big Mafioso; he was their boss. He demanded the money. I told him I couldn't pay anymore. The minute I said it, he punched me in the face and continued to beat me. He was like a wild animal. I was curled up on the floor trying to protect my head." He stopped, fighting back the tears.

"Did you call the Police?" Salvatore asked.

Julio wiped his eyes with a handkerchief, then shook his head from side to side. "They can't do anything; they won't do anything. Half of them are on the take."

Salvatore placed a hand on Julio's shoulder and gently asked, "What can I do to help you my friend?"

Julio raised his eyes to meet Salvatore's. "Salvatore, it was your son, Hugo, who did this to me."

Salvatore's mouth dropped open, his face blanched. "How can you say this, how can you be sure, Julio, you don't know my son."

"It was your son. I met him with Pat a year ago and I saw him more than once with you at St. Bart's. It was your son, Salvatore, I'm positive of this."

Salvatore dropped his hand from Julio's shoulder and with the firm grip of a laborer he took both his hands into his own. As he spoke tears welled up in his eyes. "I am deeply sorry that this pain was caused by my flesh and blood. I am shamed and humiliated by his actions. I will do whatever it takes to earn your respect and forgiveness."

Julio spoke with deep emotion in his voice. "Salvatore, you are a good man. This was not your fault, it was the fault of the Mano Nera, the fault of the Mafia of Domenico Zarragga. You don't need my forgiveness and you have always had my respect. It is your son who needs your forgiveness, but I'm afraid they own him, my friend. They own his body and soul." With this final utterance Julio Martini made a slight bow and walked toward his car.

Pat Lofredo stood silently by, watching his friend. He knew there would have to be retribution.

"Pat, tell me, where is this Cadiallac Club my son runs?"

Lofredo had a pained expression on his face. "Salvatore, why do you want to go there? It does no good, see him at your house. Wait a while. Now your blood is up. Don't go there."

"Pat, tell me or I'll go and find it any way."

Lofredo shook his head and exhaled through pursed lips. "It's on Charles Street, next door to the Columbia picture show."

"Thank you." Salvatore turned and walked toward his car.

"Salvatore, I'll come with you," Lofredo called out as he started walking after Salvatore.

"No, Pat," said Salvatore holding up one hand in protest, "he's my son. I will do this alone."

Hercules peered through the peephole. He did not recognize the gray-haired man dressed in Sunday clothing who stood waiting on the other side.

"Yeah, whaddaya want?" he called out with his usual impatience.

"I'm here to see Hugo Rossi," came the reply.

"Yeah, well I don't know you, and until somebody tells me you're okay, you ain't comin' in here"

"I'm his father. I need to see him."

Hercules Baffoni's brain slowly began to register the significance of this new visitor. "Oh, yeah, Mr. Rossi. I'm sorry. Sure, come on in." The sound of chains rattling and bolts sliding signaled the door opening. Salvatore stood in the open doorway. Several pairs of listless eyes turned from the bar to look at the tall, powerfully built man as he took several steps into the room.

"Where is Hugo, please?" Salvatore's spoke softly, with the simple tone of someone being received in an unfamiliar home.

"He's in the office in the back, Mr. Rossi. I'll show you."

"No, that's all right, thank you, I can see where it is." The door to the office stood partly ajar. Hugo sat talking with Vinnie Marfeo and Buster Zito. Salvatore pushed the door open. The three men looked up to see Salvatore framed in the doorway. Hugo was shocked at the sudden appearance of his father. He rose and walked from behind his desk.

"Pa, what are you doing here? Is everything all right?" He stood before his father, still struggling to comprehend the meaning of his visit.

"No, Hugo, everything is not all right. Tell me, do you know Julio Martini?" Hugo's expression gave him away. He turned to look at Marfeo and Zito who tried to act nonchalantly and failed. Hugo hesitated.

"No, Pa, I don't know this guy, why?"

"Salvatore's closed fist shot from his left hip in a backhand, knuckles smashing into Hugo's right cheek. The force of the blow knocked him off his feet, falling onto the desk behind him. Marfeo and Zito were taken by surprise. Zito moved to assist Hugo. The movement caused Salvatore to cock his fist reflexively. Hugo righted himself and stood holding his jaw, his face flushed, stunned by the blow and suffering from the humiliation of such a public affront to his manhood. There was an uneasy silence in the office and in the outer room. No one moved. Hugo stood massaging his face and struggling to regain his dignity. His father had never laid a hand on him in anger before.

Salvatore stood looking at his son—his only son, whom he had hoped one day would become a lawyer or doctor or perhaps follow in his own humble footsteps. Whatever he chose to do with his life, certainly he would be a man who would bring pride and dignity to the name of Rossi. Standing there now, he could barely contain the hurt and anger that it had come to this—a confrontation over his criminal behavior. He repeated the thought to himself, "criminal behavior." How could this be? In the eyes of God, how could this be! This was not the son he had raised. This was someone else. Someone he did not know. When finally he spoke his words fell like hail, shattering the deafening silence.

"You and your tough, manly friends viciously beat a simple man trying to make a living for his family, for his future in this country. You did this for money." His voice rose even as he felt his heart break. "If you go near this man ever again, then you deal with me, do you understand this?" For a brief moment their eyes locked, and in that moment they both knew that everything that had once existed between them was changed forever. There was no reply, no movement. Salvatore walked toward the door. He paused and pointed his finger at Hugo. "From this day, you no longer are welcome in my home!"

Marfeo and Zito looked at one another. Marfeo raised his eyebrows in a silent gesture nodding toward the office door. They left Hugo, head in hands, sitting at his desk as they quickly closed the door behind them. Hugo sat staring at his desk considering what to do next. There was the problem of rationalizing the incident to his men, of maintaining his reputation. He muttered to himself in anguish, "Pa, Pa, why the hell do you have to fight everybody's battles, God damn it!" He vowed to himself to mend fences with Salvatore. He would visit with him, convince him that it was all a mistake.

He opened the office door and motioned for Zito and Marfeo, who were sitting at the bar, to return. "Listen, you guys know my father, he has a temper. He means nothing by it. That's the way he is." Hugo studied their faces for any sign of objection, but Zito and Marfeo only nodded agreeably, clearly eager to avoid conversation. "And by the way," he continued, feeling encouraged by silence, "let's forget about the Martini guy. He's peanuts. We got bigger things to do deal with." Again, the young men merely nodded in agreement. Hugo clapped his hands on the shoulders of his two lieutenants and forced an awkward smile. "All right, then, let's get to work. Somebody's got to watch the store."

Domenico Zarragga was aging. Estimates of his age were between seventy-one and seventy-five, no one knew for sure. He sat behind his desk facing Hugo. They were alone in his office.

"I heard about your father visiting you at the Club. He never changes. Your father, always defending the underdog. That's why I always respected him. Have you talked with him lately?"

Hugo was uneasy in his chair. "No, Dom, but he'll get over it. I'll talk with him."

Zarragga rubbed the stubble of his cheek. "I called you here for another reason. He paused and leveled his gaze directly into Hugo's eyes. There was no body movement as he spoke. "We haven't heard from the Hammer in a couple of weeks. That's not like him. Giusto went over to his house. There was no answer so he popped the lock and the apartment looked like he was still around. You know anything about this?" Zarragga shifted in his chair and leaned forward, his hands crossed on the desk as though in prayer. "Listen," he continued, "before you answer the question, I want you to know something. Martella was an unstable man. He would obey my commands, and a man in my position needs men like him to do what needs to be done. But..." — he paused and took a deep breath, "a man like the Hammer has no friends and is destined to end his own life violently, no doubt while trying to end someone else's life violently. I had no special attachment to him. In fact, he was becoming a liability with his craziness. Now you can answer my question."

Hugo stared blankly at one corner of Zarragga's desk, not speaking for a full minute. Zarragga sat back in his chair, his fingers tent-like against his purple lips. "He tried to kill me," Hugo began at last. "He waited for me to leave Mary's apartment and charged out of the darkness like an insane man, slashing at my head. He was an animal. I defended myself." Hugo described the details of the killing as Zarragga nodded understanding. Finally Zarragga rose from his chair and walked from behind his desk to Hugo's side. He placed a hand on Hugo's shoulder.

"This was destiny, Hugo. In his craziness he saw Mary McKenna as his girlfriend. Giusto told him to forget about it, but when you're crazy...." Zarragga tapped his head with his index finger. "I'm glad you told me the truth, Hugo. I knew you had a fight with him and I suspected you killed him. Don't worry, there are plenty of Martella's at my disposal. A lotta guys are looking to make their bones. Did you tell anyone about this?"

"No, I didn't, no one."

"Good," said Zarragga, taking a thin black cigar from his shirt pocket. "Go back to the club, business as usual, *capece?*"

Hugo stood, a look of contrition on his face. "Dom...thank you."

Zarragga embraced him. "Don't worry about it. This business we're in, sometimes things like this happen."

He tried to insert the key into the apartment door. It wouldn't fit. He tried another key with the same results. He heard Baby Hugo crying, heard Angie's footsteps treading toward the baby's room.

"Angie, please open the door. C'mon, I have to use the bathroom." He pounded on the door with a closed fist. "Angie, c'mon, open the door before I kick it in!" He heard the deadbolt turn. The door opened slowly to reveal Angie—red eyed, tear-stained face—holding Baby Hugo, gurgling and smiling and reaching out to his father, who ignored him. "What the hell is wrong with you? Why did you change the lock? Are you nuts?"

She turned her back to him, the baby peeking over her shoulder. "You either leave her or go live with your *putana* on the East Side. And if that's what you want, I want a divorce."

Hugo was stunned. "What the frig are you talking about? What do you mean?"

"One of your friends ratted on you, put a note in the mailbox. What's her name, Mary McKenna?"

Hugo masked his surprise and challenged the note. "That's a crock of shit. That's someone causing trouble, that's what this is. It's a lie."

"I believe it. She's listed in the phone book. I called her, she hung up on me."

His body acted of its own accord. He spun her around and slapped her twice. She fell to her knees clutching Baby Hugo who thought the whole incident was playtime as he shrieked with laughter. Angie sat on the floor sobbing and murmuring that it was over, all over. Hugo cursed, slammed the apartment door behind him, cursed again, and ran down the stairs.

It was three thirty on a Tuesday afternoon. The autumn sun cast a dim yellow light on the walls of the small, warm bedroom as it buried itself in the west. Hugo sat propped up on one elbow marveling at the pink, perfectly formed body that curled next to his own. Her long lashes fluttered as she spoke.

"You know I have to go to work." Her smile was dazzling. "Why don't you just move in with me? You're here all the time anyway."

He sat up on the edge of the bed and lit a Lucky Strike, exhaling slowly. "I may have to, at least for a while. Angie threw me out of the house." He paused for a moment. "I guess I deserved it. I treated her like shit." He said it matter-of-factly, as if retelling someone else's misfortune. She suppressed a smile, her heart soaring.

"Here, I made you a key to the apartment. I have everything. All you need are your clothes."

State Police Lieutenant Vincent Venezia was assigned to a small group of plainclothes Detectives who worked almost exclusively on criminal organizations. He was a tall, ruddy, handsome man with sharp features and a thick mane of grey-white hair that belied his Italian ancestry. An athlete in high school, he still possessed a powerful physique that came from years of training and a careful diet.

Venezia had grown up on Federal Hill playing baseball and football with some of the same men he was now trying to put away for robbery and murder. He sat in State Police Headquarters in Scituate, about a half-hour from Providence, reviewing the chain of events in the recent gangland slaying of Nunzio Alberto Martella. There was not much to go on. No weapon had been found, and any one of a dozen guys wanted to kill him for various reasons, real or imagined. He was turning pages in the case folder when the buzzer phone rang loudly on his deskas Venezia reached for it.

"Vinnie, this is Buddy Monroe. How are ya?"

"Hey, Buddy, how you been, how's your rotten golf game?"

"Yeah, you can say that again. I had a terrible summer. I'm gonna give up the game and my membership at the club." Both men laughed. "Listen, Vin, the reason I called, my guy's were changing tires on one of my trailers a little while ago and they found a big butcher knife jammed in the trailer chassis. I figured it might have some connection to that guy Martella we found stabbed to death against my loading dock." Venezia came upright in his chair, nervously tapping a pencil on his desk.

"Listen, Buddy, did your guys handle the knife?"

"No, they used their heads. They were the ones who found the body, so they put two and two together, know what I mean?"

Venezia's faced nearly glowed. "Buddy, tell your guys good work. I'll be right there."

The crime lab picked up two sets of prints from the knife. It was left to Vespia to determine who they belonged to. The street was thick with rumors about the Martella-Rossi feud and the supposed love triangle. It made sense; Martella was an animal. He attacks Rossi, Rossi defends himself, kills Martella, end of story.

"Hey, Harry!" Harry Bogosian, Sergeant in Charge of the State Police Fingerprint Squad, looked up at the sound of his name being shouted across the squad room.

"What's up, Lieutenant?" Built like a fireplug, Bogosian had a bulldog's tenacity and an Armenian nose that preceded his entrance into any room.

"Listen, when you go to Providence check for prints on file from Hugo Rossi. You know who I mean?"

"Yeah, Lieutenant, that's Zarragga's fair haired boy, right?"

"That's the guy, Harry. I think we might have something there."

"You got it, Lieutenant."

Bogosian returned to Headquarters later that afternoon. Minutes later Venezia compared the prints. There could be no mistake: one of the knife prints was clearly Hugo's; a residue of blood gave them an unmistakable clarity. Venezia turned in his swivel chair and called out to detectives in the squad room. "Flynn, Nadeau, got a minute?"

"What's up?" Lieutenant Peter Flynn and Lieutenant Roger Nadeau were seasoned veterans, both spit and polish troopers, both with numerous commendations.

"I've got a perfect match on some prints from the Martella murder. I want you to go down to the Cadillac Club or wherever he is and tell Hugo Rossi we want him for questioning concerning the Martella murder. If he gives you any shit, arrest him. And listen, take two uniformed troopers with you."

There had been no resistance. Hugo Rossi awaited Lieutenant Vincent Venezia in an interview room at State Police Headquarters, relaxed, immaculately turned out, puffing on a Lucky Strike. Venezia entered the room carrying two cups of coffee.

"How are you, Hugo? I brought you a regular coffee, that okay?"

"Yeah, Lieutenant that's good, thank you."

"I'm glad you came up on your own, Hugo. That's an indication that you're a cooperative guy, you know what I mean?"

"Yeah, Lieutenant, I have nothing to hide. That's why I'm here." Hugo crossed his legs and took a sip from his coffee, conscious of striking a relaxed pose.

"Well, I'm glad, Hugo," continued Venezia in a soft, pleasant voice. "Let me tell you why I asked you to come up here. We have a butcher knife with Nunzio Martella's blood all over it. And on that same butcher knife we have your fingerprints as well. Any idea how that could happen, Hugo?"

Hugo blinked visibly. They had found the knife. "Listen, Lieutenant, I can't help you. I didn't even know Martella that well. A lot of people wanted him dead. He was an animal, know what I mean?"

Before Venezia had an opportunity to answer, there was a knock on the door and Roger Nadeau leaned into the room. "Lieutenant, his lawyer's here." The door swung open fully to reveal Thomas Stone.

"Lieutenant, so good to see you again. May I come in?"

Venezia grinned and shook his head slightly from side to side. "Well, well, if it isn't the great barrister, Thomas Stone."

Stone acknowledged the spurious compliment with a slight smile and moved to stand next to Hugo, who seemed relieved to see him. "May I sit, Lieutenant?"

"Of course, Counselor. We are civil here, you know."

"Thank you, Lieutenant. You may be aware that I represent Mr. Rossi."

"Mr. Stone, as if by magic you appear when needed. Let me assure you, if I'm ever in need of legal representation, you're my man."

"Thank you, Lieutenant, but I'm sure you'll never have need for my particular expertise. Now as to my client, do you plan to arrest him?"

Venezia stroked his chin and looked at Hugo. "Well, Counselor, I'm afraid I have to. We've got his fingerprints all over a murder weapon. I have no choice."

Stone had expected the reply. "The arraignment will be tomorrow, I trust."

"Yeah, I think we can get him set for a ten o'clock hearing."

Superior Court was located on Providence's East Side next to Brown University. The building was circa seventeen-seventy and had served at one time as the Continental Army's Headquarters during the Revolution. The wear and tear was evident everywhere, especially in the grooved and pitted oak flooring. Courtroom 201 on the second level was presided over by Justice Owen Fleming, a fifty-year old homosexual whose career was spared after being caught some years earlier having anal sex with a sixteen-year old boy in the back seat of his Buick sedan. Fleming owed his good fortune to Domenico Zarragga who had worked his magic with the

Providence Police Department to drop all charges and conveniently misplace all arrest records relating to the incident, confounding reporters from the *Providence Journal* who had been informed by an anonymous phone call that the Judge was in custody and for what reason.

The arraignment went quickly. The charge was murder in the first degree. Hugo pleaded not guilty, and to the surprise of everyone in the courtroom except Thomas Stone, he was released on ten thousand dollars cash bail posted by Vito Ferruccio.

He climbed the stairs to the third floor apartment apartment, his arms laden with toys for Baby Hugo. In the pocket of his jacket was a small gift box from Tilden and Thurber, the finest jeweler in Providence. He tried the door. It was locked. He called for Angie. There was no reply. He placed the packages on the landing floor and fumbled for his key. The apartment was empty. He checked the bedroom closet. Most of her clothes were gone, as were the baby's toys.

He plummeted down the three flights of stairs, raced to his car, and peeled a layer of rubber off the tires as he drove furiously to Angie's mother's house. The Ford came to a screeching halt in front of the Natale bungalow. Lorenzo Natale answered the loud pounding on the rear door. As he opened the door, Hugo pushed past his father-in-law into the kitchen.

"Where's Angie and the baby?" He stood in the middle of the room, his eyes darting in every direction. Francesca Natale appeared in the dining room doorway, arms folded across her chest and glaring at Hugo. She was a formidable woman. "What do you want here, Hugo? You haven't hurt Angie and the baby enough? You want them to come with you so you can treat them like dogs? Is this what you want, to cause more grief? They will stay here until you come to your senses."

There was a sudden silence in the kitchen. The only sound was baby Hugo gurgling somewhere in another room. Hugo turned to Lorenzo who raised his hands, palms up, and shrugged his shoulders. There was no choice. The mother would be on the phone to the police at the first sign of force, which would lead to a revocation of bail. He turned without a word and left the house.

Mary McKenna stood at the landing waiting for Hugo to climb the stairs. She threw herself into his arms, smothering his face with kisses. She leaped up, encircling his waist with her long legs. He carried her into the apartment, both hands supporting her rounded buttocks. He kicked the door closed and stumbled into her bedroom falling onto the unmade bed, mouths locked together.

As their breathing returned to normal, she held his face in her two hands. "I missed you. I was so worried! What's going to happen?"

"I don't know. My lawyer is talking with the Attorney General's office trying to feel them out. We don't want a jury trial. We want to enter a plea agreement with the Prosecutor for self-defense. My problem is that I don't have any witnesses, and I moved the body and didn't call the cops."

She lay there quietly; the room was silent. "They came to see me." Her voice was soft, almost distant.

"Who came to see you?" Hugo positioned himself on one elbow, a look of concern in his eyes. She turned to face him.

"Two detectives from the State Police."

"What did they ask you? Why were they here?" His forehead wrinkled with the question and she reached out a finger to smooth the spot between his eyebrows.

"I told them what I saw that night. I told them how he charged at you and you had to defend yourself with your bare hands. When they left here they went downstairs to the Goldberg's apartment. Mrs. Goldberg came up after they left. She and her husband watched the whole thing from their bedroom window."

He bolted straight up to a sitting position. "I don't want you involved. I don't want you to have to testify in court."

She placed her hand against his cheek. "Don't be ridiculous. My testimony and the Goldberg's testimony will be enough evidence to support your claim of self-defense."

Hugo got dressed quickly, preoccupied in thought.

"Where are you going now?"

"I've got to talk with Stone and find out how this affects our case. I'll see you at the restaurant tonight." He kissed her quickly and hurriedly descended the stairway, catching a glimpse of Mrs. Goldberg as she peered from her partially opened door.

Winslow Sloan, III, was of platinum pedigree. Son of a former U.S. Senator and grandson of a former Ambassador to the Court of Saint James, his was a landed gentry education: Choate School, Brown University, and Harvard Law. He radiated respect and confidence. As Attorney General of Rhode Island, he realized that his every decision could move him closer to a U.S. Senate seat, for which he hungered. Tommy Stone was aware of Sloan's ambitions, and his weaknesses, as he presented his proposal to the Attorney General and two of his assistants.

"Mr. Sloan, based on the eye-witness accounts of Miss McKenna and Mr. and Mrs. Goldberg, we propose to move for a declaratory judgement of not guilty by reason of self-defense from the presiding justice."

"Well, Tommy," Sloan brushed a thick wave of hair from his forehead and continued in his 'I'm a regular guy' voice, "you know we have the problem of Miss McKenna being Rossi's girlfriend. And then there's the problem of the Goldbergs, who are pushing eighty-years old, and they not only don't see very well, they also don't hear very well." The two young assistant AG's snickered at the remark.

"'Well, Mr. Sloan, from what I'm told by the Goldberg's personal physician, they are in excellent physical condition. And as a matter of fact, Mr. Goldberg doesn't require eye glasses."

"That's interesting, Tommy, but we still have the problem of your client confessing his act of deadly violence. The public will be crying for some sort of retribution, especially with his background of associating with Domenico Zarragga and the boys up on the Hill. You know what I mean?" Sloan eyed the other lawyer pointedly, certain that his unspoken accusation—that Stone knowingly represented common criminals—was clearly understood.

"Yes, I do, Mr. Sloan, perfectly." Stone's smile told Sloan that his point had been received, but it also signaled that it had caused him no pain, having long ago become immune to such slights. "So tell me," he continued, still smiling pleasantly, "what do you have in mind?"

"Well, we see this as a clear-cut case of manslaughter. We know there was bad blood between your client and the victim, and your client moving the body and hiding the murder weapon says it all to us. So that's how we're going to proceed."

Stone stood, reaching for his briefcase. "Thank you for your time, Mr. Sloan. It's always a pleasure chatting with you."

"No, Tommy, the pleasure was all mine. By the way, I assume your defense will be innocent by reason of self-defense."

"You presume correctly, Mr. Sloan. I'll look forward to seeing you at trial."

Hugo sat in the Victorian grandeur of Tommy Stone's law office, hanging on every word he uttered. "Hugo, this won't be easy. Winslow Sloan is looking to make a name for himself, do you follow?"

"Yes, I do. So what's our strategy? What the hell do we do?"

"You leave that to me. I have a meeting arranged with the Superior Court Judge. It's my understanding that Judge Fleming will be hearing the case and this will be a good thing for us."

Hugo leaned forward onto the edge of his chair. "Tommy, is he with us? I mean, can he be reached?"

Sloan suppressed a grin. "Hugo, he's a Judge of the Superior Courts. We will proceed on the merits of our case. And I'm certain we will prevail."

Owen Fleming would not meet with Stone in his Judge's Chambers. The meeting was to be in the second-floor men's room of the ancient Superior Court building. He entered the men's room at two-thirty, eyes bloodshot, smelling faintly of gin. His glance shot from Tommy Stone, who extended his hand in greeting, to the toilet stalls. He quickly pushed open each stall door to confirm they were not in use. His hands trembled; spittle crept from the corner of his mouth.

"What's this all about, Tommy? How much more do I have to do for Zarragga?" His voice was a harsh, raspy whisper. "I'm sick of this shit. People are starting to talk. How long do I have to remain as his personal asshole?"

Stone observed the desperation, the broken capillaries that drew a crooked road map on his nose. He felt a surge of pity for this once promising member of the Judiciary. "Owen, this is important. Otherwise I wouldn't be here. It's about the Hugo Rossi case."

The face of the sad little man suddenly brightened. "Tommy, I don't have that case on my docket! I can't help you out there."

"You will be getting the case, Owen, trust me. It will be on your docket next week."

Owen Fleming closed his eyes and shook his head as though trying to wake from a bad dream. "I should have known."

The men's room door swung open. Two court sheriffs entered, engaged in court gossip, and took positions at the urinals nodding at Fleming and Stone. A moment later the urinals were flushed and they were alone again.

The trial opened on December 3rd. The prosecutor's opening argument focused on the hidden knife and the movement of the body from the scene of the crime. There were allusions to Hugo's ties to organized crime and the bitter jealousy over Mary McKenna. The courtroom was packed. Salvatore did not attend, nor did Hugo's mother. Angie sat in the front pew holding baby Hugo, wounded by the graphic testimony given by Mary McKenna regarding her intimate relations with Hugo. Tommy Stone strode the courtroom floor attempting to destroy the prosecutor's argument.

"Ladies and gentlemen, this is clear-cut case of self-defense. Mr. Rossi was panic-stricken. He did not want Miss McKenna involved in this tragic happenstance. This is why he moved the body. The hiding of the weapon was impulsive and an ill-conceived attempt to distract himself from the violence of Mr. Martella's savage attack. We have the testimony of Miss McKenna and the testimony of Mr. and Mrs. Goldberg. At worst, Mr. Rossi is guilty of leaving the scene of a tragedy in panic."

Judge Fleming barely uttered a word during the four-day trial, sitting as though in a trance, executing his duties when necessary in a perfunctory manner. The jury deliberated for six hours. Angie spent the time walking the corridor, consoling a cranky baby Hugo while studiously avoiding Mary McKenna, who sat on a visitors' bench with the Goldbergs. The jury concluded deliberations and returned to the courtroom. Owen Fleming's voice quavered.

"Ladies and gentlemen of the jury, have you reached a verdict?"
The jury Foreman stood. "Yes, we have, your Honor."
"And how do you find the defendant?"
The courtroom was hushed with the exception of baby Hugo, who continued to express his dissatisfaction with his surroundings. Hugo stood with Tommy Stone at the defense table.
"We find the defendant, Hugo Rossi, guilty of second-degree involuntary manslaughter."

The courtroom erupted. Two reporters for the *Providence Journal-Bulletin* were heading for the exit to make their deadline when they were suddenly arrested by the loud, steady hammering of the judge's gavel. Slowly the mingling crowd quieted to the point where the judge could be heard.

"Please take your seats!" Owen Fleming's face was flushed; beads of perspiration were visible on his forehead. He fumbled with some papers on his desk. The court sheriff edged closer to the bench only to be waved away. Winslow Sloan huddled with the prosecuting attorneys, all wearing expressions of bewilderment. The room fell silent except for an occasional cough and the melancholy ticking of a massive Roman numeral clock that stood guard above the courtroom entrance.

Owen Fleming's hand trembled as he poured a glass of ice water. The courtroom waited as with one collectively held breath. Finally, in a voice oddly calmed, he began to speak. "I have listened to the testimony of the defense and the prosecution, and in my estimation the eyewitness accounts are convincing and compelling. Consequently, it is my belief that the incarceration of Mr. Rossi would be a miscarriage of justice."

Winslow Sloan lowered his head into his hands. The murmuring in the courtroom rose in a steady crescendo. Owen Fleming pounded loudly with his gavel, again admonishing the crowd to silence. "Therefore," he continued, his voice now echoing with judicial authority, "I set aside incarceration for Mr. Rossi and in its stead order his enlistment into the United States Marine Corp effective immediately, with the proviso that he will be volunteered to serve with our fighting troops in the embattled nation of Korea."

The room burst into Bedlam. "You should be impeached!" came a voice from the rear of the courtroom. "You're a disgrace!" Reporters scribbled rapidly, recording the chaotic scene. Winslow Sloan slumped in his chair, a look of chagrin on his handsome face as he stared at the departing figure of Owen Fleming, who now nudged the pressing reporters aside, hastily retreating to his chambers.

Hugo embraced Tommy Stone and stood looking for Mary McKennna. As his eyes scanned the crowd they settled on the face of Giusto Rotondo, who winked and made a thumbs-up sign. Angie had left the courthouse. Mary McKenna was also gone. Tommy Stone was collecting his paperwork from the counsel's table when a court sheriff approached with the official court order.

"What do I do now, Tommy?" asked Hugo. Curiously, the sudden flush of elation had disappeared as quickly as it had come, and now he felt only a strange sense of unease, like a child suddenly finding himself without the comforting presence of his parents.

Stone continued to read the Judge's order. "Well, my boy," he said looking up, "it seems you have three days to report for induction into the Marine Corp."

"Tommy, is there any way out of this?" It was the usual question for the usual reasons. After all, someone had always been there to fix things for him, to make to make his life easy...Salvatore, Ferruccio, Zarragga, now Stone. Surely there would be someone who would fix this, too.

Stone looked at Hugo with a steady gaze and placed a hand on his arm. "Hugo, in the first place, you're an extremely fortunate young man. You have friends in the right places. As far as Judge Fleming's verdict is concerned, he needed something to justify his decision and satisfy the sharks looking to devour his career. Do you understand?"

"Yeah, I think so."

"There's a car outside waiting for you. Mr. Zarragga wants to see you."

THE ARRIVAL THE STRUGGLE THE ASCENDANCY

"Tommy, what about your fee? I owe you my life."

Counselor Stone looked amused. "Your fee is all taken care of, Hugo. Your friends have seen to that."

Domenico Zarragga suffered from sugar diabetes, heart problems, and a nagging gall bladder. And yet for all his ailments he still ruled with an iron hand. Nothing happened in New England without his approval. His sallow complexion looked yellow in the semi-darkened office as he sat looking at Hugo, hands tented beneath his nose.

"So, my young friend," he said, dropping his hands and breaking into a wry smile, "you're going to defend your country against the Communists in Korea"

"Yeah, Dom. I'd rather be here, but it beats being in the can."

"Listen, Hugo, you won't be gone for long. I need you here, *capece?*"

"Yes, Dom, I understand, but how do you intend for me to be back in Rhode island in four or five months if I'm going to be in Korea?"

"Hugo, we have friends all over the country. In fact, we have some very good friends in Washington, so don't you worry about getting back to Providence. Remember, this isn't even a real war, it's a police action." He reached into a drawer and extracted an envelope, tossing it across the desk. "Take this, you're going to need a few buck on you." He stood and walked around the desk to Hugo. "All right, time for you to say goodbye to your wife and son. And then there's that girl you see, what's her name?"

"Mary McKenna"

"Yeah, the Irish girl, right."

Hugo embraced Zarragga, kissing him on the cheek. "Thank you, Dom, for everything. "I will repay you, I promise."

"Go ahead," said Zarragga, nudging Hugo's elbow, "Giusto's going to give you a lift to your house. Send me a postcard so we'll know where you are."

Hugo bounded the stairs to the third-floor apartment, bursting through the door. Angie and the baby were still gone. He ran down the stairs to the Ford Fairlane, which one of his men had retrieved for him from the state police barracks. The keys were in the ignition. He raced to the Natale bungalow on Hartford Avenue. No one answered the bell. He stood on the front porch scanning the neighborhood. Across the street a short white-haired man was digging for root vegetables in his garden. It was Gustavo, the sausage maker. Hugo crossed the street and leaned against the chain-link fence.

"Aay, Gustavo." The old man was hard of hearing. He called out loudly, "Aay, Gustavo!"

The old man turned slowly and walked toward the fence, smiling. "Ah, Hugo, how you doing?" He spoke with a heavy accent.

"I'm fine, Gustavo. Hey, did you see the Natale's and my wife today."

"Yessa, Hugo, I did," he replied with a sharp nod of his head, "This morning, was early, maybe eight, eight-thrity. They look like they was taken a trip. They had suitcases and boxes, and the baby, he was screamin'."

Hugo nodded, looking back at the Natale house. "Thank you, Gustavo."

"Sure, Hugo, anytime."

He slid behind the wheel of the Ford. He sat thinking, knowing he wouldn't see Angie or the baby before he left. He tapped a

Lucky Strike out of its package and lit it with the dashboard lighter. Smoke encircled his head as he sat pensively mulling his fate. Anger replaced apathy. Anger at Angie for abandoning him, anger at his circumstance, and anger at himself for allowing himself to be in the situation he was in.

The engine roared to life. He threw the shift into reverse and stomped on the accelerator. The rear tires caught on the asphalt, sending up a cloud of burning rubber. He jerked the steering wheel to the left. The Ford made a hundred-eighty degree turn. He dropped the shift into low gear and continued to burn rubber, fishtailing down Hartford Avenue toward Mary McKenna's apartment.

His heart was racing as he knocked on her door, desperate to take her in his arms and hold her close to him once again. No sound came from the apartment. It was Wednesday. He knew she wasn't working and she wasn't in school. It was unusual not to hear the radio was playing in the afternoon. He knocked again, louder. He heard the second floor apartment door open.

"Hugo, Hugo it's me, Mrs. Goldberg." He could see her face peering up the stairway.

"Mrs. Goldberg, did Mary go out?" The elderly woman turned to look into her apartment. Hugo surmised she was looking at Mr. Goldberg. "Hugo, come down for a minute, please."

He walked slowly down the stairway to the Goldberg apartment, to the open doorway where Mrs. Goldberg reappeared with Mr. Goldberg at her side wearing his usual hangdog expression. "Mary asked me to give this to you." She held out an envelope, then stood solemnly, hands crossed in front of her apron.

"Thank you, Mrs. Goldberg, Mr. Goldberg." Hugo quickly left the building, his heart racing once again—not, this time, with expectation, but with a dark, painful foreboding. He sat behind the steering wheel anxious to unseal the envelope, fearful of its contents. He stubbed out a cigarette, then tore open the envelope and began to read.

> *My dearest Hugo, Love of My Life, I'm leaving Rhode Island and returning to my parents' home. It would be impossible for me to live here without you. I thought it best not to see you before you left for Marine Corp training. I didn't think I could handle saying goodbye to you knowing I wouldn't see you for months. Please write me at my parents address, below. All my love forever,*
> *Mary.*

He sat for a long time, thoughts of her face, her scent, and their lovemaking filling his senses.

He visited with his mother on the morning before his departure for Paris Island, South Carolina. It was December 10, fifteen days before Christmas. Francesca greeted him with tears. She shook her head looking into the face of her darling boy. They sat at the kitchen sipping coffee.

"How's Pa? Has he said anything about this…my situation?"

Francesca reached for a tissue in her apron pocket and dabbed at her eyes. "He hasn't mentioned your name in this house since— you know, the incident. You know your father, with him black is black, white is white. There is no grey area. He feels hurt and betrayed. He feels like it's his fault, that he didn't point you in the right direction. He's a changed man."

Hugo's gaze locked on to his coffee cup. There was silence in the apartment. "Ma, Angie took off with the baby and her mother and father. I think they went up to Revere. I won't be able to see them before I leave." He reached for his mother's hand. "Ma, tell Angie I'm sorry. Please stay close to the baby."

Silent tears streamed down Francesca still youthful cheeks as Hugo tenderly embraced his mother. As they parted, he held her by the shoulders at arms length. "Ma, I'm not like my father. I wish I was. Life would be much more simple. Tell him...." He paused. "I'll write you when I get to Paris Island." He embraced her once again and left the apartment.

He spent the night in his apartment, alone, laying awake for most of the night. At nine the next morning he reported to the Marine Corps recruiting station at the Federal Building in downtown Providence. He signed several documents, raised his right hand, and was sworn in as a United States Marine. Two tall, muscular Navy Shore Patrol men stood by, watching silently as he turned from his swearing in ceremony. The taller of the two stepped forward, holding a pair of bright handcuffs. He spoke in a soft Southern drawl.

"Mr. Rossi, my name is T. J. Johnson, this is my partner Malcolm Lafleur. We are charged with the responsibility of transporting you to South Carolina and the United States Marine Corps base at Paris Island. Unfortunately, our procedures compel us to handcuff you until we board our train here in Providence. Please extend your hands." The cuffs clicked into place. Hugo smiled, signaling that he was resigned to his fate.

The train ride was uneventful. The cuffs were removed and Hugo was able to walk the train. Johnson and Lafleur were old hands at their job and sensed that Hugo represented no danger of flight. There were two train changes. They spent the evening in a private compartment, Johnson awake for the first part of the evening and Lafleur for the balance, waking Hugo at six.

The Southern States Flyer rolled into Columbia at 9:05. An olive drab U. S. Marine sedan was waiting to pick up Hugo outside the station. The ride to Beaufort, home of Paris Island, took six hours with a stop for burgers and coffee. As the sedan approached the compound Hugo glanced up at the words written across the archway spanning the main gate. He recognized the latin words from his time as an altar boy at Saint Bart's: *Semper Fidelis*. Always faithful. Faithful to what, he wondered.

On a brutally cold, drab December day, two weeks before Christmas, Superior Court Justice Owen Fleming closed the venetian blinds in his office, sat at his desk, poured an eight ounce glass of Dewars' Scotch, downed the scotch in four gulps, slowly opened his bottom desk drawer, reached deeply into the rear of the drawer and removed a military surplus .44 caliber handgun. He unlocked the safety lever, placed the barrel into his mouth, hesitated for a moment, and pulled the trigger.

Chapter 9

A NEW WORLD

The sedan slowed to 20 miles per hour as it wound its way past well-kept wooden barracks labeled with affiliation: Platoon 70 "A" Company 1st Recruit Training Battalion. The grounds were immaculate. The streets were full of Marine basic trainees jogging in T-shirts, boots, and fatigue trousers, rifles held at high port arms. Voices echoed from building to building in a marching cadence, "sound off—one, two; sound off— three, four; cadence count—one two, one two, *three four!*" A ramrod straight drill instructor in razor sharp khakis and a flat-brimmed campaign hat tilted forward at two fingers above the bridge of his nose barked cadence for a platoon of fatigue-clad trainees: "*Hawp, rap, hawp, rap. Left, right, left, right.*"

The sedan pulled up in front of Headquarters, Company Recruit Depot, Marine Barracks. Johnson and Lafleur escorted Hugo inside. The company clerk ushered them into the office of Captain Lawrence Wainight Prescott—a twenty-seven-year old product of Harvard's ROTC program and a Marine reservist who resented being called to active duty and having to leave his lucrative brokerage job on Wall Street. Johnson and Lafleur snapped to attention and saluted.

"Sir, Chief Petty Officer Johnson and Seaman 2nd Class Lafleur reporting as ordered with Private Hugo Rossi in our care and custody, sir!" He handed a manila envelope to Prescott, stepped back and said, "In accordance with our orders, we hereby transfer care and custody to The First Recruit Training Battalion of the United States Marine Corps." Both men saluted smartly. Prescott returned a half-hearted salute.

"Thank you, gentlemen, for delivering Private Rossi to us. You are now dismissed." Hugo stood awkwardly in front of Prescott's desk. To the left of Prescott stood Company First Sergeant Thomas Lee Jackson. Straight from a recruiting poster, thought Hugo. The hash marks on his left sleeve indicated the number of years of duty. There were several of them. Hugo was to discover that he had seen action at Beleau Wood and Chateau Thiery in France during the First World War. He was wounded in a bayonet charge across No Man's Land and had continued to fight until he dropped from loss of blood. He had seen service during the insurrection in the Philippines in 1922 and had been in the thick of battle during the Second World War at Gudalcanal and Iwo Jima. He had taken a machine gun burst across his chest while charging a machine gun emplacement and managed to survive. He possessed the Silver Star and three Purple Hearts. He was fifty-three years old And was single. His wife and his mistress was the United States Marine Corps. He lived in the First Sergeants quarters of the company's barracks. He spoke in the long slow drawl of rural Alabama where he lived as a boy.

THE ARRIVAL THE STRUGGLE THE ASCENDANCY

Captain Prescott leaned back in his desk chair and looked at Hugo with dispassionate unconcern and said, "well. Mr. Rossi, welcome to Recruit Training. This is First Sergeant Jackson. He'll assign you to a platoon. Good Luck."

Hugo nodded an acknowledgement. Sergeant Jackson unclasped his hands from behind his back, and in the slow drawl of his native rural Alabama he announced, "Follow me, ," as he opened the door to the orderly room.

He walked to Corporal Leo Ricardo's desk, the company clerk and handed him Hugo's manila envelope. Hugo stood waiting for his next order.

"Ricardo, this hyea is Private Hugo Rossi's file. We're gonna assign him to the 70th Platoon, you got that?" Corporal Ricardo shot a glance at Hugo as he reached for the manila envelope.

"Aye, aye, Sarge, I got it."

Jackson turned to Hugo. "Follow me, bwah." They exited the building, Hugo following Jackson at a leisurely pace toward an old two-story wooden barracks neatly painted in a nondescript grey. They mounted three wooden steps and entered the building. The first thing that struck Hugo was the strong smell of pine oil and bleach. The wood planking floors were almost white from the daily brush and mop scrubbings. He followed Jackson through the center of the barracks, double bunks on each side, each with an olive-drab woolen blanket and a five-inch thick mattress supported by steel springs and metal mesh. Khaki and olive drab uniforms hung in duplication at the wall end of each bunk. Footlockers lined either side of the barracks in perfect alintment. A young trainee assigned as fire guard snapped to attention as Jackson passed on his way to his quarters. He opened the unlocked door and pointed to a chair before a small desk in the spacious quarters.

The room was furnished with a military-issue wooden bedstead and innerspring mattress. Clothing hung exposed on a wall-mounted wooden rod. At the end of the rod of clothing hung four articles of civilian clothing, including a navy-blue suit. This was Jackson's home, thought Hugo, as his eyes traversed the room. Spit shined dress shoes, gleaming brass buckles, a number 10 can painted red and filled with sand as an ashtray. The room smelled of the United States Marine Corps. There were two small end tables anchoring the bed, a good-sized desk against one wall, and a six-foot bookcase crammed with books.

Jackson sat behind the desk and removed his campaign hat, placing it deliberately on the desk. He leaned back in his chair folding his hands in his lap. "Y'all don't come highly recommended, now do you, Rossi?" He spoke without emotion, his face giving nothing away.

"No sir, I guess I don't."

"How old are you, bwah?"

"I'll be twenty-one next month, Sir."

Jackson nodded, narrowing his eyes. "I'm gonna tell you the rules here one time, y'hear?"

"Yes, Sir."

"You disobey one order from any a' my drill instructors—and I don't care if they tell you to clean up shit—I'll send you back to that shit hole state you come from. And you will go to the jail where you belong, 'cause you don't belong in my Marine Corps dirtyin' it up. They ain't no second chance with me, bwah. You got all a' this?"

"Yes, Sir," repeated Hugo, this time looking down at the man behind the chair, their eyes meeting.

Jackson reached for a Dutchmaster in a box on the desk and lit it, puffing smoke toward the ceiling. "The way I understand it, you killed a man." Hugo began to speak. Jackson held up one hand removing the cigar from his mouth with the other. "Ah don't care what you did on the outside, bwah, I done some killin' myself. In fact, it proves to me you got a good pair ah chestnuts. I'm gonna assign you to this Platoon, the 70th Platoon. Sergeant Rodriguez is the man in charge. He's in the field right now. He'll get you outfitted and assign you a bunk. All right, get out there and wait till your Platoon gets back. You're gonna have some catchin' up to do cause they're a week ahead a' you."

"I'll catch up, Sir."

Jackson looked at Hugo with an appraising eye. "Ah think you will Rossi, ah think you will."

Staff Sergeant Pedro Rodriguez was a bantam cock, a hard-nosed drill instructor who drove his training platoons to the edge. A product of Hell's Kitchen in New York City, Rodriguez took an immediate liking to the tough new kid from Providence. Hugo took to the training easily. He was big, strong, and agile. There was an assuredness in his actions, and he quickly emerged as a leader commanding respect from his fellow trainees. Rodriguez recognized these qualities and appointed him Squad leader. As the days passed Hugo found that he actually enjoyed the rigorous training much as he had during high school football practice, and his physical training score was the highest in the battalion. There were no leaves or passes during training. Training had been suspended for Christmas Day, but there were no leaves or passes. Recruits could make one phone call. The rush was on to move troops to Korea for replacement duty and additional combat troops.

Hugo sat in a phone booth in the Base Exchange, waiting for the telephone operator to make the long-distance connection. The phone rang two times.

"Hello?" It was Francesca. Her voice was music to Hugo's ears.

"Ma, Ma, it's me."

The excitement in Francesca's voice was palpable. "Oh, my son, figlio mio, are you okay?"

"I'm fine Ma, I even like the training. And the food is not as bad as I thought it would be. It's not like yours, Ma. Nobody cooks like you."

"Hugo, we missed you at Christmas. Everyone was asking for you."

"I wish I was with you and the family, Ma, but there were no leaves for anyone. Even the officers stayed on base. Ma, how's Angie and the baby? Is she home?"

Francesca paused. "Hugo, she's still with Lorenzo and Francesca at their house."

"Do you see her, Ma? And the baby, do you see him?"

"They're always here or I'm there. Your father is always with the baby. He's always taking him to church or the farm to see the animals. I tell him he's too small yet to understand. Your father says that's not what's important."

Hugo's eyes misted as he listened to Francesca.

"How is Pa feeling?" He felt his throat grow tighter as he spoke. There was a pause, then an audible sigh.

"Your father is angry, angry. Angry because your not with your wife and child, and angry because he loves you. He will get over this. It will take some time, but he will get over this."

"Ma, take my address, give it to Angie. Ask her to write when she can. I gotta go. I'll call again as soon as I can, okay?"

"I love you, *figlio mio*." He knew she was crying now though she tried bravely to swallow the sobs.

"I love you too, Ma," he whispered, "pray for me."

He sat in the phone booth staring at the receiver. He reached into his trousers and extracted a yellow slip of paper. The long-distance operator came on the line. He gave her a Massachusetts number and waited for the phone to ring. "Hello?" The voice was unfamiliar. He hesitated. "Hello!" came the voice again, now more insistent.

"Ah, yes, ah, is Mary there, please?"

"No, I'm sorry, she's not in. Can I take a message, this is her mother?

"Oh, hello, Mrs. McKenna, my name is Hugo Rossi. I'm a friend of Mary's from Providence just calling to say hello.

"Ah, yes, Mr. Rossi." The south Boston accent became pronounced. "We know of you. We read about you in the papers and I'll thank you not to call here ever again." The phone went dead. He replaced the receiver, his hand not leaving it. It took five minutes to get the Goldberg's telephone number from the information operator. Mrs. Goldberg was ecstatic to hear from him. Mr. Goldberg could be heard in the background asking loud questions. Hugo gave Mrs. Goldberg his address and Mary's phone number and asked her to call Mary the next day. After several "God bless you" and a Yiddish blessing she finally rang off.

It was the fifth week of intense training. Twelve weeks were being compressed into ten to expedite the movement of troops to Korea. Hugo thrived on the physicality of daily training. He was mature beyond his years. His natural aloofness held him apart from other members of the platoon with the exception of a young Italian kid from New York who had been transferred into the 70th Platoon after missing the last seven weeks of Recruit due to a broken toe. His name was Raymond Pescatore—a short, pug-nosed, powerfully built street kid from the Bronx. He immediately latched on to Hugo as a kindred spirit, and Hugo took to the New Yorker's tough street swagger.

"Ay, Rossi, where you from?"

Hugo looked up as he cleaned his rifle. "Providence, Rhode Island. You know where that is?"

"Yeah," said Pescatore stretched out on his bunk, his head propped up on one hand, "I think we got some cousins over there. Some place called the Hill, or something."

Hugo smiled. "Federal Hill."

"Yeah, that's it, Federal Hill."

"What's their name?" Hugo asked as he continued to assemble his rifle.

"Pescatore, just like mine."

Hugo shook his head. "Can't say I've ever run into any Pescatores. There's hundreds of families up there. So, Pescatore, what did you do in the Bronx?"

"Call me Pesh, everybody does. I ran numbers, collected money, you know, stuff like that."

"Yeah, I know. I was doing pretty much the same thing until my career was interrupted by Uncle Sam."

Pescatore looked at Hugo nodding knowingly and the two young men sensed that an unspoken bond had been established between them.

After a particularly exhausting day in the field Sergeant Rodriguez told Hugo to report to Sergeant Jackson in the Orderly Room. When he arrived he found Jackson alone sitting behind his desk, sorting through papers. He closed the outer door and advanced to the desk. Jackson did not look up.

"Private Rossi reporting as ordered, Sir."

Jackson looked up momentarily and pointed to a chair in front of the desk and returned to his paperwork. Hugo sat watching him, fatigue cap in hand. Finally, Jackson laid the paperwork aside, sat back in his chair and spoke.

"Rossi, I'm gonna tell you, bwah, you have shocked the shit out a this ol' Marine. You one a *the* best men I ever trained, and this means you will be in a leadership role. No doubt in Korea, 'cause that's where you gonna be assigned. I called you in here today because I think you can save other Marines in a combat situation. You unnastand?"

"Yes, Sir.

"Good. Now I'm gonna tell you what you need to know to survive in hostile territory, and it's simple. Number one, you have to be fully aware of your surroundings at all times. Number two, you have to act as if you're surrounded by the enemy all the time, you unnastand?"

"Yes, I do, Sir."

"You know how small animals survive in the jungle?" He was looking hard at Hugo and Hugo knew that he wasn't expected to answer. "I'll tell you how. They keep an eye out for the lion, you unnastand?"

"Yes, Sir."

"Good, get back to your platoon now and get some chow."

Hugo stood, cap in hand. "Thank you, Sir, for having confidence in me."

"Make me proud, bwah, make me proud."

The letter arrived from Mary McKenna on a Tuesday afternoon mail call. He took it with anxious hands and quickly walked to his bunk, pressing the envelope to his nostrils, inhaling the scent that he knew so well. He sat on the edge of his bunk and gently opened the letter. He was oblivious to his surroundings as he read the neat cursive Catholic school handwriting. *My sweet darling, I'm so excited I can hardly contain myself. When Mrs. Goldberg called, I almost literally jumped for joy.* He lay back on his bunk and read the letter three times. He pressed the letter to his chest, the recent events of his life rushing and tumbling through his head. He was missing Angie and Baby Hugo and yet pining for Mary. His reverie was broken by Pescatore, who was cursing loudly as he read a letter from home.

"Why, this little whore, do you believe this?" Hugo turned to look at the beet-red face of Pescatore. "She's breaking up with me. She says we should see other people. What she means is she wants to poon other guys, that's what she means!"

Hugo sat up on the edge of his bunk. "Calm down, Pesh, your heads gonna explode."

"I don't give a shit about her anyway. I'm glad she shagged me because I was seeing her cousin on the side and you should see the set of jugs on this broad!" He gave a big toothy smile as he held out both hands and turned them as if air drying them.

Hugo shook his head and laughed out loud. "Boy, I can tell you're all broken up about this."

Graduation ceremonies were a week away. The ten-week training cycle had been completed by most of the platoon. There had been six drop outs, men who couldn't take the physical and mental strain. Orders would be distributed on the final day, but the rumor mill was grinding out all sorts of dream assignments: who was going to Hawaii, who was going to southern California. The mood in the barracks was at once upbeat and anxious. They had made it. Some of the toughest training in the world and they had made it.

Sergeant Rodriguez would now routinely join the platoon in the barracks after 16:30 hours when the smoking lamp was lit, sharing cigarettes and keeping up morale.

"Hey, Sergeant, you think I got a shot at being assigned to Puerto Rico? I love the weather there!" It was Arelio Gamacho. He smiled broadly at Rodriguez, one Puerto Rican to another.

"Listen, all of you swingin dicks." Rodriguez pointed at each man as he spoke. "Forget about sunshine and hula girls cause you're all gonna be on the same ship for Japan. In a couple of weeks you're gonna be freezing your asses off in the mountains of Korea. It gets pretty goddamn cold in Korea in January." For a moment the room became silent, each man reflecting on his place in a combat situation—in a real shooting war. "Okay, girls, don't take this so seriously, you had the best training in the world, courtesy of yours truly. And if you follow your training instructions, you're gonna be outstanding Marines."

"Excuse me, Sir."

"Yeah, Pescatore, what is it?"

"Is it true that Korean pussy is slanted sideways?"

The barracks erupted in laughter.

"You're never gonna find out, Pescatore. My bet is you'll be in the Brig for the duration of the war."

The orders came on graduation day. Rodriguez was right. The entire company, with the exception of four men, was shipping out for Japan in two days. The lines at the phone banks in the Base Exchange were six deep. When Hugo finally reached Francesca and told her of his assignment, there was a long silence.

"Ma, don't worry. It doesn't mean that I'll be on the front lines. In fact, I might even stay in Japan. So don't worry, you hear me?" He could hear Francesca sobbing as she spoke.

"Ma," he continued, holding back his own tears, "have you seen Angie and the baby, are they all right?"

"Yes, I see them every day. Baby Hugo is getting so big. He's always with your father. He takes him everywhere." Hugo smiled at the image of Salvatore carrying Baby Hugo from place to place, a proud grandfather.

"How is he, Ma, how's Pa?" Hugo's voice took on a low, dull tone. "Will he talk with me? Is he there?" Soft sniffling came through the receiver.

"No, son, he's not here. He's at Uncle Pat's, but he's the same. You know how he feels; you know the kind of man he is.

"Yeah, I do, Ma, I know." There was a tapping on the door of the phone booth. Hugo looked up. It was Pescatore, hands open and shoulders shrugged in the universal body language signaling impatience. "Ma, I have to go. Kiss the baby for me. I love you, Ma."

"I love you, *figlio mio*. Please be careful and write as soon as you can."

"Ma..." There was a strained hesitation.

"Yes, Hugo?"

"Tell Pa I asked for him."

"I will, my son. I will."

THE ARRIVAL THE STRUGGLE THE ASCENDANCY

The turbo-prop troop carrier carrying one hundred fifty officers and enlisted men had hopped, skipped, and jumped from California to Okinawa. Hugo and half of his training company were on board when the planes engines burped to a balky stop on the well-worn tarmac of the U.S. Navy base at the Pacific island of Okinawa. There would be no transitional stop in Japan. Troops were needed desperately to stem the tide of North Koreans and the hordes of Chinese troops pouring in from Manchuria.

On August 15, 1945, Korea was partitioned at the 38th parallel, dividing the nation in half with approximately nine million people in Russian-dominated Communist North Korea and approximately twenty-one million people in the U.S.-dominated southern half. Politics, national pride and the Cold War fermented ill will and a build up of troops on either side of the 38th parallel, until finally at 0400 hours on July 18, 1950, North Korean forces launched an attack into South Korea, preceded by a massive artillery barrage, including battalions of Russian made T34 tanks and well trained infantry. Their destination: the capital city of Seoul.

On June 30, following a United Nations Resolution for assistance to South Korea, General Douglas MacArthur, Commander of Occupation Forces in Japan, was ordered to dispatch two divisions of U. S. combat troops to Korea. The first fighting troops to arrive in Korea were drawn from the 24th Infantry Division known as Task Force Smith, taking its name from the Commanding Officer of the battalion, Lieutenant-Colonel Charles B. Smith. Meanwhile, a major build up of men, weapons, and materials was under way to wage war against the North Korean forces.

The hard-driving North Koreans, employing *blitzkreig* tactics, had won successive victories against Republic of Korea (ROK)

239

forces and U.S. troops made up of the 24th and the First Cavalry Division. Allied forces were pushed back to what became known as the Pusan Perimeter, a roughly rectangular area in the southeast corner of the Korean Peninsula. The perimeter stretched some eighty miles from north to south and approximately fifty miles from east to west. All allied troops eventually fought their way behind the perimeters lines. Pusan itself was a small coastal city on the Sea of Japan.

Allied forces found their backs to the sea. On August 2 an important addition to the order of battle against the North Koreans arrived in the form of the 1st Provisional Marine Brigade of the United States Marine Corps under the command of Lieutenant-General Walton H. Walker, an aggressive veteran of the Second World War. The Pusan Perimeter was stabilized, returning morale and initiative to the U.S. forces and allowing for men, weapons, and supplies to land via Pusan Harbor. The confounding problem confronting General Douglas MacArthur, Commander in Chief of Pacific Forces and now Commander in Chief of U.N. Forces, was breaking out of the Pusan pocket and gaining momentum against the North Koreans. His strategy was an audacious amphibious landing behind enemy lines at the city of Inchon, in close proximity to the capital city of Seoul.

The landing was code named Operation Chromite. As planning for the invasion evolved, it was decided that the 1st Marine Division and the 7th Infantry Division would shoulder the task. The 1st Marine Corps Division was made up of the 1st Marine, the 5th Marine, and the 7th Marine regiments. On September 15, against all odds and extraordinary tidal variances, the 5th Marines stormed ashore at Inchon, with the 1st Marines engaged in battle at what was called Blue Beach and elements of the 7th Marines taking the island of So-Wolmi-Do, known as Green Beach. Despite total confusion due to unforeseen circumstances in weather and smoke billowing from bombardments fires, the landing was an unqualified success. In the weeks following the invasion it became evident that the 165,000 North Korean troops who had invaded South Korea had been decimated, with estimates of only 30,000 to 50,000 able to make it back to North Korean lines.

At the end of September 1950 there were approximately 315,000 U.N. forces engaged in Korea. The first Chinese Communist forces in North Korea were reported in late October, estimated at approximately 20,000. MacArthur's headquarters in Tokyo denied this claim, stating that only a few Chinese volunteers were active in the field. On October 31, Chinese forces swept aside the ROK 6th Division at the North Korean City of Kuni-Ri. The U.S. 8th Cavalry was at Unsan some nineteen miles north of Kun-Ri along with the ROK 1st Division on their right. On the evening of October 31, U.S. Cavalrymen for the first time heard the eerie, bone-chilling sound of a cacophony of wildly blaring trumpets and the shrilling of whistles. The Chinese charged at them from behind a mortar barrage and rocket fire. General Walker ordered a general withdrawal of the badly mauled 8th Cavalry, which had lost half of its strength. U.S. forces retreated southward to the Chongchon River. The situation was grim. The 1st Marine Division had faced a humiliating retreat from the Chosin Reservoir to the southern port of Hungnan with staggering losses. It was time for a bold, decisive maneuver.

On December 23, General Walker was killed when his jeep collided with an ROK weapons carrier. Lieutenant-General

Matthew Ridgeway, the Army's Deputy Chief of Staff, was assigned Commander of U.N. Forces in Korea. Ridgeway had commanded the 82nd Airborne Division and later the XVIII Airborne Corps in World War Two. His distinguished record, including the Battle of the Bulge and the fighting in Normandy, gave a new spirit to the fighting troops. The tide began to turn, but not without thousands of bloody losses for American and U.N. forces.

The warm swampy gush of air buffeted against Hugo as he walked out of the air transport onto the portable staircase positioned against the airplane fuselage. Pescatore followed behind muttering unintelligible complaints.

"Hey, Hugo, look, palm trees. I ain't never seen a real palm tree."

The planeload of troops were milling about on the tarmac making small talk and inventorying their belongings. The accompanying officers were huddled under one of the transport's wings looking for someone in authority. A jeep suddenly appeared from behind the palm trees and came to a screeching halt in the middle of the clustering men.

"All right, gather round, men," shouted the driver as he clambered aboard the hood of the jeep, clipboard in hand. "I'm Gunnery Seargent Tuttel—welcome to Okinawa. We got a hula girl for everyone of you fightin' Marines." The troops broke out in laughter and off-color remarks. "All right, now, calm down. I'm just the welcoming committee. Turn around and you can see your barracks. The Officers Quarters are the two buildings off to the right. Pick up your gear and hike over there. There's a roster of names posted to the barracks door in alphabetical order. That's your barrack. Just pick a bunk. Hot chow in the mess hall at 1700 hours. You'll find it by the smell. You'll all have orders by tomorrow afternoon."

"Hey, Gunny." It was one of the officers.

"Yes, Sir."

"We already have orders for Japan."

"I think there's been a change in plans, Captain. Looks like General Ridgeway is calling a different play."

The Gunny saluted, started the jeep and spun out of the cluster of men toward the palm trees. The men retrieved their gear and trudged toward the squat half-rounded Quonset huts serving as barracks. Pescatore was the first in line at the first hut, running his finger down the list of names, twenty to a hut.

"Hey, Hugo, we're in the same barracks." He smiled happily as he headed to the far end of the sparsely furnished hut—rows of ugly metal bunks, thin bare mattress ticking with matching pillows, a woolen blanket at the foot of each bunk. The heat was stifling, the air unmoving. Hugo slumped onto the bunk next Ping.

"You know, Pesh, so far I don't like this friggin war." At that moment Gunnery Sergeant Tuttel poked his head into the front entrance.

"Listen up, Marines, I got warm showers if anyone's interested. We got soap, but you need some kind of towel. Follow the signs behind the hut."

The shower was refreshing. Hugo and Ping used tee shirts to dry themselves off. Dinner was canned spam, canned beans, instant mashed potatoes, and canned fruit cocktail. Exhausted, the men went directly to bed, lights went out at nine.

The Gunny flipped lights on at five and the new arrivals marched off to a breakfast of powdered eggs and more spam. Lunch consisted of orange cheese sandwiches and green Kool-aid. Pescatore devoured three sandwiches with double mustard. After lunch, as the men lounged in the shade of palm trees on the fringe of the barracks area, a Major emerged from the Officers Quarters followed by several other officers. As he approached the men he pointed to a sandy area beneath a cluster of trees and called out, "All right, men, gather round, we've got new orders."

The men quickly assembled around the officer. They stood tense and quiet as though everyone understood that the time for joking had passed. Suddenly, everything seemed very real and very serious.

"I'm Major Cushing, the senior officer accompanying you. I'm from a reserve unit from New Jersey." He paused as he shuffled papers in his hands. "I've got everybody's assignment here." He handed stacks of orders to two Lieutenants. "Okay, when your name is called, come and get 'em." The three officers called names in unison, the men responding "Yo" or "Here" as they scrambled forward for their paperwork. As they tore open the manila envelopes there arose a murmur of conversation and the occasional muttered exclamation as each man discovered the nature of his fate.

Hugo stared at his orders. He had been assigned to the First Marine Division, 7th Regiment, Alpha Company. Pescatore was peering over Hugo's shoulder mouthing the typewritten words. His eyes widened as he comprehended the orders that Hugo now held out for him to read. He consulted his own paperwork and looked at Hugo with an idiot grin.

"Hugo, looks like me and you are goin' to win this fucken war together!"

Hugo nodded. "Yeah, well, Pesh, I'm glad we're going to be together 'cause I need you to be my personal valet. You know, somebody to make my meals and wash my socks and shorts."

"Up yours with a tent pole, asshole. You're lucky I'm with you. I'll probably save your miserable fucken ginny life."

"Hey, where you white boys goin?" It was Daryl Kelly, a tall, skinny black kid from a backwoods town in Alabama. "Ah sure hope we gonna be together on accounta I gotten kinda used to y'all and the funny way ya'll talk."

Eddie Ramirez, a short muscular Puerto Rican, joined the conversation. "Where you guys headin?" Hugo liked the tough New Yorker and handed him his orders. Ramirez looked pleased "Hey, man, we're gonna be together. That's all right with me."

A shrill whistle blew, followed by the booming voice of Major Cushing. "All right, if you have any questions, I'll try to answer them. We're all flying into Korea, a place called Chechon. From that point there will be someone to transport you to your unit. Get your stuff together, air transport will be here in one hour. And by the way, for your information, the temperature in Korea is now twenty degrees below zero. When you get to Chechon they'll have a winter clothing issue ready for you. Good luck. See you in Korea."

The military air transport touched down in Chechon, a small city seventy-five miles southeast of the enemy occupied capitol city of Seoul. An army construction battalion had hastily laid down a long metal landing strip over the harsh frozen landscape to accept replacement troops and supplies as close to the United Nations front lines as possible. Driving sleet pelted the plane as it came to an abrupt stop at the very end of the improvised runway. When the safety light came on Major Cushing stood up and lit a cigarette.

"All right, listen good." As he spoke he exhaled, the bluish smoke mingling with the vapor of his freezing breath. There's a row of tents off to the right along the runway. When they wheel the portable stairway to the front exit, I want you all to run like hell for the large tent with the flags on it. That's where you'll pick up your winter gear. Everybody got that?" There was an absent-minded response as each man strained to peer out the small portholes, their first glance of Korea.

Hugo stepped onto the landing of the stairway and his body instinctively bent forward in an attempt to fend off the piercing sleet and sub-zero wind. It was like no cold he had ever known. He scrambled after the other men reaching the relative warmth of the command tent in a matter of minutes, though with their light-weight jackets and naked heads it seemed to take forever.

Duffel bags from the cargo hold were being unloaded and stacked in a far corner of the massive tent. The men stood in circles stamping feet and blowing into cupped hands, shaking away the brutal cold.

"Goddamn its cold! Ah neva bin in such a goddamn cold, mizable lookin place in all ma days." It was Daryl Kelly. "Back home in Alabama we neva git dis kina cold. It's nice'n warm all the time."

Pescatore winked at Hugo and Eddie Ramirez. "Hey, Kelly, you're so fucken cold 'cause you coon's spend so much time pickin cotton in the sun. Takes a real man from the North to get used to snow."

Kelly's face lit up in a dazzling smile. "Y'all better treat me with luvin care, Pesh, 'cause ah might be shootin you in your fat ginnie ass bafoe I shoot some Ko-rean' s ass."

A Master Sergeant appeared from somewhere in the center of the tent. "All right, gentlemen, can I have rows of ten men five rows deep on my right?" The men shuffled into position, automatically standing at attention. "At ease, men, my name is Sergeant Axel. I'm going to get you supplied and on your way to your respective outfits." The Quartermaster tent next door will issue you cold weather gear. Put it on in the tent. As you can see and feel, you're gonna need it. You can come back here and retrieve your gear behind me and then head for the deuce and a halfs warming up outside. Your outfit's designation is on a white cardboard sign on the tailgate. Good luck. Try to stay warm.

"Hey, Sarge, when do we get issued a weapon." It was one of the Lieutenants amongst the officers in ranks.

"You'll pick up your weapons when you get to your outfit, sir. Everything's up front."

Hugo emerged from the Quartermaster tent in a lined field jacket, woolen sweater, gloves, a cap with fur and earflaps, and a sleeping bag. He was followed by Pescatore, Ramirez, and Kelly. He found the truck marked "7th Reg Alpha Co." and clambered aboard with duffel bag and sleeping bag thrown ahead. Eleven men climbed into the two-and-a-half ton truck all headed for Alpha Company. It was brutally cold. The new clothing was an improvement, but not even this gear could protect them from sub-zero weather. The men huddled together on the truck's hard wooden benches, chins buried in military issue tan scarves. Breath escaped in steamy puffs.

The truck bumped and swayed on the treacherous, rutted road to Alpha Company's base camp. No one spoke, as though conversation had been frozen along with everything else. Hugo sat, eyes closed, unmoving. His thoughts drifted to Angie and Baby Hugo. He could hear the baby's giggle, see his large brown eyes, his chubby arms reaching out to him, his smile, his kicking bare feet. He was overcome with depression and the palpable feeling of regret. How did he bring himself to this? Why was he so compulsive? Why hadn't he listened to his father? He was right about everything. He was always right. Hugo could see his mother wiping her hands on her apron, smell his father's pipe. He saw Salvatore reading his paper, turning the pages, pipe clenched in his jaw, smoke wreathing his graying head. He's getting older, he thought. He wished, how he wished he had kissed him before he had left. How he wished they had at least spoken, said something to one another.

Finally his thoughts turned to Mary—to her beautiful face, her smile, her soft lips. He envisioned her flawless, naked body stretched across the whiteness of the bed linen. He could almost feel her soft skin, inhale the very scent of her.

The deuce-and-a-half began a steep climb up, then rolled into a large bivouac area tented with mess hall, mobile surgical hospital, and various administrative and supply facilities. They slowed to a stop in front of a large tent with the red flag of the 7th Regiment fluttering from a staff at the entrance. A Master Sergeant pushed the tent flap aside and approached the back of the truck. He cupped his hands to his mouth, his voice rising above the blasting winds.

"All right, men, dismount and fall in to my left."

The men awkwardly climbed from the truck, lugging their possessions, and assembled in front of the Master Sergeant.

"Welcome to 7th Regimental Headquarters and Alpha Company. My name is First-Sergeant Bowlders." He spoke with a mid-western twang. "Your Company Commander will see you in the Headquarters tent behind you, gentlemen. Move out and file into the tent on the double, it's damn cold out here."

The tent smelled of stale smoke, kerosene heaters, and unwashed bodies. The men automatically fell into a formation facing the Sergeant and a tall, lanky Captain with tired eyes, a pronounced chin, and an air of the Ivy League. He puffed on a yellow bowl pipe, left hand supporting right elbow as he drew on the pipe stem. Sergeant Bowlder spoke first.

"Gentlemen." He nodded toward the Captain. "This is our company commander, Captain John Chapman."

Chapman stepped forward, removing the pipe from his clenched teeth, using it to gesture as he spoke. "Welcome aboard, gentlemen, we need you. Let me bring you up to speed on what's happening up here." Hugo recognized the clipped tones of Boston's Back Bay, what Zarraga mockingly called the "fucking Boston Brownstones." Hugo had laughed at Zarraga's joke, but now the quiet confidence and self-assuredness suggested by Chapman's neat attire and easy manner struck Hugo as oddly comforting. "The entire regiment is on the move northward. U.S. forces and U.N. forces are on the offensive known as Hammer and Anvil. We're headed for Pyonyang. Tomorrow morning we leave to join the offensive. We're going to hook up with the 5th Calvary Regiment, about five miles from here. You'll draw weapons and ammo from the Company Armorer when you leave this tent. Sergeant Bowlder will show you where to draw weapons and where you'll bunk tonight.

"We leave in convoy trucks tomorrow morning at five. Make sure you have enough C-rations. This is what you will be dining on for the next few weeks or so. Good Luck, I'll see you in the a.m."

A happy-go-lucky Lance Corporal dispensed M-1 Garand rifles with two hundred rounds of ammunition and four hand grenades per man. "Listen, you guys." The Lance Corporal grew serious in tone. "Keep your weapon clean and dry and sleep with it in your sleeping bag muzzle down. Yah gotta keep it above freezing. Sometimes the bolt will freeze on yah when you need it most, understand? And good luck up there."

They drew extra C-rations from a small supply tent and trudged through the sleet, which continued unabated, to a ten-man bare-floored tent. Sergeant Bowlder stood hands on hips in the center of the tent. As the men entered they felt the warmth of a small kerosene stove that broke the chill, bringing the temperature somewhere above zero. Alcohol lanterns illuminated the interior well enough to make the men squint as they entered from the cold blackness of the early sunset.

"All right men, smoke 'em if you got 'em. You'll be in sleeping bags tonight and for the next who knows how many weeks. You'll be dining on C-rations tonight. For that matter, so will I. And if you have anyone to write to, I'd do it tonight 'cause you're not going to be able to do much more than march and fight gooks for the duration." The Sergeant jerked his thumb over his shoulder. "There's a head behind this tent. Remember, it's twenty below out there. Whatever you do, make it quick. And remember, we're boarding trucks at five a.m. Check your weapon, check your ammo. No loaded weapons in the tent. I repeat, no loaded weapons in the tent. Get some sleep if you can. I'll see you at revelle." Eddie Ramirez stamped his feet in the chill air of the tent. "Man, what I'd give to be in Puerto Rico right now, nice and warm, a beautiful beach. I gotta take a leak, but I'm afraid I'll freeze my dick off in this weather."

Pescatore smirked as he said, "Hey, Eddie, I don't want you pissin the bed tonight. You better go to the head."

"Yea, Eddie," toned in Daryl Kelly, "ah gotta go to and ah got more to lose than you, white boy!"

Hugo arranged his gear and unfurled his sleeping bag. He rechecked his backpack, drew out a small note pad and a pencil, and sat on his sleeping bag writing in the pale light cast by the overhead lanterns. Pescatore, Kelly, and Ramirez returned from the head insulting one another in their usual good-natured fashion. Pescatore sat on his sleeping bag rummaging through his backpack. He produced a can labeled "Beans and Franks" and a small can of wood alcohol with a wick for heating C-rations.

"Aay, Hugo, you want me to heat up a can for you? I'm starved. I'll even eat this shit."

Hugo looked up from his writing. "Yeah, please, take a can from my pack, thanks." He wrote hasty notes to Angie and his mother, including a separate letter to Salvatore. He was forced to stop every few minutes to exhale warm air onto his hands. He placed the letters with others in a basket at the tent entrance for collection the next morning.

He slept fitfully and was dressed before dawn. There was little conversation among the men. Even Pescatore sensed that they had finally arrived at warfare and the dangers that confronted them. They boarded the trucks and began the crawl northward, the numbing cold adding to the trepidations in each man's thoughts. Forty-five minutes later the three-truck convoy arrived at the lead elements of the 7th Regiment. The men dismounted the trucks, which were quickly filled with dead and wounded for the return trip.

Dawn was breaking. Troops were strung out left and right as far as the eye could see. There were 105mm Howitzer teams, heavy machine gun emplacements, and mortar teams interspersed amongst the rifle companies who had spent the evening in shallow trenches hastily carved out of snow and frozen topsoil, shivering in sleeping bags that could not withstand the sub-zero temperature.

The advance northward had been stalled by lack of ammunition and food. A supply drop by parachute was expected at any hour. Further northward, at Chipyong - Ni', Colonel Marcel Crambez broke free of encirclement with twenty-three tanks carrying as many infantry as possible and stumbled into the rear of a Chinese regiment forming up for an attack toward the advancing United Nations Armies. In the ensuing confusion, the Chinese bolted south into the muzzles of the U.N. Command's Anvil and Hammer campaign.

"All right, men, listen up." Sergeant Bowlders was standing with a clipboard in his hand. "All men assigned to Alpha Company fall in on me." Hugo and twelve other men stood loosely around Bowlders. "Okay, Rossi, Pescatore, Kelly, Ramirez and Landis, you're assigned to Platoon Sergeant Thomson." He turned and pointed to a tall, spare Marine Buck Sergeant. Lionel Thomson was a native of Portland, Maine, spoke little and when he did it was soft and in the twang of a down Easter. He greeted the men with little fanfare and even less congeniality.

"Welcome to the 2nd Platoon, Marines. I'm Sergeant Thomson. A'hm gonna try and keep you alive. We're advancing north toward Pyongyang. Make sure you have enough ammo, and make sure you keep your weapon clean and ready to fire. Your job is to kill as many Chinese and North Koreans as you can before they kill you." He looked closely at a small card in his hand and called off the names of the new arrivals. "Okay, buddy up and find a depression in the snow. Heat up some C-rations and sit tight until we get some orders."

Pescatore turned and spied a low depression next to a 50-caliber machine gun emplacement. "Hey, Hugo, c'mon, I found us a home."

Their breath came in puffs of vapor as they scraped the snow aside to expose as much bare earth as possible. They placed their field packs and sleeping bags in the depression and exchanged small talk with the two marines manning the 50-caliber. Kelly and Ramirez were less than ten feet away arguing about who was doing the most work in scraping out their depression.

"Hey, Hugo, you wanna tell this here spic that Lincoln done freed the slaves and ah think the spics is gonna be next, but till we get word from Washington, D.C., they gonna have to work."

Someone yelled "*ten-hut,*" but before any man moved to attention Captain Chapman called "at ease." He had the yellow bowl clenched in his square jaw. His eyes scanned the emplacements as he walked the line. He nodded at Hugo and continued his walk, inspecting the troops and their readiness. Toward nightfall Bowlders approached the line of emplacements, calling several groups of Marines together.

"Okay, Company A, all you men to my left and right, fall in on me." The troops crowded around, stamping feet and slapping hands together. The sunless sky was slowly darkening. "We're moving at dawn," he announced. "Try to get some sleep, and keep your weapon warm and loaded with the safety on, you hear?"

The men responded in a chorus of "Yes, Sergeant!"

"All right," he continued, clouds of vapor escaping from his mouth, "listen closely to me, we're gonna post the guard about a hundred yards forward. Men on guard will be armed with Browning automatics and carry walkie-talkies. If you see anything coming at you from the front of your position, take the flare gun you'll be carrying and fire it over the target. You want to aim pretty high so the flare stays up there for a while, everybody understand? The flare guns are loaded and ready to fire. The safety is clearly marked next to the trigger housing. Any questions? Okay, there'll be two men to a post, two hours on, four hours off. The following men have the duty tonight." He named off six teams of men.

"Okay, you can take your posts at sundown. Heat up some C-rations, check your ammo, and stay awake. I can guarantee you they will harass us tonight and every night. You'll hear trumpets, whistles, and screaming. Don't let that scare you. They're four-foot little skinny bastards with antique sub-machine guns. We got them on the run now. What they're trying to do is slow our advance. Stay vigilant."

The men retreated to their shadow positions. Pescatore stood with Hugo silently scanning the surrounding snow-capped mountains as the pale sun fell behind the tallest peak.

"Hugo, this is one miserable friggin place."

"Yeah, Pesh, I know. C'mon, let's heat up some beans and franks and dig in for the night."

They ate quickly. Pescatore followed Hugo to their position, muttering to himself as he walked. They settled into their sleeping bags, huddling close to increase body temperature. Hugo dozed fitfully, his M-1 by his side. Pescatore snored loudly. The jagged front line was eerily quiet, the only sound the changing of the guard.

They came at four a.m. The first sounds that penetrated Hugo's semi-conscious haze were the blaring of trumpets and the chatter of Browning automatics. He clumsily leapt from his sleeping bag, adrenaline coursing through his bloodstream. His total focus was on the flare-lit span of open, snow-covered sloping and rutted terrain in front of him. He felt no cold; was not aware of Pescatore next to him.

The guards abandoned their posts and retreated to their lines, firing bursts from their machine guns as they back pedaled for safety. Hugo watched as both guards were cut down as they ran for cover. It was then that he saw them, thousands of North Koreans and Chinese infantry bearing down on their front lines. In the burning glow of the flares he saw for the first time the grey padded-cotton uniforms and fur-lined caftan caps, their flaps pulled down tight around their heads or flapping wildly like some menacing bird of prey. Wide eyed he watched as the sneaker-clad hoard churned the snow—whistles shrieking, trumpets blaring, their screaming battle cry designed to overcome fear in a coordinated chorus of bravado.

The allied lines erupted in a thunderous cacophony of artillery, mortars, heavy machine guns, and the unmistakable sound of hundreds of M-1 rifles in rapid fire. Hugo was brought to full focus by the commanding voice of Captain Chapman patrolling the line with a bullhorn in one hand and a 45-caliber pistol in the other.

"Fire at will! Aim, slack, squeeze, make every shot count!" He strode the line, fearlessly giving direction and encouragement to his men. Hugo's rifle was pressed to his right cheek in a kneeling position; his sights were filled with a screaming Chinese infantryman firing bursts from a Tommy gun. He squeezed the trigger of the M-1. The soldier was less than two hundred feet away. The 30-caliber shell tore into his chest. He was brought up short as the shell slammed him to a stop. The Tommy gun flew from his hand as he fell face first into the snow. Hugo carefully took down four more grey clad figures as the flares slowly extinguished.

The artillery ceased and by degrees the sounds of the battle abated. Hugo heard the staccato bursts of Allied machine guns and the intermittent barking of rifle fire. Moments later the entire battlefront became strangely silent. Hugo peered over the snow bank shielding him and Pescatore from view.

"Hugo, what's out there, I can't see nuthin." Before Hugo could answer the popping sound of flare guns and the slow descent of green phosphorescent balls under a mini parachute revealed a battlefield littered with North Korean and Chinese dead. The attacking troops had vanished into thin air. Sergeant Bowlders walked the line talking with the troops, giving instructions as he went along.

"Okay, men, stand down. Reload your weapons and settle into your positions. I don't think we'll see anymore action tonight. We'll check on the dead gooks in the morning light."

Hugo slumped down against his sleeping bag and fumbled for a cigarette, offering a Lucky Strike to Pescatore. Neither man spoke as they held tightly to their weapons. The rush of adrenaline still made them impervious to the cold. Pescatore took a deep drag on the Lucky, exhaled through his nose, and spoke first.

"Hugo, I don't mind tellin ya, I was scared shitless when they started all that friggin screamin and whistle blowin. What about you?"

"Yeah, Pesh, I was a little nervous myself. They're crazy little bastards and they don't give a damn if they get killed."

"Yeah, you can say that again. Hey, Hugo, you think any of them are alive out there?"

"No, Pesh, I think they're all dead. And by tomorrow morning they'll be frozen solid. Let's get in these sleeping bags and try to get a few hours shut eye."

"Yeah, Hugo, that's if we don't wake up frozen. Must be a friggin million degrees below zero. Good thing it's not too windy."

The tide had turned for U.N. fighting forces. General Lin Piao, Commander of Chinese communist forces and the Korean Peoples Army, was replaced by General Peng Te-Huai. Rumors abounded that Lin Piao had been wounded in action. Some said the strain of watching his army fight itself to destruction had exhausted him. General Peng took command of an army decimated by aggressive air and artillery assaults and further hampered by thin supply lines and an inability to support his troops with artillery or air cover.

Peng was a ruthless leader and forced his troops to mount massive suicide attacks against overwhelming U.N. superiority. While losses were heavy, this tactic slowed the U.N. advance long enough to allow Peng to resupply his forces and to rebuild a fractured army with fresh replacements, bringing his troop level to some seven hundred thousand.

Hugo lay in his sleeping bag hugging his rifle, losing the battle to keep from shivering. He slept for minutes at a time, the emotional impact of the recent carnage replaying in his mind. Dawn broke clear with the promise of sunshine, which would warm the air by ten degrees. Company cooks who had been pressed into service as infantry rifleman somehow had managed to brew hot coffee in two twenty-gallon stockpots. The aroma wafted through the chill air, bringing the men of Alpha Company to the lighted fires and steaming coffee pots with canteen cup in hand. Captain Chapman strode from one group of men to another.

"You Marines did a good job last night. Get used to these midnight attacks. They got close last night. We know they're having supply problems, but there's so damn many of them all they need is six rounds of ammo each and they become firepower. Keep your weapons clean and loaded. And remember, safety on."

Sergeant Bowlders stepped forward and cupped his hands around his mouth. "All right, you U.S. Marines, mount up. Platoon Sergeants fall in on me."

Hugo and Pingitore gulped the remainder of lukewarm coffee, replaced the canteen cup, lit each others Lucky Strike, and rolled sleeping bags into compact rolls shaking off snow and dirt and strapping them to backpacks weighted by C-rations, first-aid packs, and dry socks. Sergeant Thomsen trudged back from the impromptu Platoon Sergeants' meeting with First Sergeant Bowlders and Captain Chapman.

"Second Platoon, fall in on me." The men formed a semi-circle around Thomsen. "All right, we're headed north in one long sweeping line. We gotta take any enemy object that gets in our way. When we head out and go by those dead gooks out there,

there's no taking souvenirs. Remember, they may be alive or booby-trapped. If you hear a sound from anyone of them, call me. You got that?" The men replied in unison as they stomped their feet trying to ward off the cold. "All right you fightin leathernecks, let's move out."

The men formed a skirmish line and began the slow trek toward Pyongyang. The plain before them was littered with grey-clad Chinese forces and troops of the Korean Peoples Army, their bodies frozen blue in macabre positions of violent death—faces shot off, limbs severed from bodies, frozen clots of blood turned black, looking much like congealed jello. Sergeant Bowlders and Captain Chapman paced the company walking fifty feet ahead of the strung out troops. Bowlders dropped back to bolster the men's spirits. As Pesh and Hugo caught up with him he clapped Pescatore on the back. "How you men doin?"

Pescatore was fascinated by the death surrounding him. "Hey, Sarge, what are those cloth tubes the gooks have wrapped around their backs? What's in 'em?"

"That's the equivalent of C-rations. They got a layer of oats, a layer of millet, rice, beans, and tea—that's what they live on. They're tough little bastards and they can go for weeks on what's in those cloth tubes."

Pescatore smirked and said, "You know, Sarge, that's not a bad idea. Only what I think what we should have is my mother's pasta fazool in a can. That would keep us goin a lot better than Spam." The men within hearing distance burst out laughing. Sergeant Bowlders smiled and turned to rejoin Captain Chapman. "Pesh, if your mother sends you some of that pasta fazool, make sure I get some."

"You bet, Sarge."

Snow showers fell intermittently. Frostbite ravaged at feet and fingers, and canteen water had to be shaken regularly to break up ice crystals. The men would only relieve themselves at the warmest part of the day. Hopefully that would be above ten degrees. There was talk of the Turkish soldier who had his penis frozen while taking a protracted urination. The storyteller swore to the truth of his story.

The men became used to the evening attacks and the slaughter that came from the wild charges accompanied by blaring bugles and shrieking whistles. On the fourth night of the advance they came, materializing out of nowhere, seemingly even more troops than on previous evenings. The charging horde made it to within twenty feet of Alpha Company's emplacements. The next morning as they walked among the carnage Sergeant Bowlders pointed out their clean uniforms and full tubes of food.

"These are replacements," he theorized, "and there's probably a lot more of them on the way."

The terrain turned hilly and then mountainous. The men walked in single file through mountain passes and depressions in the rolling snow-covered earth. Chinese snipers held the high ground, occasionally wounding or killing U. N. forces. Patrols were sent up to the mountain ridges sweeping off the high ground only to have snipers re-emerge again just hours later. American prop-driven P-51 Mustang fighter planes dropped in from time to time for strafing runs, helping to keep the enemy at bay. U.N. forces no longer had the protection of the Sherman M4A3 tanks. The terrain could not support the treads of the heavy tanks, and in the mountainous region they became easy targets for anti-tank weapons.

The assault continued nonstop, making slow but steady progress toward Pyongyang. Supply lines were thinning as the assault forces made their way northward. The troops had been living on C-rations and the occasional hot cup of coffee for five days. The constant tension was taking its toll on morale, and the cold was taking its toll on hands and feet. Alpha Company had lost nine marines from sniper fire and frontal assaults. On the sixth night the men were treated to hot beef stew that was trucked to the front from the rear echelon field kitchen. Hugo, Pescatore, Edie Ramirez, and Daryl Kelly sat on sleeping bags as they wolfed down the first hot meal in a week.

Kelly smiled at Pescatore. "Hey, Pesh, does this taste as good as yo Mama's spaghetti and meatballs?"

Pescatore kept on chewing as he spoke through spoonfuls of stew. "You know, Kelly, you're the first Irish coon I ever met in my life. This food must be right up your alley, you know what I mean, Irish stew? To tell ya the truth, right now it tastes a hell of a lot better than my mother's macaroni and meatballs. Whaddaya think, Hugo?"

Hugo nodded, smiling at the banter. Pescatore turned his attention toward Ramirez. Hugo's thoughts were in Rhode Island, his mother's warm kitchen, baby Hugo's gurgling, Mary McKenna's warm body, the fragrance of his father's pipe. Hugo's reverie was broken by Sergeant Thomsen followed by Bowlders and Captain Chapman. The three squatted down in the center of the men. Captain Chapman directed his conversation toward Hugo.

"Rossi, you're a good Marine. That's why I'm here. I need a recon party to head up to those ridges and follow the rim until you locate gooks. We need to know where they are and how many there are. You'll have a radioman with you, and I want you to take three other men with you. You pick them."

"When do you want us to start, Captain?" He spoke without hesitation. There was nothing to think about or discuss. It simply had to be done.

"As soon as the sun sets. Take a B.A.R. and enough ammo, you hear?"

"Yes, Captain."

"You let Sergeant Bowlders know who's going with you." As Chapman stood to leave he placed a hand on Hugo's shoulder. "Keep you head, son, avoid confrontation. There's a lot of them out there."

"Yes, sir, I sure as hell will."

Hugo looked at Pescatore. He nodded, his eyes flashing a silent yes. He turned to Ramirez and Kelly who quickly nodded in unison. Sergeant Bowlders recorded the names in a small notebook. He placed the notebook in his field jacket and pulled out a half-pack of cigarettes from his breast pocket. He offered the pack to each man in turn, then pulled out a Zippo. He didn't speak till all the cigarettes were lit.

"You know, we have the Fifth Cavalry, the 27th Regimental Team, X Corp, the Turks, the French, thousands of men, but Colonel Crambez selected Alpha Company for this duty because of Captain Chapman and his ability to get the job done. And the Captain selected you, Rossi, because he thinks *you* can get the job done. Don't let us down, men. And good luck."

The sun was setting; the air temperature dropped precipitously. The men huddled together, squatting on their haunches as they spoke.

"Hey, Sarge." It was Eddie Ramirez. "What's the story on the Captain. He always seems like he's in another world?"

Sergeant Thomsen joined the group squatting in the tight circle. Bowlders turned to Thomsen. "Lionel, tell them about the Captain. Lionel served with the Captain in the South Pacific."

Thomsen shifted his weight for comfort. "We was Privates together on Guadalcanal, Iwo Jima, and a couple of other small islands. He's got the Silver Star, two Bronze Stars, he's been wounded twice. I watched him lead a hand-to-hand combat charge. He's fearless and a great officer. He's a Yale graduate and a lawyer and he volunteered to come here. What else you wanna know?" The men nodded in awe and respect. Sergeant Bowlders gave his instructions as they prepared for the mission.

As U.N. forces advanced northward, the terrain had changed. What confronted them now was a relatively flat plain, five hundred feet wide with high ridges on either side of the corridor. There was no better route north. The rest of the topography to either side of the pass was impassable mountain range. Thousands of troops would be advancing through this conduit with little protection from high ground.

Hugo and his team left at sundown crossing the frozen tundra and arriving at the sloping base of the ridgeline to the right of the advance. They ascended to the top of the ridge and regrouped. There was no moon; it was pitch-blackness. Hugo spoke in a whisper.

"Okay, radio man with me out front. Spread out in single file, not too close, no smoking, no talking. We'll stop every few minutes and listen for anything. Everybody got that?"

In this way they made their way northward for several hours, finally stopping for a break in the lee of an outcropping of huge boulders at the insistence of the men. The wind had picked up and they huddled together in a vain attempt at warmth. The ridgeline banked left as they laboriously trekked onward. Hugo made contact with base once to establish communications but kept radio silence for fear of being located by Chinese radio operators.

As dawn broke the men rested in a cave-like sculpture of frozen snow formed by the howling winds sweeping the mountains. They continued on traversing the ridge as it banked sharply to the left. Hugo was in the lead with Sparks, the radio man, close behind. Suddenly, Hugo fell to one knee. The men following automatically dropped down like dominoes. Hugo extracted a pair of binoculars from inside his field jacket, placed them to his eyes and whistled silently.

"Come up here, you guys, and take a look at this."

The men scrambled up beside him. Ramirez held the field glasses to his eyes and mumbled, "Holy shit, there must be thousands of them." The field glasses were passed around. Hugo turned to Sparks.

"Raise the C.O. We got something to tell him."

At the call of his radioman, Captain Chapman scrambled from his seat and pulled on a pair of headphones. "What's out there, Rossi?"

Hugo felt his heart pounding. He forced himself to breath slowly and deeply so that when he spoke his words sounded clear and calm. "Captain, I estimate there's about five or six thousand troops with light artillery, and a number of medium and lightweight vehicles. They seem to be forming up, heading our way."

"Good work, Rossi. We need to determine how far out they are. What I want you to do is start counting to one hundred slowly.

I'm going to get the radioman in the first provisional brigade on the horn. He'll be able to triangulate your position. Okay, start counting. And sit tight for a couple of seconds."

Hugo began counting slowly. Within seconds Chapman was back to the radio. "Okay, Hugo, come on home." Suddenly excited Chinese voices could be heard over the static transmission. "Rossi!" shouted Chapman, "get out of there on the double, they know where you are."

Hugo slammed the receiver down. "We got busted. They know where we are. We gotta get back, but we have to get off this ridge line. We gotta get down to the valley floor. There's more cover over there, and we can make better time." In seconds the low drone of a small single-engine plane could be heard headed their way. There was little cover available. In minutes it was over their position. Hugo trained the field glasses on the enemy encampment. There was a flurry of activity as men piled into troop carriers.

He turned and spoke to the men who were now anxiously scanning the skies. "I saw a way down about five minutes back that way." He pointed to the direction from which they had come. "Let's double time that way. Let's go!"

The way down was a precarious icy slope leading to the valley floor. Hugo was the first one over the edge. They slid most of the way down the treacherous path, occasionally breaking their acceleration with a foothold here and there. Once down they huddled together to access any damage. Miraculously, no one was hurt and they had lost none of their ammo or supplies. Daryl Kelley turned to urinate against a convenient boulder and spoke over his shoulder.

"Whadda we gonna do now, oh fearless leader?"

"What we're gonna do, Kelley, is bug outta here. We'll travel next to this mountain face until we can find some place to hide out until the sun sets."

They traveled in single file, Hugo in the lead. It was late morning when they came upon a scattering of huge boulders at the base of the mountain face forming almost a perfect circle and good concealment. The single-engine plane skimmed the ridgeline looking for them. Chinese and North Korean troops had mounted the ridgeline in search of them never suspecting that they would be able to get to the valley floor.

They settled into the small enclave sharing the few remaining C-rations and cigarettes. Sundown came with accompanying bitter cold and snow flurries. Sparks, the radioman, hobbled about limping on his right foot that was frost bitten. They needed to get to Alpha Company before dawn broke. Ramirez had frost bitten toes. Hugo surveyed the men, now listless, exhausted and freezing.

"Okay, saddle up, we're getting out of here." The men struggled to their feet and shouldered their weapons. Hugo stood watching as they awkwardly prepared to leave the meager security and shelter the enclave provided. They heard the whine of the engines first coming from the north. They looked at one another knowing full well they would be found out. Hearts pumped, senses became heightened in acuity. Hugo motioned them to crouch down. The sound of weapons cocking split the cold air.

The glare of headlights came first, casting a wavering illumination before the trucks. Two Chinese Peoples Army transports crawled slowly around the bend. Just before the enclave powerful searchlights splashed beams of light across the mountain base, glancing off the boulders surrounding the enclave. The trucks stopped. The men could hear rapid Chinese being spoken. The searchlights were trained unsteadily on the boulders as the trucks continued to advance with a number of troops walking alongside.

Hugo cupped his hands around his mouth and whispered, "They're coming in. Get ready. Get your grenades out. Go for the trucks first. They must have machine guns mounted in them. Follow my lead."

The Chinese suspected something. The chatter ceased. The trucks stopped and then, after what sounded like orders being barked, they resumed their advance slowly and deliberately. Hugo waited until they were within throwing distance. He nodded to the men and whispered, "on the count of three, no yelling, just toss your grenades. Two grenades, one after the other. Aim for the trucks. Me and Pesh will take out the one on the right, you guys go for the one on the left. Ready one, two, three!"

They stood in unison taking aim and silently heaving ten grenades. The men crouched behind the boulders as the grenades exploded in rapid succession. One truck exploded in a shower of gasoline flames. There was a screaming chorus of Chinese voices as the enclave was showered with machinegun bursts. Hugo whispered loudly, "stay down until I jump up. They're coming for us in the open."

Hugo peered through an opening in the boulders. "All right, get ready. Be careful, they've got grenades. Okay, now!" They leaped up as one, Hugo cradling the B.A.R. on his hip, ripping through the Chinese who were in the open and silhouetted against the burning truck. The other men had been issued 30-caliber snub-nosed machine guns known as "grease guns," and together they sprayed the advancing Chinese in a withering barrage. A hand grenade carried by a Chinese soldier lying on the snow exploded as death relaxed his grip on the grenade's safety handle. There was an abrupt silence as Hugo and the men ceased fire. All that could be heard was the crackling of the burning truck.

Hugo leaped over the protective ring of boulders, the others quickly following. They walked among the dead, twelve in all counting the driver of the troop carrier still behind the wheel. The explosion from the hand grenades had caved in the passenger side door, blew out the windshield, and buckled the engine hood. Hugo mounted the running board, brushed off the broken glass, and pulled the dead driver to the ground. Jumping into the driver's seat he turned the ignition, stepped on the starter, and the engine burst into life.

"C'mon," he shouted, "we got a ride." Pescatore pried open the passenger door and sat on the broken glass cursing as Hugo laughed. Ramirez, Kelly, and Sparks jumped into the rear section. The truck took off, the right rear wheel wobbling. The exploding grenades had punctured the tire and warped the wheel. They headed south, careening left and right through the darkness.

The truck's headlamps were shattered. The white expanse of the valley was blanketed in darkness. There was no visibility. The truck wobbled forward at twenty miles per hour with no windshield. The sub-freezing cold became a blast freezer, stinging Hugo's eyes and numbing his face. The men hunkered over in the open rear section of the troop carrier. There was no conversation. Pescatore burrowed his face into his jacket, cursing the cold and the war. The truck struggled forward, steam escaping from the engine from a piece of shrapnel piercing the radiator.

THE ARRIVAL THE STRUGGLE THE ASCENDANCY

They traveled by dead reckoning with the occasional ray of moonlight piercing the thick cloudbank and providing a reference for direction. They had traveled for twenty minutes when suddenly there was a pounding on the rear window of the truck cab. It was Kelly yelling over the roar of the engine and wind.

"Hey, Hugo, lookee see what's chasin us, boy. Looks like they done found their buddies all shot up back there and they be lookin for the banditos who dunnit."

Hugo and Pesh craned their necks looking out the back window to see three sets of headlamps gaining rapidly on them. Hugo's mind raced. He glanced in the rear view mirror. They were getting closer. He slammed his foot on the brake pedal, lurching to a stop, and leaped from the truck.

"Everybody out, c'mon!" The men gathered around Hugo glancing over their shoulders at the ever-closer Chinese in pursuit. "Listen to me, they're after this truck. I want you guys to take off on foot heading south. Get back on the ridge top and keep on going. I'll hold them up for awhile and then I'll be right behind you."

Pescatore spoke first. "What, are you fucken nuts. I'm not leaving you alone out here. You don't have a shot at making it out alive."

"Listen, Hugo," said Ramirez, "we abandon the truck along the ridge face. We take up positions on the high ground around the truck and we'll kick the shit out of them." Hugo looked at each man as he spoke.

"Listen to me. I'm in charge of this mission. You guys are leaving and I'll join you." The headlamps were closer. "I'll take the B.A.R. and the extra ammo. Everybody give me an extra grenade. C'mon, give me the grenades and head for the ridge line."

The lights grew closer. The men stood, unwilling to move. "Give me the goddamn grenades and get the hell out of here!." He leaped into the truck extending his hand for the grenades. The truck jerked forward steaming and shuddering, heading for the western ridge wall, distancing himself from the men as they scampered toward the safety of the eastern wall. He hugged the wall as the truck miraculously plowed forward. The lights were gaining. The terrain was rutted and studded with boulders of various sizes. The right front tire smashed into a boulder the size of a fifty-gallon drum and shuddered to a halt. Simultaneously, one headlamp popped on. Hugo frantically searched the dashboard for the light switch. It was too late. As he turned he saw the three sets of headlamps turn toward his direction. He found the headlamp switch and killed it. He abandoned the truck and ran along the steep ridge wall looking for a way up. He could hear the Chinese troop carriers' whining engines closing in. He crouched in the pitch-blackness impervious to the bitter cold, his heart beating wildly, all his senses attuned to the moment.

He watched as the personnel carriers stopped fifty yards from the abandoned truck. Powerful searchlights illuminated the wrecked truck. There was a loud Chinese command followed by the rattling blast of three heavy caliber machine guns shredding the truck apart. The guns fell silent as the personnel carriers advanced slowly toward the bullet-riddled hulk. Hugo knew he had minutes before they resumed the hunt. He ran gripping the B.A.R., the extra grenades hooked to his belt and a satchel of ammo clips slung over one shoulder. He looked frantically for a way to the top of the ridgeline to no avail. The moon broke through the blanket of clouds revealing a deep fissure in the face of the ridge wall providing the only cover to be found.

He squeezed into the narrow space, kneeling and crouching into the three-foot deep opening. He prepared for the worst, laying out the grenades and clips of ammo on the ground before him. The personnel carriers came in a staggered line, searchlights bathing the oncoming terrain and flashing along the ridge wall. He watched and crouched lower as the trucks drew abreast of the crevice. The searchlights splayed across the top of his position continuing on slowly. The last truck in the staggered formation stopped directly in front, playing a beam of light above his position. The clouds parted revealing a full moon, illuminating the snow encrusted plain. The snow reflected the moon's rays intensifying the light cast. His position was revealed as if it were daylight.

There were excited Chinese voices. The searchlight found Hugo, holding him in its beam. His instincts took over. He snapped the B.A.R. to his shoulder strafing the truck, blowing out the searchlight and flattening two tires. The vehicle's swivel mounted heavy caliber machine gun chattered loudly, bullets missing their mark wildly. Hugo threw grenades and ammo into a satchel and ran toward the rear of the truck, tossing two grenades into the open back. The grenades went off simultaneously taking out the machine gun and three Chinese soldiers. The driver's door opened and the driver staggered out, crumbling to the snow.

The two lead trucks had turned and were slowly creeping toward the burning truck. Hugo crouched behind the burning truck aware that any minute the gas tank could explode. The first truck approached from the left side of the disabled personnel carrier extinguishing its lights. The second truck came in slowly from the right side. Hugo could make out troops dismounting the vehicles. They spread out, half circling behind the burning truck, half advancing from the front. Hugo saw a dozen or so bodies advancing slowly, their leader muttering Chinese commands. He was surrounded. The only way out was through them.

He knelt on the glistening hard packed snow, his heart pounding. He pulled two grenades from the satchel, pulled the arming pins, waited two seconds and heaved them in a high arc over the burning truck in the direction of the advancing soldiers. They detonated almost simultaneously. There were screams of pain, rapid Chinese commands, and charging feet. He stood, stepping from behind the truck, the B.A.R. blazing a spray of bullets decimating the charging troops. The sound of rushing feet came from the opposite side of the burning truck. He dropped to one knee frantically reaching for a fresh clip of ammo as he ejected the empty one. He slammed the clip into place just as the Chinese rounded the corner. He leaped to his feet grasping the B.A.R. at his hip and pulled the trigger. Nothing happened.

The six Chinese soldiers came up short in their tracks. They were twenty feet away from Hugo. They were framed by the flickering illumination of the burning truck. All that could be heard was the crackling of the fire and the hoarse, vapor-filled rapid breathing of Hugo and the Chinese. No one moved. There was a rapid exchange of Chinese. They knew they had him unarmed. It was time to take revenge for their fallen comrades.

They unsheathed their bayonets and moved forward, clustered together slowly. The satchel was at Hugo's feet. He bent quickly, snatched a grenade by its arming ring pulling and tossing in one motion. It landed at the feet of the Chinese who quickly picked it up and threw it out of range. They charged, screaming in fear and excitement. Hugo stood head and shoulders above all of them. He gripped the heavy rifle by the muzzle and swung it at the mass of humanity confronting him, knocking two to the frozen ground. His foot lashed out kicking the closest attacker squarely in the groin. The three standing soldiers circled him. All that could be heard was rapid wheezing breath and the groaning of the prostrate soldiers. They circled him, bayonets glinting in the fire's light. Hugo's body was taught; his nostrils flared. There was no thought. It was all animal reaction. He had to kill to survive. He charged like a cannon shot at the attacker to his right. The rifle swung with such force the butt broke from the barrel as it split the soldiers face in a long bloody gash in his right cheek. He ripped his razor shaped trench knife from its scabbard. He was mad with power and rage. He roared as he leaped at the next attacker, slashing his throat in one fatal swipe. The last standing attacker turned to run.

He heard the sliding bolt cocking the submachine gun. The Chinese soldier he had downed with a kick to the groin screamed as he pulled the trigger. Six bullets forming a bloody pattern from Hugo's right hip to his left shoulder gushed life. He sank to his knees, fell to his side, his vision dimmed. His final thoughts were so vivid. He was far from the battlefield. He held baby Hugo aloft as he kicked his feet and squirmed in his grasp screeching with glee as Hugo swung him to the ceiling. And then there was blackness. It was then that the soldiers came with their bayonets and took their revenge.

Father Cavalaro died peacefully in his sleep at St. Bart's Rectory. He was eighty-six years old, but he had retained the spry step of a man half his age right up to the end. Mrs. Almonte, his housekeeper of thirty-six years, was in a state of inconsolable grief. She had been widowed at thirty-five and whispered rumors were that they had been lovers for years. He had celebrated early mass at St. Bart's every morning for the past ten years leaving the later masses and many of the routine duties to two younger priests assigned to the parish. His death came as a great blow to the church community. Mrs. Almonte had called Salvatore immediately after her call for an ambulance. He arrived at the rectory, Mrs. Almonte at the open door, eyes red with tears, arms outstretched to Salvatore. He embraced her gently and held her arm as they ascended the stairs to the Monsignor's bedroom. The door was open to reveal the Monsignor at peace in death, a blue tinge overtaking his ruddy complexion. He held her by the shoulders tightly as they approached the massive mahogany bed where he lay. They stood by the bedside, Mrs. Almonte sobbing quietly, tears streaming down Salvatore's cheeks. He reached out to grasp the Monsignor's cold hand and held it. His thoughts drifted to his arrival in America and to the patron and sponsor who had been responsible for his very existence in the new world. They waited by the bedside, lost in their own thoughts until the ambulance attendants entered the bedroom escorted by Father Mario Gentile, a young priest recently transferred from a parish in West Warwick. Hugo assisted Mrs. Almonte slowly down the winding stairs to the front parlor where her teary eyed daughter embraced her and led her to her waiting car mouthing a "thank you" to Salvatore as she passed.

The wake was held at the Romano Funeral Home for two days and two nights. Thousands attended from throughout the state, including the Mayor and Governor. A high mass was celebrated at St. Barts by Bishop McVinney from Sts. Peter & Paul

Cathedral in Providence. The faithful packed the pews and isles, spilling out the doors and onto the sidewalk. The funeral cortege to St. Ann's Cemetery in Cranston wound for two miles with a police escort at the head of the procession. He was interred beneath a large bare limbed elm tree that would leaf into a statuesque grave marker.

Salvatore remained as the throng of mourners dispersed. Francesca, sensing his desire to remain alone, left with Pat Lofredo and Philomena. He stood before the grave, still open. In moments workmen would cover the casket with earth. He spoke out loud: "Thank you, my old friend, for giving me life in this new country. I love you and I will miss you. You will be in my prayers every day." He made the sign of the cross, raised his collar against the chill wind, turned, and walked to his car.

Salvatore lowered his evening paper to the floor, reached over and raised the volume on the flool model Magnavox AM/FM radio. Gabriel Heater was delivering the evening news in his trademark bombastic style. Salvatore sat back in the overstuffed parlor chair and listened intently, puffing on the yellow bowl pipe, wreaths of aromatic smoke encircling the chair. Heater reported on the events unfolding north and south of the Thirty-eighth Parallel. He spoke of American losses, the advance north of United Nations' forces, and the bitterness of the Korean winter. Salvatore retrieved the paper from the floor and thumbed to the page with the map of Korea bi-sected with a line representing the Thirty-eighth Parallel. Swerving arrows depicted advancing U.N. troops with clusters of diamond-shaped figures depicting enemy forces. Salvatore studied the map, frowning at his lack of comprehension. He rose from the chair and walked to the kitchen. Francesca was busy drying the last of the evening's dinner dishes. She turned as he approached her, paper in one hand, yellow bowl pipe in the other.

"When was the last time you heard from Hugo?" Francesca almost dropped the dish she was drying. It was the first time he had uttered Hugo's name since their confrontation at the Cadillac Club. There was a slight smile of satisfaction playing about her lips as she spoke.

"He called me from Paris Island where he was training before Christmas. It's the last time I heard from him." She paused for a moment. "Salvatore..."

"Yes?"

"He said to tell you he sends his love."

He nodded, replaced the pipe between clenched teeth, turned and walked slowly to his chair in the parlor. Francesca watched for any sign of emotion. There was none. He reached over from his chair and dialed the tuning knob to the Firestone Philharmonic Hour. Concert music filled the apartment. He laid his head back and stared into a corner of the room, puffing occasionally on the yellow bowl lost in thought. Francesca studied his profile from the kitchen. She knew the pain he was in. Her heart ached for her husband and her son. Why hadn't he written, where was he, was he safe? She removed her apron and took her knitting basket from an open cupboard and joined Salvatore in the parlor, sitting across from him on a flowered sofa. She began the ritual of knit one, purl two.

She stared at Salvatore as her hands moved rhythmically.

"Why are you staring at me?"

She laid the knitting needles into her lap. "You miss him as much as I do, don't you?" He removed the pipe from his mouth slowly staring at the carpet. "He's my son, for better or worse. He's my blood, I gave him life." He lay back in the chair, eyes closed, a signal that there was to be no further discussion.

Angelina had taken a job at a small jewelry factory within walking distance of her tenement and Salvatore's house. Francesca and Mrs. Natale cared for baby Hugo on alternate days. In time, it became Francesca who cared for him on a daily basis. Mr. Natale suffered from a debilitating asthmatic condition, which had grown worse over the years, resulting in many bedridden days and requiring the attention of his wife. There was much talk of moving to Arizona or Florida.

Baby Hugo became the focus of Salvatore's life. His every action was motivated by the child in one fashion or another. On most evenings, Angie and the baby stayed the night with Salvatore and Francesca, sleeping in Hugo's room. Francesca had become Angelina's confidant, pouring out her heart to Francesca in the quiet of Hugo's bedroom as baby Hugo slept.

"Ma, I still love him in spite of everything he did. It's there. It will never go away." She had called them Ma and Pa since she started dating Hugo years before.

"I know you do, sweetheart. I know things will be different when he gets back from the Marines." She made the sign of the cross and embraced Angelina, tears misting her eyes. She sat back glancing at her grandson. "All we need now is for his father to come to his senses."

It was a snowy, bitterly cold Sunday in mid-March. The steam radiators were hissing, warming the apartment. The fragrance of roasted chicken, pasta, and brewing coffee wafted throughout the apartment. The Natales had come for the ritual Sunday meal. Lorenzo Natale and Salvatore sat on the deeply tufted parlor chairs listening to the Italian Hour broadcast by Antonio Pace in his high-pitched, rapid delivery. Mrs. Natale and Francesca busied themselves in the kitchen accompanied by the clatter preparing the meal. Oven doors squeaked open, cupboards banged, water boiled, the clatter of dishes and glasses being arranged on the dining room table by Angelina.

Baby Hugo crawled to a dining room chair, raised himself on unsteady legs, turned from the chair and gleefully launched himself across the room making four stumbling steps before crashing headlong into a dining room sideboard, his shrieking cries turned all heads. Angelina circled the dining room table and scooped him from the floor. The women gathered around Angelina, clucking and fussing over the child, caressing his head and kissing his cheek. The men looked over and smiled, their interest attuned to Antonio Pace.

Pat Lofredo and Philomena arrived with two bottles of Pat's homemade wine, a gold-medal prizewinner in local competition. Francesca announced dinner just as Antonio Pace signed off. Symphony music accompanied the boisterous Sunday feast. Pat Lofredo and Lorenzo exchanged friendly heated debate over U. S. involvement in Korea. Lofredo thought Truman was crazy for involving U. S. forces and bemoaned the fate of our young men in battle. Lorenzo wagged his finger in pronouncement, asserting that communism must be stopped wherever it rears it ugly head. His only regret was that Hugo had to leave Angelina and the baby. The cacophony of conversation went on through coffee and Mrs. Natale's banana cream pie. Salvatore sat bemused at the constantly occurring clash of opinions of Pat Lofredo and Lorenzo. The women cleared the table. The men returned to the parlor. Salvatore poured shot glasses of Anisette and searched the radio dial for Sunday afternoon entertainment.

There was a gentle knocking on the kitchen door. The women heard nothing over their interwoven conversation, the washing of dishes, and baby Hugo's demand for attention. The knock came loudly. Francesca turned from the sink, wiping her soapy hands on her apron, and opened the door wide. In the doorway stood a young, tall All-American Marine Captain wearing a somber expression and clutching a manila envelope. Father Mario was to his right. Neither man spoke for an empty second as all heads turned in their direction. The men emerged from the parlor. A frown appeared on Salvatore's face as he saw the uniformed Marine. Father Mario stepped forward. "My friends, I'm glad you are all here together. This is Captain Anderson, he was looking for Angelina. Someone told him to see me, which he did, and I brought him here knowing she would be here on Sunday." He raised his hand to Angelina, which she took. He turned to the Captain. "Captain Anderson, this is Angelina Rossi." Francesca held baby Hugo, sucking on his thumb, as he stared at the uniformed Captain.

"Mrs. Rossi, my name is Captain Lawrence Anderson of the United States Marine Corps." Angelina stood motionless, eyes unblinking. Captain Anderson hesitated for a moment, his eyes sweeping the room. He continued in a steady voice. "It is my sad duty to inform you that your husband, Hugo Rossi, Private First Class, United States Marine Corps, was killed in action in the nation of Korea on or about March 15th of this year. You should also know that Private Rossi will be receiving the Silver Star for his bravery above and beyond the call of duty. I extend the deepest sympathy of the President of the United States and the Secretary of Defense and the Commanding General of the United States Marine Corp." He stepped forward and handed the brown manila envelope to Angelina, her hands raised reflexively to grasp it. "These are Private Rossi's records, M'am. There is enclosed a report of what occurred during the action as best as can be determined." He stepped back, reached into his jacket pocket and extracted a small card. "Mrs. Rossi, you have my sincerest sympathy. This is my card. Please call me with any questions at any time." He turned to the still open door and descended the stairs. Father Mario followed, motioning to Salvatore that he would be back shortly.

He had said it all in less than a minute. It was as if he had never been there. They stood as if petrified. Angelina began to tremble and moan. "No, no, no! It was going to be all different when he came home." Her voice rose in a sobbing crescendo. "He's too young, he's too young! Why did God do this to me?" She ran to Hugo's room, a mournful guttural wail trailing her path to the bedroom. Francesca and Mrs. Natale, hearts pounding in anguish, both blinded with tears, muttering high-pitched incoherent sounds, ran after her, Francesca clutching baby Hugo to her chest. The women fell on the bed on either side of Angelina enfolding her in their arms from either side with baby Hugo crawling and gurgling on his mother's back. The three women lay there in total, inconsolable anguish, the echoing of Captain Anderson's pronouncement of finality bringing on new waves of convulsive grief. Mr. Natale sank slowly into a kitchen chair burying his face in his hands, his chest heaving, and his breathing raspy and constricted from an asthma attack as tears streamed down his cheeks. Philomena had walked dazed into Hugo's room. She sat at the foot of the bed, arms folded across her chest, rocking back and forth. Pat Lofredo turned and walked into the parlor, eyes red rimmed and talking out loud. "It's because of that son of a bitch, Truman" he shouted. "We shouldn't be there. This is what happens…" his voice trailed off to vague murmuring as he fell onto the sofa.

Father Mario and Captain Anderson talked quietly beside the Marine Corps sedan. "Father, in the envelope I gave to Mrs. Rossi it explains that there were few identifiable remains. They really did a job on him."

"I'll talk with the family, Captain. I'll find out what kind of service they prefer."

"Thank you, Father. Keep me posted so we can send in a color guard for the service whatever it turns out to be."

"I will, Captain. Thank you very much."

Salvatore walked to his bedroom with the manila envelope. He finished reading the action report, placed the contents back into the envelope and stared out of the bedroom window into the black of evening. A light snow was falling. He was cast back in time when Hugo was a boy and he would take him sledding at the foot of the hill on Plainfield Street, his nose running, cheeks red from the cold, smiling, laughing. He spoke out loud compulsively. "Oh, if I could only have him back with me for ten minutes!" There was emptiness to his being. It was as if he had vacated his body. The voice of Father Mario and Pat Lofredo roused him from the bed. He entered the kitchen to find Father Mario accompanied by Dr. Melfi. Father Mario turned as Salvatore appeared.

"Salvatore, I asked Dr. Melfi to administer some sedative to the women. I thought it was the best thing to do."

Dr. Melfi placed a hand on Salvatore's shoulder. "How are you, old friend? Do you want something?"

"No, no, Doctor, thank you for coming. I appreciate it." Father Mario donned his heavy wool topcoat and wrapped one arm around Salvatore's shoulders, squeezing tightly.

"I'll see you tomorrow. We can talk about the arrangements. Now take care of Francesca and Angelina, they need your strong hand."

The Lofredo's left in tears, promising to return the next day. The Natales followed, Mrs. Natale whimpering and Mr. Natale wheezing his way down the flight of stairs. Salvatore walked to Hugo's room. Angelina had succumbed to the sedative. Baby Hugo lay asleep in a crib next to the bed. He closed the door halfway quietly and walked to his bedroom. Francesca lay groggy from the sedative. He lay next to her, taking her into his arms. She came alert and embraced him, tears spilling from her eyes. She buried her face in his chest and spoke in anguished tones.

"We lost him, Salvatore. We lost our golden boy, our beautiful son, my only child. What do we do now, my husband? How do we go on, what do we do my sweet husband, what do we do?"

He rocked her gently in his arms. "Shh, shhh, sleep now, my sweetheart, sleep. ow we must think of his son, our only grandchild, we must think of him." She was soon in a fitful sleep.

He dressed in a winter jacket and walked the short distance to St. Bart's Church. He knelt at the altar and tried to pray. Images of Hugo flashed through his memory. His thoughts kept returning to the fateful moment at the club where he had backhanded his son and disowned him, and suddenly he came apart, crying out— "Oh, my son, my son! How much I love you! How much I love you!" A torrent of tears sprang from his eyes; his body shuddered and heaved with sobs. He looked up at the crucifix over the altar and spoke in a cracking voice. "I have now given you my son, my only son, what else will you ask of me? All I have tried to do is honor you and obey you, and you keep on taking my loved ones from me. Why, why God, why is it this way?" He lay his head on his hands at the altar rail until the dawn began to color the stained glass windows. He lifted his head, his gaze settling upon a statue of the Virgin Mary and the Baby Jesus. He rose from the altar, made the sign of the cross, buttoned his jacket and slowly walked the long aisle to the front entrance. He spoke to himself softly as he walked. "I will devote myself to my son's son. I will not fail in this. I will not fail."

Arrangements were made for a funeral service on a Saturday morning late in March. The Romano Funeral Home had received Hugo's remains and prepared them for burial. There would be no wake. The casket was sealed. The morning of the funeral dawned bright and cold. The church was filled to overflowing with people standing shoulder to shoulder in the aisles and along the rear of the church, a testament to the honor and high regard in which the community held Salvatore. The Gilborne family was there as were virtually all of Salvatore's fellow workers. Vito Ferruccio, with genuine sensitivity to the feelings of Salvatore and his family, discreetly seated himself and a contingent of Hugo's former colleagues in the rear-most pews, his aging face looking pale and grieved. Even Abe Ratsky was there, a yarmulke pinned tightly to his balding head, his wife gripping his hand in maternal pain.

A glowing eulogy was delivered by Father Mario and countless eyes glistened and women sobbed openly while the choir sang *Ave Maria*. As Father Mario concluded his remarks, a Marine Corporal in dress blue uniform made his way down the center aisle of the church on crutches. His left leg had been amputated above the knee. He arrived at the altar and spoke briefly with Father Mario who assisted him to the pulpit. Father Mario held the crutches as the Marine steadied himself in the pulpit.

"My name is Raymond Pescatore, I come from the Bronx. That's in New York City." He hesitated for a moment, gathering his thoughts. "Hugo was my best friend in the Marines. I came here today so you would know the whole story of what happened in Korea." He went on to recount the events leading up to Hugo's death. The church was in a hush. "He saved us, he was a hero. He deserves more than the Silver Star. I lost my leg in some action on the way back to our lines, but we all made it back because of Hugo. I think of him every day. I guess I always will."

His remarks over, Father Mario assisted him from the pulpit to the front pew where Salvatore had risen to greet him with outstretched arms. He embraced the young soldier, hugging him to his chest, and in that moment he felt as though a great weight was being lifted from his heart and that once again he had become reconciled with his God. The casket was carried to the gravesite by six Marines in dress blue, commands barked by a sharply creased Lieutenant. They rested the casket on a bier beneath a canopy and retreated to rifles stacked military fashion, muzzle against muzzle, a short distance away. A color guard in full dress uniform marched in lock step to the cadence of the Lieutenant's garbled rhythm, "Lef, rart, lef, rart." Two Marines carried the American Flag and the Marine Corps Flag. A third carried a brilliantly polished trumpet tucked under his right arm. They stood at attention during the short graveside service. The crowd crushed together, collars upturned, women clutching neck scarves, warm breath coming in steamy puffs. At one end of the crescent of mourners surrounding the bier stood Mr. and Mrs. Goldberg in their best Sabbath dress. Next to them stood a tall, shapely young woman in fashionable black with a broad brimmed black hat, a widow's veil concealing her face. A mane of strawberry blonde hair cascaded over the collar of her tailored coat.

Father Mario concluded the service. The color guard turned about face and marched a short distance to a large oak tree. The six pallbearers stood at parade rest, weapons by their side. A sharp command split the cold air. There was the sound of boot heels thudding together as the men came to attention, followed by the smacking of white gloved palms against rifle butts and forends. The young Lieutenant, now at attention, shouted a command, which was followed by the metallic click of sliding rifle bolts and a volley of six rifles held at a twenty degree angle focused the crowd. Two more volleys followed. The command was given to stand at parade rest. From a distance behind the oak tree came the trumpeter's mournful strains of Taps, moving many in the crowd to fresh tears. Two Marines folded the American flag that draped the coffin into a tight triangle and presented it to the Lieutenant with a precision salute. He turned to Angelina, who was seated with Salvatore, Francesca, and the Natales on folding chairs. He made a formal presentation of the flag to Angelina, bending from the waist as he made official remarks of condolence. He stepped back, saluted, made an about face, gave a succession of commands and marched the Marines to waiting vehicles. Angelina's red-rimmed eyes stared at the flag, lower lip trembling. Salvatore took her by the arm and walked her to the waiting limousine.

The crowd dispersed to cars parked haphazardly throughout the cemetery. The Goldberg's remained with the young woman in black. As the limousine carrying Angelina pulled away, the woman in black strode slowly to the bier. She reached inside her coat and removed a single red rose, raising it to her lips as she kissed it and placed it on top of the casket mouthing the words, "I love you." She turned and with the Goldberg's in the lead, walked to a Buick sedan with Massachusett's license plates. She assisted the Goldberg's into the back seat, took the drivers seat, and slowly pulled away to join the traffic exiting the cemetery.

The limousine carrying Angelina had stalled in the gridlock of cars departing the cemetery. Angelina turned in her rear seat to peer out the window for a final look at the casket bearing Hugo's remains. It was then that the woman in black caught her attention. She watched the tall shapely figure kissing the rose. She saw the strawberry blonde hair fall over her shoulders. She watched her assist the Goldberg's into the sedan with Massachusett's plates. And it was then that she knew.

Chapter 9

1957

For Salvatore, now in his sixties, time passed quickly. The birthdays and the feast days came and went with almost alarming speed; and baby Hugo, in what seemed like only a moment, became a young boy of five.

Grandfather and grandson were inseparable. Hugo's other grandparents, the Natales, had moved to Phoenix. Lorenzo's asthma was consuming him. The only remedy, said his doctor, was a dry climate. It was an emotional departure with countless hugs and kisses exchanged among family and old friends, all of whom had gathered at the airport to bid them farewell. They had been gone for five years. Lorenzo's health had been restored and they were living a modest but comfortable life in Phoenix. Lorenzo had done well in Rhode Island, owning two good-sized grocery stores and a laundromat. He had made a number of conservative investments that returned small but consistent dividends and he held the mortgage on two of the businesses he had sold.

They returned to Rhode Island every Christmas for a week and they sent money to Angelina twice a year so she could purchase airline tickets for a week's stay with them. Angelina's decision to remain in Rhode Island was prompted by her desire to be close to Salvatore, who she knew would be devastated if she moved to Phoenix with little Hugo. The boy was deeply attached to his grandfather, spending countless hours in his company. Each evening he waited impatiently at the window for "Papa" to return home from work, jumping excitedly when he saw him and waving at Salvatore who smiled broadly and waved in return.

Angelina enrolled Hugo in St. Bart's kindergarten, and Salvatore altered his work schedule so that he could walk Hugo to the noisy St. Bart's schoolyard each morning, turning him over to Mother Superior, but not without first receiving a hug and a smacking wet kiss. Hugo was generally playful and outgoing with the other boys and girls in his class, but he could be shy and reticent in large groups, particularly when older bullies antagonized the younger boys in the schoolyard. On these occasions, Hugo would retreat to an alcove at the side doorway of the school and observe with narrowed eyes and grim lips. He complained to Salvatore about the bigger "bad boys" in an anxious high-pitched voice. Salvatore held his hand firmly as they walked to school in their slow, steady gait and explained in childlike terms about good and evil, love and hatred. The child seemed to understand and would repeat, "Yes, Papa, I will" and "No, Papa, I won't." At the end of the day Francesca would wait for him at the schoolyard gate and walk him home for a snack of fresh fruit or Italian bread and provolone cheese. And on special occasions there would be a sweet or something freshly baked, like Francesca's ricotta pie.

THE ARRIVAL THE STRUGGLE THE ASCENDANCY

St. Bart's Church was a second home to Hugo. There were Sunday services, holiday preparations—and Hugo tagged after Salvatore wherever he went. The years rolled by. There was never a man in Angelina's life. She worked every day at a local jewelry manufacturing plant, finding companionship with friends and family, the center of her life being Hugo. Salvatore in his midsixties was still handsome, robust, and virile, sharing a passionate love with Francesca, who still had the figure of a younger woman. Salvatore had become an invaluable and trusted friend to Bill Gilborne. His skill at reviewing construction plans, no matter the size of the project, was legendary in the company. He worked at company headquarters overseeing operations and dealing with the never-ending problems with the laborers' union. Angelina's Uncle, Carlo Tronni, lived two houses away from Salvatore. Angelina felt she should have some independence for herself as well as for Hugo and accepted an inexpensive rental offered by Uncle Carlo for the second floor tenement. Salvatore and Francesca understood, reluctantly, her motivation. Little Hugo, on the other hand, badgered Angelina to sleep at Nana and Poppa's house as often as he could.

Hugo enjoyed the challenge of the schoolwork and did well in all his classes under the watchful, and brutal, eye of the Mother Superior, Sister Cecilia, who knew all and saw all, particularly concerning the boys at St. Bart's. One of her favorite targets was Hugo who, for no apparent reason, was frequently beaten with a yardstick, ruler, or whatever was in her grasp at the time. Hugo complained bitterly to Salvatore about the surprise beatings and hair pulling that Sister Cecilia would inflict upon him and he added that her breath always smelled of wine. Salvatore would listen patiently but unsympathetically, reprimanding him for talking badly about one of God's servants on earth.

It was in fourth grade that Sister Cecilia handed down an impossible assignment – the memorization of the entire Baltimore Catechism. The Baltimore Catechism was an outline, a treatise of the fundamentals of the Catholic religion. The very foundation of a young person's Catholic education, it was a tome in blue paperback showcasing the Virgin Mary in radiant pose on its front cover. In a cruel, tight lipped voice with narrowed eyes, Sister Cecilia threatened that any boy who could not recite the pages she asked for from memory would stay back and repeat the fourth grade. Hugo was the only boy out of twenty who passed the verbal exam, much to the annoyance of Sister Cecilia.

He had grown close to Kenny Golonio, a student in his class, as well as to his cousins, Richard and Carl Tronni, and they all shared friendships with many of the young boys living in Silver Lake. The Providence school system was bursting at the seams with students of all ages. The return of millions of World War II veterans had resulted in an unprecedented number of births beginning in 1943 through 1950. Playgrounds and baseball fields were in constant use. Various street corners were claimed by abutting neighborhood toughs and their young followers. Schoolyard games became more violent, usually resulting in the biggest bully holding sway by beating one or two boys into submission for no reason other than the desire to proclaim himself King of the Mountain. On these occasions, Hugo would retreat to the alcove and watch grimly.

Hugo had grown. He was tall for ten years of age and gangly. He and several friends joined the Boys Club, which was in the Olneyville section of Providence, a poor neighborhood teeming with Polish, Lithuanian, and Irish kids. The director at the club was a burly, jovial Polock everyone called Stash, who ruled the club with an iron hand. Hugo swam in the club's busy pool with dozens of other boys, most not wearing bathing suits. At every opportunity Stash would come to the pool and bellow, "If I catch one of you guys pissin in the pool, you're out for good. Unnastand?"

Boxing lessons were taught by a nineteen-year old black fighter who had won his class in a Golden Gloves bout in New York. He taught the basics, the rest was up to you. Hugo loved the boxing matches, two young boys wearing 16-oz gloves flailing away for three rounds. Hugo won all of the fights in his weight class and slowly gained the admiration and respect of the other ten and eleven-year olds as well as the younger teenagers. He was filling out. The older boys introduced him to weight lifting, but Stash put a stop to it, declaring that he had to wait until he was at least twelve. "Your joints aren't ready for this yet." Still, at every opportunity Hugo would sneak into the weight lifting area and quickly perform some exercises.

He was an excellent student. Angelina pressed him constantly, sat with him while he studied, watched as he did homework. She was fearful he would succumb to the street, but he never did. Rather, his religious beliefs grew deeper. He became an altar boy serving mass with Father Mario three times a week to the unending pride of Salvatore. There was baseball in the summer, football in the fall, and always his duty to St. Bart's.

It happened in the first week of the new school year of the sixth grade. A transfer from St. Ann's School in the north end of Providence was terrorizing the schoolyard at lunch break. His name was Gus Najarian. At twelve his huge bulk towered over the other children; and he recruited two cohorts who, together, would surround their victim demanding money or whatever else happened to be in his pockets.

Najarian was menacing in appearance. He was marked by his Armenian heritage—a hooknose, bushy eyebrows, swarthy complexion, and the beginnings of a five o'clock shadow on his cheeks. He bragged about "fucken the college girl on the second floor every night." His victim one afternoon was Hugo's best friend, Kenny Golonio. Hugo watched from the alcove, heart pounding, as they surrounded him. No one came to his aid. Golonio refused Najarian's demands and raised his fists in defense. Najarian's eyebrows rose in surprise. His right fist shot out landing squarely on Golonio's chin, knocking him to the ground. He raised his arms in strong man fashion turning to the circle of boys fascinated by the violence. "I'm the King of the Mountain, I'm the King, you all hear me?" The moment his fist shot out an explosion occurred somewhere inside of Hugo. Something that had been growing within him erupted. He leapt from the alcove, legs churning, arms pumping, head lowered. He charged at Najarian with a consuming fury. As Najarian turned in exultation, his arms raised in strong man pose, his stomach was exposed. At that moment Hugo's head smashed into Najarian's solar plexus, expelling every bit of air in his lungs and knocking him flat to the ground. Hugo fell upon him, savagely beating him with both fists until blood gushed from his nose and oozed from his cheeks. Hugo grasped his hair and began pounding his head against the gravel of the school yard. The circle of cheering boys came to an abrupt halt as Sister Cecilia crashed through the ring flailing her yardstick, whipping Hugo on the back and shoulders.

Salvatore was called to the school by Father Mario. Father Mario sat behind a large, dark institutional desk, fingers intertwined, hands resting on the edge of the desk. Behind him hung a large crucifix, and in a corner of the room stood the flags of Rhode Island and the United States. Sunshine streamed into the office from two large windows fronting on the boys' schoolyard below. Sister Cecilia stood to one side of the desk next to a photograph of Pope John XXIII. Salvatore knocked on the office door lightly and entered the office pushing the half-opened door fully open. Hugo entered first.

"Good morning, Hugo, good morning Salvatore." Father Mario rose as he greeted them. Salvatore and Hugo answered in unison, "Good morning, Father." Salvatore turned to Sister Cecilia. "Good morning, Mother Superior." Sister Cecilia haughtily nodded in his direction, unsmilingly. Hugo stared at the floor until prodded by Salvatore. "Good morning, Mother Superior" he said listlessly. She responded by shifting her gaze to his direction. Father Mario smiled slightly, breaking the chill in the room.

"Please, Salvatore, Hugo, be seated." They sat directly in front of Father Mario. "Salvatore, you know why I asked you to come in?"

"Yes, I do, Father. It concerns a fight in the schoolyard that involved my grandson."

"Yes, that's right. Did he tell you what happened to the young Najarian boy?" Father Mario's gaze fell upon Hugo as he spoke.

"No, Father, he didn't give me all the details." Sister Cecilia stood by coldly, eyes piercing Hugo as he stared at the floor.

"Well, Salvatore, I'm told the boy has a broken nose and severe lacerations to the right side of his face. This is very serious, very serious." Father Mario sat back in his creaky wooden chair, raised his eyebrows and threw a hand up in exasperation. "The mother wants to call the police, a lawyer. She has no money for the hospital, the doctor. She's a divorced woman with three other children." Sister Cecilia stood, head erect, smugly waiting for Salvatore's response.

"Well, Father, I agree this is very serious business, and because it is serious, I would appreciate it if you would allow Hugo to tell his version of the story."

"That will not be necessary," Sister Cecilia snapped before Salvatore had finished his last word. "I witnessed the whole violent episode, it was brutal." She stood face flushed, breathing rapidly. Father Mario raised a hand to silence Sister Cecilia.

"No, I think it's important to hear what Hugo has to say. After all, he is being accused of a serious breech of discipline. Go on Hugo, tell us what happened."

Hugo raised his head to look directly at Father Mario. His jaw was firmly set. There was a look of disbelief in his misting eyes. He turned to look out the window. He spoke in a terse, strained voice. "I did what I had to do." There was dead silence as they waited for more. Salvatore lowered his head to look at his grandson, eyebrows raised in expectation. Father Mario leaned forward.

"Well, Hugo, is there more you want to tell us?"

He shook his head. "No, Father."

Salvatore looked at Father Mario and shrugged his shoulders in exasperation. Father Mario nodded in understanding. Father Mario sat back in his chair, arms folded, staring at his desktop. He spoke as he rose from his chair. "Well, Salvatore, Hugo, let me think about this a little longer. I'll talk with you tomorrow.

Salvatore, thank you for coming in today. It's always good to see you. Hugo, you go ahead and join your class. Mother Superior, please stay a minute."

Much to the chagrin of Sister Cecilia, there was no expulsion or punishment for Hugo. Salvatore paid the boy's medical bills and Father Mario offered free tuition for the next two years. In return, the boy's mother ceased her threats against Hugo and the school.

Gus Najarian refused to accept defeat. His bullying continued in the schoolyard and on the adjacent streets after school let out. One Friday afternoon he waited two streets over from St. Bart's with six other toughs, older than himself but still intimidated by him. He knew that this was the route home taken by Hugo and his friends. Hugo, Kenny Golonio, Al Vacolla, and Richard O'Ryan slowly strode along the sidewalk, swapping baseball cards and sharing bubble gum from the card packages. It was Friday, the weekend was ahead, and the best Western of the year, *The Man Who Shot Liberty Valance*, with John Wayne, was playing at the Rainbow Theatre on Pocasset Avenue.

"Hey, you guys, let's go to the afternoon show tomorrow." It was Al Vacolla excitedly planning the next day's activity. "The tickets are cheaper in the afternoon and they got two cartoons and Superman serials." Hugo and Ken readily agreed, but Richard O'Ryan looked dejectedly at his friends. "I can't go, I have to work at my Uncle's market tomorrow, baggin orders and helping the old ladies with their groceries. Boy, I wish I didn't have to." As he spoke, Najarian and his schoolyard gang materialized from the corner of a building. The seven of them spread across the sidewalk with Gus in the center.

"Well, well, if it ain't the little azzhole and his azzhole partners who I am now gonna beat the shit out of." As Gus spoke, he held his hands on his hips puffing out his chest, a smirk twisting his corpulent lips. "You don't got nobody to stop me today, azzhole, so don't even think of runnin anywhere because you're surrounded."

In the first moments of the surprise confrontation the six toughs had filtered to the rear and flank of Hugo and his friends. Hugo's heart pounded like a trip hammer; his breathing came rapidly. He knew there was no way out except through Najarian.

"Hugo, whadda we gonna do?" whispered Kenny Golonio. All eyes were on Hugo. No one moved, no one spoke. This was obviously a showdown between Gus Najarian, who was now toying with the much smaller Hugo." Hugo's eyes bore into Najarian's.

"Whatsa matta, azzhole? You shitten your pants? Why don't you call your grandfadda. He's not too far away, heah, heah, heah." His laughter caused the other toughs to join in the taunting. "You see this, azzhole?" Najarian held himself by the scrotum. "I'm gonna stick it up your fat azz right now in front of your queer little friends."

As he spoke the towering, black-clad figure of Sister Cecilia accompanied by Sister Vivian descended upon the confrontation as if out of nowhere. Face contorted and flushed, eyes ablaze, the yardstick raised and poised as a scimitar, she shrieked, "Gus Najarian, you filthy little animal, I heard and saw everything you just did." The yardstick cut the air like a whip and smashed into Najarian's neck, instantly raising a welt. She continued raining blows on Najarian's head and torso as he backed away, crouching and protecting his head with his arms, finally turning and running for safety with his cohorts on his heels. As Sister Cecilia and Sister

THE ARRIVAL THE STRUGGLE THE ASCENDANCY

Vivian gave chase, clutching at their habits, Hugo and his friends quickly faded from sight.

There was to be no further incidents with Gus Najarian. Less than a month later he was taken out of his classroom and sent to the boy's training school after beating his mother senseless.

The news of Najarian's defeat spread like wildfire at St. Bart's. Hugo was now looked upon as the defender of the down trodden and the put upon, and he found himself involved in numerous confrontations and brawls, all under the watchful eye of Sister Cecilia, who proceeded to build her case against Hugo, documenting every incident on and off school grounds. Salvatore was summoned to school twice more during the sixth grade school year. He was not pleased.

Salvatore sat in his favorite chair puffing on his yellow bowl pipe. Hugo sat on a couch directly in front of him, eyes downcast, white knuckled, hands gripping his knees in anticipation of his grandfather's impassioned lecture. Salvatore removed the yellow bowl from his mouth and exhaled a plume of smoke. It was Saturday afternoon and Hugo was not allowed to leave the apartment.

"So tell me, Hugo, what is all this fighting business about? Is there something you should tell me about school? Are people bothering you at school? All this fighting could lead to you being expelled. Do you know this?" Hugo nodded in acknowledgment without raising his head. "Hugo, talk with me, tell me what's going on. I have to see Father Mario next week – again!"

This time Hugo raised his head and looked squarely at Salvatore, a plaintive expression in his eyes. "Papa…" he paused groping for words. "It's not what you think. I…I don't like to see my friends being beat up by a bully. It's not right. I don't like it." The words poured out. "Papa, most of the time they get jumped from behind. That's a dirty thing to do to somebody. Nobody stops it, somebody has to stop it. And it's always the older kids, the bigger kids who do this."

Salvatore listened quietly puffing on the yellow bowl. Francesca peeked into the parlor. "Ay, you two, I just took a pizza out of the oven, you can have one piece each. We're going to have dinner in a little while." The aroma of tomatoes and garlic filled the apartment. Salvatore smiled at his wife and nodded in response. "So tell me, Hugo, is it always necessary to fight these boys? Isn't there something else you can do to solve the problem? Do you tell the Mother Superior or Father Mario?"

"Papa, they don't listen to me. They think I cause all the troubles, especially Sister Cecilia. She can't wait to hit me with something. And Father Mario, he listens to Sister Cecilia. Whatever she says, he believes." The sounds of the oven door opening and closing, the clatter of dishes and the jangle of silverware emanated from the kitchen. Hugo returned his gaze to the carpet. Salvatore removed the pipe from his mouth, leaned forward and cupped Hugo's chin in his left hand raising his eyes to meet his own.

"I can find nothing wrong with someone who wishes to defend someone from a bunch of bullies or who has to defend himself from a bully. These things happen in life. I understand this. What I don't think is right is if you take it upon yourself to be a … what do you call them, oh yes, vigilante, like in those cowboy stories you like to watch on the television. The vigilantes take the law into their own hands and sometimes they're wrong. Do you understand what I mean?"

"Yes, Papa."

"Good, now what I want you to promise me is that you won't go looking for trouble at school. Will you promise me that?"

"Yes, Papa I promise. But what do I do if they come looking for me?" "Then you must defend yourself with honor, and honor means fighting fairly and never giving up the battle, *capito?*"

"Yes, Papa, I understand."

"Hugo."

"Yes Papa?"

"I will be very disappointed if you don't follow my wishes in this matter."

"Yes, Papa. I won't disappoint you."

"Good, come on, let's go to supper. I think your grandmother has a good meal for us, and I just heard your mother come in." Salvatore bent to embrace Hugo and kiss his forehead. "I love you, my little son."

"I love you too, Papa, and I love Nana, too."

With supper finished, Angie insisted, over the strenuous objections of Hugo, that he return home with her to complete the homework assigned by Sister Cecilia. Francesca intervened with the promise of a chocolate cake the next day. Salvatore had retired to his parlor chair and his newspaper. He called out to Hugo as he and Angie were leaving the apartment.

"Hugo, come here for a minute."

"What, Papa?"

"After school tomorrow I want you to meet me at the church. I need you to help me set up some chairs in the basement, and the altar needs some polishing. And don't hang around with your friends first, come over right after you get out, understand?"

"Yes, Papa, I'll be there."

Salvatore returned to his paper, pausing to fill the yellow bowl and light it. As he shook the match dead, Francesca entered the parlor with her knitting basket, settling on the couch across from Salvatore.

"You know, I heard you talking with the baby." She always referred to Hugo as the baby, and she would the rest of her life. For Francesca, it would always be Baby Hugo. "You never told him that you were angry, you never laid down the law." She busied herself with her knitting. "Why didn't you give him…"—she paused searching for the right word—"an ultimatum? You were too easy. It's as if you approved of his actions; that's what it seemed like to me." The clicking of the knitting needles was the only sound in the room. The radio was off and they rarely watched the television, even though Salvatore had bought a new color set the previous Christmas so that Francesca could watch the Perry Como Show, her favorite, on Wednesday evenings. Salvatore lowered the paper to his lap and set the pipe in a tall stand next to his chair.

"Francesca, I listened to everything the boy had to say and I weighed the positive and the negative of what he told me. I also know our grandson to be honest. I know his character. Actually, I'm proud of his motivation. And if you notice, Father Mario, through his silence, can find no wrong in what he does."

"Yes, but what about Sister Cecilia, she would call the police on him if she could."

"Well, Sister Cecilia probably should have gotten married instead of becoming a nun. I think that's her problem."

Francesca's mouth dropped open and her eyes widened in an expression of disbelief. "Salvatore, she's a good woman. You shouldn't talk about a woman who's devoting her life to Christ."

Salvatore resumed reading the paper obscuring himself from Francesca and concealing the broad smile that broke out as he spoke from behind his paper. "Don't you worry, Nana, our boy will turn out to be a good man, that I can assure you."

The rest of the school year was relatively tranquil. Sister Cecilia maintained her vigilant stalking of Hugo, reporting any real or imagined infraction to Father Mario who considered the source and placated her with promises of strict disciplinary measures. Hugo's grades were good to excellent, and he genuinely looked forward to his duties as altar boy. Father Mario broached the subject of attending a seminary to test the waters of his faith. The subject was left dangling.

Summer vacation was met by whoops and hollers as the school was let out on its final day. Hugo had completed the sixth grade near the top of his class much to the pride of Angelina, Salvatore, and Francesca. Summer was a blur of activity, full of baseball in the local playgrounds and swimming at Joslin Street Pool and Merino Park. There were rough-hewn rafts plying Silver Lake Pond, forays to the dump at the end of Silver Lake Avenue, and in the evening, beneath green and white enamel street lights, ring-a-levio and kick the can. The older boys and young men of the "Lake" staked out various corners to gather at, to socialize, and to use as a jumping off point for other destinations. This territory was jealously guarded, and members of other corners were met with hostile glares and vocal jibes as they crossed the street to avoid confrontation while walking on Pocasset Avenue, the neighborhood's main drag.

Each corner was populated by ten to twenty older boys and young men with a contingent of younger boys hanging out on the fringe, eagerly waiting their turn to be accepted into the gang. There were gangs at Pete's Pharmacy, Laurel Pharmacy, Wellington's Ice Cream Parlor, and Spotty's Spa. There was an unwritten law that applied on all the corners: You were always polite and chivalrous to the mother, grandmother, sister, or any adult member of any gang member's family, and you never caused a problem for the owner of the business who claimed the corner as an extension of his front entrance.

Vinny Testa was the uncrowned leader of the guys who hung out at the Laurel Pharmacy. Big Vinny was nineteen and lived two houses over from the pharmacy. He had been lifting weights at the Providence YMCA since he was thirteen and had developed a muscular physique. During the summer months he worked shirtless on a construction crew for Gamino Brothers and wore a dark perpetual tan from May to October. On summer evenings he held sway on the corner, turned out in a sleeveless white tee shirt contrasted against his walnut skin. His slicked-backed black hair glistened with peach pomade. Draped around his neck was a heavy gold chain carrying a large gold medallion of Madona and Child worn more for fashion than religious symbol. From his narrow waist fell cream colored or black pleated Italian slacks complemented by tassled slip-ons with no socks. He was the envy of many young men on the Avenue.

Sitting in front of the pharmacy was the object of Vinny's love—his new Chevy Impala convertible, its black paint shining to a deep, almost liquid luster, its bright red interior offset by white pin-striping. The men and boys of the corner gathered around the Chevy like a primitive tribe gathered around its sacred idol, each keeping a respectful distance, daring not so much as to lean against the holy object. Cars cruised the Avenue, their drivers calling out "aayy Vinneee!" respectfully as they passed; and as the great leader of the pharmacy corner, he acknowledged their shouted greetings and horn honking with a bellowed response, "Aayy, Nickeee!" In this manner the street theatre continued most evenings all summer long.

It was Hugo's cousin Carl who would dally on one end of the corner, furthest from center stage where the older guys dominated, after finishing his ice cream cone. He struck his own pose, cajoling Hugo, Al Vacolla, Dennis Pickles, Richard O'Ryan, and his own brother, Richard, to hang around for a while. "C'mon, we don't have to go home right away. It's still early." The boys all swiveled their heads toward Big Vinny and the older guys. "C'mon, Vinny doesn't care if we stay here. He knows all of us, we're not doin anything."

Richard O'Ryan whispered from behind his hand, "Carl, you know him, this is his corner. You have to ask him if we can stay. He's a cuckoo clock." At that moment Joey 'No Azz' Merlino set his eyes on the group. He was leaning back against the pharmacy wall, one leg up behind him supporting his balance, cigarette dangling from the corner of his mouth. "Aayy, Vinny, did we axe for company on our corner? Whadda dese little shits doin over here?" All eyes turned to Hugo and his friends. Big Vinny turned, hands on hips.

"Aayy, youse little peanuts, get ova here— now!" Hugo and his friends shuffled over to Big Vinny. "You." He pointed to Richard O'Ryan. "What's your name?"

O'Ryan's voice was changing; he almost yodeled, "Richard O'Ryan."

"What the fucks an Irishman doin up here?" cracked Joey No Azz.

"And what's your name, you skinny minny?" asked Vinny, now pointing to Hugo.

Hugo looked at Big Vinny for several seconds, taking in the clothes and the hair and settling his eyes on the big gold medallion. "Rossi," he said softly, "Hugo Rossi."

Big Vinny's face took on a subdued expression. "Your Sal Rossi's kid, ain't you?"

"No, he's my grandfather. My father was a hero in the Korean War. His name was Hugo, too; they named a square for him down a couple of streets from here."

"Yeah, yeah, I heard about that." Big Vinny cracked his knuckles as he spoke. "All right, youse guys can stay on my corner over there where you were, unnastand?" They all nodded their heads in understanding. "Now, as a condition for me letting you hang out here, if I need something youse guys are gonna run and get it, *capice?*"

"Whatever you need, Vinny. Okay, Vinny!" they all chorused together.

"All right, go back over there. Anybody bother you, you come see me." The gathering at Laurel's Pharmacy became an evening ritual, with other boys joining the corner gang always under the bemused eye of Big Vinny. It was in late August that Big Vinny was suddenly missing from the corner. His absence was conspicuous. His gregarious personality had lit up the corner; now, the nightly gatherings took on the mood of a union meeting, dull and humorless. Finally, Hugo mustered the courage to approach Joey No Azz.

"Hey, Joey, where's Vinny? He hasn't been around for a week. Is he all right?" To Hugo's surprise, Joey motioned to Hugo to come closer and divulged the scandal as if Hugo were an equal.

"What happened is that Vinny was caught bangin Mafalda Izzo. Her husband is one of the top guys on the Hill. Where is he now, nobody knows. Somebody said he drove to his Aunt's house in New Jersey and joined the Marines." Joey looked out at the street, grimaced and shook his head. "Aayy, Hugo, not a word to anybody, you got it?"

"Yeah, Joey, I got it. Promise."

Evenings were not the same without Big Vinny on the corner. The luster was gone. Joey No Azz tried to take charge but he couldn't pull it off. For one thing, Joey was homely and had the physique of Ichabod Crane. For another, he didn't own a car. The rest of the gang just couldn't accept him as the big dog. Even Joey knew it. For Hugo, the loss of Vinny signaled that the summer had come to an end. He was ready to return to school—Sister Cecelia and all.

Summer came to a close molting into an early autumn chill and the start of the seventh grade. There was a feeling of exhilaration in the air with the anticipation of the first day of school. The fragrance of burning leaves and the first glimpse of reddening oak leaves confirmed the change of season.

The first day of school was now a routine matter—the assignment of classrooms, the issuance of books, the curiosity at the arrival of new students, and the determination to do better than last year. For the first time in the history of St. Bart's there were to be mixed classes, with boys on one side of the classroom and girls on the other. This created quite a stir among the girls as well as the boys who were suddenly confronted with a desire to ogle the more developed girls, budding into their early teens, but not wishing to run afoul of Sister Cecilia or Sister Vivian.

Amy Lee Randal sat directly opposite Hugo. She was twelve years old and tall for her age. Hugo was fascinated by her golden banana curls that hung well below her shoulders. Her pink creamy complexion was set off by large brilliant blue eyes. Her family had recently arrived from Georgia and lived in a large gabled Victorian home on the best part of Farmington Avenue, a neighborhood of historic homes on the hillside overlooking the Silver Lake business district. She spoke with a soft southern drawl and was immediately hated by most of the girls in the class. Hugo, in thirty seconds, had lost his twelve-year old heart to the young southern belle.

Amy Lee worked her natural southern charm on Sister Vivian, who was the homeroom teacher. She was soon delivering messages about the school, clapping erasers clean, and ingratiating herself to Sister Cecilia with her prim and proper attitude and religious demeanor. One brisk, golden October afternoon Hugo lingered at the entrance to the girl's schoolyard as classes were dismissed. She was unmistakable in the crowd of jabbering girls. The setting sun glistening off her bobbing curls. She spotted Hugo at the entrance shuffling about, acting as nonchalantly as possible and failing miserably. She knew he was there for her. She peeled away from her friends as they exited the gate and approached Hugo. He caught his breath as she approached.

"Ha, Hugo, you waitin fa me?" She stood there in all her radiant beauty, head tilted to one side, a dazzling smile, cradling a stack of books at her waist. Hugo spun around to face her. "Oh, hi, Amy." He was befuddled, lightheaded.

"Well, are you goin to carry my books home for me?" Hugo quickly took the books from her hands, unsure of what to do next. "C'mon silly, you goin to walk with me?"

He smiled, suddenly regaining his composure. "Of course I am. Wadda you think I was waiting here for, Sister Cecilia?" They both burst out laughing, she demurely covering her laugh with one hand and casting a half-cautious glance at the convent. They walked slowly toward Farmington Avenue. She chattered nonstop and he listened in near silence, totally beguiled by her soft breathy drawl.

"You know, Hugo, ah don't know a thing about you. What does your Daddy do for a livin anyway?"

"My father was killed in the Korean War. He was a hero. As a matter of fact, they named a corner for him. It's about four streets down from here." He pointed down Pocasset Avenue as they crossed the street starting the climb toward Farmington Avenue.

"Oh, Hugo, ahm so sorry. You must miss him a lot."

"Well, I was only a baby when he went into the Marines, so I don't really remember much about him. My mother has lots of pictures though, so I know what he looked like."

"Ah'll bet he was real good lookin, 'cause you're pretty cute yourself." The words tumbled from her smiling pink lips as her glittering blue eyes watched for Hugo's reaction. "Waa, Hugo, you're turnin beet red." She stopped walking and turned to Hugo who now faced her, books in hand, lost in her mischievous smile and fluttering eyelids. "Well, silly boy, what do you have to say for yourself?"

Hugo gulped and blurted out, "You're the prettiest girl I've ever seen in my whole life."

"Well, I sure do like that." She wrapped her arm around Hugo's and they continued the slow ascent toward Farmington Avenue. Hugo was in rapture. Neither one spoke, not wanting to break the magical spell. "Well, Hugo, what does your Granddaddy do for a livin?"

"My Papa is a construction superintendent, everybody knows him. He works for Gilborne Construction, they build all over the country. He's built some of the biggest buildings in New England. In fact, he's building a hospital in Boston right now."

"My Mama says that eye-talians are the best builders in the world on account of all the building they did in Rome and the rest of Europe, especially with cement and marble."

"Well, yeah, you're mother's right. Most of my grandfather's workers are Italian."

"So what exactly does your Father do?"

"Well, he does a lot of things. He's called a consulting textile engineer. When a company has problems, they call him. Right now he's over at the Cranston Dye Works fixing some problem."

They had arrived at a stately Victorian trimmed with elegant cornices and buttresses. "Well, we're her. C'mon in and meet my Mama." Hugo followed the bobbing curls to a short flight of stairs to a screened porch and a rear door. The fragrance of baking cookies wafted through a large, well equipped kitchen. A tall attractive blond woman turned from an oven wiping her hands on a dish towel. A large black woman in a white apron looked up and smiled as she chopped vegetables on a maple block.

"Well, ha honey!" The blond woman broke into a dazzling smile. She was an older version of her daughter, thought Hugo. "You brought home one of your school friends?"

THE ARRIVAL THE STRUGGLE THE ASCENDANCY

"Ha, Mama, this is Hugo Rossi. His Granddaddy is an engineer, just like Daddy."

"Well, hello, Hugo, ah'm so pleased to meet you. Ah'm always happy to meet Amy's friends." She turned to the oven, talking as she drew open the door. "Ah have some fresh baked oatmeal cookies for you two and some nice cold milk. C'mon and sit here at the table, Hugo." They made small talk as they ate the warm cookies. Amy's mother asked about Angelina and Salvatore and rambled on about the house, her husband, and all the traveling they did because of the nature of her husband's work. Hugo found it easy to talk to this woman, and he made it a point to say "please" and "thank you" as often as he could fit them into a sentence.

"Mama, I'm goin to show Hugo the bowlin alley." Hugo was pushing the last cookie in his mouth when Amy spoke.

"All right, honey, you two have fun. Ah'll be back shortly. Ah have to pick up some groceries at the First National store."

"We will, Mama."

She left with the black woman in tow carrying a large cloth shopping sack. Amy held a curtain aside watching as the green Buick sedan pulled out of the driveway. "C'mon, ah'm gonna show you something in the basement." They descended into a dark musty cellar. There was the faint odor of fuel oil in the air. In the center of the room stood an old cast iron coal furnace that had been converted to heating oil. She reached for Hugo's hand and tugged him to the far side of the unlit basement. Running the length of the cellar wall dimly lit by two casement windows was a ten-pin bowling alley complete with pins and six dull pitted balls. The lane had long ago lost its luster and now stood as a relic of some past family history. She held tightly to Hugo's hand as they stood staring at the blank lane. Hugo could feel her quickened pulse beating against his wrist. She moved closer so that her hip touched his. He was floating in ecstatic delight. "Well, sweet boy, what do you think?" Her voice had the edge of a tremble to it.

"Boy, this is something. They had their own...." Before he could finish she pushed him against the foundation wall with her body, wrapped her arms around his upper back and placed her warm soft lips against his, kissing him wet lipped, passionately. Hugo's surprise turned instantly to excitement. He pulled her closer to him, kissing her forcefully. He felt the swelling in his trousers. She pushed her stomach and hips against Hugo, who instinctively pushed back, their rapid breathing punctuated by her small sounds of delight. She reached for Hugo's hand, their lips never parting. She drew his hand up under her plaid uniform skirt, guiding his fingers till they found their destination. Reaching down, lips still locked together, she unzipped his trousers, her hand found its destination, sending an electric spasm through his entire body.

They never heard the cellar door squeal open. Suddenly, the cellar was bathed in bare bulb luminescence. "Ha, y'all, Mama's home, ya hear? Amy, honey, you down there with your friend, Hugo? Amy, honey?"

"Yes, Mama, we were just coming up, that's why I shut the lights off. We'll be right up."

"Well, you hurry now, your Daddy will be home soon and we'll be havin dinner, ya here?"

"Yes, Mama." She smiled at Hugo as she smoothed out her skirt, tossing back her banana curls with both hands. "C'mon, you silly boy," she whispered, "we have to go upstairs." Hugo stood bewildered by the whole episode, still conscious of the swelling below. "C'mon, silly boy," she smile, "you got to put that down."

"Amy Lee, honey, your Daddy's gonna be home soon. Visitin times ova and you've got homework to do. I want you up here now, ya hear?"

"Comin, Mama." They entered the kitchen, Hugo quietly closing the cellar door, reluctant to turn toward Amy's mother, turning finally, relieved that she had her back to the kitchen busy at the sink. The large black woman smiled slyly at Hugo as she cracked eggs into a metal bowl.

"Well, I guess I'd better be going," he announced, his voice struggling for normalcy. "My mother's gonna wonder where I am." Amy's mother turned from the sink, wiping her hands with her apron.

"Well, Hugo, it was nice to meet you and y'all come back now, ya hear." "Thank you, Mrs. Randall, I sure will. Bye now."

Amy took his hand leading him out onto the screened porch. It was after five. The sun had set and the early evening had turned cool. Amy turned to Hugo, long eyelashes fluttering. "Ahm so glad you came by today, Hugo. Ah really like the way you kiss me. It really feels so good, don't you think?"

Hugo was lost for words. "I ahh...well...can I walk you home tomorrow?" He blurted the words out.

"Ah course, silly boy. Maybe we can do some more bowlin." She smiled with raised eyebrows. He smiled while inhaling deeply, his wildest hopes realized.

"Hey, where were you till this time? It's after five, you're grandfather's been looking for you. You were supposed to help him at St. Barts, what happened?"

"I ahh...umm...was at my friends house from school. I lost track of time." He looked everywhere except at Angelina as he spoke.

"So who's this friend? Do I know him?" She knew her son, knew that he was hiding something from her.

"Well, uhh...actually it's a girl...friend...Amy Lee Randall. She's new in school. I ahh...walked her home...I met her mother."

"Are they nice people, where are they from?"

"She's from Georgia. Her father's an engineer."

"That's nice, maybe you should bring her by sometime to say hello."

"Yeah, I will, Ma."

"All right, put your stuff in your room. We're going next door for dinner and you'll have to tell Papa why you forgot to meet him." She watched as he walked slowly to his bedroom, a slight stoop in his posture. "Hey, what did you do at your friend Amy's house anyway?"

Hugo turned unable to stop the blush rising in his cheeks. "Nuthin...we ahh...she umm...showed me the house, stuff like that, and her mother baked some cookies." He shrugged his shoulders.

"All right, hurry up, they must be waiting for us." She watched as he entered his room. "He's growing up" she muttered to herself.

He carried Amy's books home almost every school night, anticipation giddying his senses. Their secret trysts took place either in the basement next to the bowling alley, in her pink and white lace room, or in a large tool shed behind the old Victorian. Angelina became concerned with his waning attention to school, family, and friends. She shared her suspicions with Salvatore and Francesca.

"I think he's doing something with the little girl from St. Bart's. Maybe not all the way, but it seems to me that that's all that's on his mind these days, and he hasn't received communion for the past two Sundays." Francesca exchanged glances with Salvatore who smiled slightly as he took Angelina's hand.

"Listen, sweetheart, he's only a boy. This is called puppy love. All boys have their first crush on a little girl. It's natural. Don't you worry about it, you understand?"

"I suppose you're right." She paused bringing her intertwined hands to her mouth. "It's just that he needs a father at a time like this. Thank God, Salvatore, you're as close to him as you are. Without you I don't know what I'd do."

Francesca rose from the kitchen chair and wrapped her arms around Angelina's shoulders, pressing her cheek to hers. "Don't you worry, Angie, together we'll bring up a good man, *capito*?"

"Yes, Ma, I hope so. He's all I've got."

Salvatore picked his pipe from a pouch on the kitchen table and lit it with a long wooden match looking at Angelina through puffs of aromatic smoke. Francesca was pouring coffee. He shook the flame from the match and deposited it in an ashtray.

"Angie, you know Leo Zartanian, the plumber?"

"Yes, Pa, he did some work at my house. In fact, he had to come back a couple of times, once for the sink and another time for the tub drain. Why do you ask?" Francesca wore a half smile as she placed a dish of almond cookies on the table.

"He asked me yesterday if it would be alright if he called you."

Angelina threw her head back and laughed loudly. "Oh my God, what did you say?"

"I told him that was your decision to make, but that I had no objection to it because he's a good and respectable man."

"I don't know, Pa, he's a nice enough man, but I'm not ready for that yet, not yet, maybe someday." Francesca leaned across the table taking Angelina's hand.

"Listen, you're a young woman, you have your whole life in front of you. Go out with him, he's a widower and a very good man. We know the entire family. They're very respectable."

"I don't know, Ma, maybe. I'll think about it."

Hugo waited with anticipation for the bobbing golden curls to appear amidst the cluster of chattering girls as they emerged from the girls' double doorway. It was Monday. He hadn't seen or talked to Amy since Wednesday. He had walked to the house on Friday afternoon. The windows were dark, there was no car in the driveway. The girls came streaming through the gate, some smiling at him as if they knew something he didn't. A crowd of girls stood on the sidewalk fifteen feet from the gate entrance giggling and glancing his way, suddenly breaking into a chorus, "Haa, Hugo, Baa, Hugo!" then turning and walking away delirious with laughter. There was a tap on his shoulder. He turned. It was Mary Healy, Amy's closest school friend. She held a small envelope in her hand. "Hugo, Amy wanted me to give you this." She uttered the words with great seriousness, handed the letter to Hugo, and walked quickly away.

Hugo tore the envelope open and read. He could hear her voice in her bold, cursive long hand: *Hi, Hugo, I can't believe this is happening. Ma Daddy had an emergency in North Carolina and we're leaving Wednesday, that's today. I'm going to miss you so much, especially bowling with you, ha, ha! I hope we meet up again soon. I don't know what I'll do without you. All my love, Amy.*

Hugo felt his heart sinking into his stomach. He jammed the letter into his pocket and walked slowly home. Two days later as Angelina was preparing laundry and sorting through Hugo's dirty clothes when she came upon the crumpled note and read Amy's cryptic goodbye. She immediately called Francesca and told her of the contents. Together they speculated wildly on what the cryptic allusion might "bowling with you" mean, but both agreed that it was by God's grace that the little vixen had been forced to move away. Hugo was saved.

As the school year wore on his thoughts of Amy slowly evaporated and he put all of his energies into schoolwork and church. He had absolved himself of sin in the confessional, stammering and stuttering his way through the description of his illicit dalliance with the young southern femme fatale. His penance of twenty Hail Mary's and twenty Our Father's came as a relief.

Then, on a bright cold day in November, Hugo's small personal loss was overwhelmed and utterly annihilated by a loss of far greater proportions. The assassination of President John Kennedy rocked Rhode Island as it did the entire country. A strong-hold of the Democratic Party, Providence and its vast Catholic immigrant population was in deep mourning over the death of the Irishman who—despite all his wealth and glamour—they thought of as "one of us." Salvatore had taken the news hard, and Francesca and

Angelina wept openly in one another's arms. Not since the death of Father Cavalaro had there been such an outpouring of grief and loss at St. Bart's church. Still, not even the death of a beloved President could slow the inexorable advance of time. Soon Thanksgiving had given way to Christmas, and Christmas to Easter, so that in what seemed like no time at all the seventh grade was coming to a close. Snowfall had long since melted away, the vernal equinox was in the air, and the promise of summer edged its way into the spring seeding and planting of the many small plots of land behind the little single-family homes in and around Silver Lake. The exhilaration of summer was heightened by Salvatore's renting of a spacious three-bedroom cottage at Scarborough Beach for two weeks in July. The dates coincided with Angelina's forced, unpaid vacation when the state's many jewelry plants closed for their annual two-week period. It was a glorious summer. Hugo's cousins, Richard and Carl, were regular visitors to the cottage, and the three boys spent the long July Fourth weekend exploring, fishing, and swimming in perfect summer weather. August was filled with baseball and hanging out with friends at the Laurel Pharmacy, the corner now abandoned by the older guys who apparently never recovered from the disappearance of Big Vinny. There had been another significant loss that year, though few noted it with any public display of regret or sorrow. Domenic Zarraga had died at 78 while cavorting with a nineteen-year-old black striptease artist at his East Side apartment. The medical examiner who arrived on the scene determined the cause of death as a massive coronary brought about by severe exertion. It also stated in the report that although Zarraga had been dead for forty-five minutes, he still maintained a firm erection. It was later discovered that he injected himself regularly with prostaglandin.

THE ARRIVAL THE STRUGGLE THE ASCENDANCY

The death of Zarraga had left a vacuum in the hierarchy of the New England Mafia, and the reverberations were felt in Connecticut and New York. Zarraga had been the rudder, the firm hand, and the undisputed leader. With his death, rival factions vied for the powerful position of New England Boss. For two years the New England mob was in disarray. Dead mobsters were making lurid headlines from Boston to Providence until in a final bloodletting purge, a powerful brutal, ruthless leader emerged. His name was Raymond Salvatore Loreda Patriarca. He came to power from a lifetime of juvenile petty crime to adult murder and mayhem. He was apprenticed as a young hoodlum to Butsy Morelli, the Kingpin of crime in Rhode Island starting in the 1930s. As the Mano Nera gave way to the larger, better organized Mafia in the United States, the older 'mustache Petes' relinquished their leadership to the younger upstarts—or a young Turk looking to make a name for himself retired them to their final reward. Curiously, Raymond, as he was called, bore a striking resemblance to Zarraga. The perpetual sneer, crooked lips, and dark forbidding visage cast him perfectly in his role as a Mafia Don. It was said that when he entered a room the temperature dropped ten degrees. He operated out of the same office and business as Zarraga. Only the cast of characters changed, many of whom were the sons or relatives of older mobsters. Raymond was one of the most respected bosses in the country because of the tight control that exerted over his *Famiglia* and the great number of law enforcement officials and politicians who were on his payroll. It wasthe start of a new era for organized crime, an era of unprecedented drug distribution and theinfiltration into legitimate businesses. But for Hugo, it was the start of the eighth grade.

Chapter 10

Hugo and his classmates were now the seniors at St. Bart's School. They felt privileged and above reproach with this new status. Even Sister Cecilia and Sister Vivian seemed to relax their vigilance of the boys with the exception of when the boys and girls co-mingled for special classes or auditorium events. It was then that Sister Cecilia could be seen patrolling the aisles with the stealth of a panther. Al Vacolla was dragged from the auditorium by his hair while watching a screening of *The Robe*. He had been caught with his hand on Anna Maria Zoglio's knee. The resulting whipping with a yardstick could be heard throughout the entire school.

It was toward the end of the school year when Father Mario summoned Angelina and Salvatore to the school. Angelina took a half-day out of work to attend the one o'clock meeting. Father Mario greeted Salvatore and Angelina, who had arrived together, with genuine warmth.

"Thank you for visiting with me, Angelina, Salvatore. I think we should discuss Hugo's future education."

"Father, he's doing well, isn't he?" Angelina's anxious question prompted a smile.

"No, no, Angelina, he's one of our top students, don't worry about that. That's what I want to talk with you about." Angelina looked at Salvatore with an expression of concern. "There's a school in Chicago, it's a seminary called Sacred Heart Academy. It's run by the Scalabrini Order."

Salvatore leaned forward. "Yes, I know that place. Carlo's son, Richard, goes there. Am I right?"

"Yes, Sal, and he's doing well there. I think Hugo would do very well there, also. As you know, it's a Boarding School. The food is very good, the accommodations are excellent, and the teaching staff is the best in the country. This will also introduce him to an ecclesiastical atmosphere that may help him determine the future course of his life."

"Father?"

"Yes, Angelina?"

"What is ecclesiastical?"

Father Mario smiled sheepishly. "I'm sorry, Angelina. What I should have said was a religious atmosphere."

"Thank you, Father."

"Father?"

"Yes, Angelina?"

"What about the cost, I can't afford that kind of school."

Father Mario raised his palm, waving it left to right and shaking his head no. "The diocese will pay for all of it, even provide him with a bus ticket to Chicago." Salvatore nodded his head in agreement, turning to Angelina for her response.

"Father Mario, this is all so quick. I never thought of him leaving home." She was clearly distraught.

"Listen, Angie," Father Mario said assuringly, "you don't have to make a decision today. We have all summer to decide. I'll go ahead and reserve a space for him at the school now. If you should change your mind, just call me and we'll terminate the enrollment. Is that okay?"

Angelina smiled, her face visibly relieved of having to make an immediate decision. "Yes Father, I'm still a little concerned about him not living at home. You understand, don't you?"

"Of course I do! If it's any consolation, I went to Sacred Heart as a boy and it shaped my career. It's a wonderful place."

Salvatore rose from his chair taking Angelina's arm as she stood. "Thank you, Father, for this opportunity. I'll discuss this more with Angie and, of course, Hugo."

Within a week the decision was made. To Hugo it all seemed like a great adventure. To the adults, it was the opportunity for an excellent education and an exercise in responsibility. And to everyone's delight, he would be home for holidays and school breaks.

The summer flew by. Richard, Hugo's cousin, was excited by the prospects of having his cousin and friend attending Sacred Heart with him. They spent many quiet moments discussing the students, teachers, city, and the "crummy food" that "you don't even get enough of." In spite of it all, Richard thought it was a great place.

"Cuz, you're gonna like it. Maybe not right away because you're gonna miss home and all that, but I'm gonna be there and I'll introduce you around, know what I mean?"

"Yeah, but what are the kids like, and what about sports?"

"Well, there's a couple of azzholes there – one kid in particular, a big Polish kid, his name is Monske, but he's just a fat assed windbag. The other guys are all good kids and we got a basketball team, baseball, and football. You know, we play almost all sports, and the Brothers play right along with us."

Angelina's fears melted in the heat of Hugo's excitement. By mid-June she had called Father Mario and consented to the enrollment. There was a flurry of excitement in the household the week before his departure. Angelina was concerned for his safety and health. Francesca was concerned that he wouldn't have enough good food. Only Salvatore, ever the pragmatist, was concerned about the boy's studies; but he trusted and admired Father Mario, and he theorized that if the good Father had emerged from the school the fine educated man that he was, Hugo would also do well.

Departure day at the Greyhound bus terminal in the commercial center of Providence was full of hugs, tears, and wet kisses. Hugo and Richard would ride together, much to the comfort of both mothers. Salvatore slipped two hundred dollars in new twenty-dollar bills into Hugo's pocket, holding up a finger to his lips as a sign to say nothing of it to his mother or grandmother. He helped him stow his two suitcases in the bus's gaping luggage bay and turned to him, holding him by both shoulders.

"Do you remember what I told you about being an honorable man?"

"Yes, I do, Papa."

"Good." Salvatore embraced his grandson, his throat pulled tight and his eyes moist with tears as he recalled another parting, without hug or handshake, now more than a decade ago.

The Greyhound accelerated out of the terminal in a plume of diesel smoke and headed for Melrose Park, ten miles west of Chicago.

Hugo and Richard watched the diminishing figures of their waving families and smiled back excitedly, their faces pressed flat against the window. The bus turned a corner, the families disappeared, and suddenly Hugo felt that wondrous combination of fear and exaltation—that defining moment when we recognize for the first time that, yes, we really are, each of us, ultimately and inevitably alone.

The Greyhound had pulled out at nine a.m. with stops for food, fuel, and restrooms, arriving in downtown Chicago at six the next morning. As the bus wound through the city streets, Hugo peered through the window gaping at the sheer size of the great Midwest metropolis. Never had he seen the likes of it, not even on his trips to Boston with his grandfather. Everything was big! The streets were broad; the buildings soared to the heavens. And even at this early hour the sidewalks were filling with the scurrying forms of countless people, men and women alike, all rushng to their day's destination.

As the bus wheeled into the Greyhound terminal it joined what seemed like hundreds of others, all loading and debarking passengers in an endless rhythmn of sound and motion. Dozens of bus lines with their distinct names and colors filled the sprawling terminal yard, a great dynamic gateway to all of America. As Hugo and his cousin stood waiting for the driver to open the luggage bays, he felt a hand on his shoulder. He turned quickly to see a tall, smiling freckle faced boy with bright red hair, a clipboard in his hand

"Hey, are you Huggo Rossi? Hi Richard, he added, nodding to his old schoolmate. Richard returned the greeting with a laugh.

"It's *Hugo,* not Huggo," Richard corrected.

"Oh, I'm sorry about that, Hugo." Hugo offered his hand to the boy, a few years older than himself, taking note of his handsome navy blue blazer, a crest of the Sacred Heart Academy embroidered over the left pocket. The boy flipped through some pages on the clipboard, looking over the crowd as he scanned the hundreds of passengers. "My name is Tom Feeney," he explained. "I'm here to pick you two fellows up, along with some other kids. Listen, get your bags and wait for me under the big clock inside the station. I've got to round up six more kids, you got that?"

"Yeah, wait for you under the clock."

"Right, don't move."

Hugo and Richard elbowed their way through the bustling terminal to the center of the large terrazzo floored reception and departure hall, finding the four-sided clock suspended from the thirty-foot vaulted ceiling. Hugo placed his old leather case on the gleaming terrazzo and sat on it, drinking in the extraordinary hustle and bustle of the windy city. Aside from a baseball stadium, he had never seen so much humanity in one place at one time. Hundreds of people lined the dark wooden benches waiting for their buses to arrive or perhaps to greet disembarking passengers. The scratchy reverberation from the ancient loudspeakers only added more confusion to the milling crowd. Hugo turned to find a tow headed boy about his age lowering his luggage to the floor followed by two others. They smiled and nodded to one another. In a matter of minutes there were seven boys under the clock followed by the smiling Tom Feeney.

"All right, boys, answer when I call your name." Everyone was accounted for. "Okay, follow me. I've got a van outside. Don't forget anything, you'll never see it again."

They followed single file to the street, walking two hundred feet away from the terminal to a non-descript blue passenger van. Feeney kept up a non-stop travelogue as they drove from downtown Chicago to the suburbs of Melrose Park. A senior at the school, he was graduating in the coming spring and headed for Notre Dame. He warned the boys about the Rector of the school, Father O'Neil.

"He takes no shit, so if I were you guys, I would be on my best behavior when you're around O'Neil. Now Father Angelo, he's another story. He's a great guy and he's always there for you."

The van sputtered through the imposing black iron gates of Sacred Heart Academy, winding its way up a cement and cobblestone driveway to the main building of the small campus. Completed in 1890, the campus consisted of the main administration building, a student dormitory, two academic buildings, a dining hall, gymnasium, hockey rink, and two small utility buildings all constructed from dark red brick in the popular Federal architecture of the day. Only the hockey rink was modern, having been added on some time after the Second World War.

The boys were ushered into a large reception room in the Administration Building, joining several other boys seated in wooden folding chairs. Hugo placed his luggage against a wall with other suitcases and duffle bags and found a seat next to a congenial looking boy about his own age. As soon as he was seated, the young boy extended his hand.

"Hello, my name is Paolo Renzi, I'm from Canada."

Hugo took Paolo's hand. "Hugo Rossi, from Rhode Island."

"You say Long Island?"

"No, not Long Island, *Rhode Island*, just below Massachusetts."

The boy's face brightened. "Ah, yes, the smallest state in America, am I right?"

The other boys had struck up conversations and the room was now buzzing with voices and occasional laughter. The hubbub petered out as a tall, broad shouldered, red-faced priest with a shock of white hair entered the room and sat on the edge of the desk at the front of the room. He was dressed in a black cassock and a black tri-cornered biretta cap. He placed the biretta on the empty desk, interlaced his fingers in his lap, and waited for the room to silence.

Father Liam O'Neil was sixty-years old. He was born in Donegal and arrived in Chicago at age twelve with his entire family of mother, father, and six siblings. The hint of a Brogue still testified to his country of origin. His entire education had been at Catholic institutions, and he had excelled at all of them. He had been a standout fullback at Notre Dame University, and after graduation had spent a year with George Hallas and the Chicago Bears. He was called to the priesthood at age twenty-four and had served as Rector at Sacred Heart for the last twenty years.

In the presence of this figure, the room had grown stone silent. He stood slowly, rising to his full six foot three inches. Hugo noted the crooked nose and large gnarled hands and recalled Tom Feeney's words of caution. "Good morning, lads." He waited for a response. Tom Feeney picked it up and the boys followed suit.

"Good morning, Father."

He pursed his lips, frowned, and continued. "Welcome to Sacred Heart Academy. My name is Father O'Neil and I run the place." He placed his hands behind his back and walked slowly to the center of the room, then turned to face the seated boys. "These are the rules" he bellowed. Tom Feeney broke into a grin having heard the rules many times. "Number one, you follow all of the rules at the Academy. Number two, you pay attention in class and you complete all assignments. Number three, you will respect all priests and instructors under penalty of expulsion. Number four, you will attend Mass and Holy Communion every Sunday. Number five, there will be no fightin'. If ye must fight, you'll do it in the ring with gloves on. Number six, there will be no masturbatin'. If you're caught masturbatin, you will be expelled and excommunicated from the Catholic Church. Are there any questions?" The room remained deathly silent. "All right, lads," he declared with a wave of his hand, "now that we have an understanding, you can follow Mr. Feeney to your dormitory."

The dormitory building had four floors. The first floor housed freshmen, the second sophomores, the third juniors, and the fourth, with its tree-top views of the entire campus, was the special prevue of the seniors. Each floor had a shower room and toilets at one end of hall, barracks style. There were no doors on the toilet enclosures. Hugo shared the freshman dorm with thirty-six other boys. Cubicles lined each side of the room, leaving a broad center aisle. It was the student's responsibility to wash, wax, and buff the vinyl floor of his cubicle twice a week. There was also latrine duty. A rotating schedule of two boys cleaned the toilets, sinks, and shower room daily—and woe unto the boys who didn't clean the latrine to Father O'Neil's standard. Each cubicle had a double bunk bed, two steel lockers, two-foot lockers, and two desks with study lamps.

Hugo's cubicle partner was Paolo Renzi, the Canadian who wore a perpetual smile and had chosen the priesthood as his future. Hugo took an instant liking to him.

"Hey, cuz, how ya doin?"

Hugo turned from his locker to find Richard sitting on the edge of his bed.

"Fine, how are you doing? Are you in this dorm?"

"Na, I'm on the second floor. Say, did you get the welcome speech from O'Neil?" He grinned at Hugo, obviously amused.

"Yeah, we did, it was a beauty. Is he really that tough?"

"Naw, he's alright, he's just got this thing about jerkin off. You can do almost anything and not get expelled, but whatever you do, don't massage your weenie!" They broke out into hysterical laughter, Paolo joining in from his top bunk perch. Hugo introduced Paolo and Richard, who shook hands and quickly became friends. "Gotta go," Richard declared at last. "I'll meet you in the cafeteria at twelve for the usual slop."

The dining hall was in a separate building in the center of the campus. As Hugo and Paolo entered the building they were met by a cacophony of sound and seeming confusion as students table-hopped and engaged in practical jokes. They were shown their table by an arrogant senior with an indifferent expression. Freshmen occupied three tables in the rear of the hall, most of the new students wearing dazed expressions on their faces. As Hugo and Paolo found chairs, a voice called out, "Hugo, hey Hugo!" Standing two tables over was Albert Bruzzi whose parents owned Bella Napoli Restaurant on Federal Hill.

The raucous conversation came to a sudden halt. Father O'Neil had arrived to lead the school in a prayer before lunch. He stood at the front of the cafeteria between the serving line and the tables. He removed the Biretta and placed it on a nearby table. "All right, lads, let's all bow our heads." He waited until all heads were bowed. "Jaysus, we thank you for the food we are about to eat and we pray that this food will give us the energy to do your work in the world, and, Jaysus, we promise to finish all of our food because there are heathens throughout the world who have nothing to eat and we, your sinners, are blessed with your bounty, amen." He looked up and waited for the chorus of "Amens," which came loudly from the seniors and meekly from the new freshmen. As Father O'Neil left, the cafeteria exploded into a babble of voices and a clanging of metal trays.

Hugo joined the long line moving toward the food service hot tables. Most of the food servers were elderly women volunteers dressed in light blue aprons and white hairnets. Hugo presented his tray for his first meal at Sacred Heart. He was starving. He hadn't eaten anything but a hot dog since boarding the Greyhound in Providence twenty-seven hours earlier. The plump volunteer smiled at Hugo, placed two pieces of cold toast on his tray and smashed a large spoonful of something unidentifiable on top. Next to this she placed a glop of mashed potatoes and peas. Hugo returned to his table with the addition of a tumbler of milk and a small bowl of lime Jell-O. As he sat down, Richard Troni pulled up a chair beside him lowering his tray to the table.

"Well, cuz, whataya think?"

"Richard, what is it?"

Troni laughed through a mouthful of food. "C'mon, cuz, it's not bad, it's chicken a-la-king, try it. It's better than the shit on a shingle we get all the time."

Tom Feeney came bounding down the center aisle of the cafeteria, clipboard in hand. "Okay, guys, I'm gonna give you the royal tour of our little campus. I also have everyone's class schedule, so chow down and then follow me."

THE ARRIVAL THE STRUGGLE THE ASCENDANCY

Father Mario had left the priesthood. The parishioners of St. Bart's were in a state of shock. There had been no notice. There was no farewell to anyone. The Bishop received the news a week after the priest had hastily packed his bags and departed on a Sunday evening, driving to Boston, registering at a motel close to Logan Airport, and departing the next morning for Miami with what one witness described as "a beautiful young woman" on his arm.

Rumors erupted the moment it was discovered that Inez Latoure had abruptly left her second floor apartment on Plainfield Street a short distance from St. Bart's Church. She had moved there the previous year from Woonsocket, a small city in northern Rhode Island heavily populated with French Canadian immigrants who worked the many textile mills along the rushing, winding Blackstone River. She had come to Providence to work as a substitute teacher for the Catholic Diocese, and from time to time she would visit St. Bart's when the need arose. Inez came from a large family and had graduated with honors on scholarship from Providence College, a small but respected institution run by the Dominican order of monks.

Her beauty was paralyzing. Long, brilliantly red hair, paintbrush eyelashes framing oversized green eyes, and a small, curvaceous figure that would tempt any mortal man. At twenty-four years she had never been with a man and was determined to save herself for the man she would marry. Every teenaged boy was in love with her. The nuns and women of the various parishes looked askance at her mode of dress when substituting in a classroom. Whatever she wore became naturally provocative on her shapely frame. When it finally became known that she had run off with Father Mario, the talk was bitter.

The Sunday following the treachery Philomena Lofredo and Francesca traded theories on why Father Mario had left the priesthood while their husbands, who had remained silent on the subject, struggled to keep themselves from betraying a sly smile. Leaning over the dinner table, Philomena pushed her coffee cup aside and made her startling revelation.

"I heard," she said in a loud whisper, "that she went to confession every Saturday and she waited to go into Father Mario's confessional. Then she would tell him things to…you know…get him, get him…interested."

Pat Lofredo guffawed. "Aayy, Philomena, what the hell are you talking about, you really think she had to go in the confessional to attract his attention? With an ass like that, of course he's gonna look."

"Ha, you men are all alike. That's all it takes is a little shake of the rear end and you leave everything, is that what you'd do?"

Pat Lofredo smiled broadly. "Well, Philomena, you know she never shook it at me! Besides, I like yours better, even though it's a little fat." Philomena threw her hands in the air and looked at Francesca, her mouth open in silent protest. Salvatore sat back in his chair and busied himself with the relighting of his pipe. Philomena narrowed her eyes, sat back in her chair, and folded her arms across her ample chest.

"So, Francesca, what do you think of this whore, this *putana*. Don't you think she's to blame?"

Francesca looked at Philomena with an arched eyebrow and rose from her chair. "Philomey, as far as I'm concerned, it takes two to tango."

Salvatore leaned forward in his chair resting both elbows on the dining room table. Slowly he took the pipe from his mouth and exhaled a cloud of aromatic smoke. "Philomey, why does she have to be a *putana*? We know nothing about her, but I know that Father Mario is a good man. It could be, you know, that they just fell in love."

Pat Lofredo burst out laughing. "No, Sal, I think it was that nice ass, that's what did it." Salvatore stifled a smile and signaled Lofredo for a retreat to the parlor and the Ed Sullivan show.

A month later a postcard arrived from Miami addressed to "Mr. and Mrs. Rossi." It was short and to the point. "*Dear Sal and Francesca, Thank you for your support, your confidence, and your affection. You will always remain in my heart as dear friends. All is well, we are very happy. All my love, Mario.*" There was no return address.

The tour of the campus lasted forty-five minutes with perfunctory introductions to various faculty members and the coaches of basketball, hockey, and baseball. Tom Feeney reassembled everyone in the dining hall for final instructions and class schedules.

"All right guys, any questions.?" There were murmurs and headshakes of *no*. "Okay, then when I call your name come up and I'll give you your class schedule, and if you want to sign up for one of our teams, I've got the forms for that, too. Oh, and by the way, all classes will start tomorrow. All right, you got that?" This time there was a chorus of *yes*.

Hugo and Paolo retreated to the dorm building, walking slowly, studying their class schedules and comparing times and courses. As they mounted the short staircase to the main entrance the door burst open followed by a large boy loudly cursing and denouncing someone whose name was unintelligible. He smashed through Hugo and Paolo, striking at Paolo's face with an open-handed arm, knocking him off the stairs onto the cement walkway below. Hugo, losing his balance, stumbled onto the grass apron. The large boy continued his ranting as he stormed away from the building. Hugo righted himself and rushed to assist Paolo who lay dazed from the fall.

"Are you all right, can you get up?"

Paolo lifted himself slowly from the cement. "Jeese, what was that?"

The two friends returned to their cubicle. Paolo sat at his desk, lightly massaging the back of his head, his fingertips gently assessing the swelling that was tender to the touch.

"Paolo, are you sure you're okay, do you want to see a doctor?"

"Naw, I'm all right."

"Okay, you freshmen, any questions about your schedule or anything else? This is your last chance to speak with the oracle." It was Tom Feeney striding the barracks, looking left and right as he walked. Hugo signaled to the senior boy and told him of the incident outside the dormitory

"Was he built like a small tank with wiry hair standing straight up?

"Yeah, that was him."

"Well, that would me Monske the Monster. He's a junior, and we think he should be in a mental hospital, not here. You wanna file a complaint?" Hugo turned to Paolo.

"No, I'm all right. I've got a tough skull."

"Okay, just stay out of his way. He's always going off half cocked, you got it?"

Hugo's schedule was made up of religion, Latin, algebra, Italian, history, and biology. He was assigned to a freshman homeroom. Paolo Renzi sat across from him. The homeroom teacher, Father Angelo, taught both algebra and Italian.

Somewhere in his mid-thirties, Father Angelo was a handsome man with almost feminine features. Tall and slender, he had the build of a long-distance runner, which had been his sport in college and which he continued to practice almost daily. He had been born and raised in Manhattan's Little Italy. It was well known among the older students that his father was a senior figure in the Gambino crime family and that his two oldest brothers were involved as street soldiers. His youngest brother, Franco, had been gunned down a year earlier in a dispute between factions of the Gambino's and the Buonano family. The murder was yet to be avenged.

The young priest stood at the front of his freshman class smiling, chatting with a boy in the front row. He stood back, clasping his hands behind his back.

"Okay, everyone, welcome to your homeroom—and also your Italian and algebra class. My name is Father Angelo and we're going to be seeing a lot of one another. Did everyone get the school rules from Father O'Neil?" He smiled broadly showing large, even white teeth. The class broke into restrained laughter. "I see you have. Well, then, I won't have to repeat them. When I call your name, please stand and tell us where you're from."

Hugo liked Father Angelo enormously, and he was determined to excel in his classes. Algebra had always come easily to him, and

Italian, though admittedly influenced by an imperfect dialect, had been his second language since birth. With a little studying, he was certain he would soon be speaking the language like Victor Emmanuel.

Paolo was an ideal bunkmate. He was quiet and studious and Hugo discovered that he was an artist of unusual talents. The cubicle walls were covered with drawings and paintings produced effortlessly by Paolo's busy hands. Richard Tronni was a regular visitor to their cubicle. The boys chatted about family, joked with each other, and Richard imparted tidbits of useful advice that he had acquired during his first year at the Academy. He was often accompanied by Albert Bruzzi, a congenial, happy-go-lucky kid whose grades needed a boost.

The first days of school were consumed by constant activity. It was only toward the end of the first week as he lay in his bunk, moonlight streaming into the cubicle from the sole window, that Hugo found himself reflecting on home. he building was quiet, with only the occasional sound of snoring, sleep mutterings, and the squeak of worn mattress springs from someone tossing and turning. He lay with his hands cradling his head, staring at the full moon, thoughts of Angelina, Salvatore, and Francesca vivid in his mind. Suddenly, without knowing quite why, tears streamed from his eyes, his lower lip quivered. Turning on his stomach, he buried his face in his pillow and sobbed softly to sleep.

The next day was Sunday. He waited till eleven o'clock to call. It would be noon in Providence and he knew Angelina would be with his grandparents for Sunday dinner. The only telephones available to the students were four booths lined up on the cement walkway in front of the dining hall. On weekends they were in constant use. He waited his turn. The receiver was warm from constant use. He dropped a dime in the change slot, dialed zero, and waited for the operator. He requested a collect call, gave the number, and waited, his heart swelling with anticipation.

"Hello?" It was Francesca.

"Nana, it's me!" cried Hugo once the operator had put through the call. His eyes misted as he spoke.

"Yes, *figlio mio*, I know it's you, thank God." Hugo could hear the excited voices of Angelina and Salvatore in the background. Angelina shared the receiver with Francesca, smiling and sniffling at the same time.

"Nana, I miss you and Papa so much, I wish I was home."

"And we miss you too, my sweet boy, and we pray for you every night. Wait a second, I'll let you talk with your mother."

"Why didn't you call before this, we were worried sick?" Angelina's voice was taught with anxiety and yearning.

"Ma, they don't let us make calls until the weekend. This is the first chance I could call when you'd all be together." He turned his face into a corner of the booth as his eyes watered and he struggled to hold back the tears. "Ma, I love you, I miss you so much. I promise you I'll get good grades and I'll call every Sunday, I promise."

"I love you too, honey, and I think of you all day. Are they feeding you? How is the food?"

Hugo let escape a small laugh. "Well, it's not like yours or Nana's, I can tell you that, Ma. I guess it's like the food you get at Boy Scout camp. I wish you could send me a plate of macaroni and meatballs!"

There was a smile in her voice as she spoke. "Don't you worry, honey, when you come home I'm going to stuff you full of pasta. Did you see your cousin, Richard?"

"Yeah, he's around all the time. Him and Albert Bruzzi, they're on the second floor."

"Good, I know they're good kids." Salvatore hovered by the phone, straining to conceal his eagerness to speak. "Hugo, Papa wants to say hello, wait a second."

"Hugo, you alright, everything going well, no problems?" With the sound of his voice, Hugo realized how much he missed his grandfather.

"Hi, Papa, yeah, everything is alright. The kids are pretty good, and cousin Richard and Al Bruzzi are always around. It's okay, but I really miss you and Nana." Salvatore had all he could do to maintain his composure. There was a pause as he fought back emotion. "Papa, you there?"

He cleared his throat. "Yes, figlio mio, I'm here. You got some money left?" "Yeah, Papa, there's no place to spend it."

"Well, I'll send you a few more dollars just in case you run into an emergency. You remember all the things we talked about?"

"Yes, Papa"

"Good, alright, here's your mother."

Richard Tronni and Albert Bruzzi insisted that Hugo and Paolo try out for the hockey team, arriving at their cubicle one Friday after class and physically pulling them along to meet Father Jerome— or Father Jerry as he was better known on campus. The hockey rink was the brainchild of Father Jerry, built with money he raised from local businessmen in his strong-armed, almost military manner. In fact, as a 19-year-old Army Ranger he had participated in the most daring and bloody operation on Omaha Beach. It was his battalion that scaled the Palisades fronting the landing areas using only grappling hooks and brute strength in the face of heavy machinegun fire and hand grenades raining down on them. They succeeded in their mission saving thousands of lives, knocking out machine gun emplacements and heavy artillery installations. Of the 250 men engaged in the operation, fewer than 50 survived.

The rink was built on a shoestring. Bare cinder block walls, no locker rooms, and wooden spectator stands of only three tiers. Two bright red Coke machines, like armed sentries, stood on either side of the door. The air was cold as the four boys walked toward the spectator stands filled with aspiring young hockey players. Father Jerry's bass voice echoed in the hollow rink. He talked as he paced in front of the prospective players. Now forty-one, the years showed in the grey of his temples and the small lines at the corners of his eyes. Short, stocky, and with hardly a neck, he had the appearance of a large bulldog.

Father Jerry stopped in mid-stride and mid-sentence as Hugo and the others clambered into the stands. "You, you four assholes that just snuck in late, get down here now!" They looked at one another and slowly climbed out of the stands. Hugo and Paolo looked at one another, clearly shocked at the language they had just heard. Slowly they shuffled forward to stand in front of the coach, his massive girth covered in a well-worn grey sweat suit and black high-topped sneakers. "All right, what's your names?"

They quickly mumbled their names. "You, Rossi, where you from?"

"Rhode Island, Father," he replied, his voice louder than he had intended.

"Jesus, just what we need, another wop from Rhode Island. All right, listen to me." He turned to the stands. "That means everybody here! Any fucken-body who doesn't show up for practice or who comes to practice late is off the fucking team, everybody got that?" The would-be athletes mustered an unintelligible murmur by way of response. "I didn't hear you, girls!"

"Yes, Father!" came the reply, echoing loudly through the rink.

"All right, you four, back in the stands."

The boys leaned against the wooden railing surrounding the rink, watching a pick-up game that had gotten underway.

"Cuz'," whispered Hugo, "Father Jerry's got a sewer mouth. I never heard a priest swear like that."

Richard Tronni laughed out loud, placing an arm around Hugo's shoulders. "Cuz', you haven't heard anything yet, wait till the practices. The other thing is, he lives with a woman in town and he's got a fourteen year old son."

Hugo's mouth dropped open; Paolo's eyes widened in shock. "Jeese, why do they keep him as a priest, he doesn't act like one?"

"He's the best priest at this school," his cousin protested, "and he's the most honest. He doesn't try to hide what he does. He doesn't give a shit."

Hugo turned to Richard with narrowed eyes. "But, why doesn't O'Neil do something about him? It can't be only that he's a great teacher and a nice guy."

"Tell ya the truth, cuz', I don't know. All I know is what Feeney said and the rumor that..." Hugo eagerly stepped on Richard's sentence. "Yeah, what rumor?"

"The rumor is he's married to O'Neil's sister. She used to be a nun."

Salvatore was seventy-one years old. With hard work and a sensible diet he had the physique of a much younger man, a full head of grey streaked hair, and a youthful appearance that belied his age by a decade or more. Francesca at sixty-five remained a beautiful woman, her once girlish figure having gracefully relaxed into the fuller curves of a maturity. Her life was Salvatore and her family. They still shared a robust marriage bed, slowed by age but with the same intensity of their youth. More importantly, they liked each other and enjoyed each other's company.

It was Sunday, the Lofredo's were coming for dinner with their family. It was to be a delayed celebration of Salvatore's birthday. Angelina and Francesca busied themselves in the kitchen. It was a special meal: roast veal, Salvatore's favorite, and a rum cake baked by Tony DiLuise himself at DiLuise Bakery. Hugo had made his usual Sunday call comforting everyone with the sound of his voice and assurances that everything was fine. Salvatore, Pat Lofredo, and his son and son-in-law watched a football game until dinner was announced. Lofredo's grandchildren had accompanied their parents and sat at a small separate table bickering over their seating assignments as Salvatore poured Chianti from a jug of home made wine. Everyone agreed it was the best Sunday dinner ever.

The cake was served with coffee and espresso spiked with Anisette. After the last stanza of *Happy Birthday* had been repeated by Lofredo's youngest grandchild, Pat Lofredo began a reminiscence of their meeting fifty years earlier. The wine flowed freely. Philomena, always the nosy-body, leaned forward resting her forearms on the table. "Well, Sal, you gonna tell us what you got for your birthday?"

Salvatore smiled as he lit his pipe. He extinguished the flame of the match with a plume of smoke. "Well, Phil, you know Angelina and Francesca always get me more gifts than I need or deserve, but this year I want to give myself and Francesca a special gift." Francesca sat forward in curious anticipation. Salvatore drew on his pipe, a twinkle in his eye. Lofredo removed the Parodi from his mouth.

"Well, Sal, what's the surprise, we're all waiting."

"I'd like to go back to the old country, a visit to Italia." Francesca's mouth dropped open, her eyes wide as saucers. Philomena broke into a fractured version of the Italian National Anthem joined by Pat as Francesca rounded the table and threw her arms around Salvatore's neck. Pat Lofredo suddenly stopped and looked at Salvatore with deep concern.

"Hey, you okay with a passport and the aahh . . . you know, the trouble you had there?"

"There's no problem, Pat, thirty years ago Bill Gilborne helped me out through Senator Greene. I'm a citizen in good standing. As far as the trouble back then, Joe Calabro, you know, the lawyer, he spoke with the Italian consulate and there is no record that I was ever wanted by the Italian officials."

Philomena appeared even more excited than Francesca. "Did you get tickets yet? Where are you going to stay? What about..."

"Phil, please, let Sal tell us what he plans to do." Francesca stood to refill wine glasses. "Aayy, I'm on this trip too, you know, I think I want to see some things. We still have a lot of family in Pescara."

Salvatore raised his hands. "My wife is right. This trip is for both of us. After all, the only places we've been are Atlantic City, New York, and Cape Cod." He reached for Francesca's hand. "Whatever you want to do and wherever you want to go is fine with me, as long as I can visit the church and cemetery in Atri." As he spoke he reached for his pipe and methodically shook out the ash until the old sadness had passed. Patsy Lofredo understood.

"All right, everybody, I think we should toast Sal and Francesca's trip to the Old Country. Everybody got a drink?"

"Papa." It was Pat's grandson. "Yes, Anthony, what do you want?"

"Papa, I need some wine to make a toast."

"Okay, Anthony, I'll pour you a little bit of wine and then you make the toast, okay?"

With Philomena carping about not pouring too much wine and broad smiles around the table, little Anthony raised his glass in a theatrical fashion and mimicked his grandfathers many toasts: "To Salvatore and Francesca, may the plane stay up in the air long enough to make it to Italy." The table erupted in laughter and applause.

The Al Italia Boeing 707 glided to a perfect landing at the Leonardo da Vinci Airport in Rome. Francesca was as excited as a little girl as she craned her neck to peer from the cabin porthole. Salvatore smiled at her excitement, feeling his own sense of exuberance. He kissed her cheek as she leaned across his seat.

The cab ride to the Excelsior Hotel was harrowing. The driver was an excitable Sicilian who claimed, with wild hand gestures and a total disregard for other vehicles in his path, that he was forced to come north because "things are so bad there, there's not even enough horse shit to grow anything." When he learned that Salvatore and Francesca were from Rhode Island he jerked the ancient cab to the side of the street, screeching to a halt. Turning to the rear seat, he smacked the top of his forehead with an open palm. "*Madona mia*, my first cousin Emilio Tasoni lives there, in a place called Johnston. Have you ever met him?"

Salvatore explained that, regrettably, he had not done so and that maybe when he returned home he would call Emilio and let him know of the coincidental meeting. The cab driver smilingly introduced himself as Giuliano and insisted that he would be their guide and driver for as long as they were in Rome. He would hear none of Salvatore's protests. "There will be no charge for my service. I will be happy to take care of people from my cousin's city in America." Salvatore and Francesca exchanged raised eyebrow glances and gave in to the inevitable.

The Excelsior proved to be one of the great Belles Epoch hotels of Europe. As Salvatore and Francesca emerged from the cab, two smiling liveried doormen doffed their brimmed caps, the older of the two announcing a formal greeting. The cavernous lobby was crowned by dozens of gleaming chandeliers reflecting lustrously from the white marble floor and broad marble columns, giving the lobby the air of an atrium. Room registration was handled with elegant formality by the staff, each wearing a white boutonniere.

As the bellman opened the double Louis XIV doors to a small but sumptuous suite, Francesca gasped audibly, bringing a smile to the bellman's face. Slightly weary from their travel, they showered in preparation for dinner. Salvatore watched Francesca as she stepped from the glass-enclosed shower and began to towel her body. She sensed his stare and raised her eyes to meet his. Francesca smiled as she dropped the towel, turning slowly, arms raised as in a pirouette. Near breathless with excitement, they made love as the sun set in the Eternal City.

THE ARRIVAL THE STRUGGLE THE ASCENDANCY

The next morning they emerged from the hotel to a sparkling Roman day. Salvatore's attention was drawn to two valets arguing loudly and gesturing wildly with a cab driver who would not move his battered vehicle from the front of the elegant Excelsior. The driver held his place, leaning against the cab door, arms folded, cap at a rakish angle, a cigarette dangling from his mouth. Salvatore thought how much the cabby looked like his late uncle, Si Antonio. It was then that he realized it was Giuliano. Their eyes met. Giuliano bolted from his position, pushed past the valets, and walked quickly to Salvatore and Francesca, reaching for both of their hands.

"*Buon giorno, buon giorno*, I told you I would be here to show you the city, and I am here!" The two valets looked at one another, shrugged their shoulders, and held the squeaking doors open for Salvatore and Francesca.

The cab lurched from the sidewalk, cutting off two angry honking cabbies. Giuliano was oblivious to traffic as he began his grand tour of Rome. They first visited the Vatican Palace, where the two American tourists stood hand in hand gazing in awe at the dome of the Sistine Chapel. Then it was off to all the usual tourist stops—the Trevi Fountain, the Spanish Steps, the Coliseum, and the ancient Roman ruins. They lunched on pizza and sparkling water at a sidewalk café and continued until late afternoon, with Giuliano making non-stop commentary. He returned them to the Excelsior, insisting that they be ready at seven o'clock, as he would take them to the finest—but little known—restaurant in Rome. Again, protests were in vain.

They rested for the balance of the afternoon, showered, changed, and were waiting as Giuliano haphazardly pulled up to the disapproving glares of the valets and doormen. He drove through the city streets for fifteen minutes, then headed north out of the city, chattering incessantly about everything that they passed. The cab wound its way through a maze of narrow streets and came to a stop in front of a small, two-story whitewashed building. Giuliano scurried about, opening doors and ushering them inside.

They stood in what looked to be a parlor. From the rear of the building came the voices of children and adults. China and glassware could be heard clinking and clattering. Salvatore and Francesca turned to Giuliano, puzzled expressions on their faces. Giuliano stood, hands clasped behind his back, beaming as an attractive, slightly plump, smiling woman came through a kitchen door, wiping her hands on her apron followed by three teenaged children.

"Salvatore, Francesca, please meet my wife, Isadora, and my children, Livio, Catarina, and Natalina. Mr. and Mrs. Rossi, you are now in the finest restaurant in Rome—my home!" Salvatore bowed to Isadora and with a warm smile insisted that it was he who should be taking Giuliano and his family to dinner, but Giuliano would hear none of it. Both Giuliano's and Isadora's mother lived with them. The two venerable ladies smiled and nodded upon introduction, exposing various missing teeth, intent upon their culinary duties. When at last all were assembled at table, the party partook of food that, as Francesca said, was fit for a visiting dignitary. From quail to homemade pasta, from artichokes to zabaglione, all chased down with fresh wine in unlabeled bottles.

Conversation was a happy mixture of Italian and garbled English. Over coffee, Francesca spoke with Isadora and the mothers while Salvatore and Giuliano strolled into a small garden behind the house. Sitting on stone benches, coffee cups in hand, Salvatore puffed on his pipe, Giuliano sucking on a cheroot. It was warm for October. Salvatore studied the constellations in the brilliant, clear Roman sky. Life in the neighborhood echoed in the warm night air.

"So, tell me, Salvatore, what brings you to Italy, vacation, business?"

Salvatore removed the pipe from his mouth and looked into the lighted kitchen as his wife laughed with the women. "Well, Giuliano... by the way, is that your first name? What is your whole name?"

Giuliano smiled, shaking his head. "No, no, my full name is Giuliano Ignazio Mario Giuliano."

Salvatore nodded in smiling appreciation. "So you're Giuliano Giuliano!"

The cab driver showed his teeth as he grinned. "Si, that's me, Salvatore. So tell me why you're here."

"Well, I guess it was 1914. I had to leave this country. I lived in Atri, a small town in the Abruzzo. I ran afoul of the carabinniere, and it was either leave or spend my life in prison."

Giuliano slapped his knee. "I knew there was something I liked about you!" Giuliano knew better than to pry further.

Salvatore stood, extending his hand. "My friend, 'thank you' is not enough. How can I repay you for this wonderful hospitality?"

"Salvatore, there is no way. Just be my friend, and if I ever get to the United States, I'll look you up."

There were hugs and kisses as Salvatore and Francesca departed. Giuliano dropped them at the Excelsior where there was another series of embraces and heartfelt goodbyes before

Giuliano departed, exhaust fuming from his tailpipe as if he were a crop duster.

The ornate elevator was manned by a liveried operator in a round cap and a chinstrap neatly in place. Salvatore sighed audibly as they ascended slowly to their floor. "Did you leave the money?"

Francesca smiled. "I gave one-hundred dollars to Catarina. I told her not to give it to her father until twelve noon tomorrow."

The concierge had arranged for a rental car the next morning. There was a flurry of activity as the valets played their roles as the exclusive servants of Salvatore and Francesca, justifying a larger tip. The last valet closed the driver's door, doffed his cap, bowed slightly, and wished them a "*buon viaggio.*"

A map of Rome and a road map of Italy were tucked in the glove compartment. The traffic was light for that time of morning, and in a half-hour they were headed northeast to Abruzzi. The roads were smooth and well built. The highway signage was easy to read. There were rest stops, picnic areas, historic vistas, and restaurants clearly marked as Salvatore tried to keep pace with the lead-footed Italian drivers shooting by him at Grand Prix speed.

They stopped for lunch in Caiano, a small town midway between Rome and L'Aquila, the capital of Abruzzi. They arrived in L'Aquila at two in the afternoon, checking into the Villa D'Oro, a small boutique hotel well appointed and well managed by the D'Oro family for fifty years. Dinner was an extraordinary experience served in the small but exquisite dining room of the hotel. The entire D'Oro family, from chef to waiter, worked in the busy, stone-floored restaurant.

They left for Atri the next morning after a leisurely breakfast. The narrow road leading to Atri looked vaguely familiar to

Salvatore as he scanned the landscape. He was silent for the final hour it took to arrive in the town square. The car rumbled quietly over ancient cobblestones. He stopped next to a small fountain spouting water over a statue of vestal virgins. His pulse quickened as he surveyed his surroundings. The town had grown. The square had been expanded, now ringed with small retail shops, antique stores, two chic women's boutiques, and a movie house at the far end.

Francesca watched him, sensing his reverie. He edged the car forward, slowly. The square was busy with pedestrians and traffic. He stopped to allow people to pass and his eyes fell on the café. It was Potenza's café. There was no mistaking it. The same brick and stucco exterior, the same shuttered windows across the front of the building, the same double French doors as an entrance. The name had changed. It was now a coffee shop with waiters in white ankle-length aprons serving tourists, shopkeepers, and locals under the warm October sun beneath colorful Cinzano awnings. He started and gasped audibly as his eyes picked out two navy blue uniforms of carabiniere officers. Francesca's eyes followed his. "And so? You're not wanted for anything in Italy. You're just another tourist." He smiled and sighed deeply, releasing his grip on the steering wheel. Francesca reached over to place her hand over his. "Salvatore, you're an American citizen in good standing." He smiled, took her hand, and kissed it.

The road leading from the square to his home of nineteen years, the home he was forced to leave in 1914, was now paved and well-traveled. In a matter of minutes, the stone house came into view. Panes of glass were missing from most windows, and even at a distance he could see several holes in the clay tiled roof. Around the house the grasses and weeds had grown knee-high, and the front entrance was choked by weeds and bushes. The verdant fields that once produced vegetables and wheat now boasted grape vines as far as the eye could see, vines drooping with the weight of the rich, purple fruit about to burst with sweet Sangiovese juice for the vintner's barrels. Salvatore watched the pickers filling their baskets with the swollen grapes, their hands stained the color of the fruit.

He parked off the road on the grass and gravel edge of the property, close to what once was a stone walkway. He stared hard at the house, eyes unblinking. Francesca broke the spell, opening the car door and stepping onto the rough gravel. Salvatore emerged slowly from the driver's side, eyes never leaving the front door of the house. He walked through the high grass, trousers rustling against the vegetation. The smell of grape and the warm autumn day began the revival of old, haunting memories. Francesca walked slowly behind him. The front door was weather-beaten but still looked strong. They stood at the door. Cicadas were serenading one another in the warm sunshine. A whiff of burning grape vine perfumed the air.

"Well, are you going in?" There was concern in Francesca's voice. He slowly lifted the latch on the door and pushed forcefully. The door swung open easily. Two small starlings flitted through an opening in the roof. The stone floor was littered with straw and leaves. The fireplace on the rear wall was surrounded by old farm implements and empty bushel baskets. Cobwebs covered the overhead rafters. There was a table in the center of the room with one chair. He walked to the table and ran his hand across a corner, revealing indentations.

"This was our table," he murmured softly. Francesca moved to his side. He eased himself onto the sturdy chair and closed his eyes, transported back to the fateful evening fifty-two years earlier. With one hand on the table, he hung his head to his chest. "Oh Francesca, how I loved them, how I loved them! Still, not a day goes by that I don't think of them!" She put her hands on his shoulders, squeezing gently. They remained motionless in the old house, the buzzing of cicadas and the distant voices of the pickers adding life to the moment. He stood slowly, brushing the tears from his eyes. He reached for Francesca's hand and they walked from the house, latching the door carefully as they left.

Sangue di Cristo Cemetery was on the same road as the house. Beyond the cemetery was the Barone Santa-Gatas Villa. In minutes, they arrived at the cemetery. Sangue di Cristo Church was a short distance from the cemetery's wrought iron gates, which were artfully welded into the figures of angels sounding trumpets. Salvatore parked the car and held Francesca's hand as he tested his memory, searching for his father's stone. The cemetery had grown in fifty years but he remembered the tallest oak tree in the cemetery and walked toward it. It was a simple grey granite stone set squarely in front of the tree. They walked close to the stone to read the carved inscription. Hugo Salvatore Rossi: 1874-1914. They knelt together and prayed, Salvatore with one hand on the headstone. As they rose, Salvatore pressed his fingers to his lips and placed them on the headstone, whispering, "I love you, Papa."

They followed the neatly bordered path toward the church, scanning headstones as they walked quietly. Salvatore recognized many of the family names. The cemetery was well kept. Neatly trimmed grass rolled over sloping terrain. Cemetery workers could be seen in the distance, tools in hand. They wandered aimlessly, scanning names, stopping from time to time to examine more closely. Salvatore stood, right hand shading his eyes from the sun, his eyes set upon a tall obelisk. "Francesca, this way." He walked now at a quickened pace toward the tall rose-colored monument. He slowed his pace, walking hesitantly to the face of the obelisk. It was there.

The obelisk sat on a wide and deep grassy area. It was all of ten feet tall, wide at the base, narrowing at the top. Salvatore felt his heart pounding as he read: *This holy plot of land is consecrated by the loved ones of the town of Atri who perished in the smallpox plague of August 1914 through November 1914. May their memories remain alive and may they rest in peace. Dedicated this day, July 1, 1916, by the family, friends, and citizens of Atri.* The names followed. They were listed by family and day of death. Salvatore ran his fingers down the carved inscriptions, finally coming to rest. He read the carvings slowly, wanting to absorb each word. *Santina Maria Rossi Bianchi, age 38, widow of Hugo Giuliano Rossi, mother of Salvatore Giuliano Rossi.* There was a sickening ache in his heart as he continued. *Tina Valetta Romanelli with unborn child, wife of Nello Ottavio Valetta, age 32.* Francesca had her arm around his waist. She watched his expression. She sensed his deep connection to a past filled with tragedy and sorrow. Salvatore's head was swimming with visions of his mother, his father, and Tina—Tina pregnant with his child. His breathing came hard. He collapsed to his knees, covering his face with his hands, his whole body shuddering. The sobs came convulsively. He murmured repeatedly, "I should have been here ... I should have been here ... Oh, God, I should have been here!"

Francesca held him tightly as he rocked back and forth, slowly regaining his composure. He stood slowly, Francesca still holding him by his waist. He turned to her with reddened eyes and tear-stained cheeks. He reached for her and enfolded her in his arms, placing his cheek tightly to hers. "I love you more than life itself. You are the center of my life. You know this?"

"Yes, I know you do, and I know why you feel so attached to your past. You left so young and you left so much."

From the corner of his eye Salvatore could see a white-haired, elderly man walking toward them at a brisk pace. He held Francesca's hand as the figure approached.

"Hello, my children, I see you're visiting our smallpox monument. That's what we call it here. May I ask where are you from?" He was perhaps five-foot-eight, a slightly built man, a light ruddy complexion. He wore a gardener's apron and gardener's gloves, which he removed as he spoke, and round his neck was a priest's collar.

"We're from America, Father, visiting the gravesite of our relatives."

"I see, I see. Who would your family be, my son? I know most of the people who perished during the 'terrible time'." As the old priest spoke, a figure began to appear in Salvatore's mind. There was something familiar about the man. He had been in his company before. Salvatore turned toward the monument, not answering the priest. Francesca tugged at his hand. The old priest was looking intently at Salvatore. A narrow-eyed look of recognition appeared on his face. He wagged his finger at Salvatore. "You are Hugo and Santina's son, Salvatore, am I right, my son?"

"Yes, you are, Father, but how did you know?"

The old priest turned and walked toward the small stone house behind the church. "Come with me. We'll have a glass of wine and a little something."

He led them to a garden and pointed to a small, round cement table surrounded by four sturdy wooden chairs. He entered the house and in moments reappeared with three glasses and a decanter, followed by an elderly woman with a dish of olives, cheese, and prosciutto and a basket of fresh crusty bread. "Come children, eat, eat. Dip the bread in the olive oil, it's good for you." He waited as his guests tore pieces of bread and took their first taste of the local wine. "Well, Salvatore, you asked me how I knew it was you—you don't remember me, do you? Well that's understandable. After all, I am ninety-two years old and as we get older, we change a little." Salvatore and Francesca looked at one another in astonishment. The priest appeared to be no older than Salvatore himself.

"I know it is hard to believe. Well, I was born on Christmas Day, 1875. Isn't that right, Marietta?" The elderly housekeeper flashed a gap-toothed smile and nodded yes. "God has been good to me and I am ready for his call, which I am sure will be in the near future, or sooner! But for now, we drink, we eat, we enjoy what God offers. Come, my children, have a little more wine. I myself drink at least a liter a day. It's good for you, makes you sleep better."

The early afternoon sun was warm on their backs; the air was clean and scented by the countryside. Salvatore sat back in his chair, now relaxed, feeling fulfilled on his journey.

"Father, you never told us your name." Francesca and Salvatore waited as the old priest finished his wine and wiped the remnants of lunch from his mouth. He smiled slightly, a twinkle in his eye.

"I think you know my name. I'm sure you will recall it. My name is Rittaco, Livio Rittaco. I was the Monsignor here when the tragedy occurred, when you were in America living with my old friend, Father Cavalaro. We were in seminary together. He was my Latin teacher and my mentor." Salvatore and Francesca remained speechless, unable to grasp the reality of the priest who bore witness to the apocalypse in 1914.

"Father, I can't believe this. You were here, you saw it all, and yet I don't remember you at the church, and I was here at least twice a week."

Father Rittaco leaned over and refreshed their glasses. He nodded his head knowingly. "The monsignor you remember was Monsignor Centofanti. He was here for many years. I came here the week of your father's funeral mass. Monsignor Centofanti was assigned to a parish in America. I think it was in, ahhh...you'll have to excuse my failing memory—age, you know. Ah, now it comes to me. It was in Chi-ca-go. Many Italian immigrants were there and they needed an Italian priest for their new church. And so that's how I came here and that's why you don't remember me."

Salvatore nodded his head in understanding. "Father, tell us what happened."

The old priest raised his eyes to the crystal-clear blue sky and then lowered his head to look off into the distance. "It was a time when I thought God had forsaken us. There were a few of us who had survived the pox as youngsters and became immune. Thank God that I was able to help the sick and bury the dead. It spread like a wild fire. I don't know how it came to our village. We made a large pit; people were dying so quickly that we left it open. We wrapped the bodies, covered them with lime and gravel, and buried them in layers. There was no other way. In the second week we lost Dr. Albanese. I thought we would lose everyone in the village. We prayed day and night. I thought your mother and the pregnant girl, what was her name?"

Salvatore looked away, mesmerized by the tale and the imagery it evoked. Francesca leaned forward. "Her name was Tina, Father, Tina Valetta."

"Ah, yes, Tina. I thought they would recover, but it was their time. First your mother, and then the next day the girl. We buried everything, clothes, bed coverings, everything. I kept valuables for relatives and family members to claim, and little by little, they were all claimed. As a matter of fact..." The old priest jumped to his feet. "Wait one minute, I have something for you."

He disappeared into the stone house and in a matter of minutes emerged holding an envelope and a gold locket in his hands. He placed them before Salvatore and seated himself at the table. "Your mother gave me the locket and the girl gave me the envelope." Salvatore reached for the round, oversized locket and snapped it open. There were two colored tintypes; his father to the left and his mother to the right. He smiled and gave the locket to Francesca, who looked at him with moistened eyes. The letter was addressed to him. It was unmistakably Tina's handwriting. He held the letter with both hands. The old priest gazed at him steadily. Marietta, the housemaid, was burning dead shrubs and yard debris in a wire basket twenty paces away at the side of the stone house. Salvatore fingered the letter as he watched the smoke curl upward from the smoldering flames. He left his chair and walked slowly to the wire basket. He stood for a moment, holding the envelope in both hands, and then fed it into the flames.

The old priest watched Salvatore, nodding his head in understanding. They said their goodbyes to the jovial priest who accompanied them to the car. "And so now, my children, where do you go from here?"

Salvatore opened the passenger door for Francesca as he spoke. "We're going for a visit to Pescara, Father. My wife has many relatives there and we're looking forward to seeing them."

"Ah, Pescara, great town right on the ocean, wonderful seafood. You'll have a good time, I'm sure."

Salvatore embraced the priest. "Father, I want to thank you for making my life complete."

The old priest smiled and took Salvatore's hand in both of his. "Farewell my son, live a good life. And drink more wine!"

Salvatore was lost in thought as they left Atri for Pescara, sixty-two kilometers to the Adriatic coastline. They drove in silence for a half hour, Salvatore finally speaking softly, eyes on the road.

"I'm glad we visited Atri and the cemetery. I feel . . . I feel relieved. It was as if a chapter of my life was never finished. Can you understand?"

Francesca reached for his hand. "I understand perfectly, and I'm glad we came here, too."

Pescara was a quaint whitewashed seaside town. As they pulled into the town center a dozen of Francesca's first and second cousins converged on the car, obvious by its rental plats, and showered them with floral bouquets. Several held up a white sheet with "BIENVENUTO" written in bold letters. There was a babble of happy voices as introductions were made, kisses and hugs exchanged, and the verbal tug of war over which cousin would be hosting the first night's dinner. Francesca's first cousin Daniella, who had visited the United States several years earlier, provided a furnished apartment overlooking the Adriatic. They stayed two nights and ate and drank wine from morning to midnight, followed by glasses of sweet Limoncello. They left in a babble of goodbyes and promised to stay in touch. Phone numbers and addresses were traded and they were on their way to Naples, the Isle of Capri and, on the tenth day, a return flight to Boston from the Da Vinci Airport.

Anthony Monske had no friends at Sacred Heart. It was said that his mother and father, who owned a small plumbing company in Chicago's Polish enclave, didn't like him either. He had repeated the ninth grade and was off to shaky start for his second attempt at completing the grade. His father was more than willing to pay the tuition and made a sizeable contribution to the Academy's Annual Fundraising Appeal in the hope that the Academy would somehow civilize his brutish son. He was allowed home only for holidays. During summer vacation he was forced to attend the Catholic Diocese's summer camp, where it was sworn to by eye-witnesses that he had sex with a sheep. Paolo Renzi had become his favorite target at the Academy. Because Monske had repeated the ninth grade, he was forced to live in the same dorm room as the new freshmen. He resented this affront to his seniority and chose Paolo to vent his anger upon. Paolo accepted Monske's brutish behavior, the punches, the pushes, and the insults. The final humiliation was delivered when Monske walked into Hugo and Paolo's cubicle and tore Paolo's drawings and paintings from the partitions and wall and left the torn shreds of painstaking creativity on the cubicle floor.

Hugo arrived that afternoon to find a distraught Paolo, tears in his eyes, sorting through the remnants of his work. "Paolo, what the hell happened?" Paolo looked up from his chair with tear stained cheeks fingering the torn remnants.

"It was Monske," Paolo explained. "He's insane. Billy Riley was on latrine duty, he saw him do it."

Hugo bent to retrieve pieces of the destroyed artwork. "I'm gonna kick this crazy bastard right in his balls." Hugo's eyes became bloodshot as he spoke. He clenched his fists and held them to his eyes. "This son-of-a-bitch, I'm gonna …"

"No, no, Hugo, please, this will only lead to more problems. Please, I don't want you to antagonize him, please. You're my friend and I appreciate your concern, let me talk with him, find out what's on his mind, why he does what he does."

Hugo looked at his friend, sensing his innocence and goodness. "Okay Paolo, but he's not gonna leave you alone. He's no good and he's nuts, mark my words."

Father Angelo's classes were the best in the Academy. His method of instruction was to break the subject matter down to bite-sized pieces and ensure that every student had an understanding of the fundamentals. He had taken a liking to Hugo, who he recognized as a bright student with a quick mind. He saw in Paolo a prospect for the priesthood and seminary life. He did not see these prospects for Hugo.

Anthony Monske was a student in Father Angelo's Algebra class and he was failing miserably. He sat across from Paolo and constantly badgered him for test answers. Paolo was in a dilemma:

denying Monske the test answers enraged him and ultimately led to more harassment; reasoning with Monske was out of the question. Paolo reasoned that a new seating assignment would free him from Monske's easy accessibility. Father Angelo understood Paolo's anxiety and agreed to a new seating assignment on the following Monday, which meant that Paolo would have to endure Monske's torture for two more days.

Two days later, on Friday afternoon while Father Angelo was outside the classroom for a brief period, Monske reached across the aisle and snatched Paolo's completed test from his desk. As he frantically tried to retrieve the work, Monske shot a right fist into Paolo's face causing blood to gush from his nose. The class was in an uproar. Monske sat back in his seat with a vengeful smile on his face. Hugo turned from his front row seat to see Paolo trying to staunch the flow of blood with a handkerchief and the smirk on Monske's face. He leapt from his seat and hurtled down the aisle toward Monske who still smirking stood ready for the advancing avenging Hugo.

Father Angelo's voiced boomed across the classroom. "What is going on here? I want dead silence. Everyone, be seated immediately. Rossi, Monske, be seated now!" Monske snarled through clenched teeth, "I'll see you after classes at the Calvery Shrine where I'm gonna kill you, you little asshole."

Hugo, backing away, whispered hoarsely, "I'll be there, you fat ugly bastard."

The Calvery Shrine was an elevated circular platform sculpted to replicate a hillock with rough terrain, and with three five-foot crosses mounted in its center. Located close to a nearby street, the shrine attracted many local residents who would stop to kneel and pray. The base of the shrine was regularly surrounded by flowers, plants, and other offerings from the faithful.

Word had filtered throughout the school that the Monster was going to kill someone at the shrine after class. Paolo had left class early under the pretext of feeling ill. He ran at full tilt for the shrine clutching an object close to his body, weaving between buildings to avoid detection. A crowd surged toward the shrine with the Monster in the lead reveling in the roll of the gladiator. The crowd egged him on with cries of "Hercules," "Samson," "Goliath." He raised his hands in mock victory enjoying what he took for adulation when, in fact, it was more the taunting of the village idiot. Hugo watched the crowd advance, a knot forming in his stomach. Paolo stood off to one side sickened by the whole event. The Monster never broke stride. He just kept on coming. There was to be no prefight linguistics. At twenty paces he lunged forward, screeching foul obscenities. At the moment of no return, Hugo quickly reached down to retrieve a heavy based fourteen-inch brass candleholder that was hidden behind a vase of lilies. In one motion, he leaped upon the base of the shrine and, in a spinning motion, whipped the candleholder into the Monster's onrushing enraged face.

The blow from the candleholder caught him squarely on the bridge of his nose. His eyes rolled back in his head, his knees buckled, and he fell backward. The crowd fell silent. From out of nowhere came Father Angelo in his running shorts and sweatshirt. He knelt, quickly assessing Monske's injuries. Monske's eyes flickered open. He groaned and tried to sit upright, blood covering his face and shirt. Father Angelo looked relieved. "Okay everybody, party's over, back to your dorms, get ready for the dinner bell. Hugo, Paolo, wait for me in my classroom."

Monske had made it to his feet. He stood groggily, eyes still not focused. Father Angelo held him by his shoulders as they walked slowly toward the center of the campus. "C'mon, Mr. Monske, we're going to get you to the infirmary. Luckily, Dr. Liebowitz is still there."

The infirmary was a small building adjoining the dining hall, half of the building used for food storage and the various odds and ends that had no visible means of use. Dr. Liebowitz was a retired neurosurgeon who donated his time to the school several times a week and was on call for any emergencies. Father Angelo steadied the still wobbly Monske through the infirmary's entrance just as Dr. Liebowitz was leaving.

"Well, well, Father Angelo, what do we have here?"

"A little overzealous confrontation, Doctor. He took a pretty good belt to the head. I'd appreciate it if you would look at him." Monske took four stitches to his forehead. He was bandaged, given some aspirin, pronounced fit to leave and headed toward the dining hall with a ravenous appetite.

"Mr. Monske"

"Yeah, Fadda?"

"I'll see you in my office after dinner, do you understand?"

"Yeah, Fadda." He watched as Monske dashed headlong toward the dining hall crashing through a trio of boys emerging from the hall.

Hugo and Paolo sat in the empty classroom debating their fate as Father Angelo entered the room. They averted his gaze as he sat on a corner of his desk. He looked at Hugo and spoke calmly.

"You could now be in the custody of the police. You could have killed him. Are you aware of this?"

Hugo stared at the well-worn wooden floor. His voice was barely audible. "Yes Father, I am but ..."

"No buts, Hugo, what you did was terrible. You could have killed another human being. How can I make you understand the severity of your actions?"

Paolo buried his face in his folded arms resting on the desktop, sobbing softly. He raised his tear-stained face blotting his eyes with the back of his hands.

"Father, may I speak?"

"Yes Paolo, you may speak."

"It's my fault. Hugo did it to protect me. Monske was constantly at me. He destroyed my paintings, he punched me in the face, he threatened me, he's no good. Something's wrong with him."

Father Angelo left his perch on the desk and paced back and forth before Hugo and Paolo for what seemed an eternity. Finally, he stopped and turned to them. "This is a matter for God to decide. I want you both to visit the chapel now. There is no supper for you this evening, and I want ten Acts of Contrition, ten Our Fathers, and ten Hail Mary's. I also want you to apologize to Mr. Monske, am I understood?"

They answered in unison, "Yes Father."

"All right, get going. And one other thing, no one is to know what took place in this room and you will refuse to discuss any part of the incident. If you disobey my orders, you will be out of here in a heartbeat. Now get going."

The two boys parried the excited questions of their classmates with vague references and a refusal to talk about the incident, which very quickly became yesterday's news. Monske was lying on his bunk leafing through a girlie magazine when Hugo approached and apologized. Monske moved the magazine closer to his face for a detailed study of the female anatomy.

"Fuck you, Rossi, I'm not done with you yet. You're a dead man." There were no further acts of aggression toward Hugo or Paolo ever again.

Thanksgiving arrived with an autumn chill. The local boys went home for the holiday, while half of the students stayed on the campus and were treated to a traditional turkey dinner. Christmas break soon followed. Hugo, Richard Troni, and Albert Bruzzi took the Greyhound bus to Providence to be greeted with hugs, kisses, and shouts of joy. Angelina, who hadn't seen her son in almost four months, held him at arms length examining him closely.

"You got skinny! Don't they feed you at that school?"

Francesca agreed "Yes, you are. That's because there's no good pasta on the menu."

Hugo looked into the distance, rolling his eyes, embarrassed at the public attention. Salvatore moved in to rescue the situation wrapping his arms around Hugo and kissing his forehead.

"How's my boy, how are they treating you down there?"

"Good, Papa, but Mama's right, they don't have any good pasta on the menu."

Salvatore tousled the boy's hair. "All right, then, let's go get some of your grandmother's pasta so we can start to fatten you up."

The week home flew by and then it was the reverse trip to school. Hugo's marks remained high, his powers of concentration made studying easy. He tutored Albert Bruzzi in Math and was often called upon for assistance by other classmates. There was hockey practice, basketball practice, studies, special assignments, religious duties. It was a full schedule occupying most of his time and mind, but in the evening after lights out, when he lay quietly in his bunk staring at the moon, his thoughts more and more turned to Amy Lee Randall. He could smell the dark cellar with the faint odor of fuel oil. His nostrils flared remembering her sweet scent. At times he would roll over, burrowing his aching member into the thin mattress with the ringing admonition of Father O'Neil in his ears.

Hugo had made the honor roll. Father O'Neil presented the certificates the day before summer vacation began. Paolo Renzi was a recipient. He had elected to stay on campus for early seminarian instruction, having made the decision to enter the priesthood.

Summer vacation proved uneventful, one day following another until, incredibly, it was gone. This time the late August trek to Sacred Heart seemed quicker and less complicated. Classes resumed with the late summer heat as an annoyance. The oak and maple leaves soon donned their brilliant autumn colors and hockey and football practice was announced by the Coach's shrill whistles through the frosty air. It was toward the middle of the semester when Father Angelo gripped Hugo by the shoulder as the class was being dismissed.

"Wait a minute, Hugo. I want to talk with you a bit, sit down." The classroom was finally quiet as the last noisy student joined the throng in the corridor. Father Angelo pulled his desk chair around to sit across from Hugo. "You know, Hugo, I was looking at your grades this morning. You're one of the top students in the school, I'm proud of you." Hugo smiled shyly. "I think you'll do very well in college once you finish high school. Are you going to stay here at Sacred Heart?"

Hugo hesitated, uncertain how to respond. "I don't know Father, I'm not sure. I haven't decided about being a seminarian. It's a big decision."

The priest leaned back in his chair, crossed his legs, folded his hands in his lap and looked out at the light snow swirling around the windows, a look of melancholy in his eyes. "You know, Hugo, I had to make a similar decision when I was your age, and if I had that decision to make all over again ...." He paused, looking over Hugo's head. "Paolo has made the right decision. He's committed to the church. I don't think it's the right decision for you. I think you'd be better off as an academician or lawyer. A profession, something where you can use your God-given gifts. Well, you still have a lot of time to decide, and whatever you decide I'm sure you'll follow through on it. Go ahead, join you classmates and get ready for dinner."

Christmas break was the usual non-stop visits to relatives and friend's homes, tree decorating, and the search for the perfect gifts for Angelina, Francesca, and Salvatore with money he had squirreled away for the occasion. Christmas Eve was known as the Night of the Vigil by the Italian community. It was Hugo's favorite dinner. Francesca had prepared several seafood dishes, which was a mandatory Italian tradition. Angelina worked with Francesca for two days baking and preparing for the festive holy celebration. The Lofredos, the Troni family, and the Natale's, home from Arizona, crowded the large tenement apartment. After several courses of seafood and pasta and several bottles of Pat Lofredo's home made wine, it was time for Midnight Mass. The men, with the exception of Mr. Natale who was dragged to church, settled into penny ante poker and coffee with Anisette. Hugo sat with Angelina in the third row from the altar, which was decorated with four dozen white and blood red poinsettias. The smell of incense mingled with the fragrance of perfume permeated the air. Candles flickering throughout the church created a mystical aura for the high mass unfolding. Hugo sat thinking of Father Angelo's conversation as the full choir broke into a loud stirring rendition of "The Night when Christ was Born." He knew then that Father Angelo was right and that the priesthood was not for him. There was an inward sigh of relief knowing that his decision was final.

The return to Sacred Heart was now a familiar routine. Father Angelo was not on the campus or in his classroom. A young red-faced priest was substituting for the missing Angelo. Days passed before a copy of the Chicago Daily Times was eagerly passed from student to student. Tom Feeney commandeered the paper from a freshman and began to read aloud to an ever widening circle of students. Hugo and Paolo buffeted their way to the center of the semi circle surrounding Feeney. "The headline reads: Priest guns down Wiseguys in Snow Storm." "Then the story begins. Three soldiers in the Lastarza crime family were brutally slain yesterday afternoon by Father Angelo Gianfranco in mid-town New York City's Little Italy. Father Angelo is on the faculty of the Sacred Heart Academy in Melrose Park of this city. Eyewitness accounts report that as Enzo Gianfranco, a cappo regime in the Gambino crime family, emerged from Sal's Bakery carrying a number of pastry boxes, two gunmen approached from an alleyway and opened fire sending a fusillade of bullets into the elderly Gianfranco's stomach and chest. The gunmen ran for a waiting delivery van that was mired in snow and ice vainly spinning its wheels to flee the scene. Father Angelo Gianfranco, the son of Enzo Gianfranco, burst from the drivers side of the late model Lincoln Continental, ran to his father's side, pulled a revolver from his father's coat pocket and turned on the two gunmen now pushing the van from the rear in an attempt to free its wheels from the slippery slush. Eyewitnesses report that the younger Gianfranco ran to the rear of the van firing into the heads of the two gunmen at the rear of the van at point blank range. He then ran to the driver's side of the van, slipping and falling once into the snowy street. He pulled the van door open and fired three bullets into the head and torso of the driver who was frantically trying to escape the clutches of ice and snow." Feeney stopped reading and looked up, mouth agape shaking his head in disbelief. The circle of boys stood stunned in awe. Paolo turned to Hugo, "what would make him kill three people in cold blood like that? I don't understand, he's a man of God." Hugo looked at his distraught friend who had grown close to Father Angelo, "Paolo, it was his father. If somebody shot my father, I would do the same thing, wouldn't you?" Paolo without answering lowered his head, turned and walked slowly to the dorm. Hugo watched his friend walk away. He knew he shouldn't try to console him, it would take time.

Salvatore kept a full schedule at Gilborne Construction. He had become legendary in the company, which had grown to international proportions. He was frequently called to jobs around the country for a day or two to troubleshoot construction problems for engineers and superintendents who had worked for him when they first joined the company. He would meet Bill Gilborne for lunch at Angelos Restaurant on Federal Hill, usually on a Friday. Bill had retired from the company and lived in Jamestown in a large waterfront house with a private dock for his large powerboat. During the summer months he insisted that Salvatore take an occasional Wednesday off to fish with him, usually off Block Island. It was while returning from Block Island after a day of fishing in late August that the first chest pains began. At first he thought it was indigestion brought on by the spicy tripe and sausage that Francesca had prepared for the sea-going journey, but the pain grew worse as they neared Gilborne's dock. Salvatore massaged his chest; his complexion had paled. Bill Gilborne wore an expression of grave concern as he assisted Salvatore from the boat and into his Cadillac for the thirty-minute ride to the nearest hospital.

The Emergency Room staff quickly hooked the patient to an EKG machine and put a call in for a cardiac specialist. Bill Gilborne stayed at his side holding on to his forearm in a reassuring fashion.

"Bill, Bill." Salvatore spoke softly.

"Yes, Sal, what is it?"

"Bill, don't tell Francesca, don't call her, please."

His friend began to protest, but Salvatore shook his head. "No, Bill. I'm all right, the pain is gone now. No need to scare her. OK?"

The curtains surrounding the gurney rustled and opened to reveal a thin, balding fellow with a prominent nose and a broad, reassuring smile. He moved to Salvatore's side and extended his hand. "Hello, Mr. Rossi. I'm Doctor Ratsky. I'm a cardiologist and I'm going to examine you and evaluate your condition." Salvatore and Gilborne exchanged questioning glances.

"Excuse me Doctor, my name is Bill Gilborne, would your father's name be Abe?"

"Yes, it would be, Mr. Gilborne, and I believe he worked for you, and he also knew Mr. Rossi here."

Bill Gilborne slapped his thigh in amazement. "I can't believe it, can you, Sal? What a small world. I remember you as a little boy. You always were a smart one. How is your father?"

"He's fine, thank you. He and my mother are living in Miami. In fact, I'll be talking with him today. I'll tell him about meeting both of you. Sal, if I may call you that, Mr. Rossi, I'm going to draw some blood, and I need an x-ray and I should have some results for you in a few hours."

The tests were inconclusive. There was something troubling Ratsky on the EKG and x-ray. He made an appointment for Salvatore to take a stress test the following week and gave him a prescription for nitroglycerine tablets. Salvatore was home at five o'clock for dinner with Francesca, Angelina, and Hugo. He never kept his appointment; he never filled the prescription.

Hugo had completed the ninth grade with honors. The summer months were spent as usual. There was baseball, swimming, and the corner. The cast of characters in front of the Laurel Pharmacy had changed, but the language and the actions remained the same. The older guys still dominated the corner, but a new pecking order had emerged based on tenure. Hugo and his friends were allowed closer to the center of the activity and there was even an occasional exchange of conversation with the younger boys. Three days a week Salvatore would drop Hugo off at a job site to work with the construction crew, picking up scrap lumber, carrying tools, filling water buckets, running for coffee, and enduring the good natured ribbing from the veteran laborers. There were Sunday trips to Olivo's Beach in Narragansett with the Lofredo and Troni families. Angelina and Francesca would be up at dawn preparing an Italian feast to be devoured by the hungry swimmers from mid-morning till their sunburned departure as the sun descended into dusk. It was mid-August when he decided to broach the subject with Angelina.

"Ma, I don't want to go back to Sacred Heart. I'm not gonna be a priest so there's no reason for me to go back there." He waited for an explosive rebuke, but none came.

Angelina dried her hands on a dishtowel, turned and calmly responded, "If that's what you want, I'm not against it. Have you thought this over carefully?" Hugo nodded. "OK, but did you tell your grandfather yet?"

"No, not yet. I will tomorrow, but I know he won't care as long as I do well in school here."

Salvatore sat listening to the car radio as he waited for Hugo for the drive to a job site in Cranston. It was 6:00; work started at 7:00. The early departure gave Salvatore enough time to stop for breakfast with Hugo and share time together, talking about the job, the Red Sox, and, of course, school. This morning the diner was especialy crowded with early shift employees from the Cranston Dye Company across the street and a number of construction workers who were working the Gilborne job. They found a window booth and sat on the old tufted vinyl seats, breathing in the wonderful smell of coffee and frying bacon. Breakfast arrived in a matter of minutes.

Salvatore sipped his coffee as he watched Hugo devour his breakfast. "Well Hugo, don't you have something to tell me?"

"My mother told you, didn't she?"

"Yes, she mentioned what you wanted to do, but I want to hear the reasons from you. Your education is important, it's the foundation for your financial future, you understand this?"

"Yes papa, I do and I intend on getting excellent grades in Mt. Pleasant, that I can guarantee you."

Salvatore studied him over the rim of his coffee cup. He saw the intensity in his eyes, the resolute jaw, the determination of attitude. He placed the coffee cup on the saucer and looked his grandson squarely in the eye.

"Okay, I agree. I'd rather have you home anyway, and I know you'll give the school one hundred and ten percent."

"You know I will, Pop."

Mt. Pleasant High School was an enormous red brick structure built in 1936 for the exploding population of first generation immigrants and their many children—mostly Irish, Italian, French, Armenian, and Jewish. The students came from working-class families with traditional values of family, church, and synagogue. By 1965 the student body had ballooned to 2,200, nearly twice what it had been when Hugo's father had attended. The faculty was an assortment of aged men and women who were waiting for the retirement buzzer and a cadre of young, starry-eyed educational reformers not yet jaded by the futility of implementing their educational utopia. Into this environment stepped Hugo in the fall of 1965. Entering the tenth grade, he was fifteen years old, somewhat tall for his age, with the added muscle that had come from a summer of hard labor. His features were maturing into a handsome face topped with a thick mop of black wavy hair. There was newness to everything, from the new back-to-school clothes to the feeling that, being in high school, anything could happen and probably would. The girls surreptitiously checked out the guys, the guys openly ogled the girls. Hugo had never seen so many beautiful girls (and so many big breasts!) all in one place. "Hey, Hugo" Al Vacolla jabbed Hugo in the arm. "Look at the ass on the blonde over there with the boy's haircut, could that skirt get any shorter!" "Madonna Mia, I'm getting a hard on just lookin at her." Kenny Furst placed a hand on Vacolla's shoulder. "Aayy Al, watch what you're saying, that's Louie Tazzano's girl. You don't want any problems with him, the guy's an animal." Vacolla shook his head in disbelief. "What a shame, she's with that jerk when she could be with a great lover like me." The guffaws were drowned out by the final bell commencing classes. The students jammed the stairwells and corridors. The school was huge, the corridors were cavernous. Hugo felt insignificant, a minnow with bigger fish.

The corridors rang with shouted greetings, laughter, and the clanging of lockers. The mob swept Hugo, Al Vacolla, and Kenny Furst toward their assigned homerooms. Hugo grasped Vacolla's arm. "I gotta take a leak, where's the boys room?"

Kenny motioned to indicate it was around the corner. Hugo was the first through the door followed by Vacolla and Furst. He stopped abruptly, with Vacolla and Furst stumbling around him. A muscle bound student with a five o'clock shadow was smashing the head of his victim against the chrome piping beneath a row of white hand sinks. Both combatants screamed obscenities at one another, oblivious to the intruders. The perpetrator caught the trios' movement from the corner of his eye and momentarily halted his mayhem.

"What the fuck you doin in here?" His prey squirmed free of his grip only to be recaptured. "Get the fuck out or you'll be next!"

The three boys fell over themselves backing out of the lavatory and found themselves swept up by the stream of students making their way to class. Hugo clutched at Kenny's arm.

"Who the fuck was that animal in there? He's gonna kill that kid."

Kenny grinned. "Hugo, you just had the pleasure of meeting Tarzan."

"Who the hell is Tarzan?"

Al Vacolla tapped his temple with his index finger. "He's a coo-coo clock. That's the guy we were just talking about, that's Louie Tazzano. He's in a beef every day. The only guy he doesn't challenge is that kid from Charles Street. A big kid, tough as nails, looks like he's about thirty years old. Kenny, what's his name, you know who I mean?"

"Yeah, they call him Rico. I don't know what his real name is, but you'll know him. He's got his own gang. They all sit at the same table in the cafeteria at lunch."

Al Vacolla pointed out Hugo's homeroom. "Hugh, this is your stop – 201, Mr. Panzarella's class."

The class was in session. Mr. Panzarella sat on the corner of his desk introducing himself to the new class. Hugo slowly closed the door behing him. Mr. Panzarella kept up his monologue as all eyes turned to Hugo, who quickly found an empty seat. A boyish looking twenty-five-year old, the handsome English teacher wore horn-rimmed glasses, a crew cut, and favored button-down oxford shirts. He also wore a ring that, to the disappointment of several young ladies in the class, indicated that he was married

Passionate about his profession, the young teacher seemed to be striving to single-handedly change the world for the better. Hugo sat in rapt attention listening as Panzarella compared Shakespearean characters to present day politicians and world leaders with stage-like dramatization. He immediately liked Panzarella, sensed his honesty and interest in his students. Hugo's scholarly achievements had preceded him to his new school. All of his classes were advanced, his classmates mostly bookish, bespectacled, narrow shouldered boys and an assortment of unfashionable young women bent upon college and careers. The students had names for each other. The street savvy C–students called the A–students "colleeges" and the studious students called the street savvy students "mondos" or "guidos," depending upon which particular group was being singled out. With a foot in both worlds, Hugo met the approval of both groups. He was careful not to discuss topics or use language that had overtones of intellect with his gang from the Lake, and he enjoyed the cerebral stimulation of conversation with his advanced classmates. The charade worked perfectly.

Announcements were made over the hollow sounding intercom system. The second week of classes the monotone voice of the student body president, Elliott Klitzner, announced tryouts for gymnastics, track, and wrestling. The football team had filled its quota. The basketball coach had his gallbladder removed two weeks before classes began, and the assistant coach was slow in starting up the program.

The lunch cafeteria was a hanger-sized chamber that could accommodate fifteen hundred students at a time. There were two lunches, the early lunch at twelve and the late lunch at twelve thirty, with the two times slots overlapping each other. Hot lunches were served for those brave enough or hungry enough to partake of the usual ground beef and mashed potatoes. There was a constant roar of voices, the scraping of chairs, the clattering of dishes in the echo chamber acoustics of the room. You could tell it was Friday in the lunchroom. All the Italian kids had sandwiches of tuna fish or egg salad or broccoli, and most of the brown paper bags had a large oil spot from the oily sandwiches inside. According to Al Vacolla, who had the attention of his lunch table, "this whole room stinks like one big fart!" The laughter melded into the swirling hubbub of the room. Al Vacolla kept up his chatter between large bites of his tuna torpedo.

"Hugh, I'm gonna sign up for the track team and maybe wrestling. Whaddya say, why don't you sign up with me?"

Hugo nodded in agreement, stuffing a large piece of omelette into his mouth. The bell rang for class, but they didn't part till the two agreed to meet at the end of the day in the gym.

Angelina's life revolved around her son, Francesca and Salvatore. She was thirty-three years old. She hadn's looked at another man since Hugo's death. She had no desire to socialize with the opposite sex or to befriend any man. In her mind, she was still married to the handsome rogue she had married at eighteen. She was still attractive, in spite of the fact she did nothing to enhance her appearance. She worked five days a week in the same small jewelry plant not far from the tenement apartment. She had been there for almost thirteen years, since Hugo's death. She didn't mind the drudgery, at least it was consistant. Her younger sister, Mary Troni, lived next door to Salvatore with her husband, Carlo. Mary's sole objective in life was to see her sister married again. Francesca, when prompted by Mary, would aid and abet her match making efforts. For weeks, Mary had been prodding Angie to date Domenic Cassella, who owned a successful liquor store on Dyer Avenue not far from her apartment. It was over coffee one afternoon with the enlisted aid of Francesca, that she took up her badgering of Angie. "You know, you're not getting any younger, in a few more years you'll be forty. Who's gonna want to go out with an old woman, tell me, who? Dom Cassella is a nice guy. He's single, he's only forty-five and he's got a very good business and he thinks you're the cat's meow." "Francesca, talk with this coogootz, this thick head, explain the facts of life to her!" Francesca placed her coffee cup slowly into its saucer, leaned forward and folded her hands on the kitchen table. She canted her head to one side and spoke in a motherly fashion. "You know Angie, she's right. Life is passing you by and you need to find out if there's someone out there for you. It won't hurt to go out with this man. You're only going to the Portuguese Club in East Providence. You'll be with Carlo and Mary, you'll eat, have a drink and maybe you'll even have a dance. I think you should go." Angie shook her head wearing a grim smile. "All right, okay, you win. I'll go out with him, but it's to the Portuguese Club and the home, understand?" "Yes, of course. What do you think we're gonna do, check into a motel?"

The Portuguese Club was a workingman's bar with a function hall that doubled as a restaurant and dance hall on Saturday nights. The bands were four or five piece groups from Rhode Island or nearby Fall River, Massachusetts. The cuisine was heavy with Portuguese and Italian peasant dishes and the beer was served in large glass pitchers. Domenic Cassella was a tall, stout, balding bespectacled man who had lost his wife to cancer two years earlier. He was forty-five years old and had the demeanor of a funeral director. He was thrilled at the prospect of dating Angelina who he had placed on a pedestal as he watched her walk by the plate glass windows of his liquor store fronting on Pocasset Avenue. He was hopeful that this first date would lead to more intimate socialization. Carlo, Mary and Angelina drove to Domenic's spacious ranch house that was in the Garden Hill section of Cranston, Rhode Island. Domenic insisted that they come inside for a drink and appetizers before they made the drive to East Providence. The real motive was to display his success to Angie. They were cajoled into taking the tour of the house including the basement with the party room and wet bar and the new state of the art oil burner.

The Portuguese Club was crowded with diners and bar patrons. They feasted on steamed clams, lobster and pasta, all washed down with pitchers of beer and carafes of wine. The band was called "The Unforgettables" from Fall River, five pieces including an accordionist. Domenic was totally taken with Angie. He attended to her every hint of need. His gaze never wandered long from Angie's face. The band came on at 9 pm to raucous applause and foot stomping.

The opening number was the beer barrel polka, designed to levitate the room. Carlo and Mary joined the twirling crowd on the dance floor waving Angie and Domenic on to the floor. Angie vigorously shook her head no. Domenic smiled raising his eyebrows. "I don't blame you, this is not my kind of music either. I like the slower music, you know, the standards, Big Band music. I used to play the clarinet when I was younger. I have every Artie Shaw and Benny Goodman record they ever recorded. How about you Angie? Do you like music?" Angie kept her eyes turned to the dance floor focusing on Carlo and Mary. "What did you say,

I can't hear with this loud music?" I said, "do you like music?" She turned to Domenic guiltily sensing his discomfort with her aloofness. "Yes, but not this stuff. I like Sinatra, Tony Bennett, you know, singers like that. I'm not crazy about the rock and roll that's all over the radio these days. That's all I hear all day at the shop. The kids love it, but it's not for me." Domenic nodded with a smile, relieved that they were actually involved in conversation. "I know what you mean, I can't even understand the words." The band announced a break with a drum and cymbal flourish as Carlo and Mary returned to the table. The evening ended at midnight with the remaining dancers swaying to the band warbling "Good night, ladies" and informing the dwindling crowd that they'd be back next week.

Carlo insisted that they stop for hot dogs at 'Haven Brothers' Diner on wheels at the side of Providence's City Hall. They sat on the broad granite steps to the front entrance of city hall and ate steamed hot dogs with onions and celery salt. Carlo devoured four hot dogs loaded with onion and mustard and burped all the way to Garden Hills in Domenic's new Buick Riviera. He pointed out the many features of the car to Angie, anxious to impress her, to which she nodded, oohed and aahd politely, feigning interest in the running commentary. They arrived at Domenic's house. As soon as the Buick stopped, Angie quickly jumped from the car and stood in the driveway waiting for Mary and Carlo to emerge. "How about dessert, and after dinner drink, some coffee?" He directed his conversation to Angie, eyebrows raised, brow furrowed in hopeful anticipation. "No thank you, Domenic. I'm exhausted, must be that glass of wine I had." Carlo was about to speak but was cut off by Mary's foot on his left one. Mary turned from the front seat as

Carlo accelerated from the curb. "He's a very nice guy and you can see he only has eyes for you. Why don't you give him a chance?" Angie smiled wanly, "okay, alright, I will, I will."

The gym was crowded when Hugo arrived. A long portable table were set up at one end with parental consent forms, doctor's forms, schedules, school regulations, and the like. Al Vacolla weaved his way through the crowd milling about, catching sight of smug Pete Vartanian, the wrestling coach. Built like a water buffalo—no neck, all shoulders and chest—he looked Armenian, which he was, and he had an enormous hooked nose to validate it. All the coaches wore warm up suits in the school colors. Mr. Zarlenga was the track coach. A serious young man, popular with the students, he was tall with a runner's body.

The coaches took up position behind the table appraising the students and passing out forms. Vacolla nudged Hugo. "Whaddaya gonna go out for?"

"I dunno, I think wrestling and track, what about you?"

"I think football, if I can get in, and maybe baseball, but I don't want to play second string. I think I'm good enough to start, know what I mean?"

"Yeah, you're pretty good. You should be first string."

A booming, raspy bass voice rang out. "Alright, you guys, everybody take off your shoes unless you're wearing sneakers. We just had this floor varnished and we don't want it roond, unnastand?" It was Vartanian standing behind his table, hands on hips surveying the crowd. Hugo found himself face to face with the wrestling coach. "What's your name, boy? And what makes a skinny runt like you think you can make it on my team?" Everyone within earshot turned to Hugo, some snickering, the seniors laughing at the classic Vartanian freshman jibe. "Well, you gonna answer me or what?"

Hugo stood dumbstruck and turned beet red, but in another instant his anger overcame his embarrassment. "Coach, the name is Rossi, Hugo Rossi, and I'm gonna be your best wrestler. You can count on it."

Vartanian placed his hands on his hips and smiled broadly, revealing a gap in the center of his upper teeth. "That's what I want to hear, Rossi. De-term-in-ation! I like that. Get this paperwork filled out and get it back to me A.S.A.P., you got it?"

Mr. Zarlenga smiled as Hugo worked his way to the track table. "Mr. Rossi, I like your spirit. Do you think you can give me some of that de-term-in-ation?"

Hugo smiled at Zarlenga's easy congeniality. "I guarantee it, Mr. Zarlenga. I'll give you one hundred percent, and that's a promise."

The days that followed were filled with classes and sports, and his evening found him studying to maintain his leadership in class, much to the consternation of Angelina.

"You're with the books too much, it's not healthy. Your cousin, Carlo, has a nice part-time job after school. He earns his spending money, why don't you do something like that? I can't keep on giving you spending money, and I know your grandfather is always shoving money at you and that isn't right. Do you think that's right?"

"Ma, I don't ask Poppa for a dime. I would never do a thing like that."

"Well, I still think you should help out a little, at least for pocket money."

Arthur Zarlenga looked up from the paperwork on his desk in the cubbyhole of an office provided to each coach. "Hey, Hugo, how are you, what's up?"

Hugo stared down at his feet. "Mr. Zarlenga, I'm sorry, I have to quit the team. Thank you for allowing me to become a member, but I have to drop out."

Zarlenga sat back in a creaking desk chair, eyebrows raised in surprise. "What brings this on, Hugo? I've watched you work out. You're definitely state champion material. Tell me what's on your mind." Zarlenga pulled a folding chair around to face him. "C'mon sit down and talk with me."

Hugo slumped into the chair, eyes averting Zarlenga. Slowly, reluctantly, he explained. "It's just me and my mother. I need to get a part-time job for clothes, spending money, you know, stuff like that."

Zarlenga crossed his arms over his chest, a knowing smile on his lips. "You know, Hugo, your story is not unfamiliar. Most of the kids in this school are in a similar boat. As a matter of fact, I was in the same boat. I had to work a part-time job during the school session and full time during the summer, so I know what you mean." Zarlenga leaned forward and leafed through a stack of papers on his desk, extracting a single sheet. He scanned it briefly and placed it back on his desk. "Hugo, you're in luck. We just got a notice from the School Department informing us that they approved our request for a part-time student to maintain equipment and supplies and to clean the locker rooms after practices. Now, this would be every day because you'll still be doing this for track, wrestling, and football, and it pays pretty well. And you'll still be able to practice with the track and wrestling teams. Are you interested?"

Angelina was pleased with the good news. Salvatore expressed concern that it would take time away from his studies, but Hugo assured him that the hours and location were ideal for studying while allowing him to participate in the school sports program. He accepted Hugo's assurances with the admonition that if he didn't keep up his grades he'd be picking up garbage for the city. "*Capece?*"

For all of his bluster, Vartanian took a paternal interest in all of his students and team members. He recognized Hugo's athletic abilities and cultivated them. In February, Hugo won his first indoor 220 yard dash much to the delight of Zarlenga and his teammates. Vartanian relentlessly drilled him on the gymnastics high and low bar, grooming him for the future. It was April; most days were warm enough to leave a jacket at home or to just carry one. It was only a few months until graduation and the junior and senior proms. It was while on an early morning bus from downtown Providence that he first noticed the tall blonde girl with stunning Nordic features. Their eyes caught across the bus for an instant and she showed a hint of a smile. The bus pulled up in front of the school and students lined up single file, shuffling toward the exit. Hugo stood behind her. Her platinum hair hung to the top of her well-curved buttocks. They walked across busy Mt. Pleasant Avenue, pausing for traffic.

"Good morning." He had blurted out the words, hoping he didn't sound foolish. Her smile told him he hadn't.

"Oh, hi." She clutched her books to her chest as they slowly walked toward the school entrance. "I'm Helga, Helga Swenson. I'm a senior. You're a sophmore, aren't you?"

He felt small and insignificant beside the tall, blonde Helga. "Ahh, yeah," he acknowledged with a tone of resignation.

"Well, you certainly don't look like a Sophmore, you look older."

Hugo's spirits buoyed. "Yeah, a lot of people have said that. It's the Italian features."

She smiled, showing even white teeth. "I like Italians," she said laughingly, "they're so passionate and so handsome."

He was emboldened. "Yup, that's me, handsome and very passionate." This time they laughed together.

"You know, I told you my name, but you never told me yours." She stood clutching her books, waiting for his reply. He slapped his forehead with his palm, and she giggled.

"How stupid of me! I'm sorry, I'm Hugo Rossi."

"Well Mr. Rossi, I've got second lunch today, would you like to have lunch with me?"

He was exultant. "Would I? It's the best thing that's happened to me since I got here." She smiled and turned, hurrying as the last bell rang for class.

He was useless in class all morning. He found her at the late lunch sitting with two girlfriends, chatting animatedly as he walked toward the table. They turned in his direction in unison as he neared, smiling the 'I know why you're here smile'.

"Hi, Helga." He placed his brown lunch bag and bottle of Coca-cola on the lunch table.

"Hi, Hugo. I'd like you to meet my friends. We all live in Smithfield. This is Janice Wardwell and Cynthia Lord. The two girls giggled a greeting and then abruptly rose to go. With waves and laughter they bid 'hello' and 'goodby' in a single gesture and darted off to class, leaving them alone at the table. Hugo busied himself opening the lunch bag, thinking of what he would say next. Helga kindly released him from his dilemma.

"Well, what do you have for lunch? I bet it's something good. All the Italian kids have the best sandwiches." She sat looking at Hugo, strands of pale blonde hair over one eye, full lips parted in a smile. He was excited just sitting across from her.

"Ahh, let's see, it is eggplant, would you like a taste?"

"Oh I'd love a taste, it smells so good."

He handed the torpedo roll to her. "I can't cut it, just eat as much as you like, it's really very good." Hugo watched as her lips surrounde the end of the roll. She smiled as she dabbed at the corners of her mouth with a paper napkin. "Well, whaddaya think?"

"Delicious. I've never tasted eggplant before. I usually bring pimento loaf or egg salad, you know, stuff like that." Hugo nodded his head as he devoured the roll, conscious of his mouth biting into the roll where her mouth had been. She leaned over the table, brushing back hair from her forehead. "You know, I hope we're going to see a lot of each other before graduation."

Hugo beamed with confidence. "You know it," he declared with an air of new-found confidence. "I'm not going to let you out of my sight!" She reached for his hand and held it with both of hers.

"I'm so glad we met before I graduated, at lease we'll get to know one another." As she spoke, he was held captive by her sparkling blue eyes. "You know, Hugo, every Saturday night there's a dance in Smithfield at the V.F.W. Hall. Why don't you come up this Saturday, take a friend, that boy I see you with all the time, what's his name…"

"Vacolla, Al Vacolla, he's a good buddy."

"Well ask him if he'd like to come too."

"Okay, I'm sure he'll want to go, plus he's got a car."

She scribbled her address and phone number at the bottom of a notebook page, tore it off, and handed to Hugo. "I'll see you at seven o'clock on Saturday." And, like a dream that had suddenly ended, she was gone.

The Smithfield V.F.W. was housed in an old unpainted shake shingle building with a pebble parking lot. The large hall hosted wedding parties and Bingo on Tuesday and Thursday nights. There was a bar area with a separate entrance and a full kitchen for catering. Saturday nights were reserved for teen dances. Hugo and Al Vacolla walked toward the front entrance where Helga and Janice Wardwell waited outside the door.

"Did you have any trouble finding us?" Helga smiled and held out her hand to Hugo.

"Nope, straight as an arrow up Waterman Avenue."

"Hugo, you remember Janice Wardwell." Hugo acknowledged the young woman and introduced them both to Vacolla, who he referred to as his "personal chauffeur." Helga led the way into the crowded hall, where a local disc jockey was playing 45 rpm records through two huge amplifiers. Teen Angel was blaring as they made their way onto the dance floor, crowded with local teenagers stomping, bumping, and twisting. Suddenly, the rock music segued to a square dance, and Hugo took Helga's hand and led her away from the crowd. Al Vacolla followed with Janice. "Sorry Helga, I don't square dance." Helga held her hands near her mouth containing laughter, tears of mirth forming at the corners of her eyes. Janice laughed out loud. Vacolla leaned toward Hugo and cupped his mouth to Hugo's ear.

"Hugo, these kids are a bunch of shit kickers, let's get outta here." Hugo nodded, and leaning close to Helga he asked, "Do you mind if we go somewhere else?"

"No, not a bit, it's kind of loud in here, isn't it?" Al and Janice led the way to the car with Hugo and Helga following, their footfalls crunching on the pebbled surface. Helga reached for Hugo's hand entwining her fingers with his. His heart soared with expectation.

"Hey, where we goin?" Vacolla had ground the car to a halt at the lot's driveway. Helga leaned into the front seat pointing directions. "Go up this road and take your first right." Vacolla followed the instructions, and Janice, without encouragement, slid across the seat positioning her body next to Al's. He instinctively let his right hand fall to her bare knee; she did not move it.

"Al, stop at the white house on the right." Helga exited the car before it came to a complete stop. "I'll be right back." She ran into the darkened house and emerged in a minute with a brown paper bag. She slammed the car door and fell into the seat next to Hugo. "Drive out to Waterman Avenue and take a left." Janice turned to Helga, a knowing smile on her lips. Helga pulled a full bottle of Old Granddad bourbon from the bag, unscrewed the cap, and gulped down two mouthfuls. She passed the bottle to Hugo who shook his head in disbelief at a Helga he didn't know. He gulped two mouthfuls and handed the bottle to Janice's outstretched hand. Hugo peered into the darkness, the bourbon bottle now back in his hand. "Helga, where are we goin?"

"Take a left at the white marker, Al, we're going to Randalls' Reservation, a campground for Boy Scouts." She giggled as she gulped more bourbon and passed the bottle to Janice. Suddenly, she threw her body onto Hugo, her mouth and tongue finding his. She straddled his leg, her skirt riding up to her waist, exposing her long pale legs. In their heated exchange, Hugo barely noticed the car coming to a stop, the front doors swinging open and the giggling Janice and stumbling Al Vacolla weaving off into the darkness.

The air hung heavy with the scent of bourbon and sexual excitement. Helga removed her blouse and bra, raising her skirt to reveal no panties. She threw one leg to the top of the front seat and pulled Hugo down to her. In seconds they had coupled and wild youthful lust took hold of their senses. They lay satiated, drunk, and spent, falling into a deep sleep. Hugo stirred first as the sun peeked through the forest mist. As he sat up, he watched Vacolla and Janice walking slowly toward the car, Janice carrying her shoes in one hand. Helga stirred, yawned, and smiled at Hugo. She sat up, hair tousled, breath still faintly tinged with bourbon. She leaned toward Hugo and kissed his cheek.

"Hey, what about your parents? It's morning, won't they be looking for you or calling the police?" Helga brushed her hair back with both hands and grinned. "My parents are visiting my aunt in Maine, they won't be home until Monday, so stop worrying. And Janice is staying with me, so we don't have to rush anywhere." They stopped for coffee and donuts on the way to Helga's house, dropped the girls off with parting kisses, and beat a hasty retreat for Providence before any neighbors became the wiser. Hugo bluffed his way out of Angie's anger for staying out all night and went with her to his grandparent's house for Sunday dinner.

Summer recess was four weeks away. Seniors would be graduating and Hugo would advance to the eleventh grade. He had finished fourth in his class. Jules Steiner had broken school records with his perfect grades. Hugo thought it strange that Helga hadn't mentioned the Senior Prom. When he asked, she claimed she had to be in Boston that night and couldn't go. She didn't elaborate further.

Salvatore had his summer hours at Gilborne lined up. He would work Monday through Thursday with the balance of the week off. His trips to the Swenson house became further apart. Strangely, he didn't mind. He had been feeling trapped in Helga's web of beauty and sexual promise. On graduation day after the ceremony she approached him in cap and gown and casually announced her departure for Emerson College in the fall and that she thought it best that they not see each other during the summer. "Besides, I'm going to be in Maine for July and August." Relieved, he kissed her on the cheek and wished her the best of luck.

It was a summer of hanging on the corner in front of the Laurel Pharmacy on hot night. He was now sixteen years old. The weightlifting had broadened his shoulders and packed muscle onto his frame. He was beginning to look like a man. Weekends were spent at Scarborough Beach with the gang from the neighborhood. It was the summer of discovering surfing with Al Vacolla, Kenny Furst, and anybody who could share in the expense of renting equipment and putting gas in Al Vacolla's GTO. It was also the summer of meeting Leslie Schwartz, whose father was a wealthy automobile dealer. She lived across the road from Scarborough in the largest summer home in the neighborhood. They shared a summer romance and her red Cadillac convertible. All too soon the maple leaves were turning red and gold and the joy of summer turned to the reality of returning to Mt. Pleasant to commence his Junior year.

Now in his seventies, Salvatore no longer traveled to distant job sites. Instead, building plans that needed his analytical eye were shipped to Rhode Island where he reviewed them with his fifty years of construction experience. Pat Lofredo had retired and spent most of his time getting in Philomena's way, as she was fond of saying at every opportunity.

Word of Lorenzo Natale's death came on a Tuesday evening in September. Angelina took the call from her mother and cried gently, uttering only monosyllables: "I know, Ma, I know, I love you, too. I'll take care of it, here she is." She handed the phone to Francesca who with glistening eyes then passed the phone to Salvatore, who made assurances of funeral and church services.

It was a Sunday evening, two days after Lorenzo's funeral. The Sunday dinner crowd was respectfully subdued in deference to Lorenzo's wife and daughter who had joined them for the meal. Pat Lofredo had stayed sober, and by six o'clock the guests had all left and Salvatore was sitting in his favorite chair, drawing on his yellow bowl, the fragrant haze curling about his head as he stared at the television screen, obviously lost in thought. Francesca sat across from him about to begin her ritual knitting.

"You know, my love," he began in a low, steady voice, "I should retire. We have more money than we need, I have a good pension plan, we could do a little traveling, maybe take a trip to California or mayby to Paris. You know, some of the places we've talked about seeing all these years." Francesca lowered the knitting needles to her lap and looked at him, a non-commital expression on her face. He removed the pipe from his mouth, "Well, what do you think?"

"I don't think you're serious. I think you say that now because of Lorenzo's passing."

"Yes, you're right, but how many more years do I have?"

She frowned, and seemed to want to say something, but the thought drifted away. After a moment she said, "I'll believe this only if you go in tomorrow and tell them you're retiring in one month. It's time Salvatore, it's time."

Bill Gilborne wanted to host the retirement party. He was planning for over five hundred people. Salvatore thanked him and politely declined. Instead, he said he'd rather have a small dinner at Camille's Roman Garden on Federal Hill with a few key employees and his family. There were twenty-one people at the dinner. After the presentation of the plaque and Rolex watch, Salvatore spoke "I am such a lucky man to have the love of my family and the respect of my friends." He paused and turned to Francesca "only one thing could make this evening better, he paused again, "my boy..." His voice caught, he breathed in deeply and exhaled. There was quiet around the table. "Well, thank you all for this wonderful tribute." He raised his wine glass "salute a tutti!"

They traveled to California, England, Paris and Sicily. He had never been happier or in better health. He settled into a daily routine at St. Bart's and visits to the local library and the Italo American Club.

Tarzan Tazzano did not return to school in the fall. His body was found roped to a tree in rural Foster, riddled with bullets. The rumor on the street was that Tarzan impregnated his girlfriend and took her to a local abortionist who botched the job. She lay close to death. Her Sicilian father and two brothers who owned a body shop in Johnston hunted Tazzano down, dragged him to

Foster, and did him in. The girlfriend survived. No weapon was ever found and no one was ever indicted for the crime.

Hugo resumed his duties as the Locker Room Attendant and his participation in track and wrestling. He maintained his high grade point average and the respect of his teachers and coaches.

It was two days before Thanksgiving. Salvatore and Francesca had just returned from Baffoni's poultry farm with a fresh twenty-pound turkey. Francesca announced that she needed to go to Angie's to bake pies, and Salvatore said he would take a little nap. As she started to leave she felt his hand on her shoulder. She turned to be embraced and kissed, but instead he held her at arms length. "You know, I love you today as much as I did when you were a girl, probably more."

She laughed and kissed him quickly. "And I love you, too, but now I have to go and bake pies. I'll see you in a couple of hours." He walked the short hallway to his bedroom, sat on the bed, removed his shoes and lay down looking out of the bedroom window. It was two o'clock and the afternoon snow flurries whipped by the window. The steam radiators hissed as he drifted into a dream. He was a young man and his son, Hugo, was crying because he had dropped his ice cream cone. He bent down to pick up his little boy and he kissed his cheeks and his salty eyes and told him that he would buy him another cone and the little boy smiled and threw his arms around his father's neck and kissed him.

Francesca glanced at the darkened apartment windows as she left Angie's house. She opened the gate to the cement walkway, carrying a pumpkin pie for the evening's dessert. It was Salvatore's favorite. The door was unlocked, the apartment in darkness. What made her know, she couldn't say afterward. But she did. She sat on the edge of the bed and touched his hand. It was cold. The light from the hallway illuminated his face, which had paled. She bent to kiss his lips, whch were tinged with blue. She lay next to him and wrapped her arms around his lifeless body. She talked of their youth and their love for one another. In time she called Father Joe who rushed to the house in sweatpants and his college sweatshirt. The house was soon full of disbelieving relatives and friends. There was the smell of cigarettes and fresh coffee, and somehow large quantities of food materialized on the kitchen table as though by magic. Pat Lofredo sat in Salvatore's chair, his reddened eyes and tear stained cheeks mirrored his grief. "He was a great man," he said deliberately and solemnly to no one in particular. "He was one of a kind, a legend. He could have been anything he wanted to be, but what he was most was a good man, a courageous man. I loved him, we all loved him."

At six-thirty Hugo arrived from practice. Pat Lofredo and Father Joe were standing at the gateway.

"Hey, who's throwing the party?" Hugo nodded toward the row of cars that lined both side of the street. Father Joe opened the gate and placed his arm around his shoulders. Pat Lofredo sobbed quietly and turned away. At that moment a hearse pulled to a stop in front of the house. Hugo glanced at the hearse and ran for the stairs, mounting them three at a time. He burst into the crowded kitchen and elbowed his way to the bedroom, flinging the door open. He fell on the bed, his face buried in his grandfather's chest. The sight of his pain moved others to fresh tears. The priest and Pat Lofredo gently pulled him from the bed as the funeral home staff waited in well rehearsed respect to collect the body.

It was the largest church service ever held at St. Bart's. In his will, Salvatore had insisted on simplicity. In accordance with his wishes, only Bill Gilborne was invited to speak. He delivered a heartfelt, emotional eulogy in a halting voice to an overcrowded assembly of mourners. As Hugo sat listening to Gilborne, he recalled a particular breakfast they had together at the diner and what his grandfather had said with serious emphasis "you know Hugo, if something should happen to me, you will be the man in the family, you understand this?" "Papa, don't talk like that, you're too young to even think about that." "Hugo, you just never know, you can't tell what fate has in store for you, capece?" "I understand, Papa."

The rest of the school year was perfunctory. He performed by the numbers. Teachers and coaches understood. They knew he had lost more than a grandfather. Salvatore had been the only father he had known. He accepted Bill Gilborne's offer of a summer job and worked five days a week spending most of his free time close to home. In time, he accepted the inevitability of Salvatore's passing and slowly life returned to a semblance of normalcy.

Hugo had asked Al Vacolla's sister, Eileen, to be his prom date. Eileen was as much a sister to Hugo as she was to her own brother. The prom was held at the Venus DeMilo, a sprawling banquet hall in Swansea, Massachusetts. The "Venus" as it was known, catered to three proms that balmy May evening, each event with its own large partitioned dining and dancing area, with a large foyer acting as a common socialization area, and three bars with bartenders strictly instructed to adhere to the minimum drinking age of twenty one. Many of the Mt. Pleasant and North Providence prom goers knew each other and called out to one another across the foyer that was swarming with white tuxedo jackets, all bearing pink or white carnations, and a showcase of young women creamed, colored, and coiffed, dressed in exotic raiments that exposed ripening bosoms as they flitted from one group of chattering, giggling girls to the next.

The three prom dinners all ended coincidently at the same time. Each school employed its own shaggy haired rock and roll band. The sound emanating from the bands thundered into the foyer, mixing with girlish screeches and testosterone laden shouts.

"Hugh, Hugo, over hear." Hugo's eyes scanned the crowd finally recognizing the waving arm of Tommy O'Rourke, a kid he had wrestled at North Providence. Hugo elbowed his way toward O'Rourke. Eileen was caught up with a circle of gossiping girls. "Hugo, how you doin man?"

"I'm good buddy, how you doin?" They gave one another a manly hug. As Hugo separated from O'Rourke his eyes fell upon his friend's date and he suddenly fell silent for several awkward seconds, not speaking again until he felt someone tugging at his coat jacket.

"Ayy, Hugh, that's my girl you're looking at. You look like you're about to jump her!" Tommy wasn't smiling.

Hugo recovered his emotional balance and turned to O'Rourke with a broad grin. "C'mon Tommy, I just paid you the ultimate compliment, you're with the prettiest girl at the prom."

O'Rourke preened as he clapped Hugo on the shoulder. "You couldn't be more right, Hugo, she was just voted Prom Queen. Hugh, meet my girl, Loraine Ciccone."

Loraine embarrassed by Hugo's unabashed stare, stood pink faced and with a glimmer of a smile as she extended her hand. "Hi Hugo, nice to meet you."

"Hello, Loraine, the pleasure is all mine." At that moment Eileen broke through the crowd.

"Hugh, we're gonna go to the East Side Diner for steak sandwiches. My brother's getting the car, let's go."

Hugo turned to Tommy and Loraine. "This is my buddy Al Vacolla's sister," he explained with a grin. "She's a little pushy, so I gotta go. See ya sometime, Loraine; see ya, Tommy."

Hugo turned eighteen the summer of 1967. He had graduated with honors in June and now he felt the physical and mental euphoria that comes with being eighteen years of age. Angie expected he would take a full-time job with Gilborne and follow in his grandfather's footsteps.

"I think you should take a job with Bill Gilborne. They are a big company and you know you'll make progress because of your grandfather." Angie turned to Francesca, who sat at the kitchen table knitting quietly. "Ma, talk to him, explain to him what a future he could have at Gilborne."

Francesca placed her knitting basket on the kitchen table and removed her glasses. "Your mother's right, but I remember one of your grandfather's sayings. He always said education was the key to success, and he also said that we shouldn't try to live other people's lives. So what do you want to do, Hugo?"

"Nana, I want to continue my education. Roger Williams College isn't expensive. I can get a lot of scholarship money and its close by at the YMCA on Broad Street." He enrolled that fall as a freshman with Vin Pella, a kid from the neighborhood who drove an ancient Chevy convertible that leaked on rainy days.

The college leased classroom space from the "Y," and the students had free use of the gymnasium and exercise equipment, which Hugo and some classmates made use of almost daily, especially the weight room. At five ten Hugo was not particularly tall, but he was muscular at a trim hundred and eighty pounds. The class work came easy to him, all his test papers came back A or A+, and yet he felt as if he was drifting, that there was nothing to hang on to, no future. He was bored with college life. There had to be more.

It was late on a Friday afternoon. Hugo, Al Vacolla, and Donald Penta were lifting weights amid a crowd of sweating, grunting, cursing, and bellowing young men exhorting one another to hoist more weight for more repetitions. Penta wiped beads of perspiration from his face as he spoke to Hugo. "Hugh, how you doin, you like it here?"

Hugo pursed his lips together and shook his head. "Nahh, I dunno. I don't think I'm gonna stay. I can't get into it. I dunno what I'm gonna do. What about you, waddaya gonna do?"

Penta responded in a strained voice as he pushed the heavy metal weights from his chest. "I'm gonna join the Marines." He sat up from the weight bench and caught his breath. "Yeah, they got a buddy program. Your buddy stays with you for the whole time you're in the Marines."

Hugo and Al looked at one another. Hugo was the first to speak. "Waddaya think?"

"I dunno, I never really thought about it, what about you?"

Two days later they were speaking to a recruiting sergeant, who assured them that they would be together during their enlistment so long as there were no emergencies. He painted a glowing picture of Marine Corp history and it was the place for real men, and the two teenagers bought it hook, line, and sinker.

He broke the news to Angelina and Francesca the same evening.

Angelina's jaw dropped, her eyes widened almost in terror. She shrieked her response "No, no, you can't go, what's the matter with you? Are you stupid, they're sending Marines to that country near China, what's the name…?"

Francesca sat at the kitchen table folding her hands. "Vietnam, Angie, it's in Southeast Asia. I just saw a news story about it on the TV. They're sending more and more soldiers there every week, it's not a good situation, that's what the TV. said."

"See what I mean, I need you here with me. I don't have good memories of your father in the Marines, only bad memories." Hugo moved to Angie and embraced her; tears welled up in her eyes as she rested her head on his shoulder.

"Ma, I don't want you to worry. You know me, I can take care of myself. And besides, not every Marine is being sent to Vietnam. I'll send you money every month, and I'll save you a lot of money on food."

Angie threw her head back and laughed in spite of the tears. Francesca took both of their hands, kissing Hugo's and then Angie's. "It's time for a prayer to Saint George, he's the patron saint of soldiers and he'll protect our dear boy."

Chapter 11

PARIS ISLAND

Don Penta picked up Al Vacolla at 6:50 am and Hugo at 7:00 as he stood on the sidewalk in front of his house. It was a cold December day. Vacolla's heater never worked very well and the interior of the car was frigid. Hugo held a small gym bag containing a change of underwear, socks, and toilet articles as instructed by the recruiting sergeant. Al Vacolla pulled the collar of his jacket up and turned to Penta. "Donald, this fucken junk is freezing, fix the heater for crissake."

Penta smiled through a swallow of coffee he held as he drove. "Shaddup, you're lucky I picked you up, azzhole." There was a feeling of excitement amongst them; an adventure was unfolding before them. They were three eighteen-year-old provincial young men about to become fodder for the Marine Corp legend. Penta's Pontiac turned into the Fields Point shipyard in Providence, a former World War Two ship-building facility encompassing fifty acres. Where once thousands of men worked on naval vessels to fight the Germans and Japanese, now the combined services utilized a small number of rusting Quonset huts for physical exams and induction administration. Here the boys had passed their physicals and received their inoculations two weeks earlier. Now two grey Navy buses stood idling beside the main hut. A group of obvious recruits stood to the side of the buses, collars up, puffs of vapor escaping their mouths as they spoke. Penta parked the Pontiac in a marked space, slid the keys under the floor mat, and the three young recruits approached the waiting basic trainees. A fat, weary, chain-smoking Navy Chief Petty Officer began a roll-call as they approached the waiting group.

"Awright, all you guys goin to Parris Island, line up single file with your orders out for my inspection." The aged Navyman grunted as each set of orders were held out to him, and he pointed to one of the idling buses. The three friends found seats on the sparsely occupied bus and waited for the driver to board. A young sailor in Navy blues and a peacoat boarded their bus, consulted his clipboard, and once again called the roll asking for a show of hands as each name was called off. The driver slid behind the wheel, closed the front door with a cumbersome lever, shifted into the wrong gear and jolted forward.

"Hey buddy," called out Vacolla, "where we goin?"

The driver yelled over the roar of the engine. "I'm takin you guys to Quonset Naval Air Station. There's a MATS plane waiting for you to take you to Parris Island."

It was Vacolla again. "What's MATS mean?"

The driver yelled back. "Military Air Transport."

The MATS, they discovered, was a converted cargo plane with only the bare essentials of comfort. An enlisted man in blue dungarees passed out a ham and cheese box lunch with tepid coffee.

The excitement of the early morning has passed, and now they sat silently, lost in their own thoughts and lulled by the drone of the plane's engines. The aircraft landed smoothly at Savannah Airport shortly after midnight. Two Marine Corp buses waited on the tarmac as the plane disgorged its passengers. One bus was already filled to capacity. The passengers joined a group from another aircraft and once again stood at what passed for attention to the disgusted glare of the Sergeant calling the roll.

"Awright, awright ree-croots, ma name is Sergeant Berniece Edwards. Now, if one a you ree-croots sez one thing bout my name, ahm gonna blow your balls off with this her 45 caliber pistol. Y'all unnastan what I just said?"

There was a murmur of yes sirs, yes Sergeant, yes Corporal. Seergeant Berniece Edwards was a tall black sinewy man with snake like features and an evil disposition. He slapped a riding crop against his left palm as he walked in long slow strides before the loosely assembled recruits. His campaign hat was tipped three fingers above the bridge of his narrow nose. He was Marine Corp starched and creased. His spit shined black shoes glistened in the headlights of the gaseous buses. "Ahh feel sorry for you boys, ahh rilly do, cause yo is about to enter hell here on earth." He stopped, turned, spread his feet, placed his hands behind his back gripping the riding crop and stood, head slowly swiveling from left to right. The command came as an explosion from his lungs "GET – THE – FUCK – ON – THESE – BUSES!! Move, move, move!"

They scrambled for the buses, jamming the doorways, stumbling for seats. The buses jolted forward leaving the airport grounds and picking up Route 21 to the city of Beaufort. Crammed together in the darkness, the only light was cast by the occasional lighting of a cigarette. There was no conversation, only apprehensive thoughts of what lay at the end of the bus ride. Vacolla and Penta had been forced onto the second bus, and Hugo, for the first time, felt a pang of loneliness. The buses cruised by the sleeping city of Beaufort, yellow street lamps casting forlorn shadows down empty streets. Sporadic flashes of neon beer signs from the dozens of booze joints claimed the only activity in the city. Route 21 turned into 280 and finally into 80. The buses slowed to cross a short bridge facing the main entrance to Parris Island. It was three in the morning as they proceeded onto the base, the experienced driver picking his way to a reception area. The buses came to a halt beneath dim street lamps in a small quadrangle with barracks buildings on three sides. There were eight drill instructors in campaign hats and spit shined shoes standing and talking with one another as the driver cut the engine. Sergeant Berniece Edwards stared at Hugo, the riding crop smacking into his left palm. The driver pushed a large lever and the bus door sprang open. There was silence for a moment and then the savagery began. A tall rangy Sergeant leaped into the bus and yanked a recruit out of his seat, dragging him on his knees to the ground, all the while screaming "outta the bus, outta the buss now, and get on those fucken yellow footprints!"

As they emerged from the buses, they were attacked by the D.I.'s screaming obscenities, punching and kicking or using batons and in the case of Sergeant Edwards using his riding crop indiscriminately against head and body. The air was filled with brutality. "You little fucken pussys will all be dead by dawn." "You're all pieces a shit, you'll never be a Marine." "Get the fuck back on the bus now, go home you assholes, you fucken morons." The viciousness finally subsided. There were bloody noses, cuts and bruises. One young recruit was sobbing, another had retched on the asphalt to the rage of the D.I.s. "Awright assholes, fall in, stand at attention." The Drill Instructors pushed and shoved the recruits into a semblance of a formation. One of D.I.s stepped forward and bellowed "ten hut!" Sixty recruits came to an awkward version of attention. They stood motionless, some vainly attempting to perfect their stance. From the periphery of the dim streetlamps emerged a burly six-foot Sergeant poured into a custom fit marine khaki and olive drab. He paced before the now apprehensive recruits hands behind his back. He spoke in a flat monotone with a midwestern twang.

"My name is Sergeant James. I am your platoon Sergeant. One out of four of you will not be here for graduation. You ask why. Because we are gonna work you and drill you to the point you will not want to go on. But those of you who do make it will join a select few men who can call themselves United States Marines." He paused looking for a particular recruit. His eyes fell upon a baby faced, plump young man with eyeglasses. "You, fat ass, you, the fat ass with the seal beams, what's your name?"

The boys eyes widened and he stiffened. He stuttered his name. "Le.. Le..Leonard Vergenous, Sergeant."

"Did I hear you right, seal beams, your name is Leonard Vagina, is that right?"

"N.. n.. no sergeant, it's Vergenous."

"Well, your name suits you well, seal beams, cause you were the little pussy who was cryin like a little girl five minutes ago, that right pussy?"

"Y... y... yess sergeant."

"You call me Sir, ya hear, pussy?"

"Y… y… yes, sir."

"Pussy, I'm gonna personally see to it that you drop out. A'm gonna ride you into the ground, ya unnastand?"

"Yes, sir!"

James turned to his left and then to his right gesturing toward the D.I.s standing with him. "These Yoonited States Marines, the cream of the crop of our military forces, will be your Drill Instructors for the next ten weeks. My advice to you ree-croots is pay attention, jump when your name is called, and don't fuck up, because their job is to break you mentally and physically. Did you hear that pussy?"

Yes, sir."

"Louder, pussy, I can't hear you."

"Yes, sir!"

"That's better, pussy. Now I want you all to tell me you heard what I just said." There was a momentary lapse as everyone took in a deep breath and screamed "Yes, sir!"

They were assigned to one of the empty barracks buildings. A supply clerk, not happy to be there, shoved sheets, pillows, and olive drab blankets into the outstretched arms. The recruits fell exhausted into hastily made bunks. One hour later three starched and creased Drill Instructors descended upon the recruits. The lights snapped on in the blackness of the early December morning. The D.I.s strode the barracks pulling bleary-eyed recruits from bunks all the while shouting obscenities and threats to the bewildered young men. "Awright, girls, drop your cocks and grab your socks, this is your first miserable day in boot camp." "C'mon, you homos, stand at attention in front of your bunk."

"Move, move!" The recruits stood at various positions of attention and in various stages of dress. "You re-croots look lak shit, but in a couple ah weeks, doze a you who are still here are gonna look real sharp. Ma name is Sergeant Mugaridge, to ma right is Lance Corporal Williams, to ma left is Corporal Thomas. Dis morning, we gonna give you a hair removal and y'all gonna start the process of becoming Marines."

Hugo's eyes moved left to right looking for his companions, but to no avail. To his left stood a young black man straining at attention. Hugo spoke from the corner of his mouth. "Why the hell are all the D.I.s from Alabama and Mississippi?" The young black man stifled a guffaw. Suddenly, standing in front of Hugo was Sergeant Mugaridge, his face purple with rage. "Wadid you say, you little Yankee homo?"

"Nothing sir."

"Well, I heard you say sumpin to this here black boy, and yo said whatever you said whall ah was talking. Get down on the deck and give me one hunrit, and that goes for you too, Sambo."

Hugo hesitated for a moment. "One hunrit what, sir?" He never saw the backhand coming. It struck him high on the right cheekbone and dropped him onto his unmade bunk.

"Pushups, you dumb homo, get the fuck on the deck and give me one hunrit." They labored through the pushups, accompanied by the taunts of Sergeant Mugaridge. Their first lesson was how to make up a Marine bunk, followed by latrine call, breakfast, the quartermaster building for uniforms, and finally head shaving. The shaving was much like sheep shearing. It took less than three minutes. The day was filled with screaming, scowling D.I.s whose favorite encomiums were homo, pussy, shit for brains, or asshole. For all of that, somehow or other after three days the new recruits knew how to salute, dress, make up a bunk, stand in formation, understand different ranks, and, most importantly, march in step. On the fourth day they were issued their individual weapon, a spanking new M-14 rifle with a serial number that was memorized within the hour of the rifles issuance. This was a sacred moment for a marine, a spiritual moment. Sergeant James handed out typed sheets of the Marines Rifle Creed. He stood before a platoon formation and solemnly read, "This is my Rifle. There are many like it, but this one is mine." He read on as if it were a prayer, finishing the final line not lifting his head to address the recruits, as if to gain his composure. Finally, he looked up. He spoke reverently. "This is the most important prayer you will ever recite. You will all have this memorized in two days. Am I understood?"

"Yes, sir!"

Al Vacolla and Don Penta were nowhere to be found. Hugo was reluctant to inquire as to their whereabouts knowing he would incur the wrath of the D.I. he asked. There was to be a full company inspection on Thursday morning at nine. The Company Commander would inspect the four training platoons. Saturday would complete six days of training. Friday night was spent preparing for inspection, spit shining boots, and polishing brass. At nine all four platoons stood for inspection, with no rifles. The Company Commander, a balding forty-year-old Captain and a veteran of the Korean War, walked the ranks occasionally stopping to chat with a recruit. He was accompanied by the Company First Sergeant, a black muscular seasoned veteran of the Korean War. Captain Diaz stopped to inspect Hugo. He had an olive complection and spoke with a trace of a Puerto Rican accent. "Where you from recruit?"

"I'm from Providence, Rhode Island, sir."

"Where the hell is Providence, Rhode Island, son?"

"Ah, just south of Massachusetts, sir."

"Oh yeah, that's where Newport is, right?"

"Yes, right, sir."

"Well, son, are you gonna make the next ten weeks?"

"Yes, sir, without a doubt."

"That's what I want to hear. Good luck, recruit."

"Thank you, sir."

The first Sergeant studied Hugo intently for a moment and moved on to inspect the rest of the company. The company First Sergeant dismissed the formation with a brief command. As Hugo turned to return to his barracks, Sergeant Mugaridge called his name. "Hey, Rossi, y'all got to go to the orderly room and visit with top."

"Okay, Sarge, what's top?" Mugaridge sneered in disgust and shook his head in disbelief. "Yo are a dumb fuken Eye-talian. Top is the Top Sergeant, the Company First Sergeant, now get your ginny ass in gear and go see the man."

The company clerk turned as Hugo stepped through the orderly room door. "What can I do fo yo, croot?" Hugo explained. "You Rossi? OK, Right through that door."

The office door was open. Behind an olive green desk sat the Company First Sergeant shuffling paperwork. He looked up as Hugo walked in. "Sit down Rossi." Hugo took the chair directly in front of the desk. The First Sergeant placed both elbows on the desk, grasping his fist with his left hand and holding it to his mouth, staring at Hugo. "You look lak him, that's for sure."

Hugo thought for a moment, then spoke. "I'm sorry, Sarge, I'm confused, who do I look like?"

"You look lak your Pappy."

Hugo's felt a slight leap in his heart. Then, slowly, "You knew my father?"

"I sure did, son. He saved my life and the lives of three other good Marines. Your Pappy was a brave, fearless, smart Marine. We all respected him; we all liked him and would have followed him into any situation. He was a born leader." First Sergeant Daryl Kelly went on to describe the mission in Korea fifteen years earlier. "Your pa was a hero, son, I hope you have half the stuff he had. I expect a lot from you during training, and don't think because of my respect and friendship with you pappa that ahm gonna cut you any slack, you got to think again, son, you got that?"

"Yes, sir, I got that. Then, softly, "Sir, can I ask you a question?"

"Shoot."

"Well, when I enlisted, I enlisted on the Buddy Program with two buddies, Al Vacolla and Don Penta, but they're not in my platoon."

Kelly smiled. "Well, son, the needs of the U.S. Marine Corp trumps any deal you think you had, so don't push it, unnastand?"

"I got ya, sir."

"Awright, get back to your platoon and show me some stuff!"

Reveille was four-thirty. It was the same every morning, lights snapped on, screaming D.I.s, rush to the latrine, five-mile run, Chow Hall. He never saw Vacolla or Penta again. Boxwood Taylor was from Trenton, New Jersey. He was coal black with the biggest, whitest teeth Hugo had ever seen. His bunk was next to Hugo's. Boxwood laughed at everything. He was big and rawboned. It was an hour before lights out. There was the hum of conversation in the barracks. The acrid scent of brass polish and boot polish permeated the air. Several recruits were busy writing letters. Hugo turned to watch Boxwood spit on the toe of his boot as he swirled polish into the supple leather.

"Hey, Boxwood, where you from anyway?" Boxwood turned flashing his Cheshire grin. "Ahm from Jersey, Hugo, Trenton. Where you from?"

"Rhode Island. You know, the smallest state in the union."

"Yeah, I got a cousin who lives in South Providence, you know where that is?"

"Yeah, sure, that's a colored section in Providence."

"Hugo, what's wrong with you, man it's not colored no more, it's black, ahm a black man."

"Okay, Boxwood, that makes it easier." They liked each other. There was an instant bonding between them. "Hey, Boxwood, you notice that big kid down the end of the barracks, what's his name ... ahh Fredericks, that's it. You know he's about six four?"

"Yeah, I know who you mean, why?"

"I think the kid is gonna have a nervous breakdown."

"Why you say that?"

"I saw him in the latrine last night, he was shakin like a leaf and he was talking to himself."

Boxwood thought for a moment. "You know, Hugo, I think these D.I.s pick out some recruits who they purposely try to break and they ain't fuken breakin me, that I can tell ya for certain."

Hugo smiled and nodded his head in agreement. "I'm with you, buddy."

It was the fourth week into training. The routine remained the same, reveille at four-thirty, five-mile run, Chow Hall, classes on Marine Corp history and the M-14 rifle, close-order drill, chemical warfare, and everyday physical training until exhaustion—push-ups, pull-ups, sit-ups, squat jumps, all to the cacophony of screaming D.I.s. It was on a Saturday morning during the five-mile run that Hugo committed the mortal sin. Captain Diaz lived on the base in officer housing. His two teenaged daughters delighted in displaying themselves in provocative outfits to the young recruits. This day saw them costumed in short-shorts and t-shirts that were obviously a size too small. As the platoon jogged by, Sergeant James, accustomed to the distraction, bellowed "eyes front, eyes front!" The temptation was too much for Hugo. As the the men passed girls bent forward and puckered their lips in a mock kiss. Hugo, with the instinct of an Italian boy from Silver Lake, smiled and blew a kiss to the giggling teenagers. Sergeant James pulled up beside Hugo jogging in lock step. He looked at Hugo with death in his eyes. "You mizable rotten piece of shit, ahll take care a you when we get back to the barn."

The early January sun was rising as the platoon neared their barracks. Sergeant Mugaridge dismissed the men for chow. "Not you Rossi, in the barracks. Sergeant James wants to see you, boy." Hugo was expecting the worst as he stepped through the barracks door. He never saw James or the fist that brought him staggering to his knees. As his head cleared and eyes focused, he looked into the maniacal eyes of Sergeant James, teeth bared, snarling his speech. "Get up you ginny mutha fucka, ahm gonna show you

THE ARRIVAL THE STRUGGLE THE ASCENDANCY

what happens to a recruit who disobeys my orders, especially when it comes to the Company Commander's daughter." Hugo raised himself, wobbly to a standing position. James had positioned his footing for the telling blow when Sergeant Mugaridge gripped his arm and whispered in his ear. "Well, Rossi, you worthless piece of shit, Sergeant Mugaridge just saved your ass and he's now taking your sorry ass over." Hugo ran for one hour at High Port arms around the battalion parade ground. He never looked at the Captain's daughters again.

Leonard Vergenous was officially referred to as pussy by both the D.I.s and his platoon members. Leonard took perverse pleasure in his sobriquet. He felt more a part of the team and was more determined than ever to succeed and perform as well as any other recruit. He had lost fifteen pounds in four week and was beginning to feel confident in his physical abilities. He didn't dare tell anyone that his father was a gynecologist.

"You know, pussy, I thought you were nothing but a fat, sloppy, four-eyed mama's boy." Sergeant James was addressing morning formation. "But you surprised me, pussy, you're just sloppy and four-eyed."

"Yes, sir, this recruit is sloppy and four-eyed, but soon I'll just be four-eyed, sir."

James stroked his chin and smiled in spite of himself. "We'll see, pussy, we'll see."

It was seven weeks into training. It became more intense, night maneuvers, map reading, hand-to-hand combat, and the exhausting obstacle course. The D.I.s were more relaxed, it was now more instructional. They had become more like coaches, with the exception of Sergeant James, who still took the hard line in every phase of training. None of the recruits were allowed calls home for the first four weeks. The discipline and training were so harsh that it was a matter of physical and mental survival that occupied everyone's thoughts, but in the quiet of the evening, after lights out, the warmth and love of Angelina and Francesca overcame Hugo no matter how hard he tried to remove the thoughts of home from his head. It happened on a Wednesday morning. The barracks lights snapped on at four-thirty. Within minutes a commotion arose in the latrine. As Hugo walked quickly toward the latrine, he heard excited voices calling out. "Somebody call for an ambulance!" "Get the Padre, too." "Get Sergeant Kelly down here." Hugo raised himself above the ring of recruits formed about the body of Fredericks, blood pumping from his left wrist as Sergeant Mugaridge attempted to tie a tourniquet to his upper arm. A bloody bayonet lay by his side. Within minutes Private Fredericks was on his way to the base hospital. Three recruits were assigned to clean up detail in the latrine and the day began one-half hour late. Sergeant James instructed the platoon to sit in a circle on the ground that afternoon during a break in a hand-to-hand combat training sessions.

"Awright you just witnessed one of your own, a recruit who could not stand the gaff, take the coward's way out. He would never make a Marine. He couldn't even kill himself the right way." He stood with his hands on his hips surveying the circled seated platoon. "Soo... here's what we're gonna do. Ahm gonna teach you how a real Marine would commit suicide." And for the next hour he selected various recruits and simulated bizarre methods of taking one's life "the right way."

It was over. Ten weeks of close-order drill, Marine Corp. history, the Rifle Prayer, forced marches, the screaming D.I.s. They had made it. Leonard "Pussy" Vergenous was ecstatic. He was a United State Marine. At the graduation ceremony as Sergeant James shook Pussy's hand, the tough-ass Marine actually smiled. "Pussy, ah nevah thought you would make it. You surprised the shit outa me, congratulations." Captain Diaz addressed the company before dismissal. "I'm proud of you men. You have what it takes to be a Marine, and all your life you will honor the Marine Corp motto, *Semper Fidelis*."

Sergeant James bellowed for order and paced before the platoon. "All you baws are movin out tomorrow for Camp Lejeune. You'll be goin to Infantry Training Regiments, that's I.T.R. for short. They're gonna teach you about automatic weapons, explosives, and advance techniques, so start packin cause you're not comin back."

"Sergeant James?"

"Yes, Pussy."

"When do we get a permanent assignment?"

"Pussy, right now I wouldn't assign you to a shithouse. You'll find this all out after I.T.R."

"Got ya, Sarge."

The Infantry Training Regiment coupled with Advanced Infantry Training was the Masters degree for combat bound Marine grunts. It was eight weeks of intensive training in all weaponry and tactics, honing the skills of the still green and untested basic training graduates. It was another step in becoming a warrior in Marine khaki. Finally, word came down that orders were in and would be handed out at the next morning's formation.

There was a special formation after breakfast. The I.T.R. Company First Sergeant called names as he pulled thick manila envelopes from a portable file. Each man responded as his name was called and stepped forward for his envelope. The formation was dismissed. The newly minted Marines tore open their envelopes to find their destination. Boxwood held his officially sealed orders shipping him to Vietnam with a stop at Camp Pendleton, California. He re-read the orders three times shaking his head and grimacing as he turned to Vergenous. "Where you goin?"

"I guess we're all goin to Vietnam." Vergenous looked over Hugo's shoulder. "You comin with us, Hugo?" Hugo finished reading the orders, turned to Vergenous, and nodded."

Marine Corp. Base Camp Pendleton in San Diego was the major staging area for the Marine Corp. as it filled the ranks in Vietnam with replacements for the Marines killed, wounded, or whose enlistment was up. Men left in clusters or individually filling a military air transport plane, orders in hand. It was located on a beautiful strip of San Diego coastline, a stones throw from Tijuana, Mexico. Hugo was assigned to Camp Horno 1st Marine Regiment, 1st Battalion. Boxwood and Pussy were assigned to the same barracks as Hugo, and the three exchanged smiles and back slaps at their good fortune. At rollcall the next morning to everyone's surprise envelopes were passed out to the new arrivals granting two weeks' leave commencing on the coming Friday. It would be the last time home for many of the young Marines anxious to see loved ones and friends.

It was good to see his mother and grandmother again, and he tried to smile and appear cheery as Angelina and Francesca did their best to add pounds to his lean, taught frame, cooing over him at every moment. But, curiously, he discovered that he was anxious to return to California. His home was no longer in Silver

THE ARRIVAL THE STRUGGLE THE ASCENDANCY

Lake, his home was the Marine Corp. The old friends he met seemed distant and uninteresting, a world away from where he had been and who he had become. Nothing of his old world seemed real or of any value. Over the strenuous objections of his mother and grandmother, he left for California after a ten-day stay, eager to be with his fellow Marines.

He arrived at Camp Pendleton technically with three days still left of leave. He rented a car and drove to San Diego center along the Pacific coastline, stopping to enjoy the majestic Pacific beaches at Huntington Beach and San Clemente. He went to Mass in San Juan Capistrano at a Mission built in the early 1800s. It was an early morning mass sparsely attended. The priest celebrated the Mass in Latin and Spanish. The stimple stucco interior was cool and dimly lit by red glass votive candles and early morning sunlight illuminating stained glass windows. His thoughts turned to Vietnam and what he would find there. Would he see action, would he kill enemy troops? He was totally oblivious of the church emptying. He sat in the silent sanctuary finally emerging from him spiritual trance and stepping into the eye-squinting sunlight.

Boxwood and Vergenous arrived in time for Monday morning rollcall and the beginning of training. The screaming and insults were over, the instructors treated the new Marines with respect and an easy manner. Days were filled with instruction in all available weaponry, tactics, map reading, and combat strategy. Nights and weekends were free. The surrounding small towns catered to Marine and Naval personnel. Tijuana was just twenty minutes south. Boxwood, Vergenous, and Hugo were a constant trio on base, but after three nights they were looking for more than the base could offer.

"Hey, Boxwood, whaddya say we go into Tijuana, get a drink, some burgers, see the ladies? There's a bus that comes by the front of our building I think every hour."

Boxwood broke into a Cheshire cat grin. "You say ladies, man? I need a lady bad." Hugo motioned toward Vergenous who lay snoring on his bunk fully clothed, eyeglasses half off his face.

Hugo shook his head as he spoke. "You wanna take him with us?"

"Yeah, let's wake him up, he'll start cryin if we leave him behind." Hugo grabbed the toe of his boot. "Pussy, come on, we're goin to Mexico, you in?"

Vergenous sprang up rescuing his glasses before they fell to the floor. "Yeah, yeah, I'm in, when we leavin?"

"Get cleaned up, we're leaving in a half hour."

The bus stop, not far from the barracks entrance, was serviced by the county's civilian bus line. It transported military personnel through various connections throughout the San Diego/Tijuana area. A dozen young Marines were waiting at the stop when they arrived. The air was filled with good natured ribbing and boasting of the upcoming sexual exploits. The bus pulled up to the stop, doors hissing open. Before the anxious borders ascended the three steps into the bus, the white haired black driver held up his hand. "Wait a minute, boys, I need to tell ya that Tijuana is off limits for the time being. When you get to the border, the MP's won't let you get across."

The grumbling and expletives spilled forth. Most of the disgruntled Marines abandoned the bus stop, assessing their options. Hugo mounted the first bus step. "Driver, you got any suggestions, you know, we're lookin for a few beers, maybe some pretty ladies."

THE ARRIVAL THE STRUGGLE THE ASCENDANCY

The driver winked and smiled. "C'mon in, boys, I'm headed to Ocean Breeze, a fine beachfront town, and on the outskirts is the Little French Palace. You'll find everything you're lookin for there."

The ride was brief, cutting through some backroads and ultimately arriving at what looked like a typical seaside town, with a strip of storefronts and garish signs running down what was clearly the main street. As Hugo, Boxwood, and Vergenous stepped off the bus and followed the flow of the crowd, civilian and military alike, two of Ocean Breezes' finest leaned against the black and white patrol cars, all too used to the activity of the bus arriving from Pendleton. The two Sheriffs could have come from central casting. The older of the two, a Sergeant, wore a tan ten-gallon Stetson. He was well near six feet with a huge protruding stomach obscuring his pistol belt. His jowly face was beet red and his sweaty neck measured twenty inches. His partner was a carbon copy, one hundred pounds lighter. The Sergeant puffed on a cigar as his squinted eyes followed Hugo, Boxwood, and Vergenous. As the jovial trio passed the patrol cards, Hugo's eyes made contact with the Sergeant's jowly face.

"Hey Bawz, hold up a minute, c'mon ovah hyea." The Sheriffs remained leaning against the patrol car, ankles crossed. Hugo, Boxwood, and Vergenous looked at one another and warily walked toward the patrol cars. "Well, well, what we got here, Percy, is three faan lookin Marine re-croots, don't we Percy?"

The younger Sheriff took out a Lucky Strike, tapped it on the side of a Zippo lighter, lit the cigarette, exhaled and finally answered "well Sergeant, it sho do look that way, cept fo the black boy here." He sniggered as he spoke. The Sergeant canted his head sideways and squinted as he spoke to Hugo. "You know bawz, folks roun hyea don't take it too kindly when they see whites and blacks together, you know what I'm talking about bawz?" Boxwood felt a rush of anger welling up in him. He simultaneously realized where he was and succeeded in acting casually. Hugo sensed the issue and spoke, mustering a smile.

"Ahh...well, officer, I understand your concern, but we're just gonna get something to eat, maybe buy a few things and head back to the base." The Sheriff smiled sardonically. "Okay, baws, you know we'll be patrolling these streets lookin fo trouble. Y'all enjoy Ocean Breeze." As they distanced themselves from the Sheriffs, Boxwood could contain himself no longer. "Those rotten fucken rednecks are dumb as dirt and you know they have sex with animals and their sisters." Vergenous stepped into the conversation. "Yeah, and usually the animals are better lookin than the sisters." They erupted in hilarious choking laughter. Boxwood wrapped his arm around Vergenous's shoulder. "Pussy man, you're the best!"

They ate cheeseburgers and fries at the Rainbow Café, drinking three pitchers of beer. Boxwood endured a few curious stares, but the café was too busy to make any difference and he was one of several black Marines. Afternoon gave way to night and the trio, now fueled with alcohol, found themselves on the outskirts of Ocean Breeze at the Little French Palace, the largest and busiest whorehouse in the county. The bouncers working the door were the human equivalent of buffalos with mean dispositions. One was field hand white, the other was cotton pickin black. The field hand spoke first. "What you baws want in hyea, you lookin a get boozed up and laid, that right?"

Vergenous realized this was his moment. "No, sir, we're just going to have a few beers and head back to Pendleton, if that's okay with you?"

The buffalos looked at one another, the cotton pickers face split into a wide grin showing a scattering of large white teeth. "Well, that's right nice a you baws. Well now, if y'all want to go in it's five bucks a piece and mind your manners in there and I specially mean you, niggah." The cotton picker waved his finger at Boxwood as he spoke.

The interior of the Palace was dark, smoky, and jammed with young and old from Pendleton. The large Wurlitzer jukebox on an elevated platform blared twanging country and western music. There were at least fifty or sixty young and not so young scantily clad women lining the walls, sitting with potential customers and plying their trade along the fifty foot bar. Hugo led the way to one of the two vacant tables. Within seconds, two white girls in their late teens, only recently acquainted with shoes, pulled chairs to the table. A third woman somewhere in her forties sidled up to Boxwood and sat next to him placing a hand on his knee. She was showing some hard mileage but still attractive in a slutty fashion. Hugo and Vergenous were engrossed in conversation with the southern belles as drinks arrived at the table. She tightened her grip on Boxwood's knee and slid her hand toward his inner thigh. She bent near and whispered into his ear. "You wanna drink now honey or you wanna take me upstairs and show me that long black snake a yours?"

The effect on Boxwood was prominent. "Well, you know, it all depends, mam, what do you charge?"

"Well honey, for you it's on sale tonight. It all depends on what you're buyin." And the lady bluntly spelled out the menu. "Take your choice, honey."

Hugo and Vergenous were in heated negotiation as Boxwood rose from the table and followed her toward a stairway leading to rooms on the second and third floors. She pulled him by his right hand as they cut through the crowd. A table of Hell's Angels teetered in their chairs, loudly proclaiming their superiority over the Marine Corp. Suddenly a deep southern voice boomed out "Hey, niggah, where y'all goin with my wife, you sumbitch?" A sweaty red-faced wall of drunken tattooed biker came stumbling toward Boxwood, fist cocked, frothing at the mouth. He bellowed incoherently as he swung wildly at Boxwood with a right hand followed by an equally ineffective left. He stood with legs apart to steady himself as he prepared another assault. Hugo and Vergenous turned toward the commotion as the tableful of bikers converged on Boxwood. He saw his target and drop kicked the wall's scrotum dead on target. The wall's eyes rolled back in his head as he crumpled to the floor. The Little French Palace was under siege as Hugo, Vergenous, and Boxwood crashed through a fire exit, the two buffalo in pursuit. They dodged the cars in the parking area and headed for the dense woods across the highway. The buffalos came up short at the highway, turning abruptly to face fifty bikers and Marines in a free for all once again attempting to determine the age-old questions of who is the tougher man.

They made it back to Ocean Breeze center on foot, catching the last bus to the base at one am. Boxwood chuckled to himself all the way back, occasionally grunting "took care of that big cracker."

They decided to stay on base Sunday. Hugo was a regular at the base Catholic Chapel. His faith was his strength. At Sunday Mass he prayed with intensity. It was as if he expected a call to arms by Jesus himself. Lenny Vergenous disappeared after Sunday lunch at the company Mess Hall. It was puzzling to Hugo and Boxwood. Hugo asked some of the men who bunked close to Vergenous if they had seen him since lunch, but no one had.

The Monday morning formation was groggy-eyed as stragglers joined the formation in hurried steps. Three men were marked AWOL. One of them was Vergenous. Sergeant Williams paced back and forth before the platoon. "Where's ma boy, Pussy? Anybody see my little Pussy?" Williams caught Hugo's eye "You Rossi, you seen him anywhere?"

"No Sarge, I haven't. I saw him yesterday afternoon in the Mess Hall, that was the last time."

Williams stood at the front of the formation hand on hip, stroking his chin. Hugo turned to find Boxwood who motioned toward town and frowned. Williams assumed his normal demeanor and flipped through his clipboard. "All right, back to business. We'll see if our boy Pussy shows up this afternoon so ah can stick my ten and a half up his chubby ass." Hugo pulled Boxwood aside after the platoon was dismissed. They talked as they walked to the Mess Hall for breakfast. "Boxwood, I've got a funny feeling he's in town. He probably fell in love with one of the ladies at the Palace."

"Yeah, well Hugo, if he's with one of those whores, you know she's got all his money and she's probably got some mean assed boyfriend or pimp."

"Boxwood, we gotta go look for him. He's a good shit and he's gullible." They badgered Williams until he relented and allowed them a pass to town at two pm with the admonition that he would not call the military police until the next morning. The battered cab dropped them at the front door of the Little French Palace. The doors were open airing out the previous night's smoke, booze, and obnoxious perfumes. A lone bartender stood cutting fruit for his bar set-up as they approached. He smiled as he spoke. "Sorry, boys, ah cain't serve ya till we're open at five o'clock."

Hugo leaned against the bar as he spoke. "That's okay. Actually we're looking for a buddy of ours, he's AWOL from the base and we're worried about him."

The bartender stopped cutting fruit, but the knife still twirled in his hand. "Well that's pretty serious stuff, y'all got a picture of him?"

"No we don't, but he's a short chubby guy, wears eye glasses and smiles a lot." The bartender nooded, put down the knife, and flashed a knowing smile. "Well you baws are in luck. Ah think ah know where your boy is. He was hangin here chasin Jewel Lafontaine last night and spending money like it was water. Evabody loves the guy and evabody was callin him Pussy.." Boxwood and Hugo turned at the same time and headed for the front door. Hugo stopped in his tracks and turned to the bartender.

"Hey, what did you say that girl's name was again?"

"That was Lafontaine."

"Do you know where we can find her?"

"Yeah, she's got a trailer a couple a miles from here at the Shangri-La trailer park. You can't miss her trailer, it's the pink one. And by the way, please don't tell her I told you all a this." The tired black cab driver and his tired cab delivered them directly to the Shangri-La and the pink trailer. The cabbie idled his engine while Hugo and Boxwood approached the trailer door emblazoned with stylized lettering that read "Jewels House of Love." Boxwood pounded on the door. Country and western wailed from the heart of the trailer. Boxwood pounded again. The door opened to reveal a thirty-year-old, bleary-eyed, platinum blonde with large voluptuous breasts barely restrained by a cheap Japanese kimono. She was drunk and stoned and wobbly on her bare feet. "Y'all gotta come back baws, ah got some business ahm finishing up raht now. See y'all tomorrow afternoon."

Hugo held the door open firmly as he spoke "Jewel, we're here to get Pussy, he's AWOL and he's in trouble." Boxwood slipped by Jewel who exploded in anger. "Hey, you niggah, you get outa ma house now, ahm callin the goddamned police on you and this here cracker, ya here me niggah?"

Vergenous lay spread eagled on the pink satin sheets of Jewel's heart shaped bed. He was completely naked, drunk, and stoned. Hugo followed Boxwood to the bedroom with Jewel screeching in his ear. "Yo friend Pussy here s'been fucken me for two days and ah want my money for anybody goes anywhere!" Hugo rounded up Pussy's clothing and found his billfold in his shoes, completely empty.

"Well, Jewel, looks like you already took all his money, so we'll be goin now." Jewel stood in the narrow corridor, arms and legs outstretched, kimono wide open showing a once attractive body. "Ah want ma money." Boxwood staggered forward with the semi nude Pussy pushing Jewel aside. Hugo followed with what was left of his uniform as Jewel opened her mouth to scream her demands.

Hugo put his finger to her lips. "Shhh...I'm not going to call the M.P.s and report that you rolled my friend, so just calm down and we'll be gone.

Pussy was at formation the next morning. Sergeant Williams barely looked at him and nothing ever came of the matter. Hugo sat on the edge of his bunk polishing a brass buckle. "So Pussy, considering the fact that we saved your ass, are you gonna tell us about your adventure?" Pussy looked up from his book with a jack-o-lantern grin. "Hugo, Boxwood, she did everything you can think of to me for two days and I mean everything. She even used tools of her trade. You know I'll be going back."

It was time. The incessant call for more troops came in daily to Camp Pendleton. Vergenous and Boxwood were leaving a day ahead of Hugo. He accompanied them to the air base at Miramar. There were military aircraft and civilian aircraft taking on hundreds of Marines, all heading for Vietnam. They exchanged hugs and backslaps and made promises to catch up with each other. As they parted, Boxwood held up his right fist as he turned. "Hey man, remember, *Semper Fi*, *Semper Fi*, man." Hugo watched them as they boarded the plane, wondering if he would ever see them again. He never did, the war swallowed them up.

Chapter 12

VIETNAM

The Pan Am Boeing 727 was filled to capacity with military personnel all debarking for Danang Airport. Hugo had checked his sea bag into the luggage bay and carried on a small gym bag with personal articles. He sat next to two Air Force recruits who laughed and joked in a Texas drawl all the way from California. The stewardesses, who were all as young as the majority of passengers, were more than accommodating. Blonde, skinny, and in matching blue skirts, they reveled in the attention they were receiving from the planeload of young men. The Captain's voice informed the passengers that they would be landing in approximately fifteen minutes and he directed the cabin crew to prepare for landing. The 727 banked into a long circular maneuver to align with the runway. Seatbelts were snapped on and tightened and the plane descended to tree top level. As the jet glided to a landing Hugo noticed bomb craters, burnt out trucks, and vintage aircraft nosed over or missing engines. A portable aluminum staircase was jostled into position. As Hugo passed through the doorway, the scorching sun caused him to mutter to himself "holy fucken shit." He followed passengers walking toward a deteriorating low-slung building with a simple sign identifying it as a terminal. He trudged toward the terminal building with two hundred other passengers, the asphalt soft from the searing heat.

The first sounds were a sputtering of small explosions emanating from one of the largest ammo dumps in Vietnam two hundred yards to the left of the terminal. The terminal bound crowd slowed, looking left. The explosions came in quick succession, a deafening roar of ammunition, bombs, and jet fuel turned into an inferno spewing shrapnel and unexploded munitions as far as the terminal and beyond. A panic took hold of the passengers running helter skelter looking for refuge from shrapnel whistling through the air. The two Texas airmen fell to the asphalt mortally wounded along with six others. Hugo ran, head down toward the corner of a metal Quonset hut, heart pounding, ears ringing and in a state of confused panic. He crashed into the corner of the building burying his head in his arms. The staccato chatter of 50 caliber machine guns mixed with the sound of shrieking jets strafing the jungle surrounding the ammo dump added more fury to the surreal moment. Various sized vehicles raced by the Quonset hut loaded with troops heading out of the compound. From a distance he heard someone screaming at him. He opened his eyes to see a Red Cross truck over laden with what he assumed to be nurses and doctors. "Hey, Marine, off your ass, let's go, let's go." It was a sooty-faced woman in her fifties. She wore a steel helmet strapped to her chin and a baggy olive drab t-shirt. The truck lurched forward picking up speed rapidly. Hugo lunged forward racing for the tailgate, helping hands hoisted him aboard. He collapsed next to a young marine with a bandaged torso and head, an I.V. held precariously by a nurse in the speeding rocking truck. The truck slowed, the mood among the passengers lightened. A nurse called to one of the doctors still in operating room garb. "Hey Doctor Zeke, I think you soiled yourself when that first explosion went off." He called back with a cupped hand "Yeah, Nurse Cupcake, you wanna change me?" The truck erupted in laughter and more ribald comments as they swung off the truck to the beach sand. Two dozen more various types of vehicles pulled onto the beach sand, people piling off, apparently familiar with the area. Hugo stood alone looking for someone in charge. He saw a Master Sergeant, clipboard in hand calling out directions.

"Hey, Sergeant" he called out as he jogged toward the only person who looked like he knew what was going on.

"Yeah, what's up Marine?"

"Sarge, I just got off that Pan Am flight and things started blowing up. Next thing I know somebody hauls me onto a deuce and a half and I'm here with no sea bag, no rifle, nothing."

The Sergeant raised his eyebrows knowingly and nodded in sympathy.

"Okay buddy, we're gonna take care of ya. You got any orders?" He fumbled with a shirt button and pulled out folded orders. The Sergeant scanned the paperwork. "You gotta report to H.Q. 3rd Marine Division, but we're not goin back till tomorrow a.m. or until somebody gives me some orders. There's a deuce and a half about six trucks down. See a Corporal Mooney, tell him I told you to pick up a poncho liner to sleep in. We'll be staying all night. I'll show you where to go in the morning.

"Hey, Sarge, where are we anyway?"

"They call this China Beach, this is where the nurses and doctors come to play. Boy, I've seen some things here…um…umm" his voice trailed off.

He entered the field Headquarters of the 3rd Marines unshaven, unwashed, and hungry. A large black Master Sergeant read his orders and checked a roster of new arrivals. "Well, Marine, welcome to Nam. Why don't you get over to the Mess Hall, get some breakfast. and come back. By that time I'll have figured out where you belong."

Hugo returned an hour later, still dirty and unshaven, but feeling the warm comfort of a full stomach. "How was the breakfast, Rossi? We got a couple of cooks who worked at some big time hotels in New York."

"It was good, Sarge, but it looks like I won't be staying for dinner."

"I'm afraid not, Rossi. You'll be goin up to Dong Ha, that's in Quang Tri Province, a real vacation paradise. You'll be leaving in about twenty minutes."

The ride north to Dong Ha was bone rattling and dusty. Hugo sat alone in the rear of an open sided three-quarter ton truck. His eyes wandered the verdant landscape and acres of swampy rice paddies with black clad farmers wearing cone shaped hats or bandanas against the searing humid sun. They stooped and tended to the rice plants slowly and methodically with whole families working together as their parents and grandparents had done before them. Hugo marveled at the beauty and tranquility of the countryside contrasted by the violence of armies clashing with one another over old rivalries.

The truck arrived in a cloud of dust at 3rd Battalion 4th Marines Dong Ha, Quang Tri Province. The Battalion headquarters was ringed with white painted rocks. The Battalion pennant lay limp against its staff. The heat bore down on Hugo as he walked toward the headquarters tent. Sweat poured from his forehead and soaked his olive-drab fatigue shirt. The tent sides were rolled up to allow some relief from the stifling heat. A large rotating circular fan droned futiley against the one hundred ten degrees registering on a circular thermometer mounted at the entrance to the headquarters. "What can I do for you, troop?" A tall, skinny Lance Corporal turned from a typewriter as he spoke. His nametag read Bumpp.

"Rossi, Hugo Rossi. I'm reporting for duty." Bumpp turned to a worn clipboard and ran his finger down a list of names stopping at Hugo's. "Yup, this is you, Rossi. Y'all come in from Okinawa?"

"Yeah, I came in yesterday, almost got blown up in Danang."

"Yeah, we heard they had some trouble down there." Bumpp stood up and extended his hand. "Well, Hugo Rossi, let me be the first to welcome you to the absolute asshole of the world. Ma name's Bumpp, Billy Lee late of Geneva, Alabama. "Ah'm the Battalion clerk. Let's see where we're gonna assan you. Rossi, you're gonna be assaned to Mike Co. Good bunch a boys. You're gonna report to Master Sergeant Demopolous, he's a good ole boy, been around for awhile. Let's see, you're gonna need a weapon, ammo, and some Vietnam duds. There's a quartermaster hut to the left as you leave here. They'll fix you up with everything. When you get back ah'll have a ride for you up to Mike Co. It's about ten minutes up the road, if you can call it that."

"Bumpp, let me ask you something, is it always this hot here?"

"Better get used to it Rossi, this is what it is."

A bored pot-bellied supply Sergeant scanned Hugo's orders and slowly issued clothing, helmet, and supplies. He directed him to the Battalion armorer who issued him an M-16 rifle, twenty magazines of ammo with twenty rounds for each clip, and four hand grenades. The ride to Mike Company took about fifteen minutes. The jeep driver pulled up to the company headquarters, waited for Hugo to unload, and sped off leaving Hugo in a cloud of hot dust. He stood in the doorway of the headquarter tent, which was empty. The tent flaps were raised for the nonexistent airflow. He turned to see a tall young man in a sweat stained t-shirt and a fatigue cap emblazoned with Captains bars. Next to him strode a short bull-necked. Broad-chested man in this thirties, also t-shirt clad, with First Sergeant written all over him. Hugo snapped to attention as they approached and held a salute. "Private Hugo Rossi reporting for duty, sir."

"All right Rossi, at ease. It's too friggin hot to be formal in this sun. C'mon inside the headquarters. I'm Captain Vanarsdale and this is 1st Sergeant Demopolous."

To Hugo's surprise, Demopolous extended his hand. "Good to have you with us, Rossi. That's Italian, isn't it?"

"Yeah Sarge, one hundred percent."

"Good, where you from?"

"Rhode Island, sir, not to be confused with Long Island." Demopolous smiled showing large square teeth slightly spaced.

"Yeah, I know where it is, we're neighbors. I'm from Pawcatuck, Connecticut. Got a big Greek family back there. Everybody's in the pizza business. Captain, I'm gonna assign this man to Hightower, he needs a couple a guys." Vanarsdale nodded in agreement while lighting a cigar. The 3rd Platoon had returned from a patrol the day previously and were scattered about in a semi-circle fifty yards away seeking relief under a stand of trees.

They were bare-chested or wore sweat soaked khaki colored tee shirts, busy cleaning rifles or machine guns. Staff Sergeant Mike Hightower stood talking and gesturing to two Corporals as Hugo and Demopolous approached.

"Hey, Gregg, you bringin me a good man here?" He smiled lazily as he spoke, running his hand through his thick black hair. "Yeah, Mike, I think he is. Say hello to PFC Hugo Rossi."

"Welcome aboard the 3rd Platoon, Rossi. Find a tent with an empty bunk and drop your gear, meet some of the guys in the platoon." The platoon was a cross section of America, young men from every walk of life, college graduates, high school drop outs, young black men from the ghetto, young Hispanic men from the barrio, and white bread young men from insular communities. They were from California to Maine.

"Rossi." It was Sergeant Hightower walking slowly in the fetid air.

"Yeah, Sarge?"

"You're gonna be assigned to bravo squad. The squad leader is right under that tree." He pointed toward a tangled mass of trees. "Name's Corporal Mendez, report to him when you drop your gear."

"Right, Sarge."

Mendez was a short wiry Mexican American from Phoenix. He wore a perpetual smile. "Welcome aboard, Rossi, glad to have you with us." He turned to the squad scattered under the shaded area. "Listen up men, this here is Hugo Rossi, he's now one of us, show him the ropes." There were feeble smiles and hand gestures. Hugo stood scanning the area feeling awkward.

"Hey, Hugo, c'mon over, take a seat over here." Hugo sat down on the scrub grass next to a large shirtless black man sipping lemonade from a canteen cup. "You look warm man, get your cup and grab some a dat bug juice over there. Got a lotta ice in it, nice n cold." Hugo drained the canteen cup and returned for a second helping. The black marine extended his large hand. "Ma name is Leon LaFleur, ahm from Louisiana. Ah must a had a French massah back when my great grandmother was pickin cotton and sugar cane." He roared with laughter, slapping his thigh. "This here guy next to me is Reginald Coxwain, helluva name for a black man, ain't it? We call him snake cause he's so tall and skinny. Over there to your left is Billy Riley, he's from Boston. Ah cain't unnastand a word that boy says. Next to him is ole Polack, ah cain't pronounce his name, that's why we call him Polack, he's from Chicago. Then we got over there under that tree Bushell ass brown, next to him is Mendoza, then there's Rizzo, ah think he's eyetalian like you, then we got Louis Ramsey, we call him Boots, ah don't know why. You'll get to know everybody soon enough, that's if you last long enough in this shithole of a country."

"Thanks for the introduction, Leon. What do we do up here every day?"

"Well, buddy, we're supposed to go out on patrols and search and destroy the NVA and the VC. That's the North Vietnamese Army and the Viet Cong. The VC are the real dirty little assholes. Most of them are down south. They're like the militia and they're harder to kill than cockroaches."

"You ever kill any, Leon?" Leon smiled, took a sip of bug juice, and turned to look at Hugo with squinted eyes. "Yeah, man, I surely did. I don't know how many, but I know I did. I wish I could kill em all, but I need help, that's why you're here Rossi. I figure you're replacing Bobby Tripp, he stepped on a mine a couple weeks ago and bam, he was scattered all over the place. He was a good ole boy, only eighteen years old. You stick with me. I'll show you the ropes."

"All right, listen up everybody." It was Corporal Mendez. "We're goin into the boonies for a while, tomorrow morning at six sharp. Check your pack for C-rations, stock up on ammo, and fill your canteens. And turn in early tonight. Riley, Polack, Bateman, you got the first watch, report to the O.D. for posting and keep your eyes and ears open."

Hugo turned to his new friend. "Leon, where are we headed tomorrow?"

"Well, I figure we're goin up to Vandergrift, that's like a combat base. Most likely we'll relieve the platoon up there and sit tight up there fore who knows how long. That puts us out front of evabody. If you're very unlucky, you get to be an F.O. For you greenhorns, that means forward observer."

There was no hot chow for Mike Company. Dinner was canned beans and hot dogs with canned peaches for dessert, and there was boiling water for Nescafe coffee. Hugo lay on a bunk with a ticking mattress. The tent flaps were rolled up and replaced by mosquito netting, which did little to impede the flying insects. He used his arm as a pillow and stared at the full moon. For the first time, he smelled Vietnam. The moist smell of jungle vegetations, of human waste drifting from the slit trench latrine, the noxious odor of t-shirts wrung of sweat and hung out to dry for the next day's wear. There was a sudden wave of loneliness that overcame him. He was alone, he was a dispensable number, a throw away soldier. He knew nothing of fighting as a Marine. He had never fired his weapon on a battlefield. He thought of death and how it might come. Would it be a sniper, would he be taking a shit and be shot in mid bowel movement? He was too young. He thought, I haven't made love to enough women. He thought of Angelina and her soft eyes, her loving caress. His was a feeling of total, debilitating helplessness, and as he had done on so many other occasions of insecurity, he prayed. He prayed himself to an uneasy sleep.

The 3rd Platoon humped its way to Vandergrift combat base three hours away. The Northeast Monsoon season was at its apex, drenching the jungle and the advancing Marines intermittently on a daily basis, adding to the miseryof jungle warfare. They walked in single file through the wet steamy vegetation, the oppressive heat and humidity drenching every man with rivulets of sweat. They carried full field packs, extra canteens of water, extra ammo, M-16 rifles, M60 and 50 caliber machine guns, and as many grenades as they could pin on their webbing straps. Hugo walked behind Leon taking his lead. Leon talked over his shoulder in a whisper. "Captain Vanarsdale gets pissed if we announce our arrival to Charlie." He chuckled as he wiped sweat from his brow streaming from his helmet with his crooked finger. The trail in places was barely passable, bamboo and tall grass tore at fatigue trousers, equipment grew heavier with every mile walked. All that could be heard through the murky sweltering air was the heavy breathing of marine grunts wary of booby traps and ambush and the ruffle of webbing and backpacks against clothing and skin. The point man who scouted two hundred yards forward of the platoon reported back to Captain Vanarsdale that there was a clearing ahead. The platoon sprawled about under the shade of the jungle foliage along the perimeter of the small clearing. The sounds of backpacks and helmets being cast off came almost in unison. The men fell to the jungle floor for momentary relief. Word was passed, there would be no smoking. Hugo sat next to Leon who gulped from his canteen thirstily.

"Hey, Hugo" Hugo turned to his left to see a young freckly faced marine extending is hand. "My name's Ronnie Haliday. They call me Doc, I'm the platoon corpsman."

"Glad to meet you, Doc, but I hope I won't need your services while I'm out here." Leon leaned over to talk to doc.

"She-it, Doc, tell him there's no charge for house calls or bandages. Rossi, this little fucker Doc here is a hero, he saved two of our guys two weeks ago." At that moment Hugo felt something fall onto his neck and slide into his fatigue shirt followed by another that attached itself to the back of his neck. He leaped to his feet, ripping the four-inch large black worm from his neck. "Leon, what the fuck are these things?" He reached inside of his shirt searching for the other visitor. Leon and Doc exchanged knowing smiles.

"Ma man, welcome to the Nam jungle. Them's what's known as leeches or blood suckers. Ya just gotta grab em before they dig in, right Doc?"

"Yeah, pull em off right away." Doc sat cross-legged sucking on an unlit cigar. He scanned the jungle as he spoke. "You know, Hugo, this country is absolutely beautiful and cruelly vicious."

Polack joined the conversation with Boots. "Ayy, Hugo, Doc's right. This fucken shit hole of a country is really vicious. Bout a couple a weeks ago one of our guys gets attacked by a tiger, a fucken tiger. Do you believe it?" Boots Ramsey raised both hands. "Wait a minute, let me tell you guys just how shitty this country really is. Not too long ago there was a marine platoon on patrol in Quang Nam or some little village down south and these guys are hot, thirsty, and tired and this little girl comes out with a glass filled with what looks like ice and a bottle of Coke and she fills the glass for some poor grunt. Naturally, he gulps it down and it turns out the ice was pieces of glass and the little girl she just stands there smiling. I heard they wasted the entire fucken village."

"All right, everybody saddle up, we're back on the trail, no talking and no smoking, let's go." They arrived at Vandergrift in late afternoon drenched in sweat, thirsty, and tired. The 2nd Platoon swapped jibes with the incoming Marines, fell into single file formation, and started the trek back to Dong Ha. The combat base was the most forward outpost in Quang Tri Province—the tip of an arrow protruding into the thick jungle and exposed to attack at any given moment. The Platoon took up positions in a sand bagged enclave with bunkers and heavy caliber machine guns scanning the perimeter. Claymore Mines were planted at strategic locations, vegetation was cleared surrounding the base to inhibit ambush. A forward observer was posed a hundred yards forward and one posted rearward. The days droned by. There were occasional sorties probing the thick foliage insuring that there was no buildup of Viet Cong militia preparing an assault. The days were unbearable, wet and stifling, followed by evenings of temperatures in the low seventies. Piss warm water was drawn from two four hundred gallon olive drab trailer-mounted water tanks. Food was C-rations. The lucky men washed themselves with green bottles of antibacterial phisohex. The effect was fleeting. They relieved themselves in open slit trenches shoveling lime over the waste to no avail. Days turned into a week of enduring steam room heat and drenching rain, and endless attempts at avoiding red ants and other crawling biting insects and snakes. Days consisted of cleaning and re-cleaning weapons, avoiding the sun as much as possible, and talking about food and sex.

The sweltering heat of the boring day dragged into another night of intermittent sleep. Hugo lay against the burlap sack perimeter wall rolled into a poncho liner staring at the sky, hands clasped behind his head. From the darkness came the shrieking, twittering, and grunting of the nocturnal jungle creatures. Bats swept silently overhead sensing prey. From time to time a fleet of choppers would swoosh through the skies delivering troops and supplies. "Rossi, wake up, up an at em." It was Corporal Mendez, clipboard in hand.

"Yeah, Mendez, I'm awake."

"Okay, little screw up in assignments, you're on guard duty for four hours, let's go. You're gonna relieve Mendoza." He followed Mendez a hundred yards east of the base. "Halt, who goes there?" Mendoza's perfect white teeth gleamed in the moonlight as he smiled at his relief. "Hey, Mendez, amigo, you brought the FNG."

"Yeah, he's gotta pull his load." After a few minutes of instruction, Mendez turned to leave with Mendoza. As they did Hugo whispered, "Hey, Mendoza, what's FNG?" He flashed a smile. "That's you, man, fucken new guy."

He sat in the hollow of a ring of tall shrubs and gnarled bent trees. Every sense was alive. He checked his grenades, the ammo clip on the browning automatic rifle. He fingered the flare gun. Every shadow, every snapping twig was advancing VC. His relief came at two. He lay wrapped in his poncho liner sleepless. He thought of his father, his heroism, his courage. Could he live up to this?

Corporal Mendez roused Bravo Squad as he walked the enclave perimeter. "Everybody up, we got a formation. Everybody up, let's go, let's go." Darkness gave way to the breaking dawn as Sergeant Hightower strode to the front of the assembled platoon. "Morning men, I got word this morning that the company is headed out for a while to do a little humpin the boonies." There were groans and mumbled curses, sounds of exasperation.

"Captain, we gonna get a chance to get back to the bunker line first, I need more medical supplies."

"No, Doc, I'm sorry. I wish we were. We're gonna get supplied by chopper. I'll make sure your order gets on board, see me when we're done here." The medic nodded in assent. "Alright, men, get your gear in order, looks like we'll be here for another full day till the company arrives and then we do what we get paid to do – find the enemy and engage." The men returned to the humdrum activities of the sweat soaked, rain soaked day resigned to forty or fifty days of c-rations, no showers and the threat of death with every footfall.

Leon placed his massive hand on Hugo's shoulder. "Hugo, man, we gonna bust your cherry on this trip. All it takes is a month of humpin and bumpin the boonies and your ass ain't no virgin no more. Ain't that right Snake?"

"Damn straight, Leon, and I expect you gonna watch my black ass pretty closely cause I'm short. I only got 115 days and a wake up call left in this mutha fucken shithole."

Three Sea Knight choppers hovered over the base camp the next afternoon landing one at a time in the clearing to the rear of the perimeter sand bags. The wump, wump, wump of the beating blades was deafening and sent clouds of dust into the super heated air. The chopper blades twirled lazily never stopping as c-rations, water, ammo, weapons and medical supplies were unloaded. A canvas sack of mail was hand carried to Sergeant Hightower. In minutes, they were airborne beating their way back to Danang. The 3rd Platoon had been without a Platoon leader for almost two months, since 1st Lieutenant Sal Colangelo had been hit with a dozen pieces of shrapnel in a surprise mortar attach while on patrol. He had recently sent a post card from the Navy hospital in San Diego. A new Platoon leader was coming up with the company the next day. Mail call produced a dozen letters for Hugo all but one from Angelina. He sorted through the letters stopping at the unfamiliar handwriting and read the return address. He slowly recognized the name and murmured to himself. "Lorraine Ciccone, the dance." The faint smell of perfume emanated from the envelope as he cautiously opened it. He noticed that the letter had been forwarded from two previous bases. She had gotten his address from Al Vacolla's sister. She hoped he was fine and in good health, was he with good people, what was Vietnam like, and she finished with "please write when you can." He sat back against the sandbag wall, closed his eyes, held the envelope to his nostrils and recalled the evening and how beautiful she was. He was physically stirred by the thoughts of that evening. He sighed audibly and stuffed the letter into his backpack. Angie's letters poured out her love for her son. She was very worried, why hadn't he written, was he all right, did he have to fire his gun, was he getting enough to eat, did he have any new friends? Nana was feeling fine, she still pushes herself every day, she goes to church every morning, sometimes she talks softly to herself as if she were having a conversation with papa, she still misses him terribly, I can't wait for you to be home. He wrote Angie for a half hour cross-legged writing on a piece of scrap plywood. He included a separate note to Francesca. He sealed the envelope and sat back against the tree trunk at his back. Thoughts of his mother and grandmother were overpowering, tears welled in his eyes. He quickly swiped at the corners of his eyes with the back of his hand. The faint scent of perfume drifted from his pack. He reached for Lorraine's letter and began to write.

The next morning during a c-ration breakfast, a SeaHorse chopper corkscrewed to a landing, blades still twirling, and newly minted Annapolis graduate and Quantico trained 2nd Lieutenant Ebenezer Watson dropped to the ground with bag and baggage. The chopper spiraled skyward in a cloud of dust as the new Platoon leader juggled his rifle and equipment in quick time to the sand bagged perimeter. Hugo and the rest of the Platoon watched as Hightower presented himself to the new Lieutenant with a crisp salute. "Mutha fucka can't find his ass with two hands," Boots Ramsey mumbled.

"Look at this little skinny, spit shined honkey white boy." It was Bushell Ass Brown shaking his head as he spoke. "We gonna have to show this boy how to shit in the woods." Hightower called a formation to introduce Watson. It did not go well. He stammered, he sweat profusely in the heat. He had a baby face, he was tall, pale, and skinny and yet he had made it through Quantico OCS.

The entire company arrived a day late. Vanarsdale, Platoon leaders, Demopolous, and the Platoon Sergeants huddled squatting in a circle in a corner of the encircling sand bags for twenty minutes. Maps were on the ground. Vanarsdale kept on pointing and gesturing toward the north. The mission came down through Hightower. "We're goin out tomorrow morning in three columns, about a half mile between columns that's so we won't be shooting each other's ass off. We're goin out for about six weeks, get some rest."

The columns left at dawn in single file, each column breaking new ground. As they left the combat base, a Platoon from Foxtrot Company filtered into the void. The column strung out in a long line. The heat was unbearable, sweat poured out from beneath Hugo's steel helmet, the salty perspiration stinging his eyes. His shirt was drenched down to the waistband of his trousers, bamboo plants and saw grasses tore at the legs, booby traps could be anywhere. This was the Viet Congs backyard. This was Charlie's neighborhood and the dinks didn't want anyone in their backyard. They were two hours out of the firebase when two muffled detonations threw everyone to the jungle floor. Hugo felt something tear through his fatigue trouser leg. His heart pounded furiously as he scanned the brush around him fingering the M16 ensuring the safety was off. Leon was ten feet ahead of him, he looked back and speaking to no one cursed "fucken gook, homemade land mines." The column cautiously rose to its feet. Leon dropped back to check on Hugo.

"How ya doin?"

"I'm okay, I just put a hole in my pants leg." He pointed to the sharp pointed piece of bamboo protruding from the ground.

"Rossi, you are one lucky grunt, that piece of bamboo could have killed you, the tips got poison on it man."

"Leon, why out here with booby traps and mines, this is out in nowhere."

"Cause Charlie's in the area and this is what they do, man. This is their little insurance policy. They know sure as shit that we're in the neighborhood."

The sun was setting as the column came into a clearing to rest for the evening. They dined on cold c-rations and warm canteen water mixed with fruit juice powder. The temperature dropped to seventy-two degrees. Hugo removed his tee-shirt and wrung the sweat from it as tightly as he could. He hung the shirt on a tree branch ready for the next day's wear. He rolled himself into his poncho liner using his pack as a pillow and fell into an exhausted sleep only to be awakened by a giant rat nibbling at his boot. He leaped to his feet, M16 in hand. Three rats scurried into the underbrush as Hugo stood cursing under his breath.

"Hey, Rossi." It was Rizzo now awake and propped on one elbow, "they're not bad grilled on a bun." Sleep came fitfully for the entire Platoon. Breakfast of hot instant coffee and c-ration ham and egg chunks were heated on blue trioxin heat tablets. There was barely time for a bowel movement in the dense jungle. It was every man for himself; no latrines were dug the night before. The columns moved out before the heat of the day reached its peak. The columns were in uncharted bush, areas that had not been touched by U.S. forces. The heat of the day brought salty sweat to sting eyes and drain energy from the plodding columns. By later afternoon, the platoon broke into a large valley dotted with untended rice paddies. The column straggled onto a hard packed gravel road paralleling the rice paddies. "The fuckers know we're here, they pass the word faster than a phone call." It was Leon now cradling his M16 with the safety off. "There's gotta be a gook village up ahead, you can count on it."

THE ARRIVAL THE STRUGGLE THE ASCENDANCY

Second Lieutenant Ebenezer "you can call me Ben" Watson dropped back to inform the column that they were coming into a small village. The platoon broke from its column formation and gathered on a plateau overlooking a small village of thatched huts. Hugo counted the rooftops. There were eighteen thatched roof buildings, fifteen appeared to be living quarters and the others appeared to be storage and meeting buildings. Sergeant Hightower stood apart from the platoon talking with Lieutenant Watson, his eyes scanning the village as he spoke. This was Watson's first time in the boonies and his expression and body language conveyed his uncertainty. The word came down, Bravo squad would enter the village, and the rest of the platoon would form a perimeter around the village. Corporal Mendez took the lead calling out as he entered the center of the cluster of buildings in a halting Vietnamese "come out, we will not harm you." He called out three times. There was an eerie stillness in the air. Every man was a tensed spring. The heat of the day coupled with raw nerves and rapid breathing had the squad soaked in sweat. Mendez nodded to Riley and then to the hut door. "Kick it in and check it out." Riley's boot smashed the door and popped it open, he crouched looking slowly inside left and right. He entered and emerged "empty, no food in there either." They searched each hut finding nothing. Sergeant Hightower and Lieutenant Watson came into the village. Hightower studied the large hut at the end of the village. "Mendez, two guys at the front door, the rest in back of the building." Mendez pointed to Hugo and Leon motioning to the front door of the building. Leon whispered as they jogged in a crouch toward the building "there's gotta be fucken gooks in the building, never seen it fail." Leon never broke stride as he jump kicked the door in. There was a sudden outburst of wailing and sobbing. A babble of screeching Vietnamese voices filled the air. Hugo was stunned as a dozen elderly men and women streamed from the building and two young women hugging infants in their arms fell to their knees inside the doorway crying hysterically and choking out the same Vietnamese phrase repeatedly. "Leon, what the hell are they saying?"

"I dunno Rossi, who the fuck can understand these gooks?"

"I can speak the language Private, I'll interrogate them." It was Lieutenant Watson squatting in front of the women. In moments they had calmed down and were gesturing wildly with their hands. Watson assisted them to their feet and walked them to the squatting circle of elderly men in the center of the village. He spoke with the men obviously asking questions. They babbled furiously pointing northward, shaking heads indicating no or yes. "Lieutenant, whatta we got here?" asked Hightower as he walked with Watson back to a cluster of troops waiting for orders.

"The women said the younger men were forced to go north with the VC and the other women in the village were walking to another small village north of here."

"What about weapons, Lieutenant, what did they say?"

"They said there's nothing here. The VC took everything with them."

"Lieutenant, that's a crock of shit. They got stuff here, it's hidden in caves or brush, I'm telling ya." Watson bit his lower lip unconsciously as he looked around the village and at the cringing villagers. He knew he should be decisive, show leadership, he faltered, his head was spinning. "Lieutenant, we gotta torch this place, they can't think there'll be no reprisal."

THE ARRIVAL THE STRUGGLE THE ASCENDANCY

"Sergeant, I know these people, I lived in Hanoi as a boy. My father was a Diplomat. I know the language and customs, I went to school here for six years."

"Lieutenant, they knew we were coming. I've never seen a village this far north that didn't have connections to the VC." Watson wavered awkwardly, pulled himself together and barked out his order.

"Sergeant, form up the column, we're headed out." Hightower muttered under his breath "yess, sirrr." As the column formed up preparing for the word to move out, three objects came tumbling out of the shadows cast by the dense vegetation. The thud of hitting earth was followed by a loud clicking sound. "Grenade, grenade, take cover." The explosions came almost in unison spraying shrapnel at a maiming level. At the moment of confusion, a saw grass camouflaged cover was thrown off a pit revealing a dozen VC firing automatic weapons and a mortar quickly positioned and fired. The surprise tactic worked. As the platoon scrambled for cover, the VC emptied the pit crouching into the underbrush to be joined by a contingent of black pajama clad young men. The VC deployed in a semi-circle a hundred yards from the Marine column now condensed in the cover of the dense jungle growth. The cries and moans of wounded Marines reverberated from the jungle growth. The VC poured automatic fire from Ak47s into the platoon's position keeping heads down. Hightower leaped up behind a tree to survey the situation and shouted his orders as he swung a B.A.R. around the tree emptying a clip. "Return fire, return fire, burn those bastards, grenades, grenades." The platoon came alive, the firepower withered the vegetation and fogged the air. Hightower crawled to Hugo's position tapping on his helmet as he sprayed the VC perimeter with his M-16. "You okay, Rossi?"

The firefight was deafening as Hugo shouted his reply. "Yeah Sarge, I'm good." "Atta boy, stay with it."

Hightower crawled or ran crouched along the line formed by the platoon. Hugo's heart was in his mouth, his breathing came in rapid bursts. Every sense was attuned. He automatically ejected ammo clips and reloaded in one lightning motion. He vaguely heard Leon's voice over the ebbing din. "Rossi, Rossi, slow down boy, save your ammo. It looks like they hit and run." He looked at Leon, coming back to his senses. He turned back to scan the thickly forested enemy line There was no movement. He felt relieved. Under the intense pressure of the firefight, he hadn't wavered and he had slipped into a state of total focus.

"Rossi, man, you did okay. Ah think you're gonna make it." Leon clapped him on his shoulder smiling a broad grin.

"Leon, what's next?"

"I dunno, man, these fucken dinks will do this off and on tryin to knock us off one at a time. Ahm telling you man, these gooks are persistent." Mendez crouching low passed the word to hold position until the area was clear of VC. Twenty minutes passed and the column reformed, heading north. Doc Halliday and another medic were tending to three wounded Marines who were in various stages of pain. Bloody bandages covered chests, arms, and heads. Two Marine lay dead, half of one man's face blown off, the other still oozing blood from a machine gun strafing across his chest. As the column pushed on, Sergeant Hightower and Lieutenant Watson stood off to one side. Hightower obviously angry, the cords in his throat tightening as he spoke. Smatterings of the conversation drifted from a distance. "Coulda got everybody killed." "I got the combat experience." "Never gonna happen again." He saluted Watson, turned, and joined the advancing column of men. They slogged through the jungle, heat drenched in sweat, hungry, in a constant state of high anxiety, not knowing when the next confrontation would erupt and who would be killed or maimed. The following evenings were sleepless, filled with jungle sounds and crawling and flying insects. The consolation was the camaraderie that develops among men in combat situations. Hugo felt like he belonged, like he was valued. On the tenth day, three Sea Horse choppers spiraled down delivering fresh water and supplies. There was no mail. The wounded and dead Marines were evacuated earlier on the same choppers. The days dragged by. Water could not be used for washing, that luxury occurred only if a stream or small pond were stumbled upon. Two weeks into the mission Hugo drew outrider detail with Bushell Ass Brown. The detail consisted of reconnaissance of the right flank of the column scouting a hundred yards from the main body of troops guarding against a surprise ambush. Hugo carried his M-16 with extra ammo clips, extra grenades, and a walkie-talkie. Bushell Ass toted the B.A.R with extra magazines stuffed into his web belt. They walked ten feet apart, vision and hearing sharpened and heightened by the thought of stumbling upon Charlie. Hugo kept a compass heading of north, correcting position as they crept silently through the denseness. They smelled it first, the distinctive odor of cigarette smoke. They came to a statue like halt slowly sinking to the ground. They looked at one another, listening to faint VC voices. Hugo motioned to Bushell Ass to move forward. They peeped through thick foliage at a dozen black pajama-clad VC taking a break in a small clearing. They were all smoking as they spoke quietly in rapid fire Vietnamese pointing north and in the direction of the columns movement. They appeared to be drinking tea. Their Officer commanded their attention as he made hand motions indicating the direction of attack. Hugo tugged at Brown's sleeve and they crept backward with eyes on the clearing. "Rossi, we gotta take em now before they take off on us and do some damage." Hugo stared in the direction of the VC, eyes narrowing. "C'mon Rossi, we gotta move before they do, what a ya doin?" he hissed.

Hugo cleared a small patch of earth with his palm. "Listen, this is what we're gonna do." He drew a small diagram of the plan of attack. Hugo worked his way silently to the opposite side of the VC clearing. At precisely the same moment, they pulled the pins on three grenades and threw them into the center of the VC group. The grenades exploded in quick succession. As the grenades were airborne, he quickly fingered the walkie-talkie shouting a warning "VC, VC on the right flank." Bushell Ass stood feet apart, the B.A.R. cutting a swath across the clearing. V.C. dropped from the lethal explosions and the withering fire coming from two angles. Bushell ass had moved into the clearing, the B.A.R. bucking and smoking in his grip. He had lost his sense of consciousness as he screamed over the blasting weapon, "C'mon you mutha fuckas, c'mon you dink mutha fuckas, ah'll kill ya all." The retreating VC now in the bush began to return fire, bullets ripping at trees and branches kicking up dust at Brown's feet. Hugo ran back to Brown calling out to him, "Get down, get back to cover!" Bushell Ass couldn't hear. He stood reloading and firing in an altered state of consciousness. Before Hugo could get a hand on him, two shells tore into Brown's torso knocking him off his feet. The VC fire became more intense. Bushell Ass lay moaning on his back gripping the B.A.R., blood pumping from two bullet holes in his upper right chest. Hugo ran to Brown, gripping his collar with two hands and dragging the big man into the bush. The smoke was settling on the clearing. Four VC lay dead, one lay mortally wounded calling out in a gurgling voice. The VC had disappeared. There was to be no surprise attack this day. Hugo broke open his first aid packet pouring sulphur into Brown's wounds and holding a gauze compress tightly against his chest. The sound of rattling weapons and footfalls was followed by Doc Halliday and the entire platoon forming a perimeter under cover of the bush. Two stretcher-bearers and Halliday brought Bushell Ass back to the company, now dug in and waiting for action. Corporal Mendez and Snake walked into the clearing checking the dead VC. Mendez turned to the moaning VC and put him out of his misery with a 45-caliber bullet to his forehead. The column halted for the day.

Captain Van Arsdale and First Sergeant Demopolous made their way to the 3rd Platoon to see the wounded and Hugo. "You saved some lives today, Rossi. You and Brown displayed some courageous actions. I'm gonna put you in for a commendation."

"Thank you, sir, but it was Bushell Ass who did all the firing. He was like a wild man out there."

"Well son, looks like he earned a ticket home if he makes it."

Hugo gripped Brown's hand as he awaited the Sea Horse Chopper spiraling out of the sky. "Bushell Ass, buddy, you're gonna make it. You just got the million dollar wound."

Brown looked up from the stretcher resting on the ground with heavily sedated eyes, smiling slightly as he spoke. "Yeah. Man. ah'll be thinking of you while ahm ridin some warm pussy." The chopper settled down, and in seconds lifted off again.

"Men, our orders are to participate in a combined operation a.k.a. Operation Prairie." Captain Van Arsdale delivered his message with little emotion. "Our objective is known as the rock pile. It's heavily fortified and it's defended by NVA. They're regular North Vietnamese troops. They're trained and they're battle tested. This is not going to be a cakewalk, so be prepared for a rough fight. We got supplies being choppered in tomorrow and the next day. Check your weapons and check your first-aid kits."

Billy Riley had stumbled upon a good-sized lagoon fed by a twenty-foot long waterfall. The water was cold, clear, and the entire company refilled canteens, swam, and showered in the torrent of rushing water. Hugo lay in the jungle darkness wrapped in his poncho liner feeling clean for the first time in weeks. He thought of Angelina and Francesca. He couldn't recall their faces, hard as he tried. He prayed as he did every day. He wondered what a bullet wound felt like, who would be wounded or killed in the upcoming battles, and finally he drifted off to a restless sleep.

"Rossi, wake up. Troop, it's room service." Sergeant Hightower squatted beside Hugo, a smile playing over his lips. "C'mon, troop, we got bacon, eggs, pancakes, what's your pleasure?"

Hugo sat up in the early morning darkness. "Hey, Sarge, what's up?"

"You're gonna be on point today with Billy Riley. Eat your c-rations and report to the Captain. Captain Van Arsdale sipped at a steaming cup of instant black coffee as he pointed out landmarks on a large field map. "You guys got enough water, enough ammo?"

"Yes, sir," Hugo and Riley answered in unison.

"You got your compasses, walkie-talkies, and flares?" Again, they replied in the affirmative. "Okay, you're gonna stay on a heading due north from this point. I'm gonna give you this map with grids on it. You'll notice there's landmarks you can't miss, at least that's what I'm told. You maintain radio silence unless you see or hear something, then do your best at figuring out what grid you're in. You're gonna be ahead of us by about two hours, we're headed for those two hills right there." He pointed to the map tapping his forefinger from left to right. "That's hill 400 and 484. We gotta take Mutter Ridge, that's what this advance is all about. You boys got any questions? Okay, get going, good luck, and don't take any stupid chances."

After an hour of trudging through jungle undergrowth, the canopy of trees soaring as high as a hundred feet turned the jungle floor to dimness. Billy Riley made the first comment, almost whispering. "Rossi, I'd love to be in a Boston snowstorm right now." He stopped, removed his helmet and mopped his face with his shirtsleeve.

"Yeah, I'm with you buddy, only I want to be in Rhode Island."

"Hey, Hugo, I never told you, but I got cousins who live in Providence."

"C'mon, where do they live?"

"I think they call it South Providence."

"Yeah figures, that's where all the Irish come from." They stood sipping from canteens, helmets on the jungle floor, mopping sweat from their brows. Hugo checked his watch, two hours had elapsed, the column would be heading out now. The soaring canopy of trees gave way to hilly terrain and open space. They fell to their stomachs as a small village came into view. Hugo peered through bamboo shoots and whispered to Riley who scanned the village with binoculars. "Billy," he whispered hoarsely, heart pounding furiously, "that's regular army NVA."

"Yeah, I can see em. Looks like a company or whatever the fuck they have for an organization, and their movin out, headed north. Looks like we'll be tanglin with these slopes soon." They watched until the village cleared out. Hugo keyed the walkie-talkie and gave a report to Captain Van Arsdale followed by three "yes, sirs."

"What did he say?"

Hugo unfolded the grid map and pointed to a mountainous area. "We gotta advance to this point, radio back our observations and wait." They trudged through heavy vegetations, the faint sound of rumbling vehicles drifting in and out of hearing range. They arrived at what appeared to be the map location, slow rising hills in every direction. They found a pocket in the midst of heavy vegetation and settled in for the night, feasting on cold c-rations and tepid canteen water.

Mike Co. arrived the next morning and formed a staging area a hundred yards behind Hugo and Riley's encampment. They joined the rest of the company as the choppers arrived with water, food, and ammo. Hugo delivered his observations to Captain Van Arsdale, Lieutenant Watson, and Sergeant Demopolous. Word filtered down to the NCO's, the battalion would form a skirmish line. Alpha, Bravo, and Charlie Co's were to the left of Mike Co. There would be an early morning assault on Hill 400. Marine jets would soften the hill in the predawn hours, followed by a frontal assault. Sergeant Hightower made the rounds of clusters of troops ensuring that weapons were ready for actions. Tension was high, all that could be heard was the sound of rifle and machine gun bolts sliding open and closing as weapons were cleaned and oiled. More ammo was issued, first aid kits were checked. For those whose stomachs were not up in knots, dinner was cold c-rations and powdered fruit drink or water. As darkness fell, Van Arsdale and Demopolous met with the NCOs and laid out the plan of attack. Van Arsdale sat on an ammo crate with officers and NCOs spread in a semi-circle before him.

"My job and your job is kicking the gooks off that hill as quickly and as painlessly as possible." He paused to light a cigar. Demopolous passed around a bottle of Canadian Club that had suddenly materialized. "Keep your men moving. Remember, these are trained seasoned NVA. They're not militia or country bumpkins. I don't want any heroes making stupid moves. They know we're here, they can smell my cigar and they know we're coming.

Hugo sat in a tight circle with Corporal Rudy Mendez, Leon Lafleur, Snake, Billy Riley, and Boots Randolph. "Follow my lead tomorrow, I don't want to lose anyone of you guys, you understand me?" Mendez looked into each man's eyes as he spoke. "Now try to get some shut eye, we got some fightin to do real early." The early morning darkness was pierced by shrieking phantom jets spraying Hill 400 with bombs, rockets, and 20-millimeter shells spewing forth at 4,000 rounds per minute. The air show continued for an hour as the sun climbed toward its apex. Mike Co. started its one mile trek to the base of the steep, heavily forested hill. Bravo squad was the first to crest a level plateau to the next slope. Suddenly, the air was filled with the burping of machine gun fire and the crackle of rifle fire. Muzzle flashes lit up the darkened jungle, the smell of gunpowder assailed nostrils. Hugo and Boots Ramsey crawled to a clump of thick bushes as hand grenades tumbled by them detonating further on. The whump, whump of mortar fire was added to the blistering salvo now sweeping the entire company and stalling the advance. Boots hugged the jungle floor, turning his head to Hugo. "What the fuck did those fly boys hit? The dinks musta been hiding in caves." Hugo peered intensely at muzzle flashes erupting from what appeared to be a camouflaged log bunker one hundred yards and twenty degrees to their left.

He looked to his left to see the rest of the squad pinned down by the intense fire, puffs of dirt forming a pattern as the heavy machine gun raked the earth searching for a body to pierce. Hugo caught the eye of the crouching Corporal Mendez. He hand signaled his intention, Mendez nodded and signaled a thumbs up and turned to speak into his walkie-talkie.

"Boots, we're gonna take out that machine gun nest."

"Rossi, are you fucken nuts?" He answered his own question. "Yeah, you are, no doubt about it, okay, how?"

"We gotta get up the hill on their blind side. Mendez will draw fire, and we'll rush the blind side and toss in grenades." Ramsay grimaced, shook his head, grunted his approval, and made the sign of the cross. Minutes seemed like hours as they ran up the hill from covering tree to covering foliage. Hugo no longer heard the raging battle, he no longer controlled his movements, and his instincts now took hold. In minutes it was over. Hugo rushed the bunker from its blind side as Mendez and the remainder of the squad opened fire on the bunker to divert attention. Ramsey was on his heels as they lobbed four grenades into the bunker opening. One grenade came flying out of the bunker followed by two tumbling NVA. Ramsey snapped his rifle to his shoulder and emptied a clip of ammo at the escaping VC before they could stand. The bunker exploded with a roar igniting machine gun shells that spewed forth haphazardly. The NVA had zeroed in on them, shells smacked into dirt and hissed by them as they retreated to the safety of a clump of towering trees, the thunk, thunk, thunk of machine gun and rifle shells making them hug the base of the trees. Mortar shells began to fall on the battalion, there was no way to move forward. Suddenly, at treetop level, two phantom jets, engines screaming, released rockets and strafed the hilltop. The battalion started its climbing assault. By late afternoon, the 3rd battalion had control of Mutter Ridge. The assault had cost twenty dead Marines and many wounded. The VC had left about a hundred dead on the hill as they fled into the dense jungle.

They lined up the dead Marines and assisted the wounded as the choppers dropped down to bag the dead and evaluate the wounded. The Third Platoon sat or lay exhausted and spent from the exhilaration of battle. VanArsdale and Demopoulos walked among the troops, patting backs, shaking hands, and feeling good about the victory. VanArsdale approached Hugo and Boots Ramsey, a smile on his face. He had been in the thick of action and looked ragged and worn. His 45-caliber pistol was slung low on a web belt hanging from his waist. "Rossi, you and Ramsey here saved the day, I want to personally thank you." Both men snapped to attention and saluted smartly.

"Thank you, Sir." Hugo spoke for them both. "We did what we were trained to do, Sir."

VanArsdale and Demopoulos shook their hands. As VanArsdale turned to leave he paused, "and by the way, you're both now Corporals."

The next morning they started the trek back to battalion headquarters, bedraggled, filthy, stinking, and hungry. They discarded their uniforms and took hot showers for the first time in weeks. New fatigues, socks, and underwear were issued to each man. The hot meal was hot dogs, beans, and canned brown bread, and it tasted better than sirloin steak. The ten-man tents had wooden floors and bunks with mattresses. Billy Riley fell on a bunk and smiled. "Boys, this is better than the Copley Hotel back in Boston." Hugo took the bunk next to Riley, stowed his retrieved sea bag at the end of his bunk with his rifle and equipment. He sat on the bare mattress staring into space.

"Hey Rossi, what's goin on with you?" It was Doc Haliday finding a seat on Hugo's bunk. "You okay, man?"

"Yeah, I'm okay, I just can't stop thinking about the guys we lost today. I'm happy it wasn't anyone from our platoon, but these guys were eighteen, nineteen. One guy had two little kids." His voice trailed off as he grimaced and shook his head in resignation. Haliday draped an arm over his shoulder.

"You know, Hugh, it could have been me or you or Billy or any one of us. It just wasn't our time."

"Yeah, tell it to those poor bastards."

He lay awake that night, his thoughts drifting home. He missed his mother, he missed his grandmother. He closed his eyes and tried to visualize them, but he couldn't. He was overcome by a deep sense of sadness. He would never see them again, he would never marry, have kids, live out his life. Slowly, anger and defiance welled up in him. He sat up on the edge of the bunk and murmured under his breath: "Fuck it, fuck it, I'm not going out like a lamb to slaughter, no way, no fucken way."

The mail chopper delivered bags of letters that had been following the battalion for weeks. Hugo had seven letters at mail call, all from Angelina and Francesca and one from a return address he didn't recognize. Angelina missed him terribly and filled her letters with family small talk. Francesca was ailing, doctors hadn't arrived at a diagnosis yet, but she was in good spirits. Francesca's letter was a grandmotherly loving lecture on taking care of yourself, are you getting enough to eat, and we're praying for you. He lay back in his bunk examining the female handwriting of the unknown letter, the envelope giving off a faint whiff of a perfume he recognized. It was from Lorraine Ciccone. His spirits soared. He savored the young feminine, lighthearted prose. He closed his eyes and pictured her lips and smile. He felt himself being stirred by the image of her breasts. He quickly wrote to Angelina with a page for Francesca. As he wrote to his grandmother, he realized she was now seventy. He took his time with the letter to Lorraine. He wanted her to view him as intelligent, well spoken, and as a combat Marine, as an American hero defending his nation.

They were headed into the boonies again. This time they were ferried into the jungle by Sea Stallion choppers with a capacity for forty combat-laden Marines. They were headed for unchartered territory looking to seek and destroy. Hugo was now a Corporal and a Squad Leader. The hot humid days rolled into one another. The choppers delivered water, ammo, and c-rations. It was up one hill, down another, sweating, stinking, hungry, itchy sore assholes, fungus feet, and dysentery. They passed a number of small villages and farms. There was evidence of VC activity in some of the villages, but no VC to be found. Lieutenant Watson was becoming increasingly erratic in his behavior. With each village or farm search, he would visibly tremble and become hostile to the farmers and villagers. They had been on the mission for six weeks when an observation plane radioed the position of a farming hamlet. Watson was ordered to take Alpha and Bravo squads to investigate.

"Man just another fucken wild gook chase. We get there, listen to everybody screamin and jabberin in gook talk, watch the fag Lieutenant shake in his boots." Billy Riley spit the words out of the side of his mouth in disgust. "Then we gotta listen to Lieutenant Fag tryin to act like a real man."

Snake threw his arm around Billy's shoulder. "Riley, how dare you talk about an officer and a gentleman like that?" It was a forty-five minute trek through rough jungle terrain before they came to the hamlet in a large flat plain. Twelve thatched roofed buildings of various sizes, cultivated fields, and irrigated rice paddies lay beyond. The appearance of the Marines at the outskirts of the village caused a great commotion. As Sergeant Hightower and Lieutenant Watson approached the center of the compound, the two squads fanned out, weapons at the ready. Watson was sweating profusely, hands visibly trembling. The village elders came forward slowly and solemnly. There were three older men in conical field caps and improvised sandals, wet from the rice paddies. Watson barked at them in their native tongue, a snarl to his voice. "Where is everyone in the village? Call them out now or you will pay for this insolence." The elders nodded, fright now in their eyes. They turned and called to the village residents, some emerging from thatched huts, others hesitantly approaching from the heavily forested area ringing the village. They assembled around the elders, eighty-four men, women, and children. Watson began his interrogation of the elders in a loud and threatening manner. "Have Viet Cong been here, are there weapons hidden here?" Some of the women began wailing and sobbing, children clung to their mothers skirts crying.

"Answer me, answer me, you pigs." The elders began jabbering simultaneously "no, no, no one has been here." "We haven't seen anyone." "We are peaceful, we want no trouble, please don't harm us." Hightower was growing uneasy with the confrontation and Watson's behavior.

"Lieutenant, we'll do a search of the hooches and shake the village down."

"Okay, Sergeant, get on it." The sun beat down on the village, drenching the Marines in rivulets of sweat. Flies swarmed over bare skin. Alpha squad rummaged through the hooches, while Bravo squad ringed the villagers. Watson waited with Hightower, a forty five-caliber pistol hanging in a sweaty palm. The village smelled of pickled vegetables and the faint odor of human waste drifting from the latrines hidden from sight. Hightower kept his eyes on Watson, who was sweating profusely.

"Sergeant, what's taking them so long? Maybe they found some weapons or hidden VC."

"I don't think so, Lieutenant, give em a few more minutes." Hugo rounded the corner, heading toward the group.

"Wadid you find, Corporal?"

"Nothing Sergeant, at least nothing that's in sight."

"They're hiding stuff here, they all do." Watson spoke with clenched teeth as he turned to glare at the elders.

"Lieutenant," said Hightower, "there's no doubt that VC came through this village, they probably have cousins here, but these people are just farmers, I know, I've seen a hundred villages like this. These people have no choices in this shitty war."

Watson turned to the elders, pistol leveled at the leader. "Where are the weapons?" Where are they hiding? Tell me or I'll burn the village to the ground." The elders shouted their denial, hands gesturing, and a look of anguish in their faces. Panic overtook the villagers as they raced to protect their homes. Watson turned to Hugo. "Corporal, torch the village." Hugo looked at Hightower who shook his head no. "Corporal, torch this fucken village now, goddamnit, now!"

"I got a problem with that, Sir, can't do it." Hightower stepped in front of Watson "Listen Lieutenant ......" Watson pushed by Hightower, a zippo lighter aflame in his hand as he approached a large hut closest to the group. The village leader ran to Watson imploring him not to torch his home. Watson ignored him, Hightower followed behind determined to stop him. The old villager crying, grabbed at Watson's arm holding the forty-five. Watson pulled his arm free in an upward motion intent on setting the old man's home ablaze. As he did, the pistol fired, blasting a jagged wound into the old man's chest. For a moment everything came to a standstill. The old man crumpled to the ground clutching at his chest and gurgling incoherently. Hightower rushed to Watson and ripped the pistol from his grip. Doc Halliday ran to the old man searching for a pulse. There was none. The villagers erupted in fury. The elder's wife fell upon his body sobbing wildly. There was nothing to do, nothing to say, they backed out of the village leaving behind another casualty of war.

Hightower totally ignored Watson as they continued on their mission. That night, Hugo set his poncho liner down next to Doc Halliday. "Doc, what about today, this war is nuts, what they hell are we doin here anyway?"

"I dunno, Hugh, I just don't know."

"You know, Doc, I don't think the Lieutenant's all right in the head."

"Yeah, Hugh, I agree, but what do you do with him?"

"I guess that's gonna be up to Captain VanArsdale. I'm sure he's gonna hear the whole story."

"Hugh, waddaya gonna say if they question you about it?"

"I'm gonna tell them what I saw, the truth."

The temperature during the daylight hours held at one hundred to one hundred ten degrees. At night it dropped to sixty-five or seventy degrees. The days dragged on. Through dense towering trees, up one hill, down another, always hungry, always thirsty, wondering if a sniper's bullet would get you, or a snakebite. Adrenaline provided the energy to keep going and peak the senses. An observation plane had spotted VC or NVA activity on a hill in Mike Company's sector. It was another non-descript piece of real estate that harbored enemy, and need to be eliminated. On the map it was located as Hill 486. The 3rd Platoon were the first Marines advancing on to the lower slope. Hugo led a squad of men single file through the thinning jungle. Two hundred and fifty-six men spread across the base of the hill in random formation. Mike Company slowly made its way toward the plateau of the hill, hearts pounding, mouths dry, safety's unlocked, fingers tensed on triggers. The first sounds emanating from the hill were thunk, thunk, thunk. In seconds, rocket propelled grenades found their mark; dozens of Marines were killed or wounded. Mike Company opened up with everything they had as they picked up the pace toward the hilltop. The hillside was ablaze with automatic weapons fire firing blindly in the direction of the rocket propelled grenades. Rudy Mendez was down, a bullet through his windpipe.

Hugo took the remainder of the two squads to the right side of the hill and advanced from tree to tree until they had surmounted the plateau. The NVA were in the process of dismantling mortars and heavy machine guns. They were fleeing the hilltop as Hugo and the two squads opened fire with M16s, machine guns, and grenade launchers. There were ten dead NVA after the smoke cleared. The Marines collected their dead and wounded and radioed for evacuation choppers. The Company was spread across the hilltop smoking, quietly talking, and coming down from the adrenaline high. Hugo sat with his squad members assessing the damage done. "Doc, how many guys did we lose?"

Halliday held his face in his bloody hands as he sat on a fallen tree trunk. He removed his hands and looked at Hugo with exhausted, sunken eyes. "Last count was twelve dead, six wounded. One guy might not make it."

"What happened to Lieutenant Watson?"

"He got shot in the back, they don't know how it happened, coulda been a stray from our side."

"Naw, that mutha fucka got shot by Hightower," said Snake as he raised himself to one elbow. "Hightower hates that mutha fucka and he shot him pretty bad, but he didn't kill him, just wanted to get rid of him, that's what he did." Everyone nodded in agreement. Pollock sat up from his prone position, "You know the tragedy is that white bread piece a shit just got a ticket home and he's goin home like some kind a hero."

They spent the night on the hilltop plateau. At dawn the choppers came in to return the company to Battalion headquarters. There was no time for instant coffee or c-rations. The squads piled into Chinook helicopters hovering inches from the ground

THE ARRIVAL THE STRUGGLE THE ASCENDANCY

overloading most of them. Fifteen minutes into the flight the pilot turned and yelled over the rotor blades and wind from the open doors. "I gotta drop you guys off at an Army base. I think it's part of the 2nd Battalion. I gotta pick up wounded up north, so sit tight. Deuce and a halves will take you to your base."

They were dumped off at the 503rd Infantry base in a flurry of noise and dust. Hugo stood with the remnants of two squads, the beating blades of the chopper a fading sound. He felt like an alien on an Army base. He took stock of his nineteen men, sweat stained, mud stained, piss stained, torn and tattered fatigues, battered boots, their faces unshaven and haggard. They carried various weapons, hand grenades, and ammo. Hugo shook his head in frustration as he turned to look at his surroundings. The aroma of bacon and fried eggs wafted through the morning air, They were just a hundred feet from an Army Mess Hall. He motioned his men to follow as he walked to the front of the Mess Hall. Sitting on a slight rise, a long wooden stairway led to a double-doored entrance. They stood at the end of the stairway like a band of renegades watching starched and polished Army personnel enter and leave. There was dead silence as they entered the dining room. For a moment the young men felt uncomfortable, then suddenly a large Staff Sergeant in kitchen whites stepped forward and bellowed in a booming voice, "Make way for the Marines, boys! We got ourselves some real heroes here!"

The truck arrived that evening to pick them up and deliver them to 3rd Battalion Headquarters. There were hot showers, new fatigues, underwear, and socks. VanArsdale and Demopoulos stopped by on a tour of the platoons checking on the condition of the men. The 3rd Platoon lay about in what shape they could find, sipping cold lemonade, smoking, and waiting for 1200 hours when mess call was sounded. A small Sea Horse Chopper circled the Battalion and slowly corkscrewed to a landing in a vacant space to the left of the platoon and the ten-man tents. Hugo watched lazily as a neatly dressed Sergeant and Gunnery Sergeant dismounted the chopper and approached the Platoon, official looking clipboards and manuals clutched in their hands as they walked to the first troops they encountered. They stopped ten feet from the circle of troops lounging in various states of undress. The Gunny Sergeant's head swiveled slowly from side to side taking in every detail.

"Listen up! My name is Gunnery Sergeant John Lightner, this is Sergeant Schumer. We're from Division Headquarters, and gentlemen, you look like shit, worse than that, you look like the worst shit I have ever seen and I am gonna write you up to reflect what I see, which in turn, will reflect on your Platoon Leader and your Company Commander."

Hugo came to his feet. "Sarge, we just came out of the boonies after two months and two fire fights. We lost fifteen men that I know of and this is our first day back. This is a bunch of bullshit." His voice rose to a loud growl. "If I were you guys, I'd get the fuck back on that chopper cause you now have a lot of pissed off Marines to deal with." The Platoon was on its feet watching events unfold.

"What's your name Corporal?" The Gunnery Sergeant's face had turned beat red.

"Rossi, Hugo Rossi."

"Well boy, I'm gonna see if we can get your court martialed, how you like them apples?" The smirk on the other Sergeant's face conveyed the message that they could not care less about those fifteen young men cut down in the budding stage of their lives and could not care less that the rest of them had not also been killed. All we're interested in, their faces made clear, is shitting on you today because we can. The rage in Hugo came up from the soles of his feet and exploded through his nostrils. He flew through the air, his right fist smashing squarely into the jaw of Lightner, who immediately collapsed to the ground in one motion. He turned to the shocked Schumer, who collapsed under a rain of left and rights to the head and torso. Lightner had recovered enough to reach for Schumer, pull him to his feet and retreat to the chopper. In moments, they cleared the treetops and were gone.

Doc Haliday draped an arm over Hugo's shoulder as he spoke. "Hugh, I think you just fucked up big time." Within forty-five minutes three MPs in a jeep came for him. He was hustled into 3rd Battalion Headquarters into the presence of Colonel Sid O'Connor, a legendary blood and guts Commander who had earned a battlefield commission during the Korean War. Hugo stood at attention before the Colonel's desk, the two accusing Sergeants stood to his left. The Colonel sat back in his chair

"All right, son, I heard the Inspectors' story, now stand at ease and tell me your version." Hugo explained what had happened and how and why he lost control and he offered his apology. "Well son, the facts are that you struck two non commissioned officers and something's gotta be done about that, you understand me?"

"Does this mean I could be court martialed, sir?"

"I'm afraid so, Marine."

In two quick steps he was in striking distance with an overhand right fist that came crashing down on the nose of Gunnery Sergeant Lightner. Lightner staggered as blood from his nostrils spurted on to his fatigues. In seconds, three MPs had Hugo in handcuffs.

Colonel O'Connor stood behind his desk shaking his head. "What the hell is wrong with you, boy, aren't you in enough trouble, you need more?"

"Well sir, I figure if I'm already in trouble, I might as well finish the job."

One of the MPs drove him to a large wooden-floored tent and sat him on an empty bunk. He removed the handcuffs. "Sit here, I'll be back for you. The head's a couple of rows of tents behind you."

Hugo lay back on the bare mattress, hands behind his head, one foot on the floor. "Why am I such a fuck up, why can't I let shit go?" he thought as he closed his eyes. "I'm gonna be in the fucken brig, and I'm never leaving this cesspool I'm in." He dozed off dreaming of Angelina. In the dream, she was crying hysterically, blood gushing from her nose and eyes. He awoke sweating and startled.

A jeep pulled up to the tent. The MP who had delivered him to the tent came in carrying an ice-cold six-pack of Coca Cola, which was as rare as hen's teeth. "Rossi, this coke is for you from the Colonel. He said job well done. The MP sat on a bunk across from him and removed his helmet. "Hey Rossi, you spare one of those?"

Hugo was in a state of shock. "What the hell is this all about?"

The MP swallowed the coke in one continuous motion, burped loudly, wiped his mouth with the back of his hand, and gave his attention to Hugo. "I was in the Colonel's office while he was talking to his Executive, and he said "why should I discipline a brave Marine whose a killing machine and besides that, those two guys from Division were assholes for doing what they did to good fighting troops just back from a two-month mission. The MP stood smiling broadly. "C'mon, you killin machine, I gotta drive you to your outfit."

There were two more search and destroy missions. In the sporadic actions, Doc Haliday was severely wounded while tending to a fallen Marine and Polock was killed by a land mine. In the cool of the evening, Hugo lay in a poncho liner fascinated by the magic of the heavens, stars so close you could touch them. As always, his thoughts turned to Angelina and his grandmother, who he prayed would stay healthy until he came home, if he ever made it home.

"Rossi, Hugo Rossi!" It was Ridley, the Battalion Clerk.

"Over here, Ridley." Hugo swung his legs to the floor and sat up on the side of his bunk.

"Rossi, how are ya buddy, get packed, I got your orders right here and you, my man, are goin home."

Hugo ripped the paperwork from Ridley's hands. He read the orders with a huge smile creasing his face. "You know, Ridley, I knew I was close, but this is a surprise."

"Yeah, buddy, a nice surprise. Listen, a chopper's gonna pick you up at 1400 hours. Get your shit together and come over to the orderly room, you gotta sign some paperwork." There were hugs and handshakes as he bid farewell to the 3rd Platoon. He was one of three Marines leaving the Battalion that day.

The Sea Knight chopper waited in a landing circle, rotors turning slowly. Riley, Snake, Ramsey, and the remainder of Bravo Squad accompanied him to the chopper, which was already revving its rotors, anxious to leave. He turned before he boarded, cupped his hand and yelled, "I'll never forget you guys. *Semper Fi!*"

The squad stood in the dust and weeds, craning their necks upward as the chopper twisted its way skyward heading for Danang Airport. There he boarded a military air transport vehchilce and at seven fifteen the following morning he arrived at Miramar Air Station in San Diego. An olive drab bus transported fifteen men to a transitory company at Camp Pendleton where he was issued new uniforms, underwent a through physical that included a teeth cleaning, and then gorged himself on hamburgers, pizza, and french fries. On the seventh day, he boarded a commercial airliner in freshly starched and tailored Marine khakis for a flight to Camp Lejune, North Carolina. He was assigned to an advanced infantry training battalion working with recent graduates of Basic Training who in all likelihood would be headed to Vietnam. He had seven months left on his enlistment.

Chapter 13

DECEMBER, 1969

The Eastern Airlines flight touched down at Theodore Francis Green Airport at 3:00 p.m. He hadn't told anyone he was coming home. He took the first taxi in line and gave the address. It was a cold overcast day in December, just before Christmas. He wore his Marine greens with dress shoes. His cap was pitched at two fingers above his right eye. As the cab sped toward Silver Lake, his head swiveled left and right like some tourist from the Deep South. He felt alien, disconnected. What was normal was the heat and impending death of Nam. He over tipped the cabbie, stood on the sidewalk in front of the tenement house, his duffel bag at his feet. He looked up and down the street, now falling into darkness. He looked up at the second floor. The lights were on. Suddenly he felt nervous, even guilty. His joy at returning home was tempered by thoughts of those he had left behind—men who he had slept with, ate with, men who had become brothers. He quietly mounted the stairs, dropped his duffel bag, and knocked on the door. He heard muffled voices and suddenly the door sprang open. Angelina stood wiping her hands on her apron. Her mouth dropped open and she threw herself into his arms, weeping quietly. Francesca stood behind her waiting her turn to embrace him, her head tilted to one side, rivulets of tear drops running down her cheeks. Angelina released her son as Francesca replaced her in his arms, cooing in Italian over and over: "Why didn't you call and tell us you were coming, you *mascalzone* you!"

"I wanted to surprise you and Nana, and I didn't want anyone else here except the two of you." Within twenty minutes he sat down to a heaping plate of pasta, sausage, and meatballs. He ate until his stomach could take no more. They sat on either side of the table watching him eat, joy beaming from their faces. They sat in the living room; the black and white television tuned to the evening news, images of rioting college students and tear gas clouds filling the screen. He watched with mixed emotions until a rioter set fire to an American flag. He moved to change channels, but Angelina beat him to the power knob and turned the TV off.

"Come on, sit with me and Nana and tell us what went on over there." For a half hour he did his best to sugar coat his time in Nam and, to his relief, succeeded. He kissed them goodnight and went to his bedroom, which Angelina had kept as he had left it. He slept until past 11:00 and awoke to the fragrance of sizzling bacon and percolating coffee. It would be Angelina and Francesca's mission to feed him to death.

He dressed in jeans and a battered leather jacket. He walked to St. Bart's Church, knelt in a front pew, and prayed earnestly, thanking the Almighty for his safe return. He sat back in the pew. The church was quiet, the scents were familiar, incense, candles, and church smells. Two older women in black walked down the center aisle, one assisting the other. They went to a bank of flickering votive candles encased in red glass holders and lit two candles, dropping the required donation into a metal box that reverberated throughout the church. He genuflected as he left the pew making the sign of the cross. He stood outside the church deciding what to do next. He turned and walked to the Laurel Pharmacy. It was a grey day, damp, cold snowflakes falling intermittently. A black fifty-seven Ford crunched to a stop next to him as he walked.

"Rossi, you fag, you made it!" He turned to see the smiling face of Don Penta.

"Don, you got uglier."

"Yeah, but not as ugly as you, c'mon get in." They exchanged handshakes and half hugs in the car. They sat in Spotty's Spa talking quietly over coffee, sharing experiences in Vietnam. "You know Hugh, I thought me and you and Vacolla would get through our tour together."

"Yeah, well you know, it's what the Marines needed. I sure coulda used you guys on more than one occasion."

"Yeah, me too, buddy." They fell silent for a moment; Penta stared through the storefront plate glass window. "One afternoon, we got jumped by V.C." He paused for a second, "we lost nine guys, all kids for crise sake, all kids. My closest buddy took it in the face, he died in my arms, eighteen fucken years old." He wiped tears from his eyes with a coffee stained napkin.

"It's okay, Don, I know, I saw the same things. It's alright."

"When did you get home?"

"About three weeks ago, I still feel like I'm in Nam."

"Yeah, I know what you mean."

"What about Vacolla, is he back yet?"

"I dunno, I don't think so, but he should be home now or pretty soon."

"Are you working yet?"

"Naw, I'm collecting an unemployment check for sixteen weeks, after that I'll worry. You should go down and apply, they don't hold you up, you get checks right away."

"Yeah, I'll go tomorrow."

Hugo had accumulated a little money with mustering out pay and some savings. He bought a fifty-eight Chevy Bel Air and some new clothes. He visited with relatives, caught up with friends, went to a few of the new discos around the state, and tried to push Vietnam as far back in his memory as possible.

Al Vacolla finally came home. He had made a diversion to Southern California, but the pull from Rhode Island brought him home. There was a reunion of sorts of old friends at Coffee's Café in Silver Lake. Of the fifteen childhood friends who showed up, six had been to Nam. They ate and drank until closing. No one talked about military service.

Francesca died in April. She had developed lung cancer and was hospitalized at a special wing at Rhode Island Hospital. Her death was the final link to a happier time in Hugo's life. For weeks he stayed close to Angelina, understanding her anguish and lonesomeness. As he sorted through his grandmother's belongings with Angie, he marveled at her beauty as a young woman. He talked for hours with Angie, trying to capture his own biological essence. She told him about his father and his grandfather, the story of Salvatore's arrival in America, his father's gropings for fame and fortune, and, finally, how his father had died in Korea and how his fellow soldiers felt about him. He also learned that his father had received the Silver Star. It was a revelation; and it connected him to a legacy, which he vowed never to betray.

With his unemployment benefits coming to an end, Hugo was restless to do something productive. He had enrolled at Rhode Island Junior College in January because of its low tuition and proximity to Silver Lake. The course work in General Studies was easy and he enjoyed academia. His Uncle Carlo had friends at Monroe Construction and he started work as a laborer as the semester came to a close. The work was back breaking, but soon he began to enjoy the feel of his own physical strength and the easy camaraderie of the construction workers.

"Hey cuz, Yoogo, cuz!" It was John Riccitelli, his cousin calling from his car in traffic. He signaled he would be back in a second. Hugo watched from his lounging position against the outside wall of Andy's Omelettes on Federal Hill. The car pulled to the curb, the driver's door sprang open, and a smiling John Riccitelli walked into a warm embrace from his friend and cousin. "When did you get home?"

"Just before Christmas. I found out you were in Las Vegas, what happened?"

"Aaayy, it's not what everybody thinks it is. The wise guys got me a job as a valet, there's a bunch of guys from the Hill out there so I had a connection. The money was good but by the time I duked everybody, paid my apartment rent, spent money on showgirls and eating out, and don't forget I'm a poker addict, I was not only broke, I was in debt. And then, guess what, the loan sharks got me! So I'm back home working for a house builder. Money's good, and I'm back living with my mother for a while." They brought each other up to date on their exploits over pepper and egg frittatas and cokes. "Hugh, I wanna take you over to George Stomponato's Karate Studio on Charles Street, it's got the best Karate guys in the state. I joined a couple of days ago, and it's not easy to join." Hugo agreed. "Alright, I'll pick you up at five."

George Stomponato was legendary in Kenpo Karate circles. While stationed in Japan as an Air Force mechanic, he befriended a Japanese civilian employee at the base whose brother was a cult figure in the Asian world of Martial Arts, having taken the sobriquet Sun Tzu after the ancient practitioner and author of *The Art of War*. Stomponato proved to be an apt student and slowly became the favorite of Sun Tzu. He took his discharge in Japan and stayed for another year studying and teaching Kenpo Karate. He returned to Providence in 1960 and opened his studio in the rough and tumble neighborhood of the North End. It was a mark of courage and toughness to be selected as a student at his school. The studio was on the second floor above a bakery and warehouse, a former banquet hall that had hosted hundreds of weddings of the Italian immigrant community from the early twentieth century. Standing at the door of the studio as they approached was Johnny "Mo" Lamana, a lifelong friend and one of Stomponato's earliest students. He enveloped Hugo in a bear hug, kissing his cheek.

"I heard you were back, it's great to see you buddy. This is where you belong." They stood on the sidewalk renewing a friendship. Lamana was a substitute teacher in Providence, was considering law school, and was working part time as a bouncer. The money was good and you had your pick of the women. "I told your cousin I wanted to introduce you to George, he's quite a character. Let's go upstairs." The sound of bare feet on floor mats and the slapping of flesh against flesh could be heard loudly as they climbed the stairwell. A roar came from the studio.

"Is this what I taught you? Are you two assholes tryin to make an asshole out of me? I should break both of your legs! Siddown and watch the next match." Stomponato glanced round as they entered. Lamana pointed to Hugo and nodded toward him. Stomponato motioned to his office with a flick of his head. The office was festooned with trophies of all sizes, posters of past and upcoming events, and a life-size erotic poster of Raquel Welch. Stomponato entered the office, pulled out a swivel chair, and sat behind a large black desk with the yin-yang symbol affixed to its front. He wore his Masters Doji uniform with a black belt. His Fu Manchu moustache, beard, and ten-inch braid suited his muscular wiry frame. Lamana broke the silence.

"Sensei, this is Hugo Rossi, the man I told you about." Stomponato stared at him with half closed eyes. "So… you're a man, a Marine, just back from Nam, a tough guy, that right?"

Hugo felt his anger rise. Who was this actor making a fool of him? He turned to his cousin. "Cuz, I don't need this fucken kid shit, I'll see ya later." His hand reached for the doorknob to the office.

"The first lesson you failed Rossi, you lost your composure, you revealed your weak point. I know about you, I know how to get to you." Hugo turned to see Stomponato sitting back in his chair, hands clasped into a steeple. "I can teach you how to overcome yourself, that's if you can pass the second test." Lamana nudged Riccitelli's elbow.

"Yeah, what's the second test?" Stomponato walked to his office door and opened it and pointed to a section of blue floor mats.

"Get in the center of the mats."

Hugo hesitated a moment, then walked to the center of the cluster of mats not knowing what to expect, senses alert, heart beating rapidly. Suddenly, three uniformed students came off the wall of the studio surrounding him. Out of nowhere came an elbow to his right cheek. He struck back at the elusive figure, flailing wildly. A blow to the side of his head sent him reeling to the edge of the mats. He charged at the larger of the three Dogi clad figures, connecting with a wild left overhand hook, and then they converged upon him beating him with feet, elbows, and fists. He crumpled to the mat, regained his senses, and slowly stood up, wavering and bloodied. He beckoned the larger figure to advance upon him but Stompanato came between them. "Okay Rossi, you passed the second test, the most important one. This is the test that reveals your balls, and I think you've got a pretty good pair. Do you want to study with me?"

The classes at the Stomponato studio were designed to weed out those students who did not possess an inner determination, a desire to win at all costs. With his natural instincts, Hugo progressed rapidly. In spite of his hectic schedule, his grades were in the top five percent of his class. He had designed a class schedule that enabled him to work out of the Laborers Union Hall, study at the Stomponato School, and hit the books to maintain his class position. He still attended Mass with Angelina every Sunday morning and still felt close to the church. There was a spiritual part of him that nagged at his conscience that demanded obeisance. He hid this side from his friends; his karate skills were now at a level where observers took note. Stomponato would watch his workouts with older students showing no emotion but inwardly recognizing his natural talent.

"Rossi, come into my office." Stomponato stood leaning against a filing cabinet, left hand supporting his elbow as he stroked his Fu Manchu. "You're ready to move up. Next week we have an in-house tournament. You win the match, you earn a brown belt, you lose the match....well, it'll take a *long* time for you to come up again."

"Geo...Sensei, who am I matched against?" The older man paused and looked up from his desk with the faintest trace of a smile "Rico, and you're gonna fight full contact."

At six foot two and well over two hundred pounds, Rico Costanzo was a favorite of the wise guy hierarchy and an up and comer in La Cosa Nostra. Hugo laughed. "So this is to me my debut and my swan song all at the same time, huh?"

Word of the fight spread in Karate circles. The match was the last of a Saturday afternoon. The overflow crowd was hushed as both fighters, barefoot and in Dogis, took to the center of the mats. Sensei Stomponato held each fighter's forearm and with head bowed recited his mantra in guttural Japanese that only he understood but was nonetheless impressive to the crowd. He stepped back, dropped his hand in a chopping motion, and the fighters assumed their opening stance. They circled each other warily. Rico wore his most menacing face as he feined a kick and a lunge. He closed rapidly, blocking a straight punch and smashing into the side of Hugo's head with a right hook. Hugo reeled to his left, regaining his footing as Rico missed with a spinning roundhouse kick. The crowd came alive, shouting strategy and encouragement to the underdog, Hugo. He landed a quick lunge punch catching Rico off guard. In minutes, it was no longer the ballet of Karate, it was an all out street fight. The crowd was wild, the Sensei stood leaning against a support beam, arms folded, expressionless, watching the mayhem unfold. He did not move to stop the combatants. They flailed at one another, finally falling to their knees, arms heavy, dripping with sweat, until neither one could raise an arm or rise from the mat. They slowly collapsed to the mat, bloody, beyond exhaustion, drenched in sweat.

Stomponato approached the mat and announced his decision in dramatic stentorian tones. "I declare this match a draw."

Angelina lived for her son. With Francesca gone he was the focal point of her life; she needed someone to care for, and who better than her only son. Hugo was concerned for her. He still accompanied her to mass every Sunday and most Sunday's they had dinner at home or at one of his aunt's homes. He was drawn to the Catholic faith, there was something that fulfilled him, that uplifted him. He could not explain his feelings, but they had always existed, and lately they seemed to become even stronger. He had been wanting to hold a conversation with his mother about his plans and one Sunday he sat at the kitchen table and spilled his feelings. "You know, Ma, you need to get out more, the movies, the Senior Center at the church…"

She cut him off abruptly. "Are you crazy, I'm not gonna hang out with those old people? Besides, Elsie DeFusco goes there and I remember she used to flirt with your father. She's nothing but a putana."

THE ARRIVAL THE STRUGGLE THE ASCENDANCY

He had a full schedule, work, school, and karate and yet, there was always time for a new lady and there were many new ladies. He was handsome, well built, and charming. And he had a sense of humor, much of it self-deprecating, which was appealing to women. He was totally unpretentious. He often thought of Lorraine Ciccone, the fragrance of her letters remained in his nostrils. He thought of contacting her, but something held him back, though he didn't really know why. Was it because she was beautiful, was it because he was afraid of rejection? He mused to himself that one of these days he'd bump into her.

Stomponato's school was gaining a national reputation and attention. There were competitive matches throughout New England and along the East Coast. The school was undefeated, and Hugo had developed a reputation as a ferocious fighter who had evolved a kicking style that came to him naturally. His jumping, thrusting, snapping and roundhouse kicks were lightning fast and difficult to defend against. They had finished a two-hour workout at the studio. They were all drenched in sweat sitting against the wall sipping cokes. George Stomponato walked from his office reading a letter as he approached the exhausted fighters. He looked up from the letter grim mouthed. "Gentlemen ...we have been invited to compete in Kansas City by the Missouri Karate Association. We can enter six fighters. Gentlemen, this is big time, they have nationally ranked fighters down there and most of the competition is filmed for television. I'll post whose going on the bulletin board and I'll also post who you will be matched up against." Rico stood up as Stomponato walked back to his office. Clenched fists on hips and in his booming voice he asked, "Awright, who wants to work out for a couple more hours?"

He graduated with honors from junior college and was granted a full scholarship with room and board to the University of Rhode Island, a land grant college in a pastoral setting an hour out of Providence. Hugo was now twenty-three-years old and a Vietnam Vet. By all standards, he was an old man on campus. He had absolutely nothing in common with the eighteen or nineteen-year-old freshmen who he rubbed elbows with or the juniors he attended classes with. He was assigned a dorm room and a roommate from Patterson, New Jersey. Schmuel Zelzer was a short, thin, bespectacled Orthodox Jew, the son of a Rabbi with a large Orthodox Congregation in Patterson. Hugo first encounter with Schmuel was as he visited the dorm to locate his room. He opened the door to find Schmuel at prayer clutching his prayer book, eyes closed, rocking back and forth and repeating a chant in Hebrew. He opened his eyes as he sensed Hugo standing in the doorway and leaped from the chair, his face coloring.

"Oh excuse me, I'm sorry, I, I…"

Hugo interrupted his halting conversation. "No need to be sorry, I think prayer's important for the soul as well as the mind." Schmuel smiled with a sigh of relief and a shrug of shoulders. Hugo, extended his hand. "My name is Hugo Rossi, and it looks like I'm your roommate." Hugo liked his roommate immediately. His open sensitive face, his obvious religious nature, and his quiet demeanor were honest and refreshing. The two young men talked for an hour, getting to know one another, and then headed to the dining hall. Schmuel selected from the small kosher offering and seemed pleased with the brisket. Hugo ate indiscriminately. They returned to the dorm and talked into the evening until Schmuel excused himself, donned a prayer shawl, and retired to one end of the room, his back to Hugo, and said his evening prayers.

Hugo awakened at daybreak to find Schmuel already at study. "Schmuel, what time did you get up?"

The younger man smiled shyly. "About three. I really don't need a lot of sleep."

Hugo used the showers at the end of the hall, which was deserted at six in the morning. He dressed and headed back to Providence on traffic-free roads. The construction work was drying up, there were fewer and fewer days when a job was available through the Laborers Union Hall. He would need to find something that paid well and still allowed him to attend school on a full-time schedule.

The roster for Kansas was posted. He heard excited voices and congratulatory remarks, some with a tinge of jealousy and dejection. "Hey Rossi, you're goin." It was Lamana, smiling as he pointed to the mimeographed roster. "Aayy, and guess who you're paired up with?"

Hugo pushed through the gawkers to read the roster and his heart sank into his stomach. He re-read the roster twice, covering is face with both hands and emitting a groan. He turned to Rico who stood watching for his reaction. "I'm fighting Sam Price. He's only number one in the country."

Rico and Lamana draped arms around his shoulder. Rico wore a knowing smirk as he spoke. "Ross, my best advice to you is to buy a gun."

"Hugo, he's bigger than you, he has more experience than you, and a very big reputation. Even his ego is bigger." Stomponato paced back and forth in his office half in thought as he muttered to Hugo. "But you, you're quicker, just as strong, and you're ten years younger. Does that answer your question?"

Kansas City was still marketing itself as a cow town for the tourists, who saw it as the last vestage of the old Wild West. Hugo and his team checked into the Round Up Motel, which boasted vibrating beds and color TV. Stomponato had rented a van with seating for nine and enough room for equipment. They drove to the Kansas City Sports Arena, an older facility once the primary venue for major sporting events in the city, now relegated to schmaltzy wrestling matches, fading entertainers, and occasional boxing or karate tournaments. The team stood in the open arena as workmen checked lighting and sound systems. Tomorrow they would stand here again, their reputation on the line.

They had dinner at Willy's Wood Grilled Steakhouse and devoured large T-bone steaks with baked potatoes and the all-you-can-eat salad bar. Stomponato called for attention as the last gnawed T-bone hit the steel sizzle plate. "Gentlemen, because you're good, you made it to championship competition. This is one of the top fights in the country, if not the world. You're going to follow in the footsteps of fighters who competed here like Joe Lewis, Chuck Norris, and Victor Moore. At this meet, we're up against Demetrius Havanas, who's number one, and other top fighters from around the country. None of you have a black belt. You have brown belts and purple belts." He paused and looked around the table, his voice just above a whisper. "For this match, you will all fight as black belts because you're tougher and smarter than the competition, and because you all have something that is an unaccountable attribute." He paused for effect. "You have lion hearts!"

The Civic Center was jammed with the sort of noisy spectators that have frequented physical contests since the days of ancient Rome, though now the trumpets were made of plastic, not brass, and banners that looked more like an NFL football game than the banners of the Imprerial Empire. An announcer in a badly fitting tuxedo walked to center stage and rang a gong, reducing the pandemonium somewhat. In his best Madison Square Garden voice, he announced the names of the competing groups to the cheers of the fans. The four judges took their seats as the referee signaled to the first contestants. The contests were fast and brutal but clean. Three two-minute rounds determined a winner or a tie. All the contestants were skilled and gave the crowd their monies worth. After the eleventh match-up, the referee signaled to Stomponato, who held his match-up roster, finger scanning the names as the ref did also, nodding in agreement they parted.

Stomponato returned to his waiting fighters. "There's a change in the line up, some guys didn't make it in. Rico, you're in first. When the ref signals, you're up against Bill Finch. He's from Texas and a mean bastard, so watch yourself." The signal came. Rico circled Finch as taught as a coiled spring. He spun away from a flying sidekick and came out of the spin with a powerful roundhouse kick that brought Finch to his knees. He finished him off with straight punches, vertical punches, and a final roundhouse punch. He was awarded the match.

At the sight of Rico's match Hugo had become an adrenaline fueled machine, primed to explode as he faced off against the supremely confident Sam Price. Price was ten years older, fight savvy, and was a master of mat strategy. Hugo exploded upon him with kicks, punches, and foot sweeps. Price purposely drew foul after foul staying his distance from the now enraged Hugo. Hugo was disqualified. He walked to his teammates dejected, head down. There were shoulder hugs, pats on the back, reassuring words. Stomponato looked straight ahead as he spoke. "He had you before you stepped onto the mat. It starts in your head first."

The matches became increasingly furious as the victories fell to the boys from Rhode Island. There was no pretense; it was straight full contact, no holds barred. Hugo redeemed himself fighting an enormous black from Atlanta. The judges awarded the match to the battered and bloodied young black man who, clutching Hugo to his chest, said into Hugo's ear, "Man, you are one tough son of a bitch, wop. You won the fight, I want you to know that."

Tom Cotorno fought and beat Demetrius Havanas while suffering from a broken jaw, dislocated shoulder, and exhaustion. Havanas was number three in the country. Rico with no thought to form or rules beat Bill Finch into the mat but limped back to his team with a broken foot. Despite the many injuries, the victories could not be denied, and they were awarded First Place in the Tournament. The Awards Ceremony followed the conclusion of the Tournament. Trophies and cash prizes were presented to individual performers and teams. In his acceptance speech, Stomponato mustered all of his dignity but succumbed to a recurring stutter of speech when in the spotlight. He thanked the officials, Tournament Promoters and all the participants and finally, his team. It all went smoothly until he began to extol the fighting of Tom Cotorno who was affectionately known as Benny. "I want to especially recognize Tom Ba, Ba, Ba, Benny Cotorno." He went on to laud his accomplishments as the local sports reporters took notes furiously. The next day's sports page was headed "Ba, Ba, Ba, Benny and the Jets Sweep Karate Tournament." There was a champagne steak dinner celebration at 'Willy's' that evening and the next morning they boarded a plane for Rhode Island. Hundreds of fans cheered as they entered the terminal of T. F. Green Airport. They had returned as local heroes. There was a photo session with Governor Noel and countless invitations to sports association groups and events. Stomponato had discovered that Hugo had a natural ability at kickboxing. He worked with Hugo and refined his style to a professional edge for use in future competition.

His grade point average at U.R.I. was in the top ten percent of his class with little studying. Schmuel could be found in the dorm room or library, nose in a book, eyeglasses perches precariously on the tip of his nose. He cultivated few friends but seemed in awe of Hugo who had come to have a genuine affection for the studious, gentle young man. It was a Wednesday evening, he had a late class and decided to have an early dinner on campus. He looked for Schmuel in the dorm, but he wasn't there. He entered the dining hall, busy for a Wednesday evening. He scanned the busy tables, his eyes taking in Schmuel, head down, and hands in his lap, his kosher meal before him untouched. Across from him sat three leather-jacketed skinheads, their voices inaudible until he drew closer. "So tell me kike, when you suck pricks does the Rabbi make them kosher or do you just suck the Rabbi's prick?" It was the bigger of the three and the obvious leader speaking. Schmuel's face reddened as he remained motionless. "Kike, is it true that your father fucked your jewell sister and you were the result?" They chuckled, snickered and leaned across the table menacingly warming to the moment. Hugo positioned himself squarely behind them, feet apart, arms hung loosely by his side. The ugliest and skinniest of the three turned to appraise him; he turned to the main antagonist and whispered lowering his head. The big bulldog looking skinhead turned slowly sizing up Hugo, his earring and heavy neck chain contrasting against his all black outfit. He sneered as he began to rise and spoke. "What the fuck are you, another heeb or maybe he's your piece of ass?" He rose from his seat slowly and menacingly. Hugo uttered not a word as the large skinhead was half standing, he leaped toward the wide-eyed skinhead and smashed his nose and mouth with a solid contact front kick. The sound of bones breaking and teeth cracking was followed by gushing blood. He thundered unconscious to the floor. The cohort to his left jumped to his feet, a tire iron materializing in his hand. He attached, Hugo spun out of the way of the powerful swipe coming out of his spin with a kick to his stomach as the skinhead doubled over, he stepped back and executed two front snap kicks to his head. He fell to the floor whimpering in pain. The third and least threatening of the cohorts had fled for his life. The Campus Police arrived with an ambulance. Both men were still unconscious. Hugo stood with his arm around Schmuel who was visibly shaken. Students clustered around them, patting Hugo on the arm or shoulder and thanking him for defending Schmuel. Slowly a small chorus of applause turned into thunderous applause with hoots and cheers for the man who single handedly dealt the campus Nazis a devastating blow. "Hugo, do you think those boys will be all right?"

THE ARRIVAL THE STRUGGLE THE ASCENDANCY

Schmuel stood hugging himself, a concerned expression wrinkling his brow. "Schmuel, they would have tortured you if they could and you're now worried about their health. I hope I put them in a hospital, the dirty bastards deserve it." "No, no Hugo, I thank you from my very soul for rescuing me from them, but if vengeance supercedes forgiveness, we are less than civilized beings." Hugo looked at Schmuel with a bemused smile, shaking his head in disbelief. Captain Casey of the Campus Police asked Hugo to sit down and give his side of the story. He recounted the details of the altercation as Casey took notes. Schmuel waited a distance away talking with some Jewish students. Casey finished his note taking, looked at Hugo and sat back. "You were brought up in the Lake?" "Yeah, how did you know?" "My cousin, Venny Penta went to Mt. Pleasant with you." "Yeah, Jesus Vinny, I haven't seen him since we graduated, how is he?" "He was killed in Nam, left a brand new pregnant wife. You were there, weren't you? In the Marines?" Hugo answered in a subdued voice, "yeah, I was there with a lot of other guys, I got lucky, I got to come home." A silence fell between the two men, Casey took a deep breath and took up his notepad. "So Rossi, you say they attacked you with weapons as you attempted to sit down and you were forced to defend yourself, right?" "Well no…" "Rossi, that's the way the report's going in, take care of your friend." The skinheads were expelled and the few remaining members of the Nazi party soon became mainstream students. Schmuel from that day included Hugo in all of his prayers and treated him with reverence occasionally at Hugo's annoyance. "Schmuel, you have to become more independent, you have to make yourself stand up to situations." "Yes my friend, I will, you're correct, however, I must listen to the Word of God first who teaches us to be simple, peaceful and forgiving." Hugo conceded defeat.

Stomponato's school played a large role in his life. There were more competitions, and Hugo found that there was money to be made by entering kickboxing matches throughout New England and the Atlantic states. The matches were usually on weekends and didn't interfere with his schooling, but when they started to take a toll on his grade point average he abruptly ended his kickboxing career.

He graduated with honors near the top of his class with a degree in Secondary Education. Angelina attended the graduation ceremony with his aunts and uncles. Most of the graduates had crowds surrounding them with flashbulbs blinking throughout the noisy crowd. Schmuel ran over to take Hugo's hand and pulled him severalpaces to meet his family. "Papa. Mama, this is the man I told you about, he saved me from who knows what could have happened." A tall bearded man in a yarmulke stepped forward; he wore spectacles and was dressed entirely in black with a black flat brimmed hat. "Mr. Rossi, I'm Schmuel's father, I want to thank you for interceding in my son's behalf. You are welcome in my home at any time." "Thank you ver much, Sir, that's very generous of you." He turned to Schmuel who embraced him. "Schmuel, remember what I told you about standing up." "I'll do my best, Hugo, I promise, I'll do my best." "Okay, I gotta get back to my family, good luck."

"I wish your father were here to see you in your cap and gown, he would have been so proud."

"Ma." He held Angelina by her shoulders as he spoke. "I had a dream about Nana and Papa last night. They were in a church lighting candles when I approached them, they turned and smiled at me. It was so real."

"They loved you, Hugo, it *was* real."

Johnny Lamana was teaching in the Providence school system. Through friends of friends, he helped Hugo start as a student teacher, eventually filling in as a substitute teacher at various junior high schools in the city. Lamana was working nights as a bouncer at the Gladiator and Marlowes, two of the most popular discos in town. One of the bouncers was arrested for cocaine possession, creating an opening for Hugo. The money was good and the women were even better. He worked four nights a week, and if he wanted a different woman each night, without much trouble he could have had one. The greatest problem was dealing with all the wannabe wise guys, whose usual response to a warning regarding rowdy behavior was, *"Do you know who my uncle, godfather, brother is?"*

The women arrived dressed to attract attention, but complained loudly if some young man ogled a little too long, and fights over women were a nightly occurance. It was an unwritten law that the bouncers skimmed a portion of the door money they collected, which they regarded as justifiable compensation for the aggravation of the job. It was a busy Friday night; Lamana, Rico, and Hugo were working the door and the floor of Marlowe's, located on the second level of a brick building in downtown Providence. Hugo saw her as she entered the first floor foyer with two other young women and started up the wide stairwell. He caught his breath as she came closer. At the top of the staircase she missed a step, and grabbing onto the railing to right herself they came face to face.

"Lorraine, how are you? God, it's been a long time."

She extended her hand. "Hello, Hugo, it's nice to see you. I wondered when we'd bump into one another again." Hugo fumbled for something to say, and Lorraine broke the silence by introducing her friends, Hugo made an ungainly introduction of Lamana and Rico and escorted them, without paying an entrance fee, to a corner table. He sent over a round of drinks and soon joined them. He passed a few minutes of innocuous pleasantries, but directed most of his conversation to Lorraine. As he rose to make a tour of the club, he bent down and spoke in what passed for a whisper in the hammering, thumping, screaming swirl of disco sounds. "Hey, you gonna be around for awhile?"

"Yeah, for a while."

"Well listen, I can be off around midnight, can I buy you breakfast?"

Lorraine's smile was bright and honest. "Yes, I'd love to, but you'll have to take me home, we used Sheila's car."

"Of course, I wouldn't let you walk, somebody would snatch you up."

They drove to the Yankee Clipper Diner, a chrome and glass block institution in Providence. She ordered ham and eggs and blueberry pancakes. Hugo looked at her plates in mock wide-eyed surprise. "Hey, do you work construction or is this just your midnight snack?"

Lorraine smiled and chewed at the same time. "I'm just a growing girl, can't you tell! Plus I really had nothing to eat this afternoon or for dinner, and these pancakes are delicious."

Hugo stabbed at a small section of pancakes on her dish with his fork and sat back in the vinyl booth, hand surrounding his coffee cups, his eyes locking on hers. "You know when I would get a letter from you in Nam, it had the same scent as the perfume you're wearing tonight."

"I always wear this cologne, it has a nice clean fragrance."

"Well, I must tell you that I would re-read your letters and inhale the fragrance for weeks."

She felt her face redden. To recover, she feigned searching for something in her purse. The waitress poured more coffee.

"How was it over there? If you'd rather not talk about it, I understand."

He smiled slightly and drank from his cup. "How was it…" He thought for a moment gazing over her head. "It was surreal. None of us could believe we were fighting a war with no beginning and no end in sight." He talked for an hour eliminating some of the more gruesome events. It was nearly three as he rolled to a stop in front of her house. He cut the engine, reached for her and pressed his mouth to her moist partially opened lips in a dizzying, heart pounding kiss. It was in that moment that he knew he wanted this woman. He was making a good living teaching and working as a bouncer, but something had long gnawed at him, something that left him vaguely unfulfilled. His life, he know, would not, could not be the same.

"Who's gonna take care of you? Who's gonna cook for you? What, you don't love your mother anymore?" Angelina was sitting at the kitchen table, tears coming to her eyes.

Hugo embraced her, cupped his hand under her chin "Ma, of course I love you. It's just time for me to have my own place. I'm only five minutes away, and I'll be here more than you want me here."

It was a small one-bedroom apartment, sparsely furnished but with all the amenities he required. He found himself with a renewed interest in his Catholic faith, it's philosophy and doctrines. He enrolled in Providence College's evening division for classes in theology and a distinguished lecturer series.

Summer vacation was fast approaching. It was at The Gladiator.

"You know cuz, you're gonna be out of school for the summer, I can take some time off, why don't we go to Italy. We could visit the family over there, whadda ya say? It's cheap, the American dollar is worth something like 200 lira." John Riccitelli spoke with enthusiasm. He was a tall, finely featured young man and a cousin through marriage on his mother's side. "C'mon, you may never have this opportunity again."

A week later Alitalia deposited the two young men at Leonardo DaVinci Airport. They spent hours visiting the historic icons of Rome and Florence, visited Abruzzi, and spent the night with cousins in L'Acquila and the town of Caieti. It was a warm, convivial meeting. They heard the confirmation of family lore that had spread to America. Hugo learned in detail his grandfather's exploits and path of emigration. The food and wines were intoxicating to their senses. Each small town was a new adventure. They visited the southern Italian cities of Calabria and Naples, ferrying to Sicily for a two-night stay. They were intoxicated with the country and their Italian heritage. They trained to Rome and made the connection to the overnight sleeper to Paris, indulging in

THE ARRIVAL THE STRUGGLE THE ASCENDANCY

a first class double cabin with private shower and toilet. Arriving Paris at 9:10 a.m., they were rested and ready to see the sights. Outside Gare du Nord they hailed one of the few remaining black purnel taxis for the day and toured the city. They registered at a comfortable boutique hotel off the Champs D'lysees and dined in a small family-run restaurant on quail and morels with an attentive staff hovering over the two young handsome Americans.

"Cuz, where do you want to go next?" Riccitelli spoke with his mouthful of a warm breakfast croissant, wiping the flaky crumbs from his lips with the back of his hand.

"You know, I have always wanted to visit Our Lady of Lourdes. You know, where the young girl, Bernadette, saw a vision of the Blessed Virgin and actually heard her speak."

Riccitelli shrugged his shoulders and held his palms up. "Okay, let's go. How do we get there?" It was a pleasant five hour train ride to Lourdes. The pastoral landscape with its towering rows of tall narrow poplars had a tranquilizing effect on Hugo. His thoughts turned to Lorraine. The taste of her lips. Was he ready for a permanent relationship? What was next in his life? How long would he live? He had a nagging feeling that, unlike his grandfather, he had been a taker all his life, not a giver, and he silenty vowed to change that somehow. The train arrived in Lourdes at 4:30. They found a small, inexpensive hotel near the station, ate in a small bistro, drank more local wine than they should have, walked the city that boasted more religious tourists than any other in Europe, with the exception of Vatican City, and retired for the evening. The next morning the cab ride to Lourdes took just fifteen minutes. The surly driver demanded twenty francs and waited impatiently for a tip.

Studing the tourist guide, they discovered tha the Lourdes campus was made up of the sanctuary, the grotto, the famous spring, and a variety of administration buildings. To their surprise, they learned that the town itself was home to twenty-two places of worship. The cab had deposted them in front of the Lourdes Cathedral, consecrated by Pope Leo XIII in 1879. Standing in the gravel covered parking area, they looked up in awe of the massive spires soaring above them. Following signs, they climbed the long granite stairway to the main sanctuary with its medieval vaulted entrance. As they walked the stairway, they saw crutches, canes, walkers, and a wheelchairs cast off by visitors who had come before them in search of a cure, in many instances miraculously being granted relief from pain and paralysis. They entered the enormous sanctuary, a third full. A mass was in progress with three priests on the altar. They found an available pew close to the majestic altar and sat enraptured by their ethereal surroundings. The Latin chants were answered by a chorus of choir voices that reverberated within the marble and stone sanctuary. Multicolored light streamed through the tall stained glass windows, casting a celestial aura as was their designers' intention. Hugo sat transported by the scent of inscense, the booming voices of the choir, the thundering ecclesiastical chorus of a monstrous German organ, and the vast heavenly surroundings. He felt the presence of God. He heard a voice within him repeating, who are you, who are you? He sat transfixed, unable to move in his reverential hypnosis. Riccitelli studied his cousin with a frown and gently shook him. "Aayyy Hugo, you okay? Talk to me."

Hugo turned to his cousin, eyes moist with tears of joy. "John, I've never felt so close to God. It's an overwhelming feeling.

THE ARRIVAL THE STRUGGLE THE ASCENDANCY

Riccitelli placed his hand on his cousin's shoulder and murmured, "I know, I know." They continued their journey, visiting Nice and Spain, climbing in the Pyrenees Moutains. Here again Hugo could feel the exaltation of spiritualism as he stood on a mountain peak watching the sunrise into a cloudless blue sky.

They returned home weary world travelers. Life was good. Hugo had been hired on a full-time basis by the school system. He was working three nights a week as a bouncer and he was with Lorraine every free moment. He wouldn't admit to himself that he loved her. Succumbing to such feelings, he knew vaguely, would cut him off from something of which he was not sure. He had all the money he needed, all the women he wanted, if he wanted them. He had Lorraine's love, too, and yet he still felt strangely unsettled. Months passed. To everyone in his circle he remained the same, smiling, outwardly happy Hugo. It was the chance glimpse of the newsstand copy of *Time Magazine* that inexorably altered his life. He purchased the magazine with the photograph of Mother Theresa on the cover, brought it to his apartment and read and re-read the article on the works of Mother Theresa in India's Calcutta and around the world. It was then, alone in his apartment, that he knew what his calling would be. He wrote to her in India, a passionate, heartfelt, three-page letter pledging himself to her work, volunteering himself for work in Calcutta's slums. He mailed it early the next morning and awaited a reply. Two months passed with no response. It was while watching the evening CBS news broadcast that he saw Mother Theresa being interviewed at the Missionaries of Charity headquarters in the South Bronx. He watched intently, learning that she would only be there briefly. He sat back on his sofa eyeing the phone. He sat motionless mulling the thought of calling her directly, thought better of it, and then showered and dressed for his shift at Marlowes.

"Hugh, what is it with you tonight, you're in a dream world, everything all right?" Johnny Lamana placed his hand on his friend's shoulder as he spoke.

"Yeah, I'm all right, I just have something on my mind, that's all."

"Well, what is it, can I help? Did you kill somebody, you need to get rid of the body?" Hugo smiled and gestured in futility.

"Listen, John, I've got something I need to get off my chest and I don't want my balls busted okay?" Slowly he divulged to his friend his newfound goal and of his feeling of epiphany.

Lamana was quiet. Hugo tried to read his friend's face. It showed no trace of humor. Then, taking hold of Hugo's arm, he said in a clear voice, "Hugh, buddy, if you feel that strongly about joining her, just do it, do it now. It's probably your last chance of every being this close to her, and if you don't do it you'll be kicking yourself for the rest of your life."

Hugo grasped Lamana's extended hand and mumbled a thank you as he hurried to the back office, picked up the phone, and dialed information for the Missionaries of Charity in the South Bronx. He had butterflies in his stomach as the phone buzzed from the other end. A faintly accented voice answered. It suddenly occurred to him that it was after ten in the evening. His opening remarks were stuttered. "Ah, I'm, ah, sorry to be calling so late, I hope, it's all right, I mean, it was my last chance…"

The voice interrupted, sensing his anxiety. "Oh, it's no problem, we're used to late evening and early morning calls. How may I be of service?"

He swallowed hard and slowly responded. "Is it possible to speak with Mother Theresa?"

"May I tell her who's calling?"

"Yes, Hugo, Hugo Rossi, from Rhode Island."

"One moment, Mr. Rossi."

Perhaps two minutes passed, but they were the longest minutes he had every waited, wondering if this was all real, if he was really about to speak with the possibly the most famous woman on the planet, a woman who many revered as a saint. And then he heard a heavily accented Slavic voice, soft and direct: "Yes, can I help you, Mr. Rossi?" He was momentarily stunned into speechlessness. "Mr. Rossi?"

"Yes, Mother, I'm sorry, I just can't believe I'm speaking with you, it unnerved me for a moment."

She laughed into the phone. "Oh, Mr. Rossi, I'm not that important, I don't know who is, so how can I help you, please?" Hugo poured out his heart to her for a full five minutes, telling her of his experiences at home, in Vietnam, and at Lourdes and how he felt compelled to pledge himself to her cause and to work with the poorest of the poor in India. He was almost breathless as he finished his appeal. He could hear multiple voices away from the phone and then Mother Theresa's voice. "Mr. Rossi, do you mind if I call you Hugo?"

"No, Mother, not at all, I want you to."

"Well Hugo, I'm leaving tomorrow for India on a nine o'clock flight. If you can be here at six o'clock we'll be able to talk."

Hugo's chest felt like it was bursting as he hurried past Lamana, smacking him on the shoulder as he descended the staircase. "John, she's gonna talk with me at six tomorrow morning, I gotta run."

He raced home, threw some essentials into a small suitcase, filled his tank with gas, and roared onto Route 95 to New York City. After taking two wrong exits, he arrived in the South Bronx at quarter past five. For almost forty-five minutes he scoured the dilapidated buildings of the burrough, unable to find the Missionaries of Charity headquarters. In desperation, he pulled up behind a large Hood's milk truck and walked to the driver's side. No one was in the truck, but as he turned toward his car he saw the driver emerging from a narrow door in a cement wall surrounding a building. "Excuse me, buddy, but can you tell me where I can find the Missionaries of Charity building?"

"Whadda ya mean, the nuns?"

"Yeah, you know they wear head shawls."

"Yeah, yeah I know, you found it."

"Whadda ya mean?"

"I mean they're in the building I just come out of." Hugo scanned the cement wall, coming to rest on a narrow wrought iron fence with a Christian cross in its center. He looked at his watch, exactly six a.m. He rang the ornate bell and stepped back, smoothing his hair with his palm. The large oval oak door opened to reveal a nun in habit. To his delight, he had been expected. One wall of the anteroom was covered with photographs and citations. Hugo moved from one to the next, examining the mostly black and white photos of the South Bronx in its better times. The photographs of India intrigued him most of all.

"Well, you made it, Hugo, I'm sure you didn't get much sleep!" He turned quickly, startled to see a diminutive, smiling, weather-beaten woman of indeterminate age.

"Mother Theresa?" He could not think what to say next.

"Yes Hugo, it's me. Please sit with me for a while." His pulse raced as he sat across from this woman who had given herself over to God. Her given name was Agnes Gonxha Bojaxhiu, she was Albanian from the small city of Scopje. She came from a prosperous family and was raised with both parents and three siblings. As a child her mother, a pious woman, saw to it that the children attended Mass on a daily basis. From her early youth, she knew her calling would be service to the Catholic Church, and she had succeeded dramatically in establishing the Missionaries of Charity serving the poor around the world. "So Hugo, tell me about yourself, start from your childhood, I'm always interested in learning about the way my people grew from childhood." His heart soared, she had referred to him as one of 'her people'. He spoke for fifteen minutes, recounting facts and episodes from his earliest recollections to the present time. He spoke as if selling vacuum cleaners door to door. She smiled at his earnestness. "Well, my son, you have had an interesting life for one so young. I think I would have enjoyed meeting your grandfather, Salvatore. From your story he was a very courageous man." Hugo nodded.

"He was my life's hero, Mother. I loved him and my grandmother very much. They gave me their values."

"Yes, I can see that." She covered her mouth with her left hand for a moment, rose from her chair and motioned to Hugo to wait there. She returned several minutes later with a tall, fair complextioned nun. "Hugo, this is Sister Andrea, she will be your Supervisor, that is, if you're still willing to join us as a co-worker."

He spit out the words. "Yes, Mother, I…."

She held up a hand to stop his answer. "I want you to wait until I have outlined what we need of you and what I expect of you, because you may not want to join us after I tell you of our need. I'm sure you noticed the destitute condition here in the South Bronx, there are thousands of people who are also destitute, who are close to losing their souls because they have lost all their worldly possessions. And the worst part is that they have lost the ones who used to love them. We are the only lifeline. I need you to work here in this hopeless place restoring hope; I need you to minister to the people addicted to drugs, alcohol, and crime. You will build halfway houses for the addicts; you will work with recently released convicts from the prisons. You will keep the peace between the ruthless rival gangs. Sister Andrea will provide the plan and the blueprints. You will have a partner assigned to you. I know you want to work with me in India, that will happen, but for now, I need you here and I need you here for a good length of time. You will have to leave your teaching position, your family and friends, and your comfortable life. Do you have a woman in your life?"

He smiled as he spoke. "I think I do, Mother, I hope I do."

She smiled in return. "I see. Well, she will have to visit you at the St. Pius Rectory not far from here or you will visit her in Rhode Island. We will provide you with room and board, but there is no stipend." She paused and looked into his eyes as she stood to leave. "Do you still want to be a co-worker?"

He stood and reached for her hand. "More now, Mother, than ever before." She embraced him, her eyes glistening. She held his hands as she spoke.

"God sent you to us to do his work, I know you will not fail." Before he could speak, she was gone. Sister Andrea's voice brought him out of his jumbled thoughts.

THE ARRIVAL THE STRUGGLE THE ASCENDANCY

"Well, Hugo, you're now officially a co-worker of the Missionaries of Charity. I'll need some information from you and then you can return to Rhode Island to conclude any business, pack your belongings, and return for your assignment, let's say one week from now."

His first stop was Angelina who was beside herself with frustration at the prospect of not seeing him on a regular basis. "It was bad enough when you were in Vietnam and I wouldn't hear from you for weeks, now you want to leave again. What, you don't like your home, your mother, what is it with you?"

He embraced her. "Ma, Ma, of course I love you, and I'm only four hours away. I'll be home as often as I can. I just feel that I have to do this." In the end she acquiesced with the admonition that if he didn't visit frequently, she would tell her friends that he had abandoned his mother. He dined with Lorraine at the Old Canteen on Federal Hill. He poured his heart out to her about his spiritual feelings at Lourdes, his meeting with Mother Theresa, and his compulsion to serve her. She said she understood, but she wanted him to know that she would be dating other men and that maybe he should date other women while in New York. There was a tinge of ambivalence in her voice as she maintained her nonchalance. They parked outside of her house and devoured each other's lips before reluctantly parting.

Sister Andrea had made arrangements for him to live at the St. Pius Rectory on 145th Street in the center of the South Bronx. It was a small room with one equally small closet. There was a bed, a desk, a chair, one window and no television. The toilet and shower facilities were at the end of the hall. The Rectory was populated by priests, Christian Brothers, various travelers on religious missions, and co-workers. The food was surprisingly good, and it was served seven days a week, three times a day. A knock on his door interrupted his unpacking. It was Sister Andrea with a young man in tow. "Hugo, I'd like you to meet your partner in your mission, this is Flavio Zambarano, an Italian boy, like you."

Flavio stepped forward smiling, extending his hand. Hugo sized him up as he shook his hand. He was younger than Hugo, two inches taller, handsome, with a mop of black curly hair and thin as a rail. "Nice to meet you Hugo, looking forward to working with you." Appearances aside, the accent was positively New England, Boston.

"Nice to meet you too Flavio…"

"Call me Zam," he interrupted, "everybody does. I'm right down the hall, by the way, next to the toilet!"

They met the next morning with Sister Andrea and a large black man in his early sixties. "Hugo, Flavio, I'd like you to meet Washington Adams, he will provide you with all the information you will need to construct, staff, and recruit residents for the halfway houses you will open here in the South Bronx." Sister Andrea left the room after wishing them good luck.

"Alright, boys, you can call me Pops. I've been called that so many times I finally adopted it as my nickname. This is how it works, you find a likely abandoned building large enough to accommodate twelve residents, in pretty good shape, and you turn it over to Stan Rosenberg's construction company. In the meanwhile, you go to City Hall and request the property as abandoned, which will be sold to us for one dollar. At City Hall you see Esmerelda Sanchez, nice lady, we have never been turned down. We normally put twelve to fifteen men in a house. We have written rules for every resident. We take anybody. They get a bed, clean linen, towels, hot showers and three meals a day. If you break the house rules one time, you're out. Am I understood on this point, it's important?" They nodded in agreement and voiced their approval. "Alright, come on, we're gonna go and take a look at some of the houses we have up and running and one we have under construction."

They spent the day visiting half-way houses, witnessing firsthand the misery of drug addicts and alcoholics. Hopelessness and despair were written on the ravaged faces and in the profoundly saddened eyes. "You know, boys, we have had some dramatic success stories, and many of the people you've seen today will kick their habits, of course with your help." Pops took them to meet Stan Rosenberg and his crew working on the newest house, soon to be home to fifteen residents. He was a giant of a man, a Jew who spoke with an Irish brogue and wore a yarmulke. They drove to City Hall to meet Esmerelda Sanchez, a woman who was in a constant state of motion and high anxiety. It was six when they arrived back at the rectory. Pops pulled his vintage station wagon to the curb. "Alright, tomorrow morning, eigth a.m., right here. I'm turning over the newest house to you guys. You're going to finish it, staff it, and keep it on track." They looked at one another

"But Pops, we don't know shit about putting these houses together. How the hell are we gonna take over that new house?"

"Don't worry boys, you're gonna do just fine, you got me, Rosenberg, Esmerelda, other co-workers, and your own good common sense. You're gonna be fine."

It took a month of twelve-hour days of following Pops around, working with Rosenberg, and learning how to untangle the red tape at City Hall, but they got the job done. Recruiting residents was sometimes hampered by the Black and Hispanic gangs who were constantly at each other's throats and who terrorized the existing small businesses in the war-torn pocket of the Bronx, once home to over 300,000 Jews. The streets were mostly empty of productive families, not a building was left untouched by decay. Evenings were lit by flames from the many buildings that had been torched in hopes of collecting insurance proceeds.

Over the years the South Bronx had gone from two-thirds white to two-thirds Black and Hispanic. One of the few untouched buildings was the local New York Police precinct, the $41^{st,}$ known as Fort Apache for its solitary stand against the surreal environment it was left to protect. Evenings were resonant with the roar of the Cross Bronx Expressway, the wail of fire company sirens, and the screeching tires of police as they pursued fleeing gang members. There were killings on a weekly and sometimes daily basis. It was a complete breakdown of civil society.

Hugo and Zam became old hands at the construction of the houses, and there were more than enough willing potential residents to fill the available beds. The two partners had gained the ear and the confidence of some of the local business people, which consisted of small grocery stores, a cleaner, a drug store, and an assortment of various service businesses, all protected after closing with roll down metal shutters. They stayed because they couldn't afford to move and they had an attachment to an area they called home. Reggie Williams, a black man with a mane of white hair and a handlebar moustache, ran the Coffee Cup Restaurant, a narrow twelve stool breakfast and lunch eatery known for his meatloaf and home fries. Hugo and Zam were regulars. Reggie had taken a liking to them and the work they performed. He smiled broadly as they came through the front door.

"Well, my, if it ain't Batman and Robin, how are ya boys?" Hugo slid onto a stool and broke into a grin. "Good, Reggie, real good. I don't know how you do it Reg, but this place is always spotless. You do a great job."

"Yeah, well that comes from twenty years as a cook in the U.S. Navy. I take great pride in the cleanliness of my galley." The entrance door burst open and three young black men entered, pushing and jostling one another.

"C'mon mofucka, gimmee ma mufucken money – now!"

"Fuck yo, mufucken mutha-niggah."

Reggie reached slowly under the counter for a loaded shotgun, resting it in the crook of his arm. "I told you boys not to bring your shit in here cause I definitely will blow your assess off, you understand me?" All eyes were focused on the gunmetal blue double barrels. "Awright Reggie, man, we be goin, you can put the cannon away." The largest of the troublemakers rested his gaze on Hugo and Zam.

"Hey Reggie, why you feedin these two honkey mufucken troublemakers? They do nothin but cause trouble since they come here."

"I told you gentlemen to leave – NOW!" The trio exited the restaurant staring over their shoulders at Hugo and Zam with daggers in their eyes. Hugo swiveled his stool to face Reggie.

"Reg, who are those guys and why are they calling us trouble makers?"

"Well ya see, you two guys are bringing stability to the area and they don't want that, you're taking some of their drug customers off the streets and they don't like that, especially that. They're part of the Black gang who thinks they own the South Bronx. They call themselves 'The angels from Hell' or 'The Angels'. Their leader is an ex con who calls himself Kong, you know as in King Kong, and he's big and ugly enough to have that handle. Then we have the Spanish guys, they're just as bad and just as crazy and it's all about the same thing, money, drugs, prostitution, and shakin people down. The leader of the Puerto Ricans or whatever they are, calls himself Grande Cojones, or something like that. He's also and ex-con. It ain't easy here boys, it ain't easy."

Hugo had made somewhat of a reputation for himself at a Karate Studio in the 'hub', the most active retail center in the South Bronx. The studio was owned and run by Kim Soong, a friend of George Stomponato and a contestant in competition against Stomponato's school, where Hugo had first met him. It was a bare bones studio that catered to novices, gang members, and uptown white-collar types feeling tough and exhibiting bravado for their friends by venturing into the area. Hugo became somewhat of a celebrity, winning several matches, such that other members of the studio would visit the school just to watch him work out. It was known as a demilitarized zone; everyone was civil to one another, and Kim Soong would not tolerate swearing or boisterous acts. He was a seventh degree black belt and commanded great respect in the greater New York City karate community. Hugo began entering tournaments under the auspices of Soong, and many had cash prizes that kept him in pocket money.

Zam had taken a job with a rock band playing in small clubs in Manhattan. It came as a complete surprise to Hugo that he was such an accomplished guitar player. It also gave him someplace to socialize at no charge.

Things were going well with the houses. He had settled into a routine and it made him restless. He visited Angelina and Lorraine every three or four weeks. Lorraine was dating, but "no one special" as she put it. Though he knew the situation was of his own making, he found himself consumed with jealousy every time he left her. He called during the week and they would talk endlessly, which consumed a good part of his spending money. He knew she was waiting for him, waiting for some words of commitment, but there was some unknown impediment, some built in defense that stopped him at the brink. He yearned to tell her how much he loved her, how she was the only woman he could envision spending his life with, but the thoughts always emerged as a weak appeal to her own deep feelings. "Let's talk next week, I'm coming home. I want to see you, okay?"

"Whatever you want, Hugo, you know where to find me – maybe."

Hector Mendez was a young member of the Cojone Gang with a passion for the martial arts. He was a regular at Kim's studio, watching Hugo work out and training with two of the instructors. He was hesitant to approach Hugo, but Hugo took the initiative. "Hey Hector, come on over here, I want to show you some technique." A surprised and pleased expression crossed the younger man's face as he slowly strutted his way across the studio to face Hugo.

"What you want man, why you wanna talk wit me?" Mendez looked toward the ceiling. He was a tall well-built handsome young man. From what Hugo learned, he was from a close-knit family made up of hard a working mother and father and eight siblings. "Look man, I don't care who knows I'm talking with you, I'm here for the karate, know what I mean, I'm here for the sport, unnastand?"

Hugo nodded and smiled. "Look, I think you have potential, you wanna train with me?" Hector's chest visibly expanded, he controlled the smile that was spreading across his face. He hesitated as not to appear too anxious. "Well…yeah man, yeah, I would like to train with you, but it doesn't mean we're gonna be best buddies."

"Don't worry about it, I'm gonna turn you into a champ, so get ready to work your skinny ass off."

The visit home to see Lorraine did not begin well. When he arrived he discovered she was out with friends at a club, not one of his favorite places, a hangout for wise guys. The bouncers all knew who he was, and he passed around the obligatory handshakes and shoulder hugs as his eyes scanned the packed dance floor. One of the bouncers, Mickey Rizzo, pointed to her table. She watched him out of the corner of her eye as he treaded his way to her table through the crush of people. She sat with three of her closest friends, heads together, feigning inattention to Hugo's advance. "Lorraine, why do you come to this bucket of blood, there are a lot of less troublesome places to go with a lot better clientele."

"Well hello to you too, stranger. You back in town for a couple of hours, and by the way don't try to tell me where I can go or can't go." He slid onto the vinyl banquette and raised both hands in mock surrender.

"I'm sorry, you're right, you're right." The three girlfriends' heads swiveled in unison from Hugo to Lorraine, relishing the repartee. "So you got time for breakfast, I'd like to talk with you about some things?"

"Well, I am here with my friends you know, I just can't leave them flat." Heads were swiveling from left to right and right to left. Linda with the high hair and giant hoop earrings, interrupted the conversation.

"Lorraine go, don't worry about us, we understand. We might see you there anyway."

They ordered English muffins and coffee, sat back and stared at one another. "Well, what's so important you wanted to talk about?"

He leaned forward, elbows on the table, staring at his coffee cup. "Lorraine, I......I love you. I need you in my life. I know it doesn't seem that way, but it's the truth. Do you feel the same about me, tell me?"

Hugo could see that she was moved, and he could feel his heart pounding in anticipation of her response. "Of course I do, what do you think I'm doing here in Rhode Island while you're in New York doing who knows what? I'm waiting for you, but how long do I have to wait?"

He reached for her hand and enfolded it in both of his. "I have a commitment, it's something I have to honor, something I need to fulfill. I can't explain it fully, it's just that I need to serve in a capacity where I can help make a difference in people's lives, people who need help because they can't help themselves, can you understand a little?"

She sat back in the booth, a slight smile on her lips. "I guess that's why I love you, Hugo, why I feel safe with you. How long will you be away?"

He took a deep breath and exhaled through pursed lips. "Well, I'm not sure how long I'll be in the Bronx, and I know that in time ..." "He paused and reached for her hand. "In time, Mother Theresa will want me to work with her in India, to work with the poorest of the poor."

"So exactly what are we talking about in time, Hugo, six months, a year, what?"

"I don't know Lorraine. I do know that I'll be in the Bronx for a while and I'll be home as often as I can. Listen, I'd like you to come up to New York sometime so I can show you what I do. We can have dinner in Manhattan and see the sights, what do you think?"

"So this is how you're gonna buy me off?"

"Yeah," he said sheepishly, "I'll do anything to hold your attention."

The months rolled by, a glimmer of stability seemed on the rise among the small businessmen in the hub and surrounding areas. There was more activity on the streets, people were out in the evening hours. It quickly changed. Kong struck first by invading the home of one of the Cojone's Lieutenants and beating him senseless in front of his young wife and son. There was a firestorm of reprisals – shootings, stabbings, and beatings. It was a war zone. It was rumored that an all out massed confrontation was about to take

THE ARRIVAL THE STRUGGLE THE ASCENDANCY

place somewhere in the Hunt's Point or the University Heights areas. It was Hector Mendez who whispered the location one day to Hugo while working out at Kim Soongs. It was to be Hunt's Point on the coming Saturday at noon. The location was a large, rubble-strewn lot, once the home a small appliance manufacturer long since gone to China and the building leveled following a massive fire. Hugo sat in his car waiting for the emergence of both gangs from the shadowed empty buildings on either side of the lot. They came like ghosts materializing as if from nowhere. He left his car and walked slowly toward the center of the combat area. He estimated that there were about a hundred of Kong's troops and about the same for Cojone's. They carried machetes, baseball bats, knives, heavy chains, pistols, and shotguns. It was, Hugo understood, a contest as to who could look the baddest. Tattoos and bandanas ruled the day. They stood twenty feet apart muttering at one another. Cojone slapped his machete against his pant leg. Kong held the head of his sledge hammer in his large left hand, glaring at Cojone.

"Wait a minute, wait a minute. Nobody's gonna die on this battlefield today." Hugo strode directly between the warring sides. "There's no need for this, you don't shit where you live and that's what you're doing, bringing shit into your neighborhood. It's time to have peace talks, work out your differences, seek some middle ground." Kong moved slowly toward Hugo, he stood a head taller.

"Listen you mufucka, you got no standing in this thing, this is between them mufucken spics and us, you hearin me?"

The word spics brought angry reprisal. "Who you callin spik, you ugly niggah. Go back to the fuken jungle where you came from." There was movement on both sides, but still tentative, as though they knew this would not end well but were reluctant to show any sign of fear. Hugo held up his hands as if a traffic cop. Kong pushed by him, moving toward Cojone.

"Hey Kong, somebody told me you fight like a little girl, that true?" Kong stopped in mid stride and turned to Hugo, slowly smacking the sledgehammer into his left palm as he walked toward him.

"You got balls, honkey, but you got no brains. You just a dumb, trouble makin mufucka and today we gonna take out these spic mufuckas once and for all and you gonna have a ringside seat."

" I got a better idea for a big tough guy like you."

"Yeah, honkey, what's that, you gonna suck my dick?"

"No, Kong, if you drop the sledgehammer, me and you will go at it and if I win, everybody goes home. And if I lose … well, then you guys can go at it, how's that?"

He dropped the sledgehammer and stood legs apart, feet firmly planted in the gravel. "You got a deal, white boy."

"Yeah, but you gotta tell your troops."

Kong shook his head in disgust and turned to his gang members. "If this little mufuken honkey beats me," he roared with laughter, "then we be goin home." In the seconds it took to turn to face Hugo, the former Marine had hurtled through the air breaking Kong's nose with a front snap kick quickly followed by a kick to his exposed throat. The enormous black crashed to the ground, blood gushing from his nose. A stunned silence fell over both gangs. Cojone stared at Hugo with bloodshot eyes, nodded his head slightly, and then waved to his gang to follow him as he slowly walked off the battlefield, turning once or twice to view Kong staggering to his feet, a tee shirt held to his swollen nose to staunch the flow of blood.

The call came at 4 a.m. Sister Imaculatta switched on the lamp at his bedside and shook him vigorously. "Hugo, wake up, wake up."

He awoke with a start. "What, what's the matter, what's wrong?"

"Put something on and come to the office, Mother Theresa is waiting on line for you." Hugo scrambled from bed, grabbing a sweatshirt and sweatpants, forgetting to put on his shoes as he bolted down the stairs to the phone. As he breathlessly entered the office, Sister Andrea looked up from the document she was reading to Mother Theresa and raised a finger for Hugo to wait.

"Alright Mother, I will, and I'll wait for your call next week. Yes, he just came in. I'll put him on." She smilingly handed the receiver to Hugo.

Hugo listened to her heavily accented voice, expectancy welling up in his chest. "I don't care about the time, Mother, it's wonderful to hear your voice."

"Thank you, my son, I called you because I need you here. Your work there is completed. I have a new challenge for you here in Calcutta, are you prepared to come here and assist me?"

"Mother, I've been waiting for this call since we first met, I will swim there if I have to." He heard her low laugh. "You won't have to swim my son, we have airline tickets and a visa for you, do you have your passport?"

"Yes Mother, I've had it for over a year, just in case."

"Good, Sister Andrea will take care of all the details, I will expect you in three weeks."

Zam had put together a bon voyage party at a small Italian restaurant, the Bella Napoli, in the University Heights section. Sister Andrea, Sister Angelica, and Sister Boniface were there in jeans and sneakers. Pops Washington was trading friendly jibes with Reggie Williams entertaining the guests. Hugo's eyes scanned the two tables provided for the party as he entered to a standing round of applause. They were all there, Stan Rosenberg, Esmerelda Sanchez with her husband, Kim Soong with his young girlfriend, and some of the house managers. Sister Andrea spoke glowingly of his service, Zam made some heartfelt remarks, and, surprisingly, Kim Soong lauded him in a halting voice as he spoke of his working with young people at his studio. The call came with clapping hands and stomping feet: "speech, speech." Hugo, smiling, raised both hands as he stood. "I want to thank all of you for making me look good, you're all so special to me and you always will be, I just wish we could all go to India together." There were hugs and kisses and a teary eye here and there. He left for Providence the next morning. Sister Andrea had booked his flight on Lufthansa out of Boston a week later. Zam helped him take his belongings to his car.

"Hugo, I'm going to miss you, buddy. Nobody else will ever bust my balls as good as you." They hugged goodbye as Sister Andrea approached them, arms held wide, enfolding Hugo.

"You're going to be a great soldier for our Lord, I know you will."

He climbed into the car without looking back and accelerated toward Providence. He surprised Angelina as she came through the apartment door, dropping her shopping bag to embrace him. "You know, you do this to me all the time, why didn't you call?"

He held her at arms length with a surprised look on his face. "Well, Ma, then it wouldn't be a surprise."

"I got a sauce with some sausage, I'll cook some macaroni, you hungry?"

"Ma, I'm always hungry for your cooking."

"So what's going on in New York, when do you have to go back, not tonight I hope?"

"No Ma, actually I'm not going back to New York."

She smiled and threw here hands into the air. "At last you came to your senses! You can live here as long as you want, I'll fatten you up." She sat next to him on the floral covered couch.

"Well Ma, I…" He thought for a moment, searching for the best way to break the news. He circled her shoulders with his arm. "Ma, I'm going to work with Mother Theresa in India. I leave next week."

She turned to look into his eyes. "I knew the minute I saw you that you would tell me something like this." She continued in a voice full of resignation. "I know it's what you want, it's, how do you say it, it's your calling." She bent over and kissed his cheek holding his face. "C'mon, put your things in the bedroom, and I'll set the table."

Lorraine sat with her eyes downcast, staring at her coffee cup.

"How long will you be there?"

"I'm not sure, probably six months to a year."

Her mouth dropped open. "You expect me to sit on my hands while you fulfill some fantasy working with that ugly little nun? Who would be crazier, me for waiting or you for going?"

He gently reached for her face and looked directly into her eyes. "There's only one woman I want in my life and that's you. I can't blame you if you decide not to wait for me, but I'll never stop loving you, you have to know that." They sat in silence for a full two minutes. She shook her head, looking toward the ceiling, exhaling through pursed lips. "I'll drive you to the airport."

Chapter 14

THE MOTHER HOUSE

Kolkata, or Calcutta as English speakers call it, has a rich and colorful history. The population of the center city is 4.5 million with the urban sprawl of 71 square miles increasing the count to over 13 million. The residents are Hindu, Muslim, Christian, Sikh, and any number of minor beliefs. There are over three thousand bustees, or slums, in Calcutta, giving rise to lawlessness and hopelessness. In 1946, ferocious religious riots pitting Hindu against Muslim led to the formation of Pakistan by it's charismatic leader, Ali Jinnah. Through the efforts of such leaders as Mohandas Gandhi and Jawaharlal Nehru, India gained its independence from Great Britain in 1947.

The Lufthansa airliner touched down at Calcutta International Airport at 10 a.m., a surprisingly modern airport glutted with travelers, blaring announcements, official whistles, the trundling of baggage carts, and the pervasive odor of curry and ginger. Hugo retrieved his one piece of luggage from the Lufthansa carousel, which was a marvel of German efficiency, and made his way through the Passport Control station. Once past Passport Control he immediately encountered dozens of men holding makeshift signs with the names of their intended passengers, a look of anxious expectation on their dark faces. He had been instructed that there would be someone to meet him, but there was no sign for "Rossi" among the throng. No matter. He'd made his way across Vietnam, he could make his way in India. He followed the signs for the cabstand, prepared to taxi to his address, when out of the corner of his eye he spied an old bearded turbaned man leaping into the air holding a white cardboard sign with the name "Rosey" written in black crayon. Hugo sprinted across the wide thoroughfare to an ancient delivery van of dubious origins. He was greeted by a bony, smiling, toothless man in traditional Indian garb. He bowed, and in a soft singsong vernacular, he said, "Welcome to Calcutta, Mr. Rosey, it is a pleasure to serve you sir." Hugo smilingly extended his hand, which was disregarded, the man instead again placing his joined palms to his lips and bowing low.

"And what is your name, sir?"

"I am called Sudha, sir. I work for the good Mother. I'm sorry, sir, I was not able to enter the airport area to fetch you, they would not allow me in."

"Why is that Sudha?"

The old man laughed as he placed Hugo's bag in the back of the van. "Well, sir, you will see that in India, there are places for all people and unfortunately that is a place that is not liking me. Come, I will take you to the good Mother." The creaking van lurched from the curb joining the wall of vehicles, carts, and bicycles that choked the city streets. The old man was amazingly nimble behind the wheel, downshifting, accelerating into what passed for a lane, working the floor shift and clutch into sharp turns all the while muttering what seemed to be angry oaths under his breath. After nearly an hour they finally broke free of the major crush of traffic onto a broad residential avenue. Suddenly, for the first time, Hugo felt the full force of the noon heat. It was early May, but the hot, hazy, humid air was stifiling. The unmarked three lane road carried a wild assortment of new Jaguars, old bicycles, rickshaws laden with outsized loads and pulled by young boys or barefoot old men, oxen drawn carts, even carts balanced on old automobile wheels. The bevy of ancient diesel tractor-trailers and buses further poisoned the air. Amidst them all, rounded yellow taxis performed death-defying maneuvers as they cut each other off vying for position. As Hugo watched it all from his window seat, the panorama that unfolded was almost surreal. Cows and oxen moved lazily on both the sides of the road, chewing on any the occasional scrap of vegetation or garbage. The ancient colonial buildings, once the pride of the British Raj, shone in a glimmering state of elegant decay, randomly interspersed among taller modern buildings of steel and glass. There were whole families in one-room shacks, bathing, eating, and defecating outdoors. There were beggars sorting through garbage, and men urinated openly against building walls, their small stream flowing into a trickle of waste running along the side the road and filling the air with its eye-watering odor. And yet, somehow he felt exhilarated. There was raw vitality to the city, a sense of expectation.

Sudha pulled off onto a long circular road, slowing and entering a driveway, coming to a squeaking stop in a small courtyard. "Well, Mr. Rosey, you are now at the Mother House for the Missionaries of Charity." The old man leaped from the van with remarkable dexterity, pulling the luggage from the rear before Hugo could do so himself. "Come, Mr. Rosey, I will take you to the good Mother, she is waiting for you." He followed Sudha to one of the two large building flanking the courtyard. He recognized the white habit with the blue striped trim that was worn by the stream of Sisters scurring about the property. Sudha led him up a short flight of stairs through the main entrance, down a long Persian carpeted hall and into a small neat office. A small woman with the white and blue habit sat behind an old desk speaking into a phone. Sudha and Hugo waited inside the doorway.

"Yes, Mr. Roy, we do have a deposit on the property and they have generously accepted our offer and it appears our solicitor, Mr. Agee Singh, will complete the paperwork by the end of this week, and we then can start our work." She paused to listen, nodding as she listened and finally, breaking into a broad smile. "Thank you, Mr. Roy, you are a wonderful man, god bless you sir. God will bless you and we will pray for your continued good health."

She placed the phone into its cradle and smilingly came around the desk, arms spread wide. She's so tiny he thought, but she lights up this room. "Hugo, Hugo, I have been waiting for you, my son, at last you're with me." She embraced him and kissed his cheek. She smiled up at him, holding his shoulders. "Sudha gave you a good ride from the airport?" She chuckled as she cast a glance toward Sudha, who bowed, palms clasped to his forehead. Overwhelmed, Hugo finally found his voice.

"Yes, Mother, he gave me quite a tour, he's a very good driver."

"Well, my son, are you ready to begin your work now in India?"

"Mother, I can't describe to you what emotions I'm feeling. Just show me what needs to be done."

"I will Hugo, but now I want you to settle in and rest a little, it was a long trip and we will have time to talk and I'll give you a tour of our facilities. Sudha will take you to your quarters and I'll see you here at my office at three. Are you in need of anything right now?"

Hugo assured the nun that he was fine, and he dutifully followed Sudha across the courtyard to the other large building on the grounds, ascending to the second level to a barracks-like dormitory with ten military-style bunks on each side of the long room. For each bunk a narrow locker stood against the wall and a footlocker at the aisle end. Sudha pointed to an empty bunk.

"Is this to your liking, Mr. Rosey, sir?" As Hugo unpacked he heard voices coming from the stairwell, followed by the appearance of two young men in hospital whites entering the dormitory. They were deep in conversation and did not immediately notice the newcomer. The taller of the two was exceptionally thin and tall, with reddish hair and freckles, and spoke with a Scottish burr. The the other – short, stout, and olive complectioned seemed very excited and was waving his arms about, speaking in English in what Hugo thought was a Spanish accent. They stopped in mid conversation when they saw Hugo standing by his bunk.

"Well, well, it's our new coworker I believe, is it yee, Hugo?" Hugo smiled at the engaging Scotsman.

"Yes it is, I've just arrived."

"Good, grrreat to have yee with us. I'm Robbie MacDonald and this argumentative little man, who's usually wrong, is Dr. Luis Mendoza, late of the Philippines."

Dr. Mendoza stepped forward to grasp Hugo's hand. "Hugo, it's good to have you with us. Pay no attention to Dr. MacDonald here, he talks a lot but it's usually bullshit." They nudged each other good-naturedly.

"Well, it's a pleasure to meet you both. I'm looking forward to assisting you in your work or whatever assignment they give me."

"Don't yee worry, Hugo, therre's plenty of work to go around, more than enough." As MacDonald and Mendoza took seats across from Hugo, Sudha arrived with a large pot of steaming tea and honey rice cakes.

"Mother thought you good sirs would like some tea and I'm pleased to bring it." He placed the tray on top of Hugo's footlocker, gave a slight bow, and left.

"So how long have you guys been here?"

MacDonald answered through a mouthful of rice cake. "Three weeks today and we will probably be here for another five or six."

"Do you leave your practices and patients? How do you break away to come here as a co-worker?"

Mendoza smiled as he spoke. "Fortunately, my dear fellow, I'm on staff at the Philippine General Hospital in Manila, a very large hospital, and we regularly send doctors and nurses here every year. And Dr. MacDonald here is on staff at Stobhill Hospital in Glasgow, which does the same thing."

MacDonald took up the conversation. "So, Hugo, what do you do back in the states and where is it that ye hail from?"

"I live in Rhode Island, not to be confused with Long Island. It's the smallest state in the country."

MacDonald's eyes narrowed as he paused in thought. "Ah, yes, Newport that's in Rhode Island, the mansions, the yacht races, right?"

"That's right, Robbie," chimed in Mendoza, "a very historic town."

"So I've heard. And what is it that you do in Rhode Island, Hugo, are you in medicine?"

"No, I'm afraid not. I'm just a school teacher, secondary education."

"Ah," declared MacDonald in a loud breath, "then you're a school master, to correct your rotten English, Luis."

Mendoza held up his middle finger in reply. Mendoza leaned forward, a serious expression on his face. "So tell me, Hugo, do you have an assignment yet?" Hugo acknowledged that he did not. "Well" said Mendoza "whatever it is, you will be very busy. We all need four hands just trying to keep up with the crush of people who need assistance."

Hugo motioned toward the empty bunks. "How many more co-workers are living here?"

MacDonald counted out on his fingers. "There are seven, including us. You'll get to meet them all tonight or tomorrow, depending on what shift they're working."

"So what do you doctors do here?"

MacDonald glanced at Mendoza and grew solemn. "Hugo, I come here and I know Luis feels the same way, because it gives me an appreciation for life and the human spirit. The people we treat are the poorest of the poor, the sickest of the sick. They are people who no one else will touch. But here, because of Mother's philosophy, they receive not only medical attention but they find hope. And, not to be too sentimental, they find love as well. Many patients die here, but if they do, they die surrounded by people who know them as individuals and who care about them. I'm a surgeon, I operate all day long. I remove tonsils, appendix, gallbladders, and every other organ. There are no specialists here. I have amputated dozens of diseased limbs, mostly lepers. It is a scourge here in Calcutta. Luis does the same work only he's better at it than I am, and he's a phenomenal diagnostician."

"Mac, you only say that because it's true." In reply, MacDonald displayed his middle finger.

Hugo arrived precisely at three and was ushered into the office by an Indian nun in a white sari with three blue stripes on the sleeves. Mother put her writing aside and walked around her desk to meet her new worker. "Hugo, I want you to meet Sister Rita, she is my right hand here for administration. Unfortunately, it takes so much time keeping track of everyone and everything, we have grown so in recent years. Come, I'll give you a tour of some of our facilities. Later, Sudha will drive us to the orphanage, but for now we will walk." As the walked across the courtyard, they passed dozens of sisters who greeted the head Mother with warm smiles.

"Mother, I've noticed tha the Sisters seem very happy here, despite the misery they have to deal with every day."

"Yes, Hugo, they must be happy, they must smile, it gives confidence to the people we care for." As they rounded a corner of the building across the courtyard they came upon a dozen or more nuns washing and rinsing clothes by hand and hanging them on endless clotheslines now filled with sheets, saris, and undergarments.

"Sister, why do you do laundry by hand, isn't it time consuming and labor intensive?" The sisters went about their labors humming and occasionally breaking out into bits of song.

"Laborers we have, and it would cost us more money than we can afford to send them out or to buy expensive machines to do the work." Sudha appeared and took a position walking behind them as they made their way to the vintage van parked behind the building. "I'm going to show you our orphanage, which has grown beyond my wildest hopes. Mr. B. C. Roy has helped us immensely, he's the Chief Minister of West Bengal and a friend to us."

Despite Hugo's doubts, the vehicle and its passengers somehow arrived unscathed at Shishu Bhavan. As she emerged from the van, Mother took Hugo's arm. "Come, we will meet with Sister Rose who oversees this building and sixty-one others throughout India."

Hugo was introduced to a large, jovial woman from Belgium who, he quickly discerened, ruled the orphanages with a velvet gloved iron fist. "So you are our newest co-worker, yes?" Before he could respond, she said, "Come now, I'll show you what we do here." For the next hour, they toured the dormitories, the cafeteria, the school, and the infirmary. The facility tended to hundreds of children who struck Hugo as happy and well fed. Mother Theresa, followed by Sudha, greeted the children with a touch or a kiss on the forehead.

"Well, what did you think of our largest orphanage?" Suda was again behind the wheel.

"Well, Mother, I think India is very fortunate to have you doing the work that you do here."

"No, my son, this is all God's handiwork. Without his intervention, nothing gets done."

They emerged from the van and walked to office. "Tomorrow morning you will meet Raj Vijaya, he will be your adviser, guide and instructor." She smiled at him and took his hand. "You are going to be a wonderful co-worker, this I know. Remember, you do this work not for me, you do this work for Jesus and his Heavenly Father. And Hugo, you will not be designated as a co-worker, you will be my *Adjutor Specialis*." She smiled as she spoke, anticipating the quizzical look on his face.

"What is a..." he stumbled over the words. She reached up and placed her hand on his shoulder, "It is Latin, Hugo. It means Special Assistant."

The aroma from the small cafeteria was distinctly Indian. As he walked in, he spotted MacDonald and Mendoza sitting at a long table with four other men. MacDonald waved to him and pulled out a chair from the table. As he approached, MacDonald stood to introduce him. "Gentlemen, our newest meat for the grinder, Mr. Hugo Rossi, late of Providence, Rhode Island, somewhere near the grand city of Newport." MacDonald introduced each man as they extended their hands. "Hugo, meet Dr. Sol Lieberman from Israel, Dr. Pasquale Imondi from Italy, Dr. Donat Ragovin from Romania, and Dr. Sergei Ilyavitch from Russia, a regular United Nations of physicians. Hey, you need some food, come with me." They returned to the table with a stainless steel tray piled high with curried chicken with rice and beans.

Hot tea was delivered to the table by a young turbaned boy. Sol Lieberman smiled and spoke in a clipped English accent. "Glad to have you with us, Hugo. Do you have an assignment yet?"

"No, Doctor, not yet."

"Please call me Sol."

"Well, Sol, I'm to meet Raj, Raj…"

"Vijaya!" they volunteered in unison. "He will show you the ropes as he showed all of us," said Sergei Ilyavitch. "Hugo, you will see things you will not believe here in Calcutta, it will make you question the existence of God." The table murmured in ascent.

He was exhausted. He shaved and showered before going to bed, as was suggested by Lieberman, and was instantly asleep at 8:15. He was awakened by the lights in the dormitory being snapped on. He sat up bleary-eyed and looked at his watch. It was 4:30. Mendoza, whose bunk was next to his, smiled as he spoke. "Get used to it, Hugo, this is the time we get up, except on Sunday it's a bit later. If you want some breakfast, you better get your toilet done and put some clothes on."

Hugo filled his tray with fragrant, slightly fermented rice and white beans. At table the doctors were discussing the division of duties at the infirmary. Dr. Imondi looked up from his tray as he poured himself and Hugo a cup of steaming tea. "Sorry, Oogo, we tried to get bacon and eggs as a sort of welcome for you but we couldn't convince the cook."

"That's okay Doctor, this is very tasty."

"Please, call me Pasquale, we're all the same here. We're all doing a similar job."

MacDonald looked toward the far end of the room. "Here comes your adviser and teacher, Hugo, Raj Vijaya in the flesh."

Vijaya approached the table, extending a hand to Hugo. "A pleasure to meet you at last," he declared in a soft, melodic voice. He was tall and thin with a neatly trimmed beard, baseball cap, jeans, and a New York Giants tee shirt. "If you're finished, we should start our day, there's a lot to see and do." There were claps on the back, victory signs, and many wishes of "good luck" as Hugo followed Vijaya out of the dining room to a military style vehicle, open in the rear with a canopy top. Vijaya dropped the tailgate and pulled a large container toward himself. It was chained to an anchor that was welded to the truck floor. He unlocked the trunk and inspected the contents – bandages, vials of pills, bottles of tonics, and medical instruments. Next to the truck were three cases of bottled water and two devices that looked like hand trucks with seats and straps. Satisfied, he locked the trunk and they entered the truck. Vijaya spoke as he backed the truck onto the road. "I'm going to show you what your assignment will be from time to time. Please ask questions and I don't care how foolish you think they may be. We're going to spend most of our time in the bustees, otherwise known as slum neighborhoods. This is where we find our clients, and God knows there are enough of them."

"Raj, you speak flawless English, were you born here?" He smiled as he spoke "I left West Bengal when I was six years old and we moved to Southern California. The 'we' is my father who is a cardiac surgeon, my mother who is a gynecologist, and my sister who is a pulmonary specialist. I grew up in San Diego, went to San Diego State, got a Ph.D in Education, and decided after meeting with Mother to volunteer to work here. For the past three years I have lived here with my maternal grandparents who dote on me as if I were still six years old, and I have more aunts, uncles, and cousins than I can count. Oh, by the way, we're Catholic, and there's only about two percent of Calcutta who are."

He exited from the highway onto a road leading into a commercial district. It was nearing seven and the fruit and vegetable vendors were setting up their stands. The apparel vendors were also setting up shop with a rainbow of saris, head covering, jeans, and footwear. Everywhere the street was coming to life. As they drove on, the street took on a more forlorn appearance. On either side mounds of garbage were piled head high, with ragged men, women, and children sorting through the refuse in search of something to eat or to sell. It was mid May and the temperature at 7 am was close to 80 degrees. The air was fetid and murky as Vijaya slowed the truck to a stop at the entrance to what appeared to be a cluster of worn brick row houses. "Okay, Hugo, let's go, this will be your indoctrination into bustee living."

They entered the sprawling bustee through the remains of an arch and proceeded into an endless warren of worn brick and cement block one-room dwellings with no windows, running water, toilets, or kitchen facilities. Each dwelling was no more than 320 square feet and housed families of five, six, or more. The entranceways were open or, in some instance, had a plastic drape to afford a modicum of privacy. Cooking was done on small charcoal grills or equally small propane burners. Water came from community faucets situated with no apparent plan. Toilet facilities were open trenches or in many cases a convenient wall or corner. The air was thick with the stench of defecation, body odor, incense, and curried food. Large black flies were everywhere. The sounds of infants wailing and children yelling as they charged through the alleyways weaving through the bustee was an overload to one's senses.

"Well Hugo, what do you think of Anand, that's what this bustee is called?"

"Its astounding and a revelation. How big is the place?"

"I think it's about five square miles, there are no statistics that I can point to, it's just secondhand information."

Suddenly, from around a corner came a stampede of children "Raj! Raj! Raj!" they yelled, stumbling over one another as they raced up to him. He held up his hand as he spoke. "Okay, okay, quiet now." He reached into his pocket and threw a handful of wax wrapped bubble gum into the air, followed by another. There was pandemonium as they pushed and shoved to get to the sweet treasure. They continued their tour of Anand followed by a pack of young boys. Open doorways exposed the inhabitants in all forms of dress or undress. They washed themselves outdoors in large basins, hung washed clothing to dry where they could, and made a life with spouses, children, and relatives all within spitting distance. As they passed an open doorway they could see in the shadow of the interior two naked bodies, limbs entwined, aggressively making love. Raj turned to Hugo. "When you live this close to so many people, you become depersonalized, as you can see."

"Don't these people work, Raj?"

"Some do menial tasks, but most of them are untouchables. It's difficult to find a decent job because of the strict caste system in this country. Most who live here receive a small government stipend."

THE ARRIVAL THE STRUGGLE THE ASCENDANCY

As they turned a corner, they almost stumbled upon an elderly, emaciated man lying on his side against a building wall. He was more bone than skin, one side of his face falling in hideous drapes of discolored skin below his neck. Raj saw the look of surprise in Hugo's eyes. "Hugo, this is your first exposure to the worm disease. He ingested a particular miniscule worm, probably from foraging through garbage for food, and became infected. There is no cure. Go back to the truck, please, and get one of the hand trucks. One of the kids will show you the way out and back."

Moments later they were positioned the ravaged body onto the modified hand truck and strapping him in. "Where are we taking him?"

"We're taking him to the home for the dying. From what my experience tells me, he doesn't have long on this planet." They wheeled the dying figure out of the bustee, gave him water and a vitamin pill, which he could not swallow, and drove him to the hospice, which was next to the Hindu Temple of Kali. As they backed into the rear of the Hospice, volunteers and Sisters gently placed the man on a gurney and wheeled him into an Emergency Room for washing, disinfecting, and assessment. Hugo followed Raj through the large, scrupulously clean, white-walled room lined with fifty beds on each side. The second floor duplicated the first.

"Raj, what kind of treatment do they receive here?"

The older man shook his head wearily. "It's really nothing more than pain management and making them comfortable in clean surroundings. Those who come here rarely leave alive."

They returned to Anand. It was now slightly past ten and the temperature had climbed to 90 degrees. They transported three teenaged pregnant girls to the Missionaries Shishu Bhavan

Orphanage and Home for Unwed Mothers. They returned again to find a young man gasping, sitting against a wall, bleeding from a stab wound to his stomach. His mother and sisters had feebly attempted to staunch the flow of blood. They bandaged the wound and transported him to the dispensary. "Raj, what about the police, shouldn't they be notified?"

Raj laughed aloud. "This is Noman's Land for them, Hugo. They figure what happens in the bustee, stays in the bustee. Incidentally, we have our own Mafia in Calcutta and they're very active in prostitution, selling cheap labor, and anything else they can do to make an illicit buck. One of their big money makers is selling little girls to pedophiles and also making porno movies. They're a nasty bunch of bastards." For the next three days they visited a shantytown, two more bustees, and patrolled the side streets in seamy neighborhoods looking for the sick, the hopeless, and the despondent. They did not lack for candidates. On the fourth morning Raj met Hugo by the truck at six thirty. They checked the medical supplies, water, hand trucks, and blankets. Vijaya looked at Hugo, smiled, and dangled the truck keys in front of his face. He reached for Hugo's hand and placed the keys in his palm.

"You're no longer a virgin, my friend, get out there and screw up."

"You mean just me? Alone?"

"Yes, just you, alone. You know what to do, go out and do it, just remember what we've done together and don't hesitate to ask the kids to help you if you need it. And here, take this." He handed him a small brown bag. Hugo opened it and looked inside "Bubble Gum!"

"Yeah, that's some insurance that the kids will help you when you need them."

Hugo knew the routes well enough to get into the bustees and shantytowns and get back to the missionary with his sick and crippled cargo. He pulled off the main highway into a bustee half the size of Anand but plagued by all the same human indifferences. It was called Valkunth, which according to Raj meant Paradise or Heavenly, he wasn't sure which. As he parked the truck, the grimness of the living conditions and the name Paradise made him shake his head. Compared to this, Silver Lake was the Riveria. As he ventured through the narrow winding walkways, he was assailed by a mob of young boys. He followed Raj's example and threw handfuls of bubble gum in the air to screams of delight as the crowd tumbled and fought over the sticky treats. Out of the corner of his eye he spotted a thin boy with cascading blond streaked curls almost obscuring his monstrous sky blue eyes. He smiled at the boy and beckoned him to his side. They boy reluctantly shuffled up to Hugo, head down. He reached into his pocket and handed the boy a lump of bubble gum. It quickly disappeared into his mouth as he smiled up at Hugo. "What's your name, my little friend?"

The bubble burst as he answered through the mouthful of gum. "Avik, my name is Avik Roy."

"How old are you?"

"I'm eight years old."

"Do you live her Avik?"

"Yes, that way." He pointed in a direction indicating that it was some distance away. Hugo extended his hand.

"Well my friend, it's a pleasure to meet you." Avik grasped the outstretched hand and shook it vigorously.

"Thank you, sir." As Hugo continued on his tour, he was closely followed by Avik snapping and chewing the bubble gum loudly.

It was a busy day. He transported men and women to the orphanage, the hospice, and to the infirmary. On each return to the bustee, Avik would be waiting to accompany him through the narrow alleyways of the slum. Sister Rita was waiting for him as he pulled the truck into the missionary parking area.

"You've been working hard, Hugo."

"Yes, Sister," he admitted wearily, "I'm tired and hungry."

"Well you should be, you have been doing a tremendous job, but for the next two or three days, I need you to work with the surgeons at the infirmary and to assist us in the home for the dying. Report to Dr. Lieberman tomorrow morning at the usual time, he will give you instruction."

Hugo sat with Lieberman as he wolfed down an unidentifiable dish of predominantly rice. Lieberman briefed him as to what he would be doing the next day, it did not sound appealing. He returned to the dorm room, past pleasantries with his bunkmates, shaved, showered, and flopped into bed exhausted. His thoughts turned to home, Lorraine, Angelina. He had been excited and preoccupied with his duties, but now thoughts of Lorraine crowded all else out. He felt himself swelling. He sat up on the edge of his bunk, went to his foot locker, found his writing tablet, and wrote a passionate letter to Lorraine spelling out his address very carefully, and then a letter to Angie assuring her that the food was good and he was in good health. He deposited them in the mailbox at the dorm entrance and returned to thoughts of Lorraine. The next three days were spent mopping and sponging up blood, washing and disinfecting bodies, and in two or three cases actually assisting in removing an arm or a leg. In the home for the dying he disinfected bodies, sanitized beds and floors, and transported the living into the home and those who had died he helped prepare for cremation.

Returning to his routine patrols, he found himself frequently at Valkunth. Invariable upon his arrival, Avik would be waiting with a beaming smile and glittering blue eyes. He developed affection for the boy and allowed him to ride with him to other slums and shantytowns. He would stop at food stalls and buy rice, chickens, fish, vegetables, and other foodstuff for Avik to take to his mother and sister. Though the boy had no formal schooling, there was no question that he was bright. "My sister is so smart, she teaches me all things," he explained with a toothy grin.

The chapel at the missionary was small and was staffed by visiting priests from all over the globe. It served the sisters and co-workers who lived and worked at the missionary and anyone who needed spiritual uplifting, confession, or a quiet place to meditate. The current visiting pastor, who would spend a year at the missionary, was from Spain. He was a tall, athletically built man, a former soccer player. Now in his fifties, he had served his church in many parts of the world. His name was Arturo Segovia. He preferred being called Father Arturo. Hugo enjoyed spending time with the priest, who was realistic about his calling and philosophical about life. He had taken to dining with the priest whenever he could and discussing the day's events and sharing Arturo's wry humor. From time to time, Arturo would ride with him and Avik patrolling the streets and bustees, sharing the duties of the mission. After a particularly grueling day on patrol, Hugo sat across from Arturo at the dinner table, toying with his food.

"What's wrong with you," the priest asked, "you usually can't get the food in your mouth fast enough."

Hugo sat back, tapped the stainless steel tray with his fork and spoke. "You know Father, I don't know how much more misery and pain I can experience. Life is not supposed to be so, so difficult, so hard to live."

Arturo smiled reached over and patted his hand. "You know, Hugo, I spent some time in Israel some years ago and I found that our Jewish brethren have learned how to cope with adversity better than most people; maybe it's because they have had so much of it for so long. I have a Rabbi friend, Avi Shulman, and he told me the story of a Jew who was drowning and as he sunk to the bottom of the lake, his thoughts were how he could adjust to living under water. The moral of the story is accepting what you can't change and adapting to your situation. The misery you deal with is something you can't change, but you can help some of the people in miserable circumstances. Like Mother says, "One, one, one. She means one at a time."

Hugo smiled and sat back in his chair. "You know, Arturo, you make it almost sensible."

He spent two more days working with the surgeons before he resumed patrolling the bustees, shantytowns, and streets. It was July, with temperatures over 100 degrees for days on end. The air was thick with auto exhaust mingled with the offensive odors of the streets. Father Arturo had arranged for a call to the United States on the coming Sunday morning at 6:00 a.m. With the time difference, it would be 3:30 p.m. in Rhode Island. Hugo had written Lorraine with the day and time, but he could not rid himself of the nagging fear that she would not be there to take his call. Holding the phone he felt his stomach twist in antipation.

With the sound of Lorraine's voice Hugo's fears vanished. It was her, the woman he loved, and he could tell her that now, tell her all the things that he had been storing up since he first left Rhode Island what seemed so long ago. But could he make her understand, he wondered? Could she understand and forgive, or was he asking more than was reasonable or fair?

"Lorraine, please, I love you, I want you to be my wife. We'll have a lifetime together. I promise you, I'll be home by October." He spoke of the work he was doing, the people he served, of the nuns, the doctors, of Father Arturo and little Avik. He seemed to lose himself as he spoke, lost in a feeling of rapture that he hoped, prayed Lorraine would understand, if only a little. Finally he stopped, and the phone was so silent he feared that the call had been disconnected. But then he heard a faint sound, a sob, and he knew it was going to be alright.

"Hugo, I do understand, and I love you even more for it."

It had been a particularly grueling day. He had transported five men and one women, including two lepers, back to the Home for the Dying and the infirmary. Avik rode with him, keeping up a non-stop chatter. He had become a valuable assistant and guide, running errands, interpreting when necessary and scurrying back and forth to the truck for supplies. As Hugo dropped him at the entrance to Valkunth he ducked down in his seat, hiding himself from the three nattily dressed young men who glared at the truck and spoke among themselves as they walked to a Mercedes sedan gleaming in the sunshine.

"They are bad men," Avik explained. "They do bad things to people."

"Avik, listen to me, there are bad people all over the world, you just stay away from them and if someone tries to hurt you, you tell me, okay?"

"Okay."

"You promise?"

The boy stared at the windshield. "Yes, I promise."

Mother Theresa toured the facilities in Calcutta every free opportunity. Her constant companion was Sudha walking behind in his unobtrusive obsequious manner. On occasion she would, out of necessity, visit the banking district in Calcutta to solicit funds or sign documents. Hugo and Raj were asked to accompany her on a visit to the American Express Bank whose manager was from Pawtucket, Rhode Island. It all happened in a split second. As they emerged from the ancient van and walked toward the glass and steel modern bank building, two young bearded and turbaned men who had been following in a plumbing company truck, raced down the sidewalk toward them shouting in Arabic "Allah Akbar, Allah Akbar" their shrill screams and the specter of wild-eyed turbaned and robed men brandishing long daggers momentarily froze the party, except Sudha who charged the onrushing assadins leaping into the air, his foot smashing into the face of one as his left arm swept out to grab the beard of the other, as his feet landed firmly on the concrete, he instantly circled behind his bearded captive and twisted his neck. The sound of bones cracking could be heard reverberating off the glass building. The assassin fell to the pavement, his neck grotesquely bent to one side. He turned to advance on his first victim now standing groggily with his dagger by his side.

The loud voice of Mother Theresa brought everyone back to consciousness. "No Sudha, enough, enough. God will deal with them." He turned, bowed and returned to his station slightly behind her. The Police came moments later and took a report from Raj. They spoke Hindi with Sudha, conferred with each other and allowed him to go on his way pending further investigation. That night, he sat with Raj and Father Arturo at a dining hall table and in a voice filled with amazement, asked about Sudha. "I couldn't believe how quickly he reacted and with no regard for danger and the way he took both of them out, I couldn't believe it was Sudha, where did he come from?" Father Arturo smiled knowingly as he spoke. "Mother found him twenty years ago at death's door. He was totally wasted away, living in an alley, rats nibbling at his torso. She nursed him back to health and he has dedicated his life to her. He has no family that we know of and he's of the untouchable caste." "You know those guys who attacked us this afternoon were radical Muslims. They wanted to make a point by assasinating Mother, but they never expected Sudha. I saw him do a similar thing two years ago, he's amazing." "You know Raj, he doesn't look that physical." "Well, I found out that he studied Kalari Payattu for years. It's an ancient form of martial arts and he's obviously good at it. He also runs ten miles a day and does push-ups, pull-ups and sit-ups. Two hundred each, every day." Hugo shook his head in wonder as he spoke. "Wow, I know who I'll be calling for help if I ever need it." "Do you think the Police will charge him with murder?" "No" said Father Arturo. "She's a National Treasure and Sudha took two bad people out of polite society."

He waited at the entrance to Valkunth for Avik for fifteen minutes, pacing around the truck. He asked some of the young boys if they had seen him, but they had not seen him for some days now. On the third day after distributing his bubble gum he recruited one of the boys to take him to Avik's house. As they approached, he noticed it was one of very few houses with a door, a metal door. He thanked the boy with a bonus of bubble gum and knocked on the door. There was no answer. He knocked again, this time louder and called out his name. Slowly, the door opened slightly. Avik peered from the slit, casting his gaze downward, saying nothing. Hugo's eyes widened in concern as he studied Avik's face. His eyes were blackened, his cheeks were bruised, his lip was cut, and his nose had a welt on one nostril.

"Avik, open the door, who did this to you?" He gently pushed the door open as Avik backed away, his head down, tears welling in his eyes. Hugo dropped to his haunches, placing an arm around Avik's shoulder as he spoke in a tender, soothing voice. "Avik, tell me, I'm your friend, I want to help you. Who did this to you and why, was it some of the boys here or was it a relative, tell me Avik."

The boy wiped the tear from the corner of his left eye with the back of his hand and spoke softly and hesitantly. "It was...it was... the bad men, the Mafia. You saw them when I was ducking down in the truck. They're the ones, there were three of them."

"But why? Why did they do this? What was the reason?"

A young feminine voice responded behind him. "Because he wouldn't tell them where I was." Hugo turned still on his hunches to view a young woman, perhaps eighteen or nineteen standing at the rear of the dark room. He slowly rose to his feet, his eyes struggling to see in the darkened room. Hugo could see that she had the same tawny complexion as her brother, and ringlets of golden hair cascading down her back. Her lips were overfull with long, dark lashes framing her sparkling eyes. She was dressed in a colorful tangerine Sari and sandals, but even in the pale light of the interior, Hugo could see that she had the figure of a mature woman. When he spoke, he could not suppress a smile of appreciation.

"Hello, my name is Hugo..."

"I know who you are, Mr. Rossi. I'm glad we finally meet so that I can personally thank you for all that you do for Avik and for me, I will find a way to repay you."

"No, no, there's no need... ah, excuse me. I'm sorry Avik never told me your name."

Her smile revealed small even white teeth. "My name is Riya, Riya Roy."

"Riya, there is no need to repay me for anything. I like having Avik riding with me, and he's a great help to me as well." Avik beamed with pleasure as Hugo spoke. "Tell me Riya, how long has this been going on?"

The young woman motioned for Hugo to sit at the table in the center of the room as she prepared tea from the small propane stove. "It started two years ago. The Dada who controlled the Valkunth brought the moviemakers here with the gangsters. The moviemakers produce pornographic movies and the gangsters invest money to make the movies. They also have discos and nightclubs where they require many young women to work as prostitutes." Hugo noticed that she spoke in a mild Indian cadence, but that her English diction and vocabulary were flawless, obviously schooled by nuns. "They come regularly looking for young women to put in the films and work as prostitutes. The leader of these evil men is called Rakesh Kumar. He is a killer, his street name is Mercy. That, no doubt, is because he shows none. In the beginning, the Dada would come to see me, he said that Mercy wanted me for himself and that I would be paid handsomely and I would live like a Queen."

"And what did you tell him?"

"I told him no, of course, and that only made Mercy more insistent to the point where he started to come to my house to find me."

"What did you do? How did you avoid him?"

"The Dada felt pity for me, he would warn me when he would be coming and sometimes the young boys would warn me, and I would run and hide at my Aunt's house. Two months ago, the old Dada disappeared and the man who moved up is looking to gain favor with Mercy so there are no more warnings from that source."

He felt the anger welling up in him, his jaw muscles tightening, his hands clenching. "Riya, I want you to be very careful in your travels. I'm going to see what I can do to put a stop to this. I'll stop by tomorrow if that's okay with you."

"Yes, please do. I would like that and I would like you to come for dinner. I'm a very good cook." His heart sang as she spoke, a smile wreathed his face. As he said goodnight, he shook her hand. As their hands touched, he had an overwhelming compulsion to kiss her. She sensed his emotion and stared into his eyes. They stood locked in a gaze until she spoke in a slightly trembling voice: "Well, then, we will see you tomorrow evening at seven."

He sighed deeply as he left. He felt deeply guilt ridden for his powerful feelings for her, and he tried to shunt all thoughts of her aside, but could not. He returned to the dormitory and wrote a five-page letter to Lorraine. As he left the breakfast hall the next morning, he found Sudha waiting for him.

"Good morning Mr. Rosey, how are you Sir?" Hugo smiled pleasantly in response. "Well, Sir, the reason for my visit is to thank you for assisting Miss Riya Roy and Master Avik Roy. Thank you again, Sir." Sudha began to turn to leave.

"Wait! Sudha, how do you know Avik and Riya?"

"They are my cousin Tanya's children."

Hugo took a moment to process this unexpected news. "Sudha, where is Tanya, is she living?

"I don't know, Sir, she just disappeared. No one knows what happened to her, she is very beautiful. If I were to speculate, I would say that she was taken forcibly to serve as a slave by some wealthy man who paid a handsome sum for her. I think perhaps Pakistan or Afghanistan, of course this is only speculation."

Hugo nodded silently pondering Sudha's reasoning. "Thank you, Sudha, it's always nice to see you."

The older man bowed with clasped hands to his forehead. "It's always my pleasure Mr. Rosey, Sir."

Hugo worked with Dr. Ilyavitch at the Home for the Dying all day. It was intense work and it was emotionally draining. He showered slowly, scrubbing away the blood, stench, and futility of the day. He arrived at Riya's home at seven carrying a basket of fresh fruit, bread, and Coca Cola. Avik opened the door slowly, his face lighting up when he saw Hugo.

"Come in, come in!" He locked the steel door deliberately behind Hugo. Riya turned to smile and greet him. "Hello, please sit, I have poured you a small glass of Sherry that I have had for many years, please enjoy it." She toiled at the propane stove, the pungent scents of the herbs and spices filling the room. They dined on rice, vegetables and a fish curry—the best that Hugo had tasted since arriving in India. Avik kept up non-stop chatter until Riya shooed him outside. Hugo watched her every movement.

"Where did you learn to cook like that, it was delicious."

She bowed her head slightly in shy appreciation. "Thank you, I learned to cook by working with my mother. She was a wonderful cook."

"Where is your mother, do you see her?"

"No" she said looking off into the distance, her eyes moistening.

"I'm sorry Riya, I don't mean to pry ..."

"No, no, it's all right. My mother is young, she is only thirty-six. She is very pretty. We think she was abducted into slavery, but we cannot be sure. She has been gone for a year now. No one has heard anything. The police came, they took a report, but we knew nothing would come of it. To the police, we are disposable people, nothing more."

"What about your father, does he know about this, do you see him?" She went into the bedroom and returned with a small color photograph. She sat at the table and handed Hugo the photograph. "This is my father." He was dressed in a military uniform; it appeared to be an officer's uniform. He was tall, well built, blonde, and handsome. Hugo looked up quizzically. She smiled gently. "He was a Captain in the British Royal Marines. His name is Liam O'Connor. My mother did laundry for the officers' quarters at the Army Base here in Calcutta. Many men wanted her, she had to fight some of them off, and then she saw my father. She said he was not like all the rest, he was a gentleman and he was kind to her. She was just sixteen years old and he was twenty-five. She fell in love with him and he claimed he loved her. He rented a small flat off the base and she lived there with him when he was here."

"What do you mean, when he was here, where would he go?"

She paused, picked up the photograph and stared at it. She spoke softly as she continued to stare at the photograph. He was married, he had a wife and a child in England. He was here on and off for many years, he would return home every two or three months on a British Air Force flight."

Hugo took the photo from her hand and examined it not knowing what he was looking for. "Riya, why was he here?"

"He was an instructor, he was training Indian Army Officers in some sort of special things."

"Did your mother know he would be leaving, did he ever tell her the truth?"

"No, but she suspected, when she first met him he was wearing a wedding ring but the next time she was with him it was gone."

"What happened to him, have you ever had contact with him?"

"I haven't seen him or heard from him in over ten years, but he did arrange for us to receive a decent government stipend, and he did get us this large living unit with amenities the other units do not have."

"Did your mother ever hear from him again?"

"Yes, she told me it was right after Avik was born. He left when my mother was nine months pregnant. She told me it was a very long letter and that he loved her but it could never be. She told me that she considered suicide but when she held Avik to her breast, she knew she would never do it."

Hugo took her soft hand. "Riya I'm so sorry that you have had to experience all this hardship, it isn't fair."

"Well, I think of all the good things I have in life and one of them is Avik, and I know our life will get better someday and I feel confident."

He continued to hold her hand; she made no move to release his grip. His eyes locked onto hers, the room was silent as they stood inches apart. He broke the silence as he said "I uhh… I have to be going. I'd like to see you again; is that all right with you?"

"Oh, yes" she replied instantly.

"Well, then, I'll be leaving. Goodnight."

"Goodnight, Mr. Rossi."

"No Riya, Hugo. Please, call me Hugo."

"Goodnight then, Hugo."

He spent the next two days working in the infirmary washing patients, emptying bedpans, mopping floors, and feeding patients. On the third day he resumed his patrols. As he restocked the truck with water and firstaid supplies, he thought he heard Avik's voice. He turned in the direction of the voice to see Avik running at full tilt toward him, arms waving and screaming.

"Hugo, Hugo they found Riya, Riya, they found her!" He threw himself at Hugo wrapping his arms around his waist, sobbing. "They took my sister. They're bad men, they will hurt her." He unwrapped Avik's arms from his waist and held him by his shoulders.

"Avik, stop crying and tell me what happened slowly."

THE ARRIVAL THE STRUGGLE THE ASCENDANCY

The boy gasped for breath, struggling to get the words out. "She was at my cousin's house last night and they came for her there, one of the older boys told the bad men where she was and he brought them to the house."

"All right, get in the truck, show me where the house is."

As they approached the cement block unit in an adjoining bustee, Avik called out. "Cousin Nandu, Nandu, open the door, it's me Avik." The door opened slowly, a man in his early forties peered out, both eyes blackened and a severely cut lip bleeding profusely. He pressed a white cotton cloth to his mouth futilely attempting to stanch the bleeding. The door opened and they entered the small room. The man's wife and three children were huddled in a corner.

"Nandu, I'm a friend, I'm with the Missionaries of Charity, and I'm here to help. Tell me what happened."

"It all happened so fast. There was a knock on the door, I opened it to see who it was. They pushed in. There were four of them. Riya had covered her head and her face and somehow managed to get out the door, running like an antelope with the four of them in pursuit. They came back a half hour later and beat me because I wouldn't tell them where she went."

"Avik, get the first aid kit out of the truck and I'll take care of Nandu's wounds." As he bandaged Nandu, he questioned him. What did the men look like? Did he remember any names? Did they have weapons? And, finally, what direction did Riya run?

"I think she ran toward the Christian cemetery, it's about fifteen minutes up the road."

They drove through the worn gates of the small Catholic Cemetery scanning the headstones and possible hiding places.

"Avik, call out your sister's name." As the truck slowly moved through the cemetery, Avik yelled out her name. "Riyaaa, Riyaaa!" Hugo stopped, the truck engine idling, when suddenly from the corner of his eye he saw the steel door of an elaborate tomb swing open and Riya running to the truck. Avik clambered from the cab and ran to her, throwing his arms around her, smiling and laughing. Hugo stood by her side, uneasy in the open area of the cemetery.

"How did you find this hiding place?" Hugo asked.

"One day I was cutting through here, taking a short cut from the bus line to my cousin's house and I saw the door open. I looked in and saw it was empty. I remember thinking it would make a good hiding place, so I picked up a bolt lying on the ground, closed the door and inserted the bolt in the latch that keeps the door closed.

"You are lucky you had this place to come to. Now let's get out of here." He started the engine and sat deep in thought, hand on the shift.

"Where are we going?" she asked.

"I'm thinking about that right now." He shifted into low gear and slowly accelerated. "I'm taking you home so you can pick up what you need for a few days, then we're going to the orphanage to see Sister Rose. I want you to stay there with Avik until I get the situation at Vaikunth straightened out." As they pulled up to Vaikunth, Hugo whispered to Avik as Riya walked ahead. "Find some of the older boys, tell them that you and Riya are back home and that Mercy doesn't scare Riya. Wait until she leaves the house with her things and is back here with me, you got that?"

"Yes, I got it," said Avik, delighted to be part of what was an unfolding conspiracy. Back at the truck, Hugo and Riya waited for Avik, who minutes later shot out of an alleyway and leapt into the cab that was accelerating before the door had closed.

"What happened?"

"I told Ajay and Ramesh. I think it was Ajay who told Mercy where Riya was hiding. He seemed very interested when I told him."

"Good boy, Avik, good work." Back at the home, Hugo explained to Sister Rose the life threatening experiences that Avik and Riya had endured. Before he could finish, she had her arm around Riya's shoulders escorting her to a room with Avik. He called out that he would be back the next day. Riya turned, smiled, waved and continued her conversation with Sister Rose. Avik broke away from Riya and ran back to Hugo.

"Why can't I come with you, I can help you?" Hugo tousled his hair as he spoke.

"Listen, I need you to stay with your sister and make sure she's okay. Understand?"

"Okay, I will," he said in a dejected voice as he turned to join Sister Rose and Riya.

Hugo found Sudha under the hood of his van muttering to himself as he wiped his hands on a grease stained rag. "Sudha, I need your help."

Sudha bowed. "Yes, Mr. Rosey, how can I be of service to you?"

Hugo related the events of the past two days and of the preceding months. Sudha nodded as he spoke with no change in facial expression. The only change was in his voice, it became flat, monotone, and cold. "I am with you, Mr. Rosey. These men are evil, there is only one way to deal with them, what do you wish me to do?"

Hugo outlined his plan to Sudha, who smiled slightly as he listened. Sudha drove them to Vaikunth at nine that evening, parking away from the entrance walk. Hugo wore a turban and carried a hideous looking rubber mask, as did Sudha. Sudha knew from which direction they would come. Vaikunth was settling in for the night as they took up positions on the sides of the low slung buildings where the walkway made a right angle turn. There was very little light in the bustee. Two hours passed, Hugo grew restless. He whispered hoarsely to Sudha, who appeared to be in a trance like state. Do you think they'll come? Maybe we should try another night, maybe we should go looking for them."

Sudha shook his head slowly and whispered back. "They will come, Mr. Rosey, they will come." Within minutes, the sound of automobiles braking on gravel announced their arrival. Four doors slammed shut. Hugo held up four fingers to Sudha, who nodded impassively. The voices were loud; they spoke English slang in the Indian singsong manner. They laughed and boasted of what they would do if this were not Mercy's woman. As they came deeper into the bustee, the voices became loud whispers. Hugo donned his mask followed by Sudha. Long shadows signaled their arrival. They turned the corner walking two abreast. Hugo and Sudha leapt out of the blackness, roaring like mad men. The tough young gang members froze. Sudha and Hugo carried three-foot lengths of heavy plumber's pipe. Sudha struck first cracking the nose and cheekbone of the figure closest to him, quickly turning and smashing the shin of another. Hugo leapt up and smashed the face of the third figure, quickly followed by a blow to the clavicle of the fourth who was trying to escape. It was over in twenty seconds. They lay panting and frightened for their lives. Hugo, not saying a word, searched them for weapons and relieved them of two pistols and six knives. He stood above them and said in a low, menacing voice: "Tell Mercy the next time you come here, some of you will never leave alive."

Hugo and Sudha left the figures lying in the darkness, bleeding and moaning. As Sudha started the engine on the ancient van, he spoke as if to himself. "They will be back, they will be back with Mercy and he will be angry and he will want to come back, no doubt tomorrow night."

"I have an idea Sudha, are you with me tomorrow night?"

"Absolutely, Mr. Rosey, absolutely."

The next morning he found Father Arturo at breakfast and set his tray down across from him.

"Good morning, Hugo."

"Good morning, Father."

"I see you've been busy at Vaikunth with the boy and his sister, an interesting story. She's a very beautiful young woman." He paused expectantly for Hugo's response. Hugo sensed the inference of the remark and his cheeks reddened.

"It's not what you may think, Father. She's a wonderful young woman whose life is in particular danger. And the boy .... well, he's a bright, special child who needs his sister. I can't lie to you, I do find her very beautiful and yes, I had a moment of moral indecisiveness. But I have a fiancé back home and, well, you know what I mean."

Arturo smiled and reached across the table to squeeze his hand in response. "Well, my friend, what is next?"

"Can we get them to the missionaries in Australia or England?"

Arturo rested his chin in his hand and appeared to be in deep thought. "I'll talk with Mother. It wouldn't be the first time something like that has happened; and I'm sure that because the request is coming from you she'll give it special consideration. You know, she thinks you're superhuman."

Hugo sat back in surprise. "Really, she said that?"

"Well, not exactly that, but words to that effect. I'll talk with her this morning; she's leaving for Africa this afternoon. I'll see you later today."

Hugo drove to Vaikunth and spent two hours driving around the perimeter, finally parking in the area where the gang members would likely park that night. He sat for an hour and thought. He drove back to the Motherhouse and found Sudha. They talked for an hour and prepared for the evening's encounter. As the sun set, they drove to Vaikunth concealing the van behind a rusting yellow school bus, its wheels and windows long ago removed. They carried a wooden soda case to a low rise below the parking area where Mercy's men would park, and lay against the embankment listening to the ebbing sounds of Vaikunth. They came at 10:30. Two new Mercedes sedans crunching to a halt, doors opening and slamming shut, loud voices heading toward Riya's home. They scrambled up the embankment with the soda case containing six Molotov cocktails and two ball peen hammers. Sudha lit the rag wicks of the bottles while Hugo smashed the side windows of the cars. The sound of the shattering glass brought Mercy and his men to a nervous halt. In an instant, both cars were engulfed in flames. As Mercy and his men came screaming and running back to the cars, Hugo and Sudha slid down the embankment and ran in opposite directions, coming up behind them. Sudha in mid stride struck first with a brutal blow to the head of his closest prey, quickly spinning with a smashing swing into the mouth of another. Hugo disabled one man, but as he turned to an onrushing attacker was confronted by a large figure who could only be Mercy. As the gangster aimed his pistol at Hugo, two shots rang out and then two more. Sudha stood with a smoking pistol in his hand, eyes ablaze. Mercy lay dead, as did another man beside him. The other three lay motionless in the heat and illumination of the rising flames from the burning cars. Young men and boys came streaming out of Vaikunth toward the blaze.

"Sudha, let's get out of here." They ran down the embankment just as one of the Mercedes exploded. As they leapt into the van, the sound of police and fire sirens could be heard growing closer. Sudha spun the wheels on the van as he accelerated onto the main road. They drove in silence as they passed police and fire apparatus headed in the opposite direction. Sudha spoke calmly as he slowed for a red light. "If we do not stop evil, evil will grow unchecked and then it will consume all that is good and beautiful in the world. They were evil men, they did not belong in society. Mother, she does not understand this. But you and I understand this. I am happy to have acted as the hand of God in ridding them of this world."

Hugo looked at Sudha, pondering his philosophy, unsure of what to say. "Sudha, what about the police?"

"The Police will be happy that Mercy and his henchmen are gone. His life was full of brutality, there will be no intense investigation."

The *Calcutta Times* headlined the gangland murder of Mercy and his henchman. There were no leads in the investigation.

Father Arturo slid his tray of rice, fish, and vegetables across from Hugo and sat down. "Well Hugo, I told you she likes you, your young friends will be off for Australia in five or six weeks. Sister Rita has already informed Riya and is obtaining visas for them, are you happy?"

Hugo was speechless, he stumbled over his words. "I don't know what to say, Father. Thank you so much, they deserve a better life."

As Father Arturo lowered his head to scoop in some rice, he said, "What do you think about those killings last night, wasn't that man Mercy, the gangster who was threatening Riya and Avik?" He looked up at Hugo, his eyes carrying a conciliatory expression.

As Hugo emerged from the shower room, Avik came running down the corridor. "Avik, what are you doing here, is everything all right?"

The boy paused to catch his breath. "Riya wants to see you, she said it was important, she said come now."

He walked to the three large buildings that housed the orphanage, classrooms, and dining hall. Riya and Avik had been assigned a small private room because of her age and tentative residency. Hugo knew the buildings well, having worked at the orphanage from time to time. He entered Riya's building through a side entrance and bolted up three flights of stairs to a long corridor. He knocked on the door of room 315. There was no answer, he knocked again. He heard the door latch slide open and the door cracked open to reveal a wary Riya who smiled happily when she saw him. She swung the door fully open.

"Please, come in, I wasn't sure if it was you, I'm glad you came." She was exceptionally beautiful in a red Sari, her hair hung in golden ringlets below her shoulders. Her full lips glistened red and her sparkling blue eyes held him captive. She was obviously nervous. He scanned the room. It was sparsely furnished, a bed, a dresser, a table with two chairs and one mirror mounted above the dresser. Bathrooms were at the end of the hall. "I asked you to come so that I" --she paused casting her glance downward— "could thank you for saving me from Mercy for arranging for our new home in Australia. Avik will have a chance to grow up as an equal and not be consigned to a third class status."

He took her hand. "There's no need to thank me, it gives me great pleasure to help you and Avik to a better life." Looking into his eyes, her lips slightly parted, she whispered, "This is the only way I can thank you." With a quick movement she slid the top of her Sari from her shoulders. Hugo's senses reeled. "This is the only way I can thank you," she said in a trembling whisper. "I have never been with a man, I want you to have me. I want to give myself to you." All that could be heard in the room was their rapid heavy breathing. He came to, and turned his back to her.

"Riya, please cover yourself, please." She pulled up her top, tears forming in her eyes. He went to her and enfolded her in his arms, resting her head on his shoulder. He pushed the curls from her face and tenderly kissed her moist cheek. "I want you to save your virginity for the man you will marry someday. That is the gift that I want from you. I want you to promise this to me."

She looked up at him and quickly kissed his lips. "I promise you I will."

"I want you to know that I have a woman at home who is waiting for me and who I love."

She smiled in understanding. "Is she very pretty?"

"Yes, she's very pretty."

"She is very fortunate to have a man like you who loves her."

He wanted to turn the conversation. "When did they tell you that you would be leaving?"

"Maybe five weeks or six weeks. When do you return home?"

"I don't know, whenever Mother decides I've done enough, I suppose."

"Then we will see you before you leave?"

"Of course you will, I wouldn't think of leaving without saying goodbye to you and Avik." As he left the building, he almost stumbled over Avik sitting on the cement stairs to the building. "Hey, what are you doing here buddy?"

"Riya told me to wait here until you left. Did you do it to Riya?" His eyebrows shot up and he chuckled as he spoke.

"What!! Did I do what to Riya?"

"You know" he made a circle of his index finger and his thumb on his left hand and plunged his right index finger in and out rapidly.

"Hey, stop that, where did you learn that?"

"From the older boys at Vaikunth."

"Well, don't do it again, it isn't a nice thing to do."

"Okay."

"Get upstairs, I'll see you tomorrow."

The next two weeks were frantic. There was a shortage of co-workers and the workload fell to whoever was on duty. Days went longer and everyone performed more than one job at a time. Slowly the new co-workers trickled in, some were returnees and some were new. Hugo worked with Raj Vijaya to indoctrinate the new workers into their tasks. Riya was working with the sisters performing the same duties, keeping the same hours. Avik was getting his first exposure to a formal classroom and not taking the confinement well. Mother Teresa had undergone surgery and was convalescing in her quarters at the Motherhouse.

It was Tuesday, around seven-thirty, when Sudha came and found him at his bunk just returning from a shower.

"Mother would like to see you."

"Right now?"

"Yes, Mr. Rosey, if you don't mind, sir."

As he walked to the Mother house, he could see lights on in Mother Teresa's office. He was greeted by Sister Rita who smiled and seemed genuinely happy to see him. "Come Hugo, Mother's waiting for you."

She sat in a huge leather chair, further diminishing her size. Upon his entry she turned and smiled, patting a chair seat next to her. "Come Hugo, sit next to me. I hope I didn't disturb you."

"No, not at all Mother, I'm always at your beckon call. How are you feeling? How was the surgery?"

She smiled at him and raised her hands in exasperation. "You know, when you age, your parts wear out or they fail to work. It wasn't major surgery, and I'll be back traveling in a few days. I'm needed in the Philippines, much poverty, much sickness, it never seems to end. I think this is God's way of testing our resolve. If someday you should decide to return to us, I think your talents would serve us best in the Philippines. Hugo, you have been an amazing man. You have gained the respect and the admiration of everyone here. Every now and again, God lays his hand on someone special, and you are one of those special people. You have performed beyond our expectations, but now it's time for you to return home. You have a fiancé or a special woman in Rhode Island?"

"Yes, Mother, I do, her name is Loraine Ciccone."

"Ahh a nice Italian girl! They make good wives, they know how to take care of a family." She stood slowly, Hugo assisting her midway. She grasped his shoulders, raised herself on her toes and kissed him on the cheek. "Sister Rita has all your travel documents and the airline tickets, you'll be flying out on Thursday afternoon. Come back to us when you can, Hugo."

He held her hands, head bowed, struggling to hold back his tears. "I will, Mother, I promise you."

"And remember, when you return, you return as my *Adjutor Specialis*!

He spent Wednesday packing his few belongings and visiting the Sisters and doctors who were still on the campus. He visited the infirmary and the orphanage. Avik was in school. He debated the idea of calling him out of his classroom but thought better of it. He asked a young sister if she had seen Riya and was informed that she was working that day in one of the many orphanages in Calcutta. She did not know which one. At dinner that night, Dr. MacDonald, Dr. Imondi, Dr. Mendoza, and Raj Vijaya sat with him and exchanged addresses and phone numbers. The doctors would be leaving in two weeks as replacements arrived. This was their second tour of duty in twelve months.

Robbie MacDonald called for silence and raised his teacup and spoke in his rich Scottish burr. "Hugo, in my life's experience, I've learned that there are people who watch things happen, and there are people who make things happen, and there are people who ask what happened. Hugo, you are one who makes things happen. We value you, we have an affection for you, and we hope you'll be back with us soon."

He was up early the next morning. Sudha would be driving him to Calcutta Airport at eleven. He hurried to the orphanage to see Riya and Avik. Riya was nowhere to be found. He found Avik in the dining hall and sat next to him as he finished his fruit juice. Avik was smiling from ear to ear as he spoke. "Can I ride with you today, I can help a lot."

Hugo tousled his hair as he spoke. "I'm afraid not, buddy, I'm leaving for my home this afternoon." Avik's face dropped, he stuttered searching for words. "But, but ... why can't you stay, Riya needs you!"

"Because it's time for me to see my family, but maybe next year I'll be back."

"But we will be in Australia, we won't see you" he said in an anguished tone.

Hugo smiled and put an arm around his shoulders. "Where did Riya go?"

"She left early this morning to work at another place, she went on a bus with other people and the Sisters."

Hugo reached for Avik's ruled notebook and tore out a page. He took a pencil from his pencil box and began to write. "Give this to Riya, it's my mother's address in the United States. I want you to write me once you're settled in, in Australia, and let me know how you're doing, okay? And make sure you tell Riya I tried to see her this morning. Oh, and one thing more, I want a promise from you-- I want you to promise me that you will go on to college in Australia."

The boy threw his arms around Hugo and would not let go. "Hey, hey, I have to go, remember your promise."

"I will," he whispered.

Sudha was waiting by the van and hurried to take his bags. They arrived at the airport in one piece. Sudha hurried to take the bags over Hugo's objection. Inside the terminal, he placed the bags on the spotless terrazzo floor and extended his hand. "Mr. Rosey, my grandfather told me when I was a small boy that to be a man among men, you must confront yourself every day and you must look into your heart and find the goodness. Mr. Rosey, you are who my grandfather was speaking of. It is an honor to know you sir." Before Hugo could return the compliment, he was gone. He heard his flight number being called, picked up his bags, and hurried to his gate.

Made in the USA
Columbia, SC
05 February 2018